This book addresses critical issues in normative ethical theory. Every such theory must contain not only a theory of motivation but also a theory of value, and the link that is often forged between what is valuable and what is right is human welfare or well-being. This topic is a subject of considerable controversy in contemporary ethics, not least because of the current reconsideration of utilitarianism. Indeed, there is as much disagreement about the nature of value and its relationship to welfare and morality as there is about the substantive content of normative ethical theories.

The essays in this collection, all new and written by a distinguished team of moral philosophers, provide an overview, an analysis, and an attempted resolution of those controversies. They constitute the most rigorous available account of the relationship between value, welfare, and morality.

VALUE, WELFARE, AND MORALITY

Value, Welfare, and Morality

Edited by

R. G. FREY and CHRISTOPHER W. MORRIS
Bowling Green State University

CAMBRIDGE
UNIVERSITY PRESS

Published by the Press Syndicate of the University of Cambridge
The Pitt Building, Trumpington Street, Cambridge CB2 1RP
40 West 20th Street, New York, NY 10011-4211, USA
10 Stamford Road, Oakleigh, Melbourne 3166, Australia

First published 1993

Printed in the United States of America

Library of Congress Cataloging-in-Publication Data
Value, welfare, and morality / edited by R. G. Frey and Christopher W.
Morris
p. cm.
ISBN 0-521-41696-5
1. Social values. 2. Values. I. Frey, R. G. (Raymond Gillespie)
II. Morris, Christopher W.
HM73.V35   1993
303.3′72 – dc20   92–36143
                                                        CIP

A catalog record for this book is available from the British Library.

ISBN 0-521-41696-5 hardback

Contents

List of contributors	*page*	vii
Preface		ix
1	Value, welfare, and morality	1
	R. G. FREY AND CHRISTOPHER W. MORRIS	
2	The land of lost content	13
	SIMON BLACKBURN	
3	Putting rationality in its place	26
	WARREN QUINN	
4	Can a Humean be moderate?	51
	JOHN BROOME	
5	Welfare, preference, and rationality	74
	L. W. SUMNER	
6	Preference	93
	ARTHUR RIPSTEIN	
7	Reason and needs	112
	DAVID COPP	
8	Desired desires	138
	GILBERT HARMAN	
9	On the winding road from good to right	158
	JAMES GRIFFIN	
10	Value, reasons, and the sense of justice	180
	DAVID GAUTHIER	
11	Agent-relativity of value, deontic restraints, and self-ownership	209
	ERIC MACK	
12	Agent-relativity – the very idea	233
	JONATHAN DANCY	

13 The separateness of persons, distributive norms, and   252
    moral theory
    DAVID BRINK
14 Harmful goods, harmless bads   290
    LARRY TEMKIN

Contributors

Simon Blackburn, Edna J. Koury Distinguished Professor of Philosophy, University of North Carolina, Chapel Hill

David Brink, Associate Professor of Philosophy, Massachusetts Institute of Technology

John Broome, Professor of Economics and Ethics, University of Bristol

David Copp, Professor of Philosophy, University of California, Davis

Jonathan Dancy, Professor of Philosophy, University of Keele

R. G. Frey, Professor of Philosophy, Bowling Green State University

David Gauthier, Distinguished Service Professor of Philosophy, University of Pittsburgh

James Griffin, Reader in Philosophy, Oxford University

Gilbert Harman, Professor of Philosophy, Princeton University

Eric Mack, Professor of Philosophy, Tulane University

Christopher W. Morris, Associate Professor of Philosophy, Bowling Green State University

Warren Quinn, late Professor of Philosophy, University of California, Los Angeles

Arthur Ripstein, Associate Professor of Philosophy and Law, University of Toronto

L. W. Sumner, Professor of Philosophy, University of Toronto

Larry Temkin, Associate Professor of Philosophy, Rice University

Preface

In the last two decades, the rise of substantive ethics and, through this, the renewed development of normative ethical theories have become prominent concerns in moral philosophy. In turn, however, the development of such theories has raised to prominence issues in value theory and the epistemology of morals, and resolution of these issues has come to be regarded as vital to progress in the renewed search for an adequate normative ethical theory. In these regards, what is the relation between value and desire or preference? Do desires and preferences alone provide reasons for action? Indeed, do they provide reasons for action at all? Are judgments of value "subjective" in some way, and are they "projected onto the world"? Or are such judgments "objective," either in the sense of having truth-values independent of their conditions of verification or in the sense of representing something inherent in the world? What is the relationship between claims of "objectivity" in either of these senses and the natural properties of things in the world? What exactly is supervenience, and what supervenes on what? Is there a viable distinction to be drawn between agent-relative and agent-neutral value? Are there any agent-neutral values, and how do we tell whether there are? Are there agent-independent values as well? The growing conviction that we are unlikely to make further progress in the development of an adequate normative ethical theory or even in substantive ethics without resolving a number of these issues, has given them an air of urgency as well as prominence.

It was with these questions in mind that we held a conference on "Value, Welfare, and Morality" at Bowling Green. To it, we invited a number of philosophers who had made significant contributions to value theory and moral theory. We have supplemented their efforts here with five additional essays commissioned for this volume, also by significant figures. Our aim has been, then, not only to produce a volume that addresses fundamental questions to do with value, welfare, and morality but also to produce one that is representative of the very best work on the interlocking themes that comprise this general area of moral philosophy.

Numerous people have helped us both with the conference and this volume, especially among the graduate students, staff, and faculty of the philosophy department at Bowling Green, and we are grateful to them all. The referees for Cambridge proved helpful as well, as did our editor, Terence Moore, whose customary good advice and encouragement has once again placed us in his debt.

It is with deep sadness that we note one of our contributors, Warren Quinn, died before the appearance of this volume. While we have lost a friend, philosophy has lost a dedicated and vibrant talent. We are pleased to present here one of his best, if very last, pieces.

1

Value, welfare, and morality

R. G. FREY AND CHRISTOPHER W. MORRIS

In addition to an account of motivation, every normative ethical theory must contain an account of value, and the link that is often forged between what is valuable and what it would be right or what we ought to do is human welfare or well-being. While this linkage is not new, it has become a source of considerable controversy in contemporary ethics, not least because of the general reconsideration of utilitarianism that has been underway for some time now. Indeed, it often seems that there is as much disagreement about the nature of value and its relationships to welfare and morality as there is about the substantive issues on which our normative theories are supposed to pronounce.

Both in philosophy and the social and policy sciences, two general pictures of value and of its link to welfare and morality haunt contemporary discussions in the Anglo-American world. Both general pictures are inherited from David Hume and Jeremy Bentham and from the tradition of political economy founded by Adam Smith and David Ricardo. From Hume, there develops an instrumental view of rationality, of reason in the service of the passions; while reason can assist one in obtaining one's ends, what these ends are depends upon one's passions. This widely influential view of rationality is associated today with desire- or preference-based conceptions of welfare (and with conventionalist or even contractarian accounts of justice). From Bentham and nineteenth-century economics, there develops the rival though quite friendly view of utilitarianism, in which the focus is on aggregation of pleasures and pains over persons generally and in which reason assists one in the pursuit of this impersonal though welfarist end. As they are fleshed out and given substance, these two pictures come to form general accounts of value, welfare, and morality, and they form the background for and underlie the treatment of numerous issues in value and moral theory. It may be well, then, to indicate at the very outset of this volume some of what goes toward fleshing out these views.

The neo-Humean view – it differs in some respects from Hume's actual account of matters – starts with an instrumental conception of practical reason, according to which persons are rational to the extent that their behavior is an efficient means to their ends. These ends, however, are not discovered by reason but are determined by desire or, in contemporary parlance, preference. There are quarrels among neo-Humeans as to the coherence and other conditions (e.g., information) that rationality can impose on preferences, but these intramural disputes need not detain us now.

All neo-Humeans agree in forbidding substantive conditions to be imposed on the content or nature of preferences; rationality has essentially to do with the manner in which agents take their preferences to guide their actions. To speak, then, of the "rationality of ends" is inappropriate, for this would be to ask for something more than a purely instrumental conception of rationality and to suppose that human ends are set by something other than or in addition to preference.

Importantly, it is almost certainly the case that, while neo-Humeans reject conditions on the content or nature of preferences, they will be constrained to accept some conditions on admissible preferences if they wish to hold, as many do, that instrumental rationality is to be understood as the *maximization* of the satisfaction of one's preference, or that the measure of preference is utility. For maximization, properly understood, requires at least a weak ordering of alternatives or options, that is, a complete and fully transitive ranking of alternatives. The point is logical: One cannot *maximize* unless one can (1) compare all alternatives with respect to, for example, preference or goodness; and (2) order them in a way that satisfies transitivity. There is no greatest or best if x and y cannot be compared in the relevant manner, or if x is better than y, y better than z, and z better than x.

On the neo-Humean view, preferences guide action, with the result that action is typically explained by reference to the agent's preferences and beliefs. This conception of rationality has an explanatory function, which is widely appealed to in the economic and social sciences, which in turn is taken to testify to its explanatory power. Indeed, it might be held that this explanatory power is nowhere more apparent than in everyday life, where human action seems commonly understood and explained by appeal to what the actor believed and desired.

Neo-Humeans agree that desires or preferences provide reasons for action, though there are disagreements, related to those mentioned above, as to whether *all* preferences do; but virtually all neo-Humeans agree that *only* preferences provide reasons. This has a rather striking result: Preference-independent interests and needs provide no reasons for action, whether the interests be one's own or those of others. Of course, it is highly likely that one's interests or needs will figure among one's preferences, that is, that one will have preferences, of greater or lesser strength, with regard to the objects of one's interests or needs. But this in no way affects the point about reasons. As indicated, this claim that only preferences provide reasons for action is accepted by the vast preponderance of neo-Humeans. (It is worth noting that some neo-Humeans, such as David Gauthier, allow considerations that are not themselves preferences, albeit preference-based, to provide reasons for action.)

From this point of view, some neo-Humeans go on to interpret welfare as well-being, well-being as preference satisfaction, and the latter as the satisfaction of informed and/or self-regarding preferences. The link with welfare is then trivial. This general line of approach to welfare is characteristic of "welfare economics," a normative branch of economics; it no more treats of a preference-independent notion of welfare than does neoclassical economic theory generally.

The link between instrumental rationality and morality is more problematic. In fact, doubts are expressed by some writers as to whether a genuine morality is available to creatures who are merely instrumentally rational. For instance, it seems clear that some parts of morality, such as benevolence, might be held by neo-Humeans to be found in ordinary other-regarding preference. But other parts of morality may not be so easily accommodated, such as those associated with the virtue of justice, understood in the broad sense that includes truth-telling and fidelity, as well as respect for others' rights. For, as Plato and many others noticed long ago, justice frequently asks us to do that which we do not want to do, which it is not in our interest to do, and which it even sets back our interests to do. If this is so, if, that is, justice can require of us acts (and dispositions) that are not themselves utility-maximizing, then how is the neo-Humean account of rationality or value, based in preference, going to make room for justice? Put summarily, in a phrase of James Griffin's, what road do we follow from the good to the right?

One idea has been to adapt Hume's conceptions of justice and property to the task. Hume thought of the norms of justice and property as conventions that serve the general interest and that, as a result, one has reason to support, insofar as one's interests are included in those of the public. To be sure, Hume recognized that one's interests and those of others may be in opposition, as when one finds oneself, as he puts it, in the company of ruffians; in such situations, as between humans and animals, justice ceases to bind. Importantly, then, the mere fact that our interests are included in those of the general public does not entail that we individually have reason to support the norms that serve the public interest, as Hume's "sensible knave" and Hobbes's "Foole" both recognized. This much is evident from the variety of familiar situations that are structured like the Prisoners' Dilemma. Nevertheless, the general strategy suggested by Hume is clear, and, in one form or another, it is developed, for example, by J. L. Mackie, David Gauthier, and Gilbert Harman.

The neo-Humean, then, begins with an instrumental conception of practical rationality, constructs a conception of welfare that provides reasons only insofar as it is preference-based, and develops a conception of morality, or, perhaps more accurately, justice, as a set of mutually advantageous or agreeable conventions. Additional features of this view will emerge in the discussion of the second, utilitarian position, to which we now turn.

If practical rationality requires individuals to maximize the satisfaction of their preferences, and if morality requires of us that we be impartial to the ends of one person over another, then it might seem natural to construe morality as asking that we maximize preference satisfaction overall. Certainly, it has seemed so to many moral and political philosophers, to economists and social theorists, and to numerous social reformers, starting with the British Philosophical Radicals.

As the neo-Humean and utilitarian traditions are in various respects close allies, many of the same views regarding the relations between desires, well-being, and reasons have their proponents here as well. Early utilitarians tended to understand welfare in terms of mental states, variously adumbrated as pleasure, happiness, benefit, and so on, and to think that people were moved to action by considerations of pleasure, happiness, and the like. (This view of motivation did not *require* that agents be construed as psychological egoists.) Later utilitarians came to find the mental-state view of intrinsic value and utility too confining and shifted to a desire-satisfaction account, wherein it is true that we desire more in our lives than merely pleasure or happiness. Of course, not all utilitarians have made the switch, and some remain mental-state theorists, for whom the fundamental datum of value is any of various experiences called pleasure, happiness, and so on. And other utilitarians seem to have endorsed both views, in that they apply the desire-satisfaction view in the case of humans and the mental-state view in the case of other animals.

Moreover, some utilitarians have refused either to identify preference with welfare or to take preference instead of welfare as the object of importance for morality. For these theorists, seemingly a growing class, it is well-being, understood as something independent of preference, that is what ought to be maximized. The debate here is more complicated than with neo-Humeans; for part of what is at issue is whether one's welfare, understood as independent of one's preferences, provides one with reasons. In addition, does the welfare of others, all others, provide one with such reasons? It would seem that it must, if, indeed, we are to believe that morality demands that we maximize the well-being of all.

Talk of well-being understood as independent of one's preferences raises a tantalizing possibility: Can there be articulated an "objective" account of well-being, one that construes well-being to consist in certain factual conditions of human flourishing *and* that measures degree of success in achieving these factual conditions in some equally factual way? Some utilitarians have been intrigued by this possibility and by questions of whether individuals are the best judge of their well-being, of whether their word is final on the matter, of whether they can be deceived, and so on. Something like a measure of well-being as consisting in, among other things, caloric intake might illustrate the point: It becomes possible to plot well-being on a scale that can be applied to persons indiscriminately, and possession of such a measure would in turn seem to make it possible for one to refuse to take as definitive in the matter the individual's own statement of how well his life is going. Doctors in hospitals, for instance, frequently take themselves to have such measures, and economists and policy theorists interested in judgments of "social welfare" have commonly attempted to construct such scales.

Several points now arise of the utmost importance to the debate between neo-Humeans and utilitarians. A few words on each of these will have to suffice to show their crucial relevance.

First, as traditionally understood, utilitarianism is a maximizing theory that would have us maximize total preference or welfare satisfaction, that is, the greatest total amount of satisfaction distributed across all persons or, rather, all sentient beings. Let us call this the greatest total good. Some versions of the theory are "internalist" and claim that we each have reason to seek the greatest total good. Other versions are "externalist" and claim only that the greatest total good is the goal of morality; whether each of us has reason to seek it is a contingent matter. All these versions, whether internalist or externalist, however, seem committed to the view that the greatest good is of value, in some way, to all persons, that is, to each and every person. Is this the case? While it is easy to realize that my welfare, or that of my family and my friends, matters to me, and relatively easy to see how the welfare of (most) members of my community matters to me, it is not obvious that the general or collective welfare, understood as the greatest total good, matters to me. If it does not matter to me, then it seems unlikely that the greatest total good can provide the motivational force to action that utilitarians, whether internalist or externalist, have thought that it provided.

Second, to claim that the greatest total good is of value, in some way, to all persons is to claim that the value of the greatest good is agent-neutral. By contrast, neo-Humeans claim that the good of others, much less the greatest total good, is of value to someone only if it is the object of one of her preferences. For them, the value of the satisfaction of someone's preferences or welfare is agent-relative. How exactly the agent-neutral/agent-relative distinction is to be drawn is a matter of increasing controversy. But the general idea is clear enough: Something has agent-relative value to the extent that it has value from particular perspectives, those of the particular valuers to whom it is valuable, whereas something has agent-neutral value to the extent that it is valuable, necessarily, from the perspective of all, or rather, of each and every valuer. (And while an agent-relative value could be a value from the perspective of all, it need not be.) Utilitarians generally affirm, and neo-Humeans generally deny, that the value of the greatest total good is agent-neutral.

Clearly, the dispute between utilitarians and neo-Humeans is of special theoretical importance. For if one could establish that there is no agent-neutral value, most versions of utilitarianism would be in trouble; whereas if one could show that there is no agent-relative value (as G. E. Moore perhaps thought) or merely that there is some agent-neutral value, most neo-Humean positions would be in trouble. The establishment of either thesis, then, would seem to carry import for the adequacy of versions of the position in question.

It is important to stress a difference between utilitarian and neo-Humean positions here. Utilitarians, as well as many philosophers who include some consequentialist principles in their accounts of morality, would appear to think that there is at least one agent-neutral value, but many seem also to hold that there are agent-relative values as well. Endorsement of the existence of agent-neutral value need not bar them from recognizing the existence of agent-relative value. Neo-Humeans, however, typically deny the existence of agent-neutral value and recognize only agent-relative value; all value whatsoever is agent-relative. This is a bold thesis that denies a possibility that many utilitarians and consequentialists allow. And it is not only they who allow it; recent work by Thomas Nagel affirms the existence of both agent-neutral and agent-relative value, without endorsing the claim that the greatest total good is an agent-neutral value.

Another interesting possibility bears mention as well: Neo-

Aristotelian virtue theorists such Philippa Foot, while antagonistic to neo-Humeanism, deny the existence of any agent-neutral value. Thus, while neo-Humean accounts entail that all value is agent-relative, it should not be thought that rejection of preference-based accounts commits one to accepting (some) agent-neutral value, as shown by neo-Aristotelian ethics. We should guard against thinking, as is not uncommon, that consequentialist theories and various neo-Kantian alternatives exhaust the theoretical options we have.

Third, it is often said today that utilitarianism does not take seriously the "separateness of persons," a charge usually contested by utilitarians. The idea, in part, is that to attribute to morality a global-maximizing structure is *ipso facto* to minimize the importance of or to accord derivative significance to the separate points of view of individuals. Put differently, to sum desire satisfactions or utilities across persons, as global-maximizing theories do, is to place less significance on the fact that these utilities are those of particular and distinct individuals. Of course, the formal requirement of utilitarianism, that each is to count for one and no one for more than one, ensures that no individual is overlooked in determining the greatest total good; but the good of any particular individual is summed with the goods of others to form the greatest total good, and the distinctness of these individuals ceases to be of fundamental moral concern.

A number of contemporary philosophers regard this failure to accord primary weight to the distinctiveness of persons and personal perspectives to be a central flaw of utilitarianism. They believe that no moral theory can be adequate if it fails to take seriously the different perspectives of separate agents. One can, in part, think of this issue as having to do with the identity of the appropriate "objects" of moral theory; utilitarians understand well-being or the good as the object of primary moral concern, whereas others, such as neo-Kantians and many contemporary natural rights theorists, take individuals to be the objects of moral theory. The central issue here, then, to use Sidgwick's terms, is between moral socialism and moral individualism.

It is important to guard against taking talk of agent-neutral value to refer to value in some agent-independent sense. Thus, when utilitarians claim the greatest total good to be an intrinsic, that is, a noninstrumental value, their critics have sometimes been led to speculate about whether there are other values, agent-independent values, that would persist even in a world of no valuers. But this is not what utilitarians take intrinsic value to be. Whatever is held by them to be valuable in and of itself in no way severs all connections with agents or sentient beings. The greatest total good is not valuable in virtue of its fostering or facilitating the realization of some other value; that is why it is said to be of "intrinsic," or better, of "ultimate," value. But that is not to say that it is an agent-independent value. Agent-neutral value refers to the fact that something is, necessarily, valuable to all agents, and that is not the same as claiming that something is valuable independently of any reference to agents at all. We should distinguish between two senses of the term 'intrinsic': Some value might be intrinsic in the sense of being "ultimate" or noninstrumental, and some value might be intrinsic in the further sense of being inherent in the world, a valuer-independent property of objects. These different senses are often conflated.

Some environmental ethicists regard the value of a functioning biotic community as intrinsic in both senses and even think that this value would persist or remain even if agents or valuers gradually ceased to be part of the picture. Neither neo-Humean nor utilitarian positions – nor, indeed, the positions of Foot or Nagel – hold much comfort for these environmentalists. This said, however, there may be a perfectly straightforward way of accommodating a portion of the Green movement without severing the link between intrinsic value and agents. We can speak of the "non-use" or "existence" value of something, which refers to people's preferences that something not be used (or consumed, spoiled, polluted) but continue to exist (as it is). Just as people value the existence of the spotted owl, so they value the existence of a particularly beautiful part of the countryside or, more generally, of unspoiled forests or unpolluted rivers. In this way, the "intrinsic" value of inanimate nature may be identified with non-use or existence value. But this value makes direct reference to people's preferences. It need not be value independent of all valuers; the part of the Green movement that seeks value of this sort in nature may find little comfort from contemporary value theory.

Neo-Humeanism and utilitarianism, then, are traditions that to a great extent dominated discussions of moral value and so ethical theory during the last two centuries, at least in the Anglo-American world. Even today, when numerous theorists depart from these traditions and when it is probably fair to say that no tradition is dominant, neo-Humeanism and utilitarianism nevertheless form the background against which those new discussions take place. Indeed, in the case of utilitarianism, it remains in all its versions the object of attack, even as its opponents attempt to spell out new alternatives, whether with respect to rightness and the adequacy of consequentialisms of different stripes or with respect to goodness and the adequacy of utilitarian value theory.

Interestingly enough, too, in view of the recent surge of interest in substantive ethics, metaethical considerations and considerations that are part of the epistemology of morals have resurrected themselves, in some forms similar to what they were in the postwar Anglo-American world and in other forms different. The matter of the "objectivity" of moral judgments is of considerable interest to many philosophers today. We might ask whether moral judgments are capable of being true (or false). Some "expressivists" and "projectivists" deny that they can have truth-values. Others disagree. Among the latter there is an additional debate as to whether the truth of moral judgments is independent of their conditions of verification.

Traditionally, it used to be thought that metaethics is, or ought to be, neutral between competing normative ethical theories. But an important point of contention between expressivists and their opponents is whether the former's analyses can in fact account for the content of our moral judgments. Can emotivist or expressivist analyses, for instance, recognize the agent-neutral or even agent-independent content of some moral judgments? The resolution of these disputes may have considerable importance for the questions we have raised about the relations between value, welfare, and morality.

The essays that follow take up a number of the above issues and numerous others as well. They not only give, collectively, an overview of the sorts of controversies sketched above, but they each seek as well to address and resolve some of those controversies. They aim, thus, to advance discussion of acutely significant issues having to do with the connections among value, welfare, and morality.

In defense of a "projective" account of the content of moral judgments, Simon Blackburn, in "The Land of Lost Content," enumerates the ways projectivism provides a better story than its rivals. Its naturalism makes metaphysical sense, he argues, as well as explaining how it is that such judgments can be known and how skepticism can arise concerning them. Additionally, sense must be made of the motivational power of ethical judgments, and this, Blackburn thinks, is a central strength of projectivism.

In "Putting Rationality in its Place," Warren Quinn raises an objection against a type of subjectivism that is influential in recent moral philosophy, what he calls "potential noncognitivism." It is the view, identified with J. L. Mackie, that morality, conceived as involving genuine beliefs, is defective and must be reconceived along expressionist lines. What Quinn wishes to attack is the part of this subjectivism that understands an individual's moral judgments as providing reasons; indeed, subjectivists think that such judgments provide reasons only because of the noncognitive attitudes that they express. Quinn questions this claim, and he sketches an alternative view that reasons are provided by the good that acts realize or the bad that they avoid.

"The moderate Humean view," as John Broome characterizes it in "Can a Humean Be Moderate?", is the position that while reason does not constrain the ends one may hold, it does require that a person's preferences be consistent in certain ways. These "moderate" requirements are the subject matter of decision theory, as many if not most practitioners view the field. A more radical Humean view is more extreme: It is the view that no preference can be irrational. Such a position does not even rule out someone taking inefficient means to achieve his ends. Broome argues that the moderate view is untenable, leaving only the extreme view to defend the field.

L. W. Sumner, in "Welfare, Preference, and Rationality," wishes to undermine both the received view of welfare as consisting in the satisfaction of an individual's preferences and the received view of rationality as consisting in the individual's maximization of her preferences. Taken together, the two views entail the view that rationality requires the maximization of one's own welfare, a position that he takes as absurd.

Drawing analogies between the role of preference in contemporary moral philosophy and that of perception in classical empiricism, Arthur Ripstein in "Preference" also attacks the uses to which the concept of preference has been put by recent philosophers. Extending antiempiricist arguments to preference-based moral theories, Ripstein argues that either they provide no account of practical reason or the good, or they presuppose an independent account of reason or good.

Without denying that one's preferences often provide one with reasons, David Copp argues in "Reason and Needs" that meeting one's basic needs is central to achieving the good from one's own standpoint and that needs and their satisfaction are independent of preference. Copp defends three theses about needs: that a person's needs are not determined by his or her preferences, that someone's needs provide him or her with reasons, and that rationality does not require one to do something that would prevent one from meeting one's basic needs.

A number of contemporary philosophers, including Copp, have appealed to second-order desire or preferences – desires or preferences about (first-order) desires or preferences – to explain or to construct basic notions. David Lewis, for instance, has recently argued for identifying valuing with a kind of second-order desire. Gilbert Harman is critical of all such attempts and argues against several recent versions in "Desired Desires." He thinks that valuing something involves desiring it and that no second-order desire need be involved; however, he does not think all desiring is valuing.

In his contribution, "On the Winding Road from Good to Right," James Griffin considers the manner in which we move from claims about well-being to conclusions about the right. He examines the way in which various limits, as of the will or of knowledge, impose constraints on the route we take from good to right. The upshot is that considerations of the good tend to be pushed into the background of our moral thought, and that a variety of norms are to be found in the foreground (e.g., those governing property).

In a major extension of the moral theory developed in his *Morals by Agreement,* David Gauthier in "Value, Reasons, and the Sense of Justice" considers morality not as an artifice but as a set of natural dispositions. The framework he now constructs is labeled "Kantian naturalism" to indicate its affinity to Kant's account of the understanding in the first *Critique.* Without making the theory of the sense of justice part of the theory of rational choice, Gauthier develops an account of this sense according to which a person's life would typically go less well were he not to possess it.

In "Agent-relativity of Value, Deontic Restraints, and Self-Ownership," Eric Mack defends a type of moral individualism, one which, in his estimate, gives proper recognition of the separate moral importance of individuals. He defends an account of value according to which all value is agent-relative, albeit objective. The agent-relativity of value is linked, Mack argues, to the acceptance of deontic restraints and correlative rights.

In "Agent-relativity – The Very Idea," Jonathan Dancy asks what it means for a reason to be agent-relative. Examining the accounts of Thomas Nagel, Derek Parfit, and others, he argues that existing analyses are mistaken. Dancy suggests that agent-relativity consists in values that are discovered by agents, without it following that they are relative to their discoverers.

It is widely claimed that utilitarian moral theories, and those with similar structure, fail to recognize or to accord proper weight to the "separateness of persons." In his essay "The Separateness of Persons, Distributive Norms, and Moral Theory," David Brink critically examines and rejects a variety of these claims. He argues that the alleged objection to teleological theories cannot provide the defense of contractualist theories that it is often held to do.

In "Harmful Goods, Harmless Bads," Larry Temkin critically examines an influential slogan, that a situation cannot be worse or better than another if there is no one for whom it is worse or better. He argues that the slogan is more ambiguous than may at first appear and that interpretations are controversial. Additionally, Temkin argues that the slogan does not support most of the particular positions it has been thought to support.

Finally, it should be stressed once again that this volume does not purport to be a summary of positions or of a literature. It focuses on the connections among value, welfare, and morality, the background for which is neo-Humeanism and utilitarianism. As will be seen, however, the essays range widely over this general terrain and speak to Kantians and Aristotelians as certainly as they do to consequentialists. Value theory knows no particular home among the schools.

2

The land of lost content

SIMON BLACKBURN

This is the Land of Lost content
I see it shining plain. . . .
A. E. Houseman

1. Ideals

What do we want from a theory of the content of ethical judgments?
A great deal. Their truth must make metaphysical sense. That includes
having an intelligible relation with the natural facts on which they su-
pervene. It must be possible to know them, and say how we do – but
also possible to make sense of various kinds of skepticism. It must be
possible to say what place they have in our lives, and that will include
making sense of their motivational power and their curiously fragile
objectivity. Because a whole philosophical industry depends on it, it
ought to be possible to say to what extent they are fit objects of difficult
theory, and to what extent such a theory would appeal to all rational
people. It would be good to know what someone must share with us to
count as using ethical terms with the same sense, and good to know to
what extent the judgments we make are on all fours with other kinds
of judgment. I consider these notions in order below.

I have long argued that one kind of theory provides the best combination of answers to all these problems. This is a "projective" theory,
starting in the same corner as traditional emotivism and prescriptivism,
but taking certain critically different options. The starting point is to
recognize a "nondescriptive" or expressive function for states of assent
to ethical judgment. Assent is thought of in terms of an attitude of some
needed kind, or what we might think of as some kind of acquiescence
to a pressure on choice and action. Gibbard calls it acceptance of a
system of normative government.[1] We need to voice such sentiments,
and we need to voice opposition to them; we need to argue and educate
and worry about which of them to encourage and discourage. The ethical
judgment stands as the focus for these transactions. It provides the
common currency of such debates. If practical life were simpler its

pressures could be voiced by a simpler linguistic method: the "Boo!– Hooray!" language of emotivism, or the simple issuing of overt pre- scriptions, as in the Decalogue. But once reflection starts up and we have to think about competing practical pressures, we need a richer language, and this is what we have. We have given the discourse what I call its propositional surface. We are pretty casual about doing that in any event: Consider the usual expression of gustatory delight "That's yummy" instead of just "yummy!"

We have become more scrupulous, or perhaps more neurotic. Voicing felt pressures on action and choice is one thing, judging surely another. Where is the content of the ethical judgment on this view? What is there to be right or wrong about? What makes such a judgment – or might it be, imitation of a judgment – true or false? What is actually being said, doubted, thought? In short, what are the contours of this land of lost content? These questions sound serious because we are used to looking for a certain kind of answer to them – a reductive account, or at least some kind of different identification of the "truth makers" for such judgments. A projective theory gives an explanation of the practice of judgment, but no useful redefinition of its content. But it tries to demystify the existence of such a content. Here is a rough guide to coping with the concerns identified in my first paragraph.

Metaphysical sense. This is one of projectivism's main boasts. It demands no more than we have to believe in anyhow – a natural world, with ourselves and our natural reactions to it. We do not have to postulate distinct facts or properties. Our reactions are to vary with natural facts. This is what they are for, and we voice this by subscribing to the supervenience of the ethical on the natural.

Epistemology. We need no distinct ways of knowing about ethical facts. We need no distinct modes of perception or capacities of reason, for example. On the other hand a projectivist can be quite relaxed about any distinct phenomenology a judgment might have – the kind of phenomenology that might lead people to talk of perceiving values, for example. Consider the ambitious case of causal projectivism. Suppose, as Hume thought, that the difference in someone who perceives a pattern of events as illustrating a causal connexion is a nondescriptive difference: It is to be thought of as a change in his organization, notably in the expectations he will form on apprehension of the event deemed to be the cause. There is no reason why this change in organization should not bring about a different "way of seeing." A sequence seen as caus- al might, literally, be seen differently. Similarly a voice heard as threatening might be heard differently, but this will be because of the different expectations and emotions generated, and it is these non-descriptive reactions that we need first to understand. Seeing a sequence differently will be seeing it in the light of the organizational or emotional tone, and there is no *a priori* limit on the phenomenological difference this could make.

Skepticism. Projectivism is sometimes called noncognitivism, but this is a pity. I think we know some ethical truths: It is better to marry than burn, better to have loved and lost than never to have loved at all. In saying this I am voicing my own attitudes, of course, but in claiming knowledge I also express confidence that the conflicting attitudes are worse, so that no improvement in my position will lead my attitudes to change. If I imagine them changing, I am at the same time imagining myself deteriorating. There are also things that we do not know, such as the right way to treat animals or manage inequalities of wealth. I have no confidence that my opinions on these things could not improve and change! In general we should be chary of claiming too much knowledge; as Nietzsche constantly insisted, such a claim has the function of shutting off examination, caution, and experiment. How much error can projectivism tolerate? Even if it can countenance an operational concept of truth and improvement, is something lost? Perhaps we want a nonoperational notion or idea of truth as possibly transcending any improvement in opinion we could muster – something that, perhaps, we cannot get to from here. Even if the projectivist can grant us, of any opinion, the possibility that it might be wrong, perhaps she cannot understand the possibility that all opinion might be wrong, and it might be thought that this closes a door that should be left open.

Of course, it is not clear that the loss is an important one. Examination, investigation, caution, and experiment go on within the system; only paralysis seems likely to ensue if we think that the system itself might be so radically out of tune that nothing recognizable from within it would count as an apprehension of truth. And we may take comfort from the thought that at least two of projectivism's main competitors – a Wittgensteinian internalism and a dispositional theory of more traditional kind – face the same problem. Eventually there has to be a residual confidence in our way of life or our dispositions to approval and disapproval. Nevertheless I think projectivism can accommodate even the global skeptic, if it wishes. Consider what I do know about my own sensibility. Its pedigree is bad; it is historically molded by ways of life it itself cannot wholly admire; it is the inheritor of centuries of distasteful ethical tone. Is it impossible that there should be a better cast to practical reason, but one which it cannot achieve, and could not even tend toward, nor recognize, because of the very flaws that its corrupt ancestry has built into it? Why rule this out? We would have to do so if we offered a definition of ethical truth, in terms of the best system achievable from here. But I deny that any such definition is needed, and if it is avoided, even global skepticism may be intelligible. The trick will be to remain thoroughly operational. This means understanding the potential range of ethical attitudes first, and dismissing the head-on question, What is truth? If thoughts about our fallibility are pressing enough, then among the attitudes we will want to acknowledge is that expressed by saying that we might be globally and totally fallen. In any case truth is given at the end, and for free: It is whatever is needed to make sense of the required range of thought. But it is understanding the ethical content that comes first.[2] My attitude here is that of Wittgenstein. When objectors are presented saying that on his account, for instance of logical necessity, they lose sight of it being true that this follows from that, he always replies that it being true that this follows from that just means that this does follow from that; it repeats the judgment, but makes itself no advance toward understanding it.

I think of this as taking seriously the idea of truth as a "regulative ideal," not as something "constituted" by (for example) membership of such and such a set of commitments.

Motivational power. This is one of projectivism's triumphs. Everybody acknowledges that assenting to an ethical judgment has something to do with motivation for or against its subject. It is not plain why assent to a judgment of fact should have this power; on the face of it, that should depend on whether one's desires engage with the fact judged. The projectivist simply tailors the attitude to the right degree of motivation. This is clearly more economical than, for example, a mixed theory that makes possession of the right attitudes some kind of odd precondition of being able to judge the moral world rightly.

A person may judge that something is right or ought to be done, be in full possession of his faculties, and be disinclined to do it. This is the point at which R. M. Hare appealed to an inverted commas use of ethical terms, but I prefer to allow real all-in cases. I think we can usefully connect akrasia with the phenomenon insisted on by Nick Sturgeon, that we allow a great variety of motivations and desires in people whom we accept as fellow users of any ethical terms.[3] Thus in one of his examples Thrasymachus and Socrates are discussing the same topic – justice – but in Socrates the belief that a course of action is just has one motivational force, and in Thrasymachus quite another. Sturgeon sees this as difficult for projectivism, just as the phenomenon of people with different standards "all the way down" was difficult for naturalism. I prefer to see it as illustrating the need to concentrate upon public, shared sense, rather than fully determinate, but possibly idiosyncratic, motivational profiles. Thus the need to communicate and to bring as many people as possible into the same conversation may stand in the way of a simple equation of valuing with a given antecedent function of desire. I return to this point in connection with David Lewis's theory below.

2. Objectivity

This comes in at least three guises and they need to be separated. Within ethics there is the objectivity of fairness and universalizability: the treating of like cases alike in the demanding sense of supplementing self-centered concerns by concerns with the egocentricity stripped out. Some people are better at this than others and some theorists think that a good ethic requires sensibilities in which self-centered concerns virtually vanish, while other theorists are more relaxed. Projectivism per se has no implications for this first order ethical topic. A sensibility that delivers attitudes only after informing itself of purely universal features of a situation may be a good thing, if we can manage it. Or, it may represent just one strand in a healthier mix.

We could leave the issue to first-order moralists, except that it does have a connection with the very possibility of ethical attitudes at all. This is seen very clearly by Hume when he talks of us correcting our sentiments by discounting the perspective created by our own particular set of interests. It is interesting that Hume talks without blushing of "correcting" our sentiments, and moral realists may scent a killing to make. Where can any notion of correctness arise, if all that we have is a menagerie of more or less selfish sentiments? Hume's answer is obvious. The functional role of universalizing is clear enough: It affords a common standpoint with which to share our attitudes or from which to issue what Gibbard describes as conversational demands on behalf of the norms we accept.[4] Hume himself described our ability to take the general view as making possible "the intercourse of sentiments" or ethical language:

General language, therefore, being formed for general use, must be moulded on some more general views, and must affix the epithets of praise or blame, in conformity to sentiments, which arise from the general interests of the community.[5]

The last clause might be debated; it suggests that Hume is a closer ally of R. M. Hare than the more general point warrants. Discounting ego-centric demands means that a kind of filter is put on an ethical sensibility, implying that it is to be responsive only to features of a situation that can be responded to equally by (some) others who have a different individual perspective. But it does not at all follow that the only features that get through the filter are those that themselves relate to the general interest. Nor is there an *a priori* priority for the ethical standpoint, since good men will in their hearts maintain more perspectival sentiments:

It is wisely ordained by nature, that private connexions should commonly prevail over universal views and considerations; otherwise our affections and actions would be dissipated and lost, for want of a proper limited object. Thus a small benefit done to ourselves, or our near friends, excites more lively sentiments of love and approbation than a great benefit done to a distant commonwealth: But still we know here, as in all the senses, to correct these inequalities by reflection, and retain a general standard of vice and virtue, founded chiefly on general usefulness.[6]

Hume is less apocalyptic about this than Bernard Williams. He certainly does not see it as putting an obstacle in front of the very possibility of ethics, and I suggest that in this he is right.

The second sense of objectivity is, I think, largely concerned with sheer phenomenology. It concerns the feeling of independence, of some-thing other ("larger") than oneself constraining choice and action. It makes a subjective source for ethics seem inadequate, and therefore incredible. In many writers it suggests tension between any kind of external "natural" theory of ethical feeling and the internal sense of ethics as a source of demands upon nature. How can contingent desires and attitudes support such categorical requirements? When justice and fidelity place stern bounds on what would otherwise be overwhelmingly tempting, how can we feel them as genuine bounds when we know them for projections of our own attitudes?

I find it hard to believe that this is a real problem. Why should a correct appreciation of the source of the virtues serve to diminish them? Why should we worry that, say, our repugnance to injustice is a senti-ment among others, with a contingent historical ancestry and function? I can understand people thinking like this: If we want boys to stand on burning decks, we had better not tell them that the navy exists mainly to bolster national vanity. But then the right answer is that if this is true, we ought not to want boys to stand on burning decks anyhow. If we do we may need to dazzle them with a mythology. But ethics in itself needs no mythology: We can form a steady ethical view of the point of a virtue. We do not have to be ashamed of ethical impulses, and when we are not, second-order reflection will not undermine them. We do not feel our appetites less because we understand their sources within us. But if we understand these sources, don't we lose a right we want, the right to judge and even coerce those who feel differently? This brings us to my third sense of objectivity, which is that associated with pressure toward convergence of opinion. It is what we need to avoid a flabby relativism. There must be a right answer, which means one right answer. We want its assurance when we judge and coerce and cajole and struggle in the swamps of first-order theory. But there is one right answer, although it does not answer every question. We all know the names of the virtues: "discretion, caution, enterprise, industry, assiduity, frugality, economy, good-sense, prudence, discernment . . . endowments whose very names force an avowal of their merit."[7] Such lists – Hume adds temperance, sobriety, patience, constancy, perseverance, forethought, and others, then mentions that there are a thousand more of the same kind – substantially answer Socrates' question, How are we to live? Live exhibiting these virtues. Any other answer will be worse. Appreciating these virtues gives us every right to judge those who lack them, and the words lie ready to hand: indiscreet, rash, lethargic, lazy, luxurious, dull. Adding "irrational" to this list only makes for confusion. The clear-sighted egoist, successful by what Bernard Williams calls the ecological standard of the bright eye and glossy coat, reasons well enough. What is wrong with him is that he is selfish, and what is wrong with that is (fairly) obvious.

But suppose someone with an inferior sensibility cannot be brought to improve: Suppose there is nothing in her motivations that gives us a foothold for effective reasoning. Does that give her a "right" to her state, implying that we should simply tolerate the difference and withdraw judgment? In spite of Gilbert Harman's advocacy I see little to recommend such a general view. A proper sensibility includes dispositions to take attitudes to human failings themselves: When people are mad, bad, and dangerous to know we have to react differently. Of course, whether such reactions invite expression in terms of righteous anger and blame is another matter, and will depend on which particular set of failings is in evidence. Moralizing against a character is not always in place, but bad characters naturally incur discrimination and disapprobation: The victim of a bad character who had no say in the matter will find the world going badly enough without any specific attribution of responsibility.

But a life exhibiting virtues will still face hard choices, and there is little prospect of unique theory determining one right answer. Further-

more, even if one theory "best explained" settled dispositions or intuitions about answers in easy cases, it need not be at all clear that this
gives it a unique authority in other cases. When we think of the historical
contingencies that may have shaped the settled answers, we may beware
of taking an explanation of these answers as an authority to follow into
uncharted waters.[8] More likely the judgment we want to make about
the uncharted waters and our sense of the best explanation of the settled
answers go hand in hand, in a hermeneutical alliance.

3. Dispositions and naturalism

Projectivism is not the only theory of ethics that uses the same ingre-
dients. Recently a more traditional "subjective" theory has emerged
that shares the metaphysics, but offers an alternative, dispositional theory of the meaning of moral predicates. It is naturalistic not just in the
sense of providing a natural explanation or placing of ethics, but in the
more ambitious, Moorean sense of "reducing facts about value to facts
about our psychology."[9] I shall take David Lewis's discussion as my
focus.[10] In Lewis's analysis "something of the appropriate category is a
value if and only if we would be disposed, under ideal conditions, to
value it." As might be expected Lewis confronts and disarms many
possible sources of opposition to this view.

What is the favorable attitude of valuing? To make the definition
useful, it should not be just that one values something by believing it
to be a value. Although the circularity that this seems to threaten is not
itself vicious, it would leave the dispositional claim at best secondary,
parasitic upon an antecedent understanding of the special activity of
valuing. Lewis himself favors "desire to desire." He considers, but rejects, going further up a potential hierarchy of desires, or in effect
bundling up such a hierarchy with a closure clause – "being such that
one has no higher order desire opposed to it" – on the grounds that it
is not contradictory to imagine persons desiring not to have the values
they do. But we can be content with indeterminacies here. "Desire to
desire" also suffers from potential counterexample: Sin may be enjoy-
able, and a person of failing appetites might desire to desire more eagerly
to possess more illicit partners while nevertheless ruefully recognizing
that her possessing more illicit partners would be a bad thing. But a
projectivist will not make a big issue out of this. He shares the problem
of locating the attitude projected without merely describing it as the
one we have when we value things.

I think we ought to be content with a quantification: To value something will require some attitude in the range of desire, socialized desire,

higher-order desire, bundled-up desire, desire that others desire, or even desire with potential for guilt or shame or self-hatred, the promise being that even if these last introduce a recognizably moral element, it too can be naturalistically explained. I see no obstacle to a naturalistic enterprise in admitting an irreducibility of valuing if the irreducibility is in turn explicable. If the explanation were that seeing something under the heading of the good is itself *sui generis,* we would be at square one. But if the explanation is that the purposes of ethics require that anyone who has some pro-attitude and expresses herself in ethical terms counts as part of the conversation, then the irreducibility is not fatal. Almost anyone sharing a language is deemed to be using words with a shared public sense, whatever the idiosyncrasies of his own cognitive structure. Similarly, anyone using ethical terms may be deemed to be part of the same conversation, regardless of idiosyncrasies in her own configurations of desire.

There is a classic dilemma for any dispositional analysis. Either the disposition gives us a genuinely natural predicate or it gives us a more complex moral predicate. If the former, Moore's open question argument still operates. If the latter, it is hard to see what is gained. In particular, a projectivist (or a realist) will be waiting in the wings to say that even if the complex predicate has the same sense as the original, it in turn needs a further theory. It would be like analyzing good in terms of right – establishing neighborhood links within the domain of the moral, but not telling us what commitment in that domain is in the first place. How does Lewis confront this dilemma? His analysis is that something is a value if it is such that we would be disposed to value it under ideal conditions. This of course looks set to fall on this second horn of the dilemma: It flaunts the value term 'ideal', and invites the reply that even if the equation holds, it gives us no theory of the moral. It only substitutes one evaluative predicate for another, rather than giving a rival theory of what value is. This will be the upshot if ideal conditions are simply "whatever conditions enable us to desire to desire only good things."

To avoid this reaction, Lewis takes the other turn. He identifies ideal conditions as "conditions of the fullest possible imaginative acquaintance." The theory thus becomes that something is a value if and only if we are disposed, under conditions of the fullest possible imaginative acquaintance, to value it. This is intended as a thoroughly naturalistic property: one in principle knowable by empirical means. And it has a number of nice features. It accords with the central place imagination plays in moral epistemology. Our canonical way of thinking through whether something is a value is to imagine, as well as we can, its realization. The definition explains why this is so (although there are cases, like eating oysters or sexual activity, where we value activities mainly by avoiding hard imaginative focus). The definition allows for some moral mistakes, since I may misidentify what we would value under such conditions; it allows for a flexible response to the problems of relativism, and it allows Lewis to doff his hat to the error theorist, who may have wanted to find a property of being necessarily such that we are disposed to value it – a property which probably has no instance.

If the only argument against this naturalistic analysis is Moore's Open Question argument, Lewis is on strong ground. For he rightly points out the difficulties in front of that argument: There are true but unobvious analyticities; wherever there are such the Open Question argument would apply; therefore it cannot be valid. In response to this reaction, the argument needs to go one more round. We frame the Open Question by conjuring a possibility: Surely we might make sense of the possibility that we would all desire to desire something under conditions of the fullest possible imaginative acquaintance, yet be wrong to do so? The object of desire would not then really be a value, and the analysandum comes apart from the analysis. The question is whether it could ever be right to identify empirically a group and a method of thought, and disallow the possibility that this group with this method is nevertheless getting the ethics wrong. The question is whether to admit this, which I shall call the Moorean possibility. Lewis's own attitude is that without corroborative detail the case is "bald and unconvincing" – a case in which our alleged power to make sense of a possibility is a poor guide to its existence.[11]

So suppose we provide some of the corroborative detail. How might it be that we are disposed to value something, under conditions of fullest possible imaginative acquaintance, yet it not be a value? Well, suppose better people than us would not be so disposed. How could that come about? Mention the old faults and flaws – bad childhoods, bad ancestry, bad genes. Under conditions of fullest possible imaginative acquaintance, turning over the issue as well as it can be turned, they value something, but because of these flaws they are wrong to do so. We can certainly make sense of this possibility in individual cases – the misanthrope, the sadist, the person whose desires are irretrievably locked onto her special interests or those of her group. We certainly seem able to contemplate the possibility that "we" are just lots of people with those kinds of defect. In fact, most of us probably think that most other people are actually in that position. After all, many people, perhaps a substantial majority in the present day, let alone in human history, turning it all over imaginatively as fully as they can, think that murdering those who write the wrong things is a value. Yet this puts no pressure at all on me to think so. There is no democracy here.

If all defects are defects of imaginative power, Lewis need not be troubled. If that is our situation, we will be bad judges of what we would be disposed to value were we able to exercise the fullest possible imaginative acquaintance, but it may remain that if we were able to exercise this power, we would identify true values. The troubling case is the one where the defect is not that, but one of misshapen desires, meaning that after the full imaginative exercise we find it easy to indulge our fanaticism, or shrug off the pains of others, or actually desire them, or otherwise exhibit depravity.

Lewis himself admits we can make sense of the fallen villain, who "cares not a fig for what he once valued, and yet he has forgotten nothing." If one why not lots; if lots, why not us? True, in other dispositional cases we see well enough why we cannot generalize. One person may taste a bitter substance as sweet, but not everybody (or at any rate not everybody all the time), for then it is no longer bitter. But I think we should not be satisfied with an attempt to block the Moorean possibility at just this point. Moral crusades and whole religions are built on the premise that our desires are the wrong ones, and it would only be if we were better that we could see values as they are. It would, I think, be quite arbitrary to draw the line just at us, admitting that we make perfect sense of the possibility that these things are true of other people, but not of us (flouting the famous Generality Constraint).[12]

Swapping intuitions about what counts as a genuine possibility is apt to lead to standoffs, unless we can provide a superior framework that more smoothly explains the virtues of the dispositional theory, but without the cost. In suggesting that a projective theory does this, I shall confine myself to three small points.

First, projectivism shares the metaphysics of Lewis's dispositional theory. But it objects to his relocation of ethical content (the substitution of a naturalistic predicate). The reason is that we must be able to combine a naturalistic metaphysics with a place for an activity – moralizing – that does not confine itself to delineating natural features. There is no need to see this as what we are doing when we are moralizing – it is not its point, and no such feature deserves to be given an analytic connection with the content of our activity. Certainly, when we think about whether to endorse some value, we go in for the imaginative exercise Lewis describes. But our aim is not to find whether the object has a particular dispositional effect on us. Our aim is not to contemplate our own dispositions, but to exercise them: Our dispositions are used, not mentioned. Our aim is to find whether to endorse or reject the value. We can usefully compare other judgments in respect of this difference: A thing will be described as red or funny or beautiful or square if it is such as to prompt these verdicts from us. But it is not true that it is the thing's relation to us that is the content of the judgment, that necessarily defines the verification conditions for it, or locates its place in our thought. We use the imaginative exercise to come to the verdict, but we do not say anything about the exercise.[13]

It might help to point the difference here with a parallel. When we consider whether an event is probable, we go in for a very similar imaginative exercise. We think of the possible evidence; we use our imaginations, we play our thoughts using our disposition to give credence to the event in the light of this imagined pool of relevant facts. Should we then say that we are really assessing a proposition (x is probable) with the following reductive an analysis: x is such that ideal imaginative acquaintance with a class of propositions counting as evidence would dispose us to more than such-and-such a degree of confidence in x? Surely not. We use our imaginative powers to come to such-and-such a degree of confidence, and we perhaps voice this by giving a verdict on x's probability. But we do not, as it were, turn our gaze through ninety degrees, and speak of the confidence we have, and I think there are clear objections to a theory that sees us as doing so.

Second, there is no getting behind the use of values as we think about moral truth. And it will be our values that we are using, of course. So is it plain that a projective vision of moral truth allows for the Moorean possibility? Not plain, because we have no sideways standpoint from which to imagine moral truth being one thing, but all our best exercises leading somewhere else. But as I explained in the section on skepticism, the possibility is one that it may be right to assert, for all that. In our own case this leaves space for due fallibilism: We do our best, and hope that it is good enough, but it remains a hope and its fulfillment is not to be regarded as analytic.

Finally, Lewis's theory has the neat feature that the exercise of fullest possible imaginative acquaintance is the canonical way to come to a verdict on value, because this is what the verdict is describing. Can any other theory protect the connection so well? My own answer is that the connection does not need the status of an analyticity (any more than it does in the case of probability). Once more, it takes a value to make a value. We value such an exercise because we value thinking things through. It is hard to imagine not doing so, but not impossible. Genghis may despise the sicklied brow that afflicts Hamlet, and put his paralysis down to the fullness of his imagination. If we disagree with Genghis, we want to think further about why we value such exercises, and we

:an do so by building on other values. We point to the disappointments and mistakes that come from ignoring them: the pleasures that turn to ashes, the free spirit whose lot is vacancy. Things go badly – this is my ethical view, and others may prefer impulsive chaos – when we don't think them through. And this, I think, is the only connection we need.[14]

Notes

1 Allan Gibbard, *Wise Choices, Apt Feelings* (Cambridge, Mass.: Harvard University Press, 1990), ch. 4.

2 The best-defended version of a deflationist attitude to truth is Paul Horwich's minimalism, expounded in *Truth* (Oxford: Basil Blackwell, 1990).

3 Nick Sturgeon, "What Difference Does it Make whether Moral Realism is True?" *Southern Journal of Philosophy* 24 (1986), Spindel conference Supplement.

4 Gibbard, *Wise Choices,* pp. 172ff.

5 David Hume, *Enquiry Concerning the Principles of Morals,* ed. Selby Bigge (Oxford: Clarendon Press, 1962), part 2, sec. 5, p. 228.

6 *Enquiry,* p. 229. See also *A Treatise of Human Nature* (Oxford: Clarendon Press, 1978), book 3, part 3, sec. 1, p. 581ff.

7 Hume, *Enquiry,* part 1, sec. 6, p. 242.

8 I differ here from the kind of conservatism that seems to lie in Susan Hurley's *Natural Reasons* (New York: Oxford University Press, 1989). The theme pervades Ronald Dworkin's work.

9 David Lewis, "Dispositional Theories of Value," *Proceedings of the Aristotelian Society,* Supplementary Volume 63 (1989): 113–37.

10 The view might be called the Princeton view: Lewis acknowledges the influence of Mike Smith and Mark Johnston. See also Mark Johnston, "Dispositional Theories of Value," *Proceedings of the Aristotelian Society,* Supplementary Volume 63 (1989): 152.

11 Lewis, "Dispositional Theories," p. 132.

12 Not that this is decisive here, as the case of bitterness shows.

13 A useful paper on the distinction needed here is Philip Pettit and Michael Smith, "Backgrounding Desire," *Philosophical Review* 99 (1990):565–92.

14 I make further remarks about a variety of dispositional accounts in "Circles, Finks, Smells and Biconditionals," in James Tomberlin, ed., *Philosophical Perspectives,* vol. 7: *Philosophy of Language and Logic* (Atascadero, Cal.: Ridgeview Publishing Company, forthcoming.)

3

Putting rationality in its place

WARREN QUINN

One kind of metaethical debate between realists and antirealists is about the character of ethical truth, with realists asserting and antirealist denying that truth in moral thought transcends our capacity to find reasons in support of our moral judgments. The antirealist in this kind of debate, no less than the realist, thinks that there is objective moral truth and knowledge. And the truth in question is not merely disquotational. Both parties think that a true moral claim corresponds, in some way or other, to the way the world is. Their disagreement, like that of their counterparts in mathematics, is about the nature of this correspondence. The antirealist sees it as a relation between the claim and the publicly available facts that could be adduced as good reasons to accept it, while the realist sees it as a relation to what he thinks of as the truth condition of the claim – a state of the world that may transcend our ability to detect its presence by way of reasoned argument. This issue is surely an important one, but it is posterior to the more fundamental question that has dominated metaethics in the last half-century. This is the question whether what lies at the heart of moral thought are beliefs capable of genuine truth or noncognitive attitudes that cannot be so assessed: feelings, emotions, desires, preferences, prescriptions, decisions, and the like.

Let's use J. L. Mackie's terms 'subjectivism' and 'objectivism' to name the opposing camps in this older debate.[1] In this essay (in Section 2) will argue against a certain common and influential version of subjectivism as it bears on the nature of reasons for action and practical rationality, and then (in Section 3 and 4) try to sketch out part of the defense of a vaguely neo-Aristotelian version of objectivism. But first

This essay was written during 1987 and delivered in the fall of that year at the University of Washington and the University of Rochester. It was revised in 1988 with the very helpful comments of Tyler Burge, Bob Adams, and Philippa Foot. It was delivered in that form to the conference at Bowling Green State University from which this collection is gathered. It benefited later from elaborate comments by Joseph Raz and interesting criticisms from Chris Morris, Mark Greenberg, and Ruth Chang.

I will try to bring out some important features of the contrasting conceptions.

1

The earlier subjectivists, notably Charles Stevenson and R. M. Hare, argued that the primary function of ethical thought and language is emotive or prescriptive rather than descriptive. Stevenson thought that the job of ethical language is to express moral feeling and so to influence the feelings and behavior of others.[2] Hare thought that a person's morality consists in the universalized principles he decides to try to live by and therefore prescribes to himself and others.[3] These authors were, in short, noncognitivists about ethical judgment. To say or think that an act is good or bad might, in a secondary way, imply certain facts about it, but its goodness or badness could never consist in such facts. Ethical concepts and judgments are on this view quite special. The concepts do not have the function of picking out properties or relations, and the judgments do not have the function of ascribing them. Their job is rather to enable us to express to ourselves or others the noncognitive attitudes mentioned above.

J. L. Mackie himself rejects this noncognitivist version of subjectivism in favor of an "error theory."[4] According to him, our ethical concepts and judgments have the same descriptive function as their empirical counterparts. The trouble is that there are no moral properties or relations answering to the concepts and no moral truths answering to the judgments.[5] For such properties and truths would be unacceptably "queer." They seem real only because we mistakenly project our own attitudes onto the world. But Mackie wishes not simply to do away with morality, but to reconstruct it. And if this reconstruction is to be done along metaphysically respectable lines, it will have to avoid the vulgar projective error. This is what he must have in mind when, speaking of the honest ethics that is "not to be discovered but to be made," he says that "the morality to which someone subscribed would be whatever body of principles he *allowed* ultimately to guide or determine his choice of action."[6] So Mackie's reconstructed morality looks something like Hare's version of noncognitivism.

This is not surprising. The subjectivists I want to consider are not, in Mackie's terms, "first order" moral skeptics.[7] They want to be able to make and "defend" moral claims. So given that the point of *belief* has so much to do with the acquisition of truth, morality – conceived as a set of false beliefs, or beliefs that can be neither true nor false – seems needlessly defective. The natural remedy is to reconceive, or remake it along expressivist lines. So, following this line of thought, I will treat all error theorists who think, like Mackie, that what lies behind and animates each sincere moral belief is a corresponding noncognitive attitude as potential noncognitivists.

But there is another aspect to typical subjectivist thought that is as essential as its noncognitivism. *It is the idea that an agent's moral judgments can and must, despite their noncognitive character, rationalize the moral choices that he makes in accordance with them.*[8] The objectivist agrees, at least when the moral judgments are reasonable. But the agreement is superficial. For we find two very different conceptions of how the rationalization comes about. The subjectivist of the kind I am imagining adopts a broadly instrumentalist (or derivitivist) theory of practical rationality that includes finding suitable means to one's determinate ends, suitable determinations of one's indeterminate ends, and suitable applications of one's chosen principles.[9] If, for example, an agent has a moral pro-attitude toward helping the poor and believes that something he can now do will relieve someone's poverty, he then has a perfectly objective instrumental *prima facie* reason to do it. And if he subscribes to the principle of keeping his promises, then he has a perfectly objective *prima facie* reason to keep this particular promise.[10]

Moral pro- and con-attitudes, whether directed to goals or to principles, thus have the power to rationalize choice. And this power is essential. For it is extremely uninviting to suppose that an agent's moral judgments – or on cognitivist accounts, an agent's reasonably correct moral judgments – could fail to provide reasons for action. For subjectivists, these reasons are provided only with the help of the noncognitive attitudes that moral judgments express. In this respect modern subjectivists have extended Hume's idea that morality produces motives only through its noncognitive content to the idea that it produces reasons only in the same way.[11]

This shows up in Bernard Williams's "Internal and External Reasons," where he includes "*dispositions of evaluation*" in an agent's "subjective motivational set" (*S*-set), the set from which all the agent's reasons for action derive through various acts of deliberating.[12] The evaluations that an agent's *S*-set disposes him to make presumably include the moral evaluations that he has internalized and made part of his way of life. But the practical reasons afforded by these moral evaluations do not derive from his recognizing them to be true. Even if he could come to see that they were false and others not flowing from his *S*-set true, he would not, on Williams's view, have any reason to follow the latter. For he would have no rational method of transferring the motivation present in his existing dispositions to the better ones.[13] Indeed he would be caught in such a bizarre dilemma (forced to accept his self-acknowledged false evaluations as reasons and unable to act on their true alternatives) that the overall position can be saved, I think, only by denying that the evaluations that flow from his motivational set can be rationally assessed as true or false. And, by our criterion, this not only makes Williams, at least in "Internal and External Reasons," a subjectivist about what must be an important class of moral evaluations, but also one who thinks that reasons follow from their noncognitive force.

Objectivists – at least of the kind I am considering – see things very differently. They agree that moral thought, at least when it is correct, provides reasons for action. But they think it does so only because of its cognitive content. What rationalizes or makes sense of the pursuit of a goal, they assert, is some way in which the goal in question seems *good*. And what rationalizes or makes sense of strict conformity to a principle is some way in which it seems that one can act *well* only by following it.

According to this kind of objectivism, practical rationality is not as different from theoretical rationality as the subjectivist supposes. Practical thought, like any other kind of thought, requires a subject matter. And for human beings the subject matter that distinguishes thought as practical is, in the first instance, human ends and action insofar as they are good or bad in themselves. The branch of practical thought that is usually called practical reasoning is the determination of how something desired as good can be obtained. In practical reasoning, thus defined, one does not critically examine the desired good to see if it is genuine or, if it is, to question whether something in the special circumstances forbids its pursuit.

These important questions belong to a more fundamental kind of practical thought that might be called ethical. Here one tries to determine what, given the circumstances, it would be good or bad in itself to do or to aim at. These questions are referred to larger ones: what kind of life it would be best to lead and what kind of person it would be best to be. The sense of "good" and "best" presupposed in this noncalculative form of practical thought is very general. In an Aristotelian version of objectivism these notions attach to actions, lives, and individuals as belonging to our biological species.

The object of this kind of thought is not in the first instance morality or prudence as these are commonly understood. For most people think that a human being may be prudent without being good, and many think that there is room for Nietzschean or Thrasymachean skepticism, according to which the best kind of human life might be immoral in one or another way. An objectivist of the kind I wish to defend sees practical thought as deploying a master set of noninstrumental evaluative notions: that of a good or bad human end, a good or bad human life, a good or bad human agent, and a good or bad human action. Practical reason is, on this view, the faculty that applies these fundamental evaluative concepts. If there is no truth to be found in their application, then there is no point to practical reason and no such thing as practical rationality.

I have already indicated a way in which subjectivists who hold an instrumentalist conception of practical rationality can be objectivists about practical reason and rationality. While they deny that ends, principles, and actions are objectively good or bad in themselves, they hold that a person acts rationally in trying to realize his own ends or maximize conformity to his own principles. On the plausible assumption that acting rationally is a natural and not merely conventional form of acting well (and acting irrationally a natural form of acting badly), and in the apparent absence of grounds for other not merely conventional forms, instrumental rationality thus becomes the one objective virtue and instrumental irrationality the one objective vice.[14] In contrast, my objectivist regards instrumental rationality, in this sense, as mere cleverness – something that may or may not be a good to its possessor or make her a better agent. If, on the other hand, someone's practical reasoning is necessarily constrained by appropriate ends and principles, and a sense of the fine and the shameful, then his cleverness constitutes a real virtue – part of his overall practical rationality.[15]

According to the objectivism I will defend, the primary job of practical reason is the correct evaluation of ends, actions, and qualities as good and bad in themselves. And what it is for something to be a reason for action follows from this. *On this view, a reason to act in a certain way is nothing more than something good in itself that it realizes or serves, or, short of that, something bad in itself that it avoids.* To the extent that one realizes or serves some such good one acts well. To the extent that one realizes or serves some such bad one acts badly. An objectivist therefore sees moral obligation as giving an agent reason to act only because, and only to the extent that, the agent will act well in discharging it or badly in neglecting it. Moral skepticism therefore comes to nothing more than the doubt that acting morally is a genuine form of acting well.[16] This is the kind of doubt with which moral philosophy began. And, on this view, it is the most important doubt for moral philosophy to resolve.

The subjectivist has a very different account of how moral judgment provides reasons for action. He obviously wishes to avoid bringing in any of these allegedly grounding concepts of actions, lives, ends, and ιgents as good or bad in themselves. He proposes instead an appeal to ϸasic and therefore cognitively uncriticizable *attitudes*. And this is what, ιs I shall now try to argue, he cannot do. As unpromising (or even "queer") as the objectivist picture may seem (and I shall be examining ϸome objections to it later), I wonder if it is not our only hope of retaining ϸhe idea of practical rationality that we want.

2

The problem lies, I think, in what the subjectivist must take these non-ϲognitive pro- and con-attitudes – these emotions, desires, aversions, ϸreferences, approvals, disapprovals, decisions of principle, and so on – to be.[17] So far as I can see, a reasonably up-to-date subjectivist would ϸresent them as functional states that, *inter alia,* tend to move an agent ιn various practical directions and therefore help explain why his having ϲertain beliefs and perceptions makes him choose, or feel inclined to ϲhoose, one course rather than another. They underlie his *tendencies* or *dispositions* to form and express feelings and to choose certain practical ιctions in the presence of various perceptions and beliefs. To say in the ιntended sense that someone has a pro-attitude toward world peace is ϸo say, among other things, that his psychological setup disposes him to ϸo that which he believes will make world peace more likely. And to ϸay that keeping his promises is one of his principles is to say that, ιmong other things, he is set up to do that which he sees as required ϸy the promises he has made.

But how can a noncognitive functional state whose central significance ιn this context is to help explain our tendency to act toward a certain ϸnd, or in accordance with a certain principle, *rationalize* our pursuit ϸf the end or our deference to the principle? How can the fact that we ιre set up to go in a certain direction make it (even *prima facie*) rational ϸo decide to go in that direction? How can it even contribute to its ϸationality? Even if a past decision is part of the cause of the psycho-ϸogical setup, there still remains the question whether to continue to ιbide by it. It is not, according to the view we are considering, the ϸpecifically moral aspect of the noncognitive attitude that gives *it* the ϸower to rationalize. Moral attitudes, whatever their special moral ear-ϸmarks, rationalize because they are dispositive functional states and not ϸecause they are moral. The underlying neo-Humean theory of ration-ϸalization is completely general. So in testing its plausibility we are free ϸo turn to nonmoral examples. Such examples also free us from the ϸdistracting worry whether a given functional-dispositional state ration-ϸalizes in a distinctively moral way. *The basic issue here is more funda-*

mental: whether pro- and con-attitudes conceived as functional states tho dispose us to act have any power to rationalize those acts.[18]

Suppose I am in a strange functional state that disposes me to tur. on radios that I see to be turned off. Given the perception that a radi in my vicinity is off, I try, all other things being equal, to get it turne. on. Does this state rationalize my choices? Told nothing more than this one may certainly doubt that it does. But in the case I am imagining this is all there is to the state. I do not turn the radios on in order t hear music or get news. It is not that I have an inordinate appetite fo entertainment or information. Indeed, I do not turn them on in orde to *hear* anything.[19] My disposition is, I am supposing, basic rather tha instrumental. In this respect it is like the much more familiar basi dispositions to do philosophy or listen to music.

I cannot see how this bizarre functional state in itself gives me eve a *prima facie* reason to turn on radios, even those I can see to be availabl for cost-free on-turning. It may help explain, causally, why I turn on particular radio, but it does not make the act sensible, except insofa as resisting the attendant disposition is painful and giving in pleasant But in that case it is not the present state that is the reason but th future prospect of relief.[20] Now at this point someone might object tha the instrumentalist subjectivist does not or need not regard basic non cognitive pro-attitudes as rationalizing their *objects,* but rather as ra tionalizing actions that are the *means* to them. So, of course, my od pro-attitude gives me no reason to turn on radios.

The picture here is of practical reason as a cognitively criticizabl mechanism for transferring motivation from the objects of attitudes t that which is "toward" them.[21] Since the ultimate objects are rationall uncriticizable, no reasons are produced for them – no reasons to hav those ends or principles or to do those things that are wanted or chose for their own sakes. But since it is possible to reason well or badly abou what will enable one to have or do those objects, reasons are produce for ancillary actions. So if, for example, one loves to listen to music – a contingent taste unassessable by reason – one's attitude does not give a reason actually to listen, but only, in the context of further intentions. to get a record down from the shelf and put it on the turntable.

I find this construction of instrumentalism, while possible, unattrac- tive. If my basic love of listening to music doesn't give me a reason tc listen, then it doesn't, I think, give me a reason to take the record down. The appeal of the view, apart from suggesting a line of escape from my argument, may come from conflating two distinct points: (a) that, on an instrumentalist view, a person's ultimate preferences are uncriticiz- able (except by reference to their compatibility), and (b) that a person's ultimate preferences do not mark off their objects as, given that he has those preferences, rationally appropriate for him. The first point is essential to instrumentalism, but the second does not follow from it. Nor is it a particularly plausible part of that view. But even if it were, my counterexample still works. For my basic noncognitive pro-attitude (conceived as a dispositive functional state) toward turning on radios seems not only to give me no reason to turn on radios but also no reason to take the necessary steps, such as plugging them in. Both seem equally senseless.[22]

But surely my disposition must strike me as odd, if only because it must strike others as odd. Perhaps then I regard it as an embarrassment and wish to be rid of it. And this might seem to make a difference that the subjectivist can exploit. It is not any old functional-dispositional state that rationalizes action, but only one that an agent is ready to stand behind or is at least not alienated from. A second-order endorsement (or the absence of a second-order rejection) is the missing ingredient.

It will be admitted, of course, that an unwelcome first-order attitude can provide the actual point of someone's doing something. A pyromaniac may hate it that he takes pleasure in setting fires, yet set another fire for that very pleasure. But perhaps the subjectivist will say that in such a case the pyromaniac's pleasure fails to give him a genuine reason to set the fire. For that he would need to approve it, or at least not disapprove it, at some higher level.

Now I think it very doubtful that a subjectivist can legitimately attach this significance to the existence or nonexistence of opposing higher-level attitudes. Here, as elsewhere, he is presupposing a significance that depends not on level but on content. An objectivist would take the pyromaniac's higher-level disapproval seriously because he would see in it an evaluation of the pleasure as bad – for example, perverse or shameful. And this would be relevant simply because someone who thinks that an attraction is bad in some such way can scarcely think that he will act well by giving in to it. So the higher-level disapproval shows that the *positive evaluation* that would normally attach to an action as pleasure-producing is canceled. The self-disapproving pyromaniac would not see the prospective pleasure as something that tends to make the torching choice-worthy. But the subjectivist, in rejecting the idea of choice-worthiness as the subject matter of practical reason, can see nothing in the higher-level disapproval except more complexly structured psychological *opposition,* and such opposition would seem to leave the lower-level attitude securely in place with its own proper force.

This point is perhaps worth emphasis. Higher-order attitudes pro and con lower-order attitudes will presumably be treated by the subjectivist as further noncognitive states of the same generic functional type – states grounding, among other things, dispositions to choose one thing rather than another in the face of certain percepts and beliefs. Rather than grounding dispositions to seek certain first-order ends such as pleasure or health, they ground dispositions to seek to be or not to be a person who has or acts toward those ends. What this picture does not explain, however, is the *authority* of the higher-level attitudes.

If the pyromaniac regards his fascination as sick and reprehensible, then he will not see it as giving him a reason to set fires. He may succumb to it as a temptation, but as he looks back on his choice he will not regard the pleasure he took as at least something positive to be credited to his choice. But on the subjectivist's view, it is hard to see why he shouldn't be consoled in just this way. For the subjectivist sees the pyromaniac as having two practical attitudes at odds with each other. His lower-level attraction moves him toward the act of pouring the kerosene, and his higher-level aversion moves him away from it. If he goes ahead he satisfies one of these attitudes, if he refrains he satisfies the other. There is therefore something to be said for and against each alternative. Without the thought that the appetite for fires is bad and therefore *without power to rationalize choice,* there seems no way to keep it from counting.[23]

Even setting this point aside, I cannot see how the subjectivist can insist that I *must* have some higher-level disapproval of my odd disposition to turn on radios. Perhaps, upbeat person that I am, I positively like my first-order attitude. But even if I do, this still doesn't seem to help rationalize my behavior. Turning on radios still seems perfectly senseless.

Perhaps a subjectivist should simply reject the example as too bizarre. According to this objection, we can make sense of someone's behavior as revealing pro- and con-attitudes only if the attitudes are ones we share to some considerable extent. So if my allegedly basic pro-attitude toward turning on radios is not rendered in one way or other familiar, it may have to be rejected. Attempts to undermine the neo-Humean theory by way of outlandish examples are thus doomed to failure.

Subjectivists may hope by means of some such argument to bring the actual implications of their theory of rational action more in line with those of objectivists who think that we make sense of an action only when we find something that seems good about it – some advantage, pleasure, boost to the ego, or the like. For the objectivist, the state disposing me to turn on radios fails for want of a point. Neither acts of turning on radios nor the state of affairs in which radios are on can intelligibly be seen as goods in themselves. But since the pro-attitude is stipulated to be basic, it cannot be rationalized by being referred to any further good, such as entertainment or knowledge.

Perhaps subjectivists can rule out motivational interpretations that are very strange. But it is difficult to see how. For I do not see how they could rule it out that I might actually engage in the odd behavior in question and that the best functional explanation would be that I had a correspondingly odd pro-attitude understood in their favorite functionalist terms. Indeed, I do not see how they could rule it out that someone might have basic pro-attitudes (conceived as such favored functional states) toward very many bizarre things (disease, pain, poverty, etc.). This is easiest to imagine in someone who desires to communicate reasonably truthfully,[24] is aware of her own eccentricity, has a reasonably accurate picture of the world, deliberates well about means toward and constituents of her largely bizarre ends, and acts accordingly. Such a person would be intelligible as desiring these strange things *if* desires were the things subjectivists took them to be.[25] And she would not be incapable of recognizing her odd ends and counterends for what they were, and for their oddity. A person does not have to be set up to strive for health to know what health is, a gloomy ascetic temperament does not rule out the knowledge of pleasure, perverse drives frequently recognize (indeed revel in) their own perversity, and so on. Such odd psychologies might, of course, be determined by an anomalous brain state. We might even come to recognize the neurological causal factors. But then the rest of us could imagine that we too might (unhappily) come to have these attitudes.

So I do not think that subjectivists can rule out the possibility of my radio case. Nor can they rule it out that, if I perform my odd routine cheerfully and without regret, my first-order attitude is unopposed by higher-order attitudes of disapproval. So they ought to see it as having the power to rationalize. But that is exactly what it seems to me not to have. It may in some way explain the fact that I turn on another radio, but it does not, in my view, go one step toward showing it to be sensible.

I have chosen a bizarre example to make my point as sharply as possible. But the argument applies, I think, with complete generality. No noncognitive, dispositive functional state of the kind under consideration can, by itself, make the contribution to rationalizing action that subjectivist instrumentalists suppose it to make. This is true even if the state points toward something good like pleasure or health. For pleasure or heath provide a point to their pursuit that does not consist in the fact that they are pursued. A noncognitive pro-attitude, conceived as a psychological state whose salient function is to dispose an agent to act, is just not the kind of thing that can rationalize. That I am psychologically set up to head in a certain way, cannot by itself rationalize my will's going along with the setup. For that I need the *thought* that the direction in which I am psychologically pointed leads to something good (either in act or result) or takes me away from something bad.

Someone might object that I am imputing to the subjectivist too narrow a conception of desire, aversion, preference, approval, disapproval, commitment, and the like – that I am focusing too exclusively on their role in explaining tendencies to *act*. These states may have other characteristic noncognitive features that better account for their rational force. Chief among these would be the pleasing light that positive attitudes, and the unflattering light that negative attitudes, cast on their objects.[26] These hedonic colors may also be lent to the idea of doing that which will make the pleasant or painful prospect more likely. And perhaps it is here that we find the rationalizing force of pro- and con-attitudes.

But how is this to be spelled out? It might be said that pleasure or pain in the prospect of having or doing something makes pleasure or pain in the reality more likely. So a person with a basic pro-attitude can expect pleasure in achieving his object and frustration in failing to achieve it, just as someone with a basic con-attitude can expect unpleasantness in getting his. And it is this that rationalizes pursuit or avoidance.

There are at least two problems that stand in the way of this solution. To the extent that a present basic pro-attitude rationalizes by virtue of a promised pleasure, then rationalization should also be present – and just as strong – in the case where the agent expects the pleasure but oddly lacks the present motivation. If I believe that I will get just as much pleasure from this piece of candy, which tempts me, as from that piece, which oddly does not, then it is hard to see, at least as far as gustatory pleasure is concerned (the typical reason for buying candy), how I could have more reason to choose the first. That I now find pleasure in the *thought* of eating or buying the first piece but not the second seems irrelevant. Or if I believe that I will feel as much psychic pain in violating a rule (in the sense of a possible rule) that I have deliberately not subscribed to (perhaps because I feel its pull on me is irrational) as in violating a rule that I have adopted, it is hard to see how the prospect of pain can give me more reason to observe the second than the first.

But there is an even more serious problem with supposing that a basic pro-attitude rationalizes by reference to the pleasure its fulfillment promises or the pain its frustration threatens. For the objects of many basic desires do not include the subject's pleasure or pain at all. Suppose, for example, I want to see famine ended in Ethiopia. I therefore take pleasure in the very idea of famine relief (and perhaps also in the idea of working toward it) and feel pained when politics stands in the way. But if I attach basic value to the end to famine, then it is the thought that doing such and such will help feed people that gives me my basic reason to do it – not the thought that doing it will bring me pleasure or save me pain. These might give me *additional* reasons, but they cannot be my basic ones.

It seems, moreover, that the pleasure one expects in getting (or working toward) what one basically wants and the displeasure in failing to get it are themselves rationally assessable. It generally *makes sense* to be pleased or frustrated in these circumstances. What more sensible thing to be pleased or displeased about? But surely the subjectivist will want to say that this good sense depends entirely on the attitude. It is rationally appropriate to be pleased at getting what one wants or displeased at failing to get it *because* one wants it. So, again, the pleasure or displeasure cannot provide the basic reason to pursue the object.

In any case, it seems to me a mistake to think of the concepts of pleasure and displeasure as purely descriptive, psychological concepts. To call an experience pleasant or unpleasant is already to bring it under an evaluative concept.[27] That is why purely psychological accounts of pleasure seem to leave it utterly mysterious *why* we should pursue the pleasant and shun the unpleasant. On one such account, a pleasant experience is, roughly speaking, one whose intrinsic character makes an agent want to prolong it. When we combine this with a subjectivist account of wanting, we conclude that a pleasant experience is one whose intrinsic character creates a functional state grounding, among other things, the disposition to prolong it. But why should anybody want to be in such a state? Suppose I tell you that if you start scratching your ear the experience will strongly dispose you to keep on scratching. Does this by itself give you reason to want to scratch? Conceived as a kind of psychological inertial force, pleasure takes on a somewhat sinister aspect. This is because the account leaves out the salient thing: that an agent wants to prolong a pleasant experience precisely because it is pleasant – because it feels good. Pleasantness is not merely that which brings about a prolonging disposition, it is what makes sense of it.

So far, I have urged that neither the dispositional nor the hedonic aspect of pro-attitudes can provide what we want in the way of reasons for action. The subjectivist might respond by taking a somewhat different tack. He might claim that noncognitive attitudes may be formed in a rational or irrational way, and that *rationally formed* attitudes can provide reasons. This might, of course, mark a considerable retreat from the familiar subjectivist position that *any* pro- or con-attitude can give a reason for action. But if the requirements of rational attitude formation turn out to be weak, the retreat may be limited. If the requirement were merely one of reasonably adequate information, then many noncognitive attitudes would provide reasons. If, on the other hand, the requirement were as demanding as Kant's generalization test, far fewer would qualify.

My response to this strategy is to deny that the kinds of noncognitive states the subjectivist means to be talking about can be made rational or irrational by the way in which they are formed. This is because I cannot see how, in the absence of objective prior standards for evaluating ends or actions as good or bad in themselves, a state disposing one to act can be any more rationally criticizable than a state disposing one to sneeze. Any factor (like having a perfectly regular character or being caused by true rather than false beliefs or valid rather than invalid reasoning) could be just as true of sneezing as acting. It's true that the disposition to sneeze can be irresistible, while dispositions to turn on radios or read philosophy papers, typically are not. But space for the voluntary seems to me in itself devoid of rational significance unless it is in the service of an agent's values.

It is often said that an attitude formed in light of true beliefs has more power to rationalize than one formed in error. And while there is something right about this, it is not something that the subjectivist can obviously make use of. Suppose, liking canned chop suey and believing it to be a typical Chinese dish, I am moved to seek more Chinese food, and in particular to try out my local Szechwan restaurant (where my bland tastes are likely to be shocked). Such examples are often taken to show the need for some informational constraint on rational desire and preference.

But surely what is ultimately bad about my motivation here is not that it is based on false belief, but that it is a very uncertain guide to food that I will find good-tasting. To the objectivist, information is relevant because without it I won't be pointed in the direction of good things, like innocent pleasure. But the subjectivist must reject the cognitive claim that pleasure is a good. For him, liking something is just another noncognitive pro-attitude. And his account of pleasure, in omitting the idea that what is liked is found experientially good, removes the sting from the criticism of my motivation to patronize the Szechwan restaurant. For if we ask the subjectivist why it's too bad that my desire for Chinese food was rooted in error, he can say only that it is because the functional state in which my desire consists will probably extinguish itself once I get real Chinese food. But this seems to miss the point. Why should cultivating a functional state that will extinguish itself be less rational than cultivating one that won't? What is so important about resistance to extinguishability?

One might agree that an informational constraint is not enough, but think that adding some other conditions will do the trick. Hare, for example, has argued that if we are going to give ourselves certain kinds of prescriptions, we must give ourselves perfectly universal ones.[28] (He thinks that moral language is analytically cut out to express just such universal commands or norms.) Yet why should someone who sees himself as choosing in a cognitive void where there is no prior truth about good or bad action, insist on giving himself universal commands? Of course *we* wish to give ourselves such commands, because we think there is a subject matter of good and bad action that, like all genuine subject matters, is to some considerable extent regular. Since we think that certain *kinds* of actions are bad — for example, sticking one's hand in a fire – we tell ourselves not to do actions *of that kind*.[29] But if we thought there were no such knowledge of good and bad action to be had, I do not see why we should want our self-prescriptions, or some set of them, to be universal. And it would make no difference if there were, which I think there is not, some special vocabulary exclusively dedicated to making such commands. Why should we use this vocabulary? Or why shouldn't we subvert it?

Of course it may be said, plausibly, that we need to cooperate and coordinate, and so need to find common norms.[30] But I do not see it as a point of subjectivists. For on their reading, this need must consist in something like the fact that with the cooperation bred of common norms we will get more of what our pro-attitudes – either independent, norm-permitted ones (e.g., my morally innocuous pro-attitude toward turning on radios) or new, norm-generated ones – point us toward. And if the preceding argument is correct, we have no reason to care about *this*. I suspect that the theoretical appeal to the importance of coordination works because we think that without common norms (or serviceable and just common norms) life with each other would be pretty bad – indecent, painful, suspiciously on guard, and too short to be meaningful. We need good common norms to live well together. If human beings didn't need to be thus coordinated, the selection of such norms would be pointless. Since they do need it, norms that make it possible, especially those that help us make the most of our human potential, have something objective in their favor.

3

But am I really claiming that desire and preference can't rationalize choice? Not at all. I am claiming instead that the subjectivist's account of desire is impoverished, leaving out precisely that element of desire that does the rationalizing. I have been careful not to raise the question whether my odd functional state is in fact a basic desire to turn on radios. That is, I have been careful not to raise the question whether the existence of a noncognitive dispositive functional state of the kind subjectivists would take desire to be is sufficient for desire. I have not raised it because I am not at all sure of the answer. What I feel sure of, and what I have argued, is that, whether or not the mere functional state is sufficient, it cannot ground reasons for action. What does that is another element (of necessity) typically present in basic desire, namely, some kind of evaluation of the desired object as good – for example, pleasant, interesting, advantageous, stature-enhancing, as decent. I am not saying, however, that desire is in general nothing more than positive evaluation. In some cases we would not speak of desire if the implicit positive evaluation did not provoke or were not accompanied by some kind of appetite that prods the will toward the object for the good that it seems to offer.[31] What seems amiss in standard neo-Humean subjectivism is the way it runs together the ideas of explanation and rationalization. The noncognitive attitude present in many cases of desire may sometimes be part of the causal account of why the desired object is pursued, but the pursuit is rationalized not by the attitude but by the apparent value that attaches to its object or to the pursuit of it. Without the appearance of the value, the attraction would be empty, as it is in my counterexample.

It might seem, however, that the view that desires and preferences rationalize only because of the value judgments they involve can scarcely be correct. Aren't there rationalizing desires and preferences that point to no real or apparent good? To answer this question I need to make some distinctions between different types of goods to be attained in action and the different types of rationalization that they involve. First and most obviously, an action may promote goods that speak in its favor *as a good action* and therefore one that ought to be done. It is in this way that considerations of health and pleasure typically support visits to the supermarket and doctor. A good such as this – one that in the circumstances tends to make its pursuit good – may be called *choice-worthy*. Some choice-worthy goods are in particular circumstances *conclusive* – they provide decisive reasons for acts that would bring them about – while others are *contributory*, providing reasons that may be overruled. Choice-worthy goods give full-fledged reasons for action. So here we may speak of rationalization in the fullest sense.

But we must also consider goods that are *not* choice-worthy. These are goods that do not ever, or at least in some particular circumstances, speak in favor of their pursuit. A plausible example is the pyromaniac's pleasure in watching a building burn. The pleasure of parent–child incest is another. No right-minded person who is capable of these pleasures would suppose that he had good reason to seek them. They are clearly not goods in the full-fledged sense, for they do not contribute to the goodness of action or life. Yet, contra Plato and Aristotle, these pleasures do seem genuine. We can imagine a prospect that has nothing in it to attract us but that, oddly, sets up in us a strong impulse to seek it. But the prospect of these pleasures, to one who can experience them, is not like that. They present such a person with a real temptation. It therefore seems plausible to regard them as some kind of experiential good. We might say that they *make intelligible,* but do not rationalize, a choice to pursue them.

Perhaps we should also briefly consider goods that are *merely apparent.* These are objects that appear good in some choice-worthy or non-choice-worthy way, but are not. Some present simple illusions, like vanilla, which smells delicious but tastes bad. Some involve symbolic connections with real goods, as in the case of someone who anxiously avoids stepping on cracks. Other cases are less psychiatric. At some emotional level all of us invest certain minor successes and failures with a significance they really lack. Such "goods" and "evils" cannot, when they fail to take us in, rationalize pursuit or avoidance. Nor can they make pursuit or avoidance intelligible, at least not in the way in which the special class of goods and evils just considered can. Yet to the extent that we are taken in, they can, in a sense, do both.

With these distinctions in mind, we may consider cases in which an inclination unadorned by any prospect of objective value might seem to rationalize or make sense of action. What about whims, for example? Can't people have whims to do that which serves not even an apparent value? I think we should not assume that they can. Philosophers' examples might, in this regard, be misleading. What we would do on whim is usually something whose value (or apparent value) can either be discerned or made the object of intelligent speculation. In some cases only the timing or means is capricious. One flies off to London for a haircut. One gets up at midnight, dresses, and goes out to seek pie à la mode. Anscombe's example of wanting to touch a spot on the wall or Davidson's example of wanting to drink a can of paint may not, I think, be all that typical. But they do count, so what can I say about them?

It seems to me a mistake to say that your wanting to drink paint counts as a whim only if there is no answer to the question what you see in it. We often, of course, put off that question by saying that it's just a whim. But putting off the question and there being no answer are different.

The smooth and creamy paint might, after all, look delicious. And the allure of this appearance might be reinforced by a perverse curiosity. You might wonder what the paint tastes like.[32] The whim might have other explanations. It might be an odd desire to do something really, if trivially, original – to break the fetters of convention if only in some silly way. Adolescents are famous for this kind of desire, and there are outbreaks of adolescence even in the apparently mature. It might have a related but even more primitive significance. Children are continually performing actions that might at first glance seem pointless but that may well aim at the demonstration, however symbolically, of what they wish to be unlimited powers of independent agency in the physical world. They empty out drawers, pick up sticks and run them along fences, skim stones on the water, and so forth. Given the vicissitudes of the human predicament, all this makes a certain sense. And adult whims might sometimes be like this. They might reflect a curiously displaced need to demonstrate the power to act outside our rutted ways.

There are other diagnoses of very odd whims that have a more exclusively psychiatric significance. The odd desire to drink the paint might focus some unconscious need of rebellion. Perhaps you drank some paint as a child and were severely reprimanded by your frightened parents. Or perhaps the drinking has a hidden sexual significance. Doesn't everything?

I think we are very reluctant to rest content with the whim as a state that merely disposes you to drink the paint. This is because we wish to treat the whimsical urge as at least marginally intelligible. And to do this we need to see the whim as pointing to something that might be or at least seem attractive from your point of view. If we can find no such value – if there is nothing that you see or seem to see, consciously or unconsciously, in drinking the paint – then however effective its causal influence, the dispositive state gives no support to your choice to drink the paint.[33] Perhaps we should treat such a disposition as a limiting and degenerate case of desire. Or perhaps we should treat it as merely resembling genuine desire and preference. But on either view, I am inclined to see whims as no exception to the general rule that desires can rationalize only by reference to the conscious or unconscious evaluation that is (typically) at their core.

But here another, perhaps more difficult, objection arises. Even if some kind of value judgment is always, or almost always, present in desire and preference, a desire or preference is often, as I have indicated, more than a value judgment. We may see the availability of certain good things but be unmoved by them, and if we are unmoved then surely we may lack at least a certain kind of reason to seek them. Some good things that leave us cold (e.g., our future health) still give us strong reasons for action, but in other cases an absence of felt attraction may affect our reasons. Both X and Y may offer the prospect of equally witty and intelligent conversation, but you may be much more attracted to the kind offered by X than to the kind offered by Y. Surely then you have much better reason to spend time with X.

According to this objection, at least some good things are rationally pursued only to the extent that they attract us. But then contrary to what I have been urging, our being moved must itself be part of our reason for pursuing them. If mere pro-attitudes are not sufficient to rationalize, they are in some cases necessary. But if so, then surely some doubt is thrown on the claim that they lack any kind of rationalizing force.

I cannot here try to consider all the kinds of cases in which reasons might seem to depend partly on attraction as well as on expected value. In cases that involve personal taste, such as taste in company, the significance of attraction might lie in its containing a foretaste of pleasure or satisfaction. Attraction to people, or for that matter to novels and paintings, promises a kind of personal pleasure in our future interactions with them. And that anticipated pleasure can give a perfectly respectable reason to seek them out.

Someone might object that such pleasure is nothing more than the consciousness of having gotten that to which one's noncognitive pro-attitude propelled one. If so, the pleasure would be a mere logical reflection of the earlier pro-attitude. But this picture seems wrong to me, although it may be encouraged by an easily missed ambiguity. An inclination might, in one sense, be said to be satisfied when its object is obtained. But it is a sad truth that this kind of technical satisfaction may lack any element of real pleasure or fulfillment. The anticipated pleasure that is part of ordinary attractions to people or art is, however, real pleasure. It might, as a matter of empirical fact, be pleasure partly caused by the previous inclination. And if it were, the existence of the inclination could be evidence for it. But even so, it is only the pleasure itself that makes sense of acting on the inclination.

There are many other cases in which we would have to look closely to see whether noncognitive attitudes were themselves providing reasons. Let me just mention one of the most puzzling. Two people may be equally supportive, kind, admirable, beautiful, pleasant to be with, and so on, but we may, because of some other difference of quality that in no way reflects well or badly on either, be fonder of the first than of the second. And when this happens most of us suppose, at least in practice, that we have greater reason to pursue the good of the first.

Why? Someone might say that the greater fondness is simply constituted by a stronger altruistic disposition. But I think the answer must be more complicated. Human beings can thrive only in various private connections of concern and identification – as with family, friends, colleagues, or acquaintances. Some of these connections are thrust upon us, but many are not. And some people simply fit better than others into the highly personal sympathetic world we have already created for ourselves. These people belong in our story and so their good is especially important to us. I cannot claim to fully understand the nature and operation of such judgments of importance. But I feel it would be a travesty to interpret them as nothing more than functionally grounded tendencies to go for some people's good over that of others.

4

My claim has been that noncognitive analyses of desire, preference, commitment, and the like cannot capture their reason-giving force. In depriving pro-attitudes of any evaluative thought, noncognitivism reduces them to functional states that, upon reflection, may show what we will do under certain conditions but not what we should do. Practical rationality, I have argued, requires a subject matter of the values to be achieved or realized in human action – a subject matter that only cognitivism can provide.

Even if I am right about this, there remains room for evaluative skepticism, which if correct, might remove actions altogether from the authority of reason. As noted earlier, Mackie and others have argued that certain evaluative judgments, while genuinely cognitive, cannot be true. There are in evaluative thought the concepts appropriate to a genuine subject matter, but the world does not, indeed cannot, furnish the corresponding properties and relations. Evaluative facts would be unacceptably queer in two ways: first, in providing motivation – in effect exercising a power over the will – and second, in providing reasons for action that do not depend on subjective inclinations. Mackie objects to the idea of motivation or rationalization (he speaks of the latter as prescriptive authority) that is not wholly explained in a neo-Humean manner. Like Hume, he thinks that genuine thought is by itself powerless to cause or make good sense of action.

Now I think an objectivist should be more or less unperturbed by the part of the argument that concerns motivation. To say that someone recognizes a value (say a moral value) that can be achieved in action is not to say that the recognition must be a spur to his will. To recognize that justice or decency requires us to do something is, in my view, to recognize that we shall act badly if we do not do it. The connection with motivation is indirect and conditional. To be unresponsive to the genuine badness of an action is to have a will that is unmoved by a conclusive reason for not doing something – a will that is, to that extent, irrational or unreasonable. If we were more reasonable, we would care more about the quality of our actions. And since most of us are not wholly unreasonable, we do to some extent care. That, I think, is what the motivational force of unconditioned value comes to. And that does not require value facts to have any "queer" power over the will. It requires instead a conception of the will as the part of human reason whose function is to choose for the best.

The other skeptical argument questions whether objective value could have rational authority. Let's begin with the objective value of ends. Why, it will be asked, should we care whether or not our ends have objective value? Why is such a concern rational? If, as I think, practical rationality chiefly consists in correctness of thought about human good and evil, a concern is rational just in case reason determines that it is a good concern for us to have. And if a concern belongs to real human virtue – the qualities that make us and our actions good – then it can hardly be denied that it is a good concern. So, on this conception of rationality, to show that we have reason to be concerned with the objective goodness of our ends it is enough to show that such concern is essential to human excellence. And while showing this may present many difficulties, it does not seem to be ruled out in advance as an unacceptably "queer" task. Something similar can be said about reasons given by the objective goodness of action itself. If, as I think, the reasons for doing an action just *are* the good-making features that it has either in itself[34] or that it derives from the good ends it serves, then the mystery of how the goodness of action can provide reasons seems to disappear. Mackie's problem depends on supposing that we start with an idea of practical rationalization or prescriptive authority that is prior to our idea of good and bad action. If that were true, and if goodness weren't in some way reducible to rationality, then we could raise the question, and so make it seem mysterious, how the mere recognition of something good about an action could give us a reason to do it. But I am skeptical of this prior conception of reasons, and therefore suspect that the real mystery that Mackie and others are circling around is how actions can have objective goodness in the first place. They suggest that the problem is how, if there were such a thing, it could give reasons. But, if I am right, the problem must be more fundamental.

In much of contemporary moral thought, rationality seems to be regarded as the basic virtue of action or motivation, one that grounds all the other virtues. This, I have been arguing, is a mistake. Practical rationality is a virtue of a very special kind. But it is not special in being the most fundamental merit of action or motivation. It is special by being the virtue *of* reason as it thinks about human good. A virtue isn't a virtue because it's rational to have it. A good action isn't good because it's rational to do. On my view, the only proper ground for claiming that a quality is rational to have or an action rational to do is that the quality or action is, on the whole, good. It is human good and bad that stand at the center of practical thought and not any independent ideas of rationality or reasons for action. Indeed, even in its proper place as a quality of practical reason, rationality is validated only by the fact that it is the *excellence,* that is, the *good* condition of practical thought. Even here the notion of good has the primary say.

But note that I have not here argued against the possibility that practical rationality makes demands on practical thought that should be understood antirealistically as requirements on the *construction* of a picture of human good and bad.[35] On such a constructivist view, we might have to begin practical philosophy with a critique of practical reason as it thinks about human good. Here I have been arguing only that the primary questions are not what it is rational or irrational, but what it is good or bad to be, seek, or do – that is, protesting the confusion that arises when the notions of rationality escape their proper place and become themselves the primary objects of practical thought.

Notes

1 J. L. Mackie, *Ethics: Inventing Right and Wrong* (Harmondsworth, England: Penguin Books, 1977), ch. 1. Mackie's introduction of "objectivism" (p. 15) as the view asserting that (intrinsic or categorical) moral values are "part of the fabric of the world" could at first suggest evaluative realism. And if so, subjectivism, which is introduced as the denial of objectivism, would be compatible with moral antirealism of the truth-admitting kind. But as Mackie gives content to the notions in the following discussion, it turns out that his subjectivism denies that moral evaluations of the relevant kind *can* be true. So the salient contrast turns out, after all, to be over truth.

2 The nub of the theory is clearly presented in Charles Stevenson, "The Emotive Meaning of Ethical Terms," reprinted in *Facts and Values* (New Haven: Yale University Press, 1963), pp. 10–31.

3 R. M. Hare, *The Language of Morals* (Oxford: Clarendon Press, 1952), pp. 69ff.

4 Mackie, *Ethics,* p. 35.

5 Mackie admits that certain claims of instrumental value can be true, but only because those claims are naturalistically reducible (ibid., pp. 50–9). Judg-

ments of instrumental value that presuppose judgments of intrinsic value must be just as badly off as the judgments of intrinsic value they presuppose.

6 Ibid., p. 106. The emphasis on 'allowed' is mine.

7 Ibid., p. 16.

8 This use of 'rationalize' is an old one that completely lacks the modern psychoanalytical idea of finding false but self-comforting reasons for what one does or feels.

9 For an example of a very broad conception of instrumental rationality see Bernard Williams's "sub-Humean model" in "Internal and External Reasons," *Moral Luck* (Cambridge: Cambridge University Press, 1981), p. 102.

10 David Gauthier, who certainly holds that moral preferences and self-prescriptions give instrumental reasons, also accepts a kind of reason applying to certain important moral situations that cannot be counted as instrumental. On his view, if it is instrumentally rational for me to be disposed to honor personally advantageous agreements (as it might be if enough people could see through any insincerity) then I thereby have a special moral reason to comply with the terms of one that I made with the honorable intention to comply. See *Morals by Agreement* (Oxford: Clarendon Press, 1988), ch. 6. Of course, if I retain my earlier honorable disposition then I have, in my broad sense, an instrumental reason that flows simply from that. For complying instantiates a pattern of behavior that I personally value. This is a typical subjectivist reason that presumably remains present in Gauthier's system. But, given the other parts of his complex view, I would still have a reason even if I had lost the disposition. This latter reason does not fall under the present discussion of subjectivism.

11 Stevenson was, admittedly, strangely silent about reasons for action. But Hare makes it clear that moral reasons come from preferences, which he certainly regards as noncognitive dispositions to choose, exposed to facts and logic. See, for example, R. M. Hare, "Another's Sorrow," in *Moral Thinking: Its Levels, Methods and Points* (Oxford: Clarendon Press, 1981), pp. 104–5. Something similar holds, I believe, for Mackie, although his discussion of reasons in ch. 3 of *Ethics* makes things a bit tricky. He there distinguishes three categories of reasons or requirements: merely external and conventional ones (like the rules of a game or social practice seen from the outside), those that spuriously purport to bind categorically and intrinsically, and those that, depending on an agent's own attitudes, bind hypothetically. The latter might be called natural reasons. And it is these that, on his account, a properly "made" morality would give the agent whose morality it was.

12 Bernard Williams, *Moral Luck* (Cambridge: Cambridge University Press 1981), pp. 101–13.

13 According to Williams, deliberation is always *from* existing motivations, bringing *them* to bear upon the possibilities of action. See *Moral Luck*, p. 109.

14 Note however that some subjectivists have backed away from this theo-

retically odd hybrid – either, like Richard Brandt (in *A Theory of the Good and the Right* [Oxford: Clarendon Press, 1979], pp. 10–16) by adopting a descriptive account of practical rationality that does not require it to be regarded as an objective excellence or, like Allan Gibbard (in *Wise Choices, Apt Feelings: A Theory of Normative Judgment* [Cambridge, Mass.: Harvard University Press, 1990], e.g. pp. 45–6) by applying an expressivist-prescriptivist account of rationality itself. For Gibbard there is no fact of the matter whether maximizing the satisfaction of one's preferences is rational, and argument can break down about fundamental questions of rationality in much the way Stevenson thought it could about fundamental questions of goodness. That such argument breaks down as rarely as it does (that there is mutual argumentative influence over even such basic matters) is a result of the fact that we have been biologically selected to be conversationally cooperative creatures. While I suspect that the substance of my antisubjectivist argument could be applied to these authors, I must postpone the complexities of that discussion for another occasion.

15 A review and minor elaboration of this quasi-Aristotelian vocabulary might be helpful. *Practical reason* is the generic faculty of which *practical thought* is the characteristic generic activity and practical rationality the generic virtue. *Practical reasoning* (i.e., *instrumental reasoning* in my broad sense) and *ethical thought* are the two main species of practical thought. If practical reasoning does not presuppose a correct evaluation of the ultimate suitability, whether in general or in the circumstances, of the desired goal or chosen principle, then its virtue is *cleverness*. For the neo-Humean, cleverness exhausts the virtue of practical rationality. If practical reasoning does rest on a correct assessment of the present suitability of the goal or principle, its virtue is, let us say, *real instrumental rationality*. And *wisdom* is the virtue of ethical thought. *Prudence* and so-called *moral goodness* are conspicuous but controversial candidate characteristics that wise ethical thought may deem the chief virtues of action.

16 Alternatively, that the so-called moral virtues are real human virtues.

17 I use the term 'noncognitive attitude' here broadly to cover all of these mental states. A decision of principle includes a pro-attitude toward the standard of behavior one has chosen and a con-attitude toward behavior that violates the standard.

18 My skepticism about this and related matters is shared by others in recent ethics, perhaps most thoroughly by E. J. Bond in *Reason and Value* (Cambridge: Cambridge University Press, 1983), esp. p. 56.

19 There are several variations on what the object of my pro-attitude might be: (a) the *act* of my turning on radios, (b) the *state of affairs* in which I turn them on, (c) the state of affairs in which they are turned on (by anyone), etc. For my purposes it doesn't matter how my state is conceived, although I will tend to use (a) for simplicity. Note that on all three interpretations, hearing something coming from a radio may be evidence that the object of

my pro-attitude has been achieved, even though hearing something is not in itself the object of that attitude.

20 We will be coming back to the question of rationalization by the prospect of pleasure or pain.

21 This possible objection, to whose subtleties I may not be doing complete justice in the following remarks, was raised by Joseph Raz.

22 Since turning on radios and taking the steps thereto (e.g., plugging them in) seem to me to stand or fall together, I will continue, for reasons of economy, to apply the question of rationalization to the former. If the reader disagrees, he may, whenever I speak of turning radios on, substitute some mere means to that end.

23 In case one is tempted to think that the force of the higher-order attitude derives from its taking account of the lower-order attitude, note that in typical cases the lower-order attitude also takes account of the higher. That is, it remains in existence despite its recognition of opposition from above. Even though the pyromaniac may hate himself, he still wants to set fires.

24 That and other familiar pro-attitudes (about communication and learning) are certainly necessary when so many others are lacking.

25 It is sometimes said that some interpretations of preferences, conceived along subjectivist lines, will simply be ineligible on the ground that neither we nor the subject will be able to justify the interpretation. E.g., that while the subject might, on perhaps frivolous aesthetic grounds, prefer normal oranges to red apples but green apples to normal oranges, she could not, for example, be understood to prefer normal oranges to red apples on high shelves but red apples on low shelves to normal oranges (at least not unless there was something more to the story – highness and lowness of shelf could simply not be an ultimate object of attachment). But again this seems to confuse the question of causation and justification. If preference is conceived along subjectivist lines as a preevaluative functional state causing one to feel and act in various ways under various conditions of belief and recognition, then there is no reason why this odd "preference" could not emerge. Indeed, the person might be bemused by her own highly unusual internal psychological economy. And to say this in no way implies that either the subject or anyone else is infallible about her "preferences" – we might come to see that it was something other than shelf height after all.

26 Here I return to a point that I explicitly put aside earlier. It may be more plausible with respect to desire and aversion than to commitment to principle. But it might also be thought that commitments (whether moral or personal) lend the prospect of their fulfillment a pleasing aspect of self-consistency and personal integrity, and their violation a disturbing aspect of incoherence and failure.

27 In *The Varieties of Goodness* (London: Routledge and Kegan Paul, 1963), pp. 63–85, Georg Henrik von Wright argued that pleasure is not merely good but is itself a kind of goodness.

28 Hare, *Moral Thinking,* pp. 1–24.

29 With perhaps an escape clause for very unusual situations.

30 A point stressed by Gibbard, *Wise Choices;* see, e.g., pp. 26–7.

31 This kind of motivating state – one that has influence *on* the will – must be distinguished from dispositive states *of* the will, forms of executive rationality (steadfastness, courage, prudence, etc.) or irrationality (distraction, cowardice, weakness, etc.) that enable or disable the will in its natural pursuit of the best course of action. On my anti-Humean conception, which has been greatly influenced by discussion with Philippa Foot and by Thomas Nagel's *The Possibility of Altruism* (Oxford: Clarendon Press, 1970), ch. 5, much rational human action comes about without the influence of motivational pushes and pulls. I see that it is a convenient time to get needed service for my car and I simply proceed to do it. All that is required is the perception of overall advantage (the safety and comfort of having a well-running car and the convenience of present service) and a reasonable degree of executive rationality. In such a case we may also speak of my desire for the advantage, but this desire is nothing more than my will's healthy recognition of its availability. Such a desire is not something the will *takes account of* in determining a rational choice.

32 When one is curious about something, the knowledge one seeks seems interesting and perhaps even important, even if at some level one knows that it is not. And it is this impression of significance (or urgency) that makes the curious behavior intelligible.

33 Unless of course it is unpleasant to resist.

34 Either directly (e.g., its pleasantness) or because of the virtue or right principles to which it conforms (e.g., its fidelity).

35 The evaluative realist thinks that every constraint on practical reason has the function of maximizing the likelihood of correspondence to a transcendent, and therefore possibly unapproachable, reality. The constructivist, in the perhaps special sense I have in mind, thinks that there are constraints that, coming from the nature of practical thought itself, must set limits on where the truth can lie and how much truth there can be. The method of reflective equilibrium as discussed by John Rawls in *A Theory of Justice* can be given a constructivist interpretation not as the best method for descrying an external or internal moral reality, but as the only systematically acceptable method of moral thought, the applications of which determine, insofar as such determination is possible, where the moral truth is to lie. Such constructivism might come, however, in two varieties. In one, the rational constraints would lead first to the identification of actions and ends as rational and therefore good. In the other, the constraints would be from the very start constraints on rational thought about the good. It is only the first kind of constructivism that I have been attacking.

4

Can a Humean be moderate?

JOHN BROOME

1. Moderate and extreme Humeans

A Humean believes that no preference can be irrational. It is not irrational to prefer the destruction of the world to the scratching of your little finger, or your own acknowledged lesser good to your greater.

An extreme Humean leaves it at that. A moderate Humean adds a qualification. Although, she says, no individual preference can be irrational on its own, some patterns of preferences are irrational; there are some sets of preferences that a person cannot rationally have together. Rationality, then, does constrain preferences to some extent.

Moderate Humeans recognize two types of constraint on preferences. One, recognized by David Hume himself, is the connection between preferences about means and preferences about ends. Suppose an action *A* will bring about one result, and *B* will bring about another, and you prefer the result of *A* to the result of *B*, and you have no intrinsic preference between *A* and *B*. Then it is irrational for you to prefer *B* to *A*.

The other type of constraint is consistency. Moderate Humeans recognize various consistency constraints. One is transitivity: If you prefer an alternative *A* to *B* and you prefer *B* to *C*, then it is irrational for you to prefer *C* to *A*. There are other consistency constraints too. *Decision theory* is generally taken to encapsulate them. Decision theory consists of a number of axioms defined on a person's preferences. Transitivity is one, and there are several others. Each is intended to specify a consistency constraint on the preferences.[1] A rational person is supposed to have preferences that conform to the axioms.

These two types of constraint on preferences really come down to one: Consistency constraints subsume means–ends constraints. Indeed,

This essay was presented as a paper at the conference on "Value, Welfare, and Morality" at Bowling Green State University in April 1990. My thanks to Donald Hubin and Philip Pettit for their helpful comments, and also to many of the participants at the conference. I should particularly like to mention Simon Blackburn, David Copp, David Gauthier, Gilbert Harman, and Edward McClennen.

the main point of decision theory is to make clear the nature of means-ends constraints. It specifies precisely what is the connection that ra tionality requires between a person's preferences about ends and he preferences about means. I described this connection just now, but m description was rough and inadequate. For one thing, I mentioned a "intrinsic preference" without explaining precisely what that means And secondly, things are almost never as straightforward as I implied You can almost never be sure what the result of an action will be; i might be one thing or something else. Furthermore, the result, whateve it is, will almost certainly be complex. It will almost certainly not be th achievement of some simple end that you want; it will have some feature you want and others you do not want. Forming a rational preferenc between two actions will therefore be a matter of weighing some good against some bads and of weighing the probabilities of some result against the probabilities of others. In this, you will be working bacl from preferences about ends to preferences about means, but the proces will not be a simple one. Decision theory is intended to describe hov a rational person conducts the complex weighing-up that is involved.

The moderate Humean view, then, comes down to this. You may rationally, have any preferences, provided only that they are consisten with each other. And what consistency requires is spelled out in decisio theory.

The extreme Humean view is unappealing. It implies that reasor leaves people unequipped for life. For one thing, it leaves them a de fenseless prey to Dutch bookmakers, money pump operators, and such like sharks.[2] But that is the tip of the iceberg. The extreme Humear view implies that reason cannot even guide people through the mos ordinary business of living. When you want a hot shower rather than ǎ cold one, rationality will not even direct you to prefer to turn on the hot tap rather than the cold one.

A moderate Humean wants to avoid this conclusion. She wants to allow reason a role in guiding people through life; she wants it to helɲ determine and modify their preferences. But she still wants the ultimate basis of preferences to be unconstrained by rationality. Her idea is thaᵗ some preferences can give rational grounds for others. When a persor has some particular preferences, reason will require her to have other particular preferences. So the person may have a reason to have some particular preference – and if she does not have it she will be irrationa – but the reason will always derive from her other preferences. A mod erate Humean respects the fundamental Humean principle that a reasor must always derive from a preference. But she supplements this principle with some requirements of "instrumental rationality," as they are ofter called. When a person has preferences that are inconsistent with one another, reason requires her to alter some of them, though it does not determine which. The moderate Humean thinks of decision theory as (in Richard Jeffrey's words) "a sort of Logic of Decision which individuals can use as an anvil against which to form and reform parts of their preference rankings."[3]

But in this paper, I shall argue that the moderate Humean position cannot really be held apart from the extreme one. I hope this will diminish the appeal of the Humean view as a whole.

2. A difficulty facing moderate Humeans

The details of decision theory are not universally agreed upon. Different versions have different axioms. But they do all agree at least on the axiom of transitivity. Transitivity is a minimal condition of consistency; if consistency does not require transitivity, it requires nothing.[4] So we may take it that all moderate Humeans believe rationality requires a person to have transitive preferences. A Humean who does not insist on transitivity is extreme, not moderate. For this reason, I shall concentrate on the transitivity axiom in my argument.

It is an interesting question how a moderate Humean might defend the requirement of transitivity. But that is not the subject of this essay. I am not concerned with the grounds of the moderate Humean's view, but with whether her view is significantly different from an extreme Humean's.

Think about this example. Maurice, given a choice between going mountaineering in the Alps and visiting Rome, prefers to visit Rome. Given a choice between staying at home and visiting Rome, he prefers to stay at home. But given a choice between staying at home and going mountaineering, he prefers to go mountaineering. Maurice's preferences seem to be intransitive, and therefore irrational. But Maurice has a defense against the charge of irrationality. In describing his preferences, I distinguished only three alternatives: mountaineering, Rome, and home. Maurice, however, distinguishes four:

H_r: Maurice stays at home, when going to Rome was the only other alternative available.
R: Maurice goes to Rome
M: Maurice goes mountaineering
H_m: Maurice stays at home, when mountaineering was the only other alternative available.

He points out that transitivity requires him to prefer H_r to M, given that he prefers H_r to R and R to M. But the choice between staying at home and going mountaineering is a choice between H_m and M, and nothing requires him to prefer H_m to M. Maurice's defense, then, is to refine the individuation of the alternatives.

It does not matter for my purposes what Maurice would choose if offered a choice between all three alternatives at once. But it adds a complication worth mentioning. Suppose he would choose Rome. This suggests he does not prefer home to Rome, though I said earlier he did. So it suggests that Maurice's preferences vary according to what alternatives are on offer.[5] This, like intransitivity, is contrary to the consistency conditions of decision theory. But Maurice can obviously handle this problem in the way he handles intransitivity. He can individuate the alternatives taking account of the choice on offer. He can treat H_r – staying at home when Rome was the only other alternative – as different from staying at home when both Rome and mountaineering were available. This will allow him to arrange his preferences in one big, unvarying order.[6]

Since the same device of fine individuation works for both problems, I shall continue to concentrate on apparent intransitivity. Maurice's defense is available to anyone who has apparently intransitive preferences. Suppose someone, faced with a choice between A and B, prefers A. Faced with a choice between B and C, she prefers B. And faced with a choice between C and A, she prefers C. These preferences seem intransitive. But let us individuate the alternatives more finely. Let us write 'A when B was the only other alternative available' as A_b, 'B when A was the only other alternative available' as B_a, and so on. Then this person prefers A_b to B_a, B_c to C_b, and C_a to A_c. And there is no intransitivity in that. It seems, then, that the requirement of transitivity is really no constraint on preferences at all. Fine individuation of alternatives will always allow a person to wriggle out of it.

That is an overstatement, however. Transitivity *does* constrain Maurice's preferences, despite his fine individuation. Because Maurice prefers H_r to R, and R to M, transitivity requires him to prefer H_r to M. This is a constraint on his preferences. To be sure, H_r and M is not a pair of alternatives that Maurice could ever have a *choice* between. If he was to have a choice between staying at home and going mountaineering, that would be a choice between H_m and M, not between H_r and M. Let us call one of a person's preferences "practical" if it is a preference between a pair of alternatives that the person could have a choice between. Then Maurice's preference for M over H_m is practical, but his preference for H_r over M is nonpractical.

The truth about fine individuation is this. It means that a person's *practical* preferences are not constrained by transitivity. Transitivity im-

oses constraints on a person's complete pattern of preferences, in-
luding her nonpractical ones. But her practical preferences form only
part of her complete pattern of preferences, and these practical pref-
rences can have any pattern at all without conflicting with transitivity.

For the sake of precision, I need to say more about this conclusion.
'ake the person who prefers A to B, B to C and C to A. Under fine
idividuation, she prefers A_b to B_a, B_c to C_b and C_a to A_c. Consequently,
ransitivity requires this of her: either she prefers A_b to A_c, or she prefers
B_c to B_a, or she prefers C_a to C_b.[7] So if my claim that transitivity does
ot constrain practical preferences is to be correct, then a preference
etween A_b and A_c, and other preferences of that sort, cannot be counted
s practical preferences. Yet at first sight, it may look as if the person
aight actually have a choice between A_b and A_c. She might be presented
rith this choice: Would you like to have a choice between A and B, or
lternatively a choice between A and C? If she decides in advance that,
rhichever of these alternatives she chooses, she will choose A in her
ubsequent choice, then this may look like a choice between A_b and A_c
between A when the only other alternative available was B, and A
rhen the only other alternative available was C. But this is not really
plausible interpretation of the choice the person is faced with, since
he alternatives available to her really include all of A, B and C. In any
ase, I do not mean A_b and A_c to be understood in such a way that the
hoice I described counts as a choice between A_b and A_c. Nor is there
ny other way a person could have a choice between A_b and A_c. So a
reference between these alternatives is indeed nonpractical. Consider
Iaurice again. Implicitly I have been assuming he is indifferent between
R_h and R_m, and also between M_r and M_h. Transitivity consequently
equires him to prefer H_r to H_m. And this is a nonpractical preference;
Iaurice could not have a choice between H_r and H_m.

Transitivity, then, does not constrain practical preferences. And it
urns out that none of the other consistency axioms of decision theory
onstrains practical preferences either. All of them yield to similar treat-
1ent by fine individuation. This point is well recognized when applied
o the "sure-thing principle," the central axiom of Leonard Savage's
lecision theory.[8] It has often been argued that rational people may have
references that do not conform to the sure-thing principle;[9] many plau-
ible examples have been produced of preferences that seem rational
ut do not conform. But it has also been recognized for a long time that
hese examples can be brought into conformity with the sure-thing prin-
iple by means of fine individuation, just as Maurice's preferences can
e brought into conformity with transitivity. Fine individuation, then,
an be used to defend the sure-thing principle against the examples.

However, it has been recognized for just as long that fine individuati(
leaves the sure-thing principle "empty" (which seems to make it a
unsatisfactory defense).[10] What this means, precisely, is that the sur
thing principle does not constrain practical preferences. I do not nec
to go into the details here.[11] The conclusion is that, because of th
possibility of fine individuation, the consistency conditions on prefe
ences do not actually constrain practical preferences at all.

This is a difficulty for the moderate Humean. She wants rationali
to guide a person in her practical affairs. But she supposes that rationali
is nothing more than consistency. And it now turns out that in practic
matters – between alternatives the person might have a choice betwee
– consistency does not guide her preferences at all.

3. A non-Humean response

What inference should we draw?

Let us consider whether Maurice is really rational. Has he real
justified his preferences by insisting on fine individuation? Certainly n(
by that alone. If we thought him irrational to begin with, because of h
apparently intransitive preferences, we shall not revise our view ju
because he points out the formal possibility of individuating the alter
natives more finely. He will have to do better than that. Having distin
guished H_r from H_m, Maurice puts them in different places in h
preference ordering. And this is what he will have to justify to us. H
will have to justify his preference between H_r and H_m.

Perhaps he can. Suppose the explanation of Maurice's preferences
this. He is frightened of heights, and therefore he would rather go t
Rome than go mountaineering. Sightseeing bores him, however, an
therefore he would rather stay at home than go to Rome. But Mauric
sees a choice of staying at home and undertaking a mountaineering tri
as a test of his courage. He believes it would be cowardly to stay a
home, and that is why he prefers to go mountaineering. (He consider
it cultured, not cowardly, to visit Rome.)

Is this enough to show that Maurice is rational? I do not know, bu
I do know what it depends on. If we are to conclude that Maurice
rational, what shall we have to say? We shall have to say he has produce(
an adequate reason – that one involves cowardice and the other do(
not – for placing H_m and H_r in different positions in his preferenc
ordering. If, on the other hand, we are to conclude Maurice is irrationa
we shall have to deny this. We shall have to say that he has not show
a difference between these two alternatives that is adequate to justi1

is having a preference between them. Maurice is rational if and only he is justified in having a preference between H_r and H_m.

Presumably we shall only take the view that Maurice is irrational if e think he is wrong about cowardice, and that actually there is nothing owardly about staying at home rather than mountaineering. Even if e think this, it would perhaps be unfair to condemn Maurice for irrationality. His preferences stem from a false belief, and there may be othing irrational about having a false belief. His preferences will be nistaken in a sense, and we might perhaps say they are objectively rational, but not subjectively so. Furthermore, even if Maurice is wrong bout cowardice, we might concede that his preferences are not irraional in any sense. They will not be irrational if, because of his incorrect iews about cowardice, staying at home will make Maurice feel bad, or it will make him lose his self-respect. Preserving his self-respect and voiding a bad feeling are presumably themselves sufficient reasons to ustify Maurice's preference for mountaineering, quite apart from the natter of actual cowardice.

But in any case, Maurice definitely cannot be convicted of irrationality xcept on the grounds that he is not justified in having a preference etween H_r and H_m. So long as it is rational for these two alternatives o occupy different places in his preference ordering, Maurice's preferences are rational. To convict him, we shall have to insist on a *rational rinciple of indifference.* We shall have to say that the difference between I_r and H_m is not enough to justify Maurice in having a preference etween the two: Rationality requires him to be indifferent between hese alternatives. This rational principle, together with transitivity, is nough to bring home the charge. The rational principle requires him o be indifferent between H_r and H_m, and transitivity requires him to refer H_r to M. Together they require him to prefer H_m to M, and ctually he does not.

It might be thought that a quite different argument can show Maurice's references to be irrational. It seems that a money pump could be perated against Maurice, however he may choose to individuate the lternatives he faces. Suppose he has a ticket to Rome. You offer to xchange it, at a small price, for a certificate to stay at home. Maurice ill accept. Next you offer to exchange the certificate, at a small price, or a mountaineering ticket. Again Maurice will accept. Finally, you ffer to exchange the mountaineering ticket for a ticket to Rome, at a mall price. Once more, Maurice will accept. So he will end up where e started, but poorer. If Maurice can be milked in this way, that is opularly supposed to show his preferences are irrational.

A money-pump argument may or may not be effective in general;

that is no concern of mine in this essay. But it certainly cannot succee
in this case. For one thing, it proves too much. If it works at all, it w
work even if Maurice is right about cowardice, and fully justified in h
preferences. But then his preferences are rational, so there must I
something wrong with an argument that concludes they are not. And
is plain what is wrong with it. Suppose Maurice is right. And suppo
he is now planning to stay at home, having turned down a trip to Rom
Then, if you come and offer him a mountaineering trip, you are by th
very action making him worse off. You are, in effect, moving him fro
H_r to H_m, which is justifiably lower in his preference ordering. Mauri
is willing to buy his way out of this position. It is as though you sto
his shirt and then sold it back to him. Rationality cannot protect Mauri
from that sort of sharp practice. So the fact that he is susceptible to
is no evidence of irrationality. The money-pump argument fail
therefore.

To generalize the conclusion I have drawn: There must be such thin
as rational principles of indifference; rationality must determine th
some differences between alternatives are not enough to justify a pers
in preferring one of the alternatives to the other. There must be the
rational principles because, if there were not, then rationality would n
constrain practical preferences at all. Consistency conditions on the
own (transitivity and the other conditions too) cannot constrain then
Rational principles of indifference are needed to give consistency a gr
on practical preferences. These rational principles must be concrete ar
specific, not formal and general like the consistency conditions. The
must determine which specific differences between alternatives are n
enough to justify a preference.

I am happy with the conclusion that there must be rational principl
of indifference. Here is a plausible one, for instance: The mere diffe
ence that in H_r Maurice has not rejected a mountaineering trip where
in H_m he has is not enough to justify Maurice in having a preferen
between H_r and H_m. If he is to be justified in his preference, there mu
be some other difference as well. The other difference Maurice clain
is that one involves cowardice and the other does not. If Maurice cann
establish the existence of a justifying difference like this, then his clai
to rationality fails. In general, it is not rational to have a preferen
between two alternatives unless they differ in some good or ba
respect.[12]

The view that there are concrete rational principles of indifference
not at all unusual. Some ethical theories imply very restrictive principle
Jeremy Bentham, for instance, seems to have believed that pleasure
the only good, and pain the only bad. Consequently, he would presun

ably have believed that if each of two alternatives gives everybody the same pleasure, and everybody the same pain, it is not rational to have a preference between the two.

4. A Humean response

A Humean, on the other hand, cannot be happy with the conclusion that there must be rational principles of indifference. Such a principle denies that certain specific preferences are rational, which is something a Humean cannot allow. She cannot allow that rationality should ever deny a person the right to prefer anything to anything else, provided this preference is consistent with her other preferences.

A Humean must therefore pay the penalty. She will have to accept that rationality does not constrain practical preferences. At first it looked as though the consistency conditions of rationality constrained them. But actually consistency conditions cannot do so without the support of rational principles of indifference. And those the Humean cannot acknowledge.

How severe is this penalty? Does it completely undermine the position of a moderate Humean? An extreme Humean believes that rationality allows a person to have any pattern of preferences whatsoever. Even a moderate Humean, we now see, has to believe that rationality allows a person to have any pattern of *practical* preferences whatsoever. So can she hold herself apart from an extreme Humean?

She can certainly defend her position. In discussing Maurice, I have been considering the constraints of rationality from the outside. I asked whether we could or could not convict Maurice of irrationality. The answer is that, if we are Humeans, we never could. Nor could we convict anyone else, however strange her practical preferences. But a moderate Humean is not interested in rationality as a criterion for condemning people from the outside. She is interested in it as a guide that helps people conduct their own affairs. So am I, of course.[13] The talk about condemnation was only metaphorical. I had in mind that Maurice could ask himself, "Am I really being rational in preferring H_r to H_m?" He could ask himself, that is, whether some rational principle of indifference requires him to be indifferent between H_r and H_m. If he concludes this preference is not rational, then he should adjust his practical preferences. This is how I see rationality guiding him.

But the moderate Humean will point out that when a person is beating out her preferences on the anvil of decision theory, she has access to all of her preferences, not just the practical ones. The consistency conditions certainly constrain all of her preferences taken together. The person may consistently have any pattern of practical preferences at all, but the pattern of her practical preferences will, by consistency, determine a lot about her nonpractical preferences. Maurice, given the practical preferences I ascribed to him, must prefer H_r to H_m, for instance, or else M_h to M_r or R_m to R_h. Conversely, if he has none of these nonpractical preferences, he ought not to have the practical preferences he does have. If he finds himself in this position, reason requires him to change some of his preferences, and he may change one of his practical ones. In this way, the consistency constraints, applied to the whole pattern of a person's preferences, may have practical effects. If a person has a particular pattern of nonpractical preferences, then the consistency conditions will limit the practical preferences she may have.

According to a moderate Humean, then, reason may guide Maurice in forming his practical preferences as follows. Maurice can ask himself, "Do I really prefer H_r to H_m?" If he concludes he does not, reason will bring him to adjust his practical preferences. From the inside, Maurice does not need to ask whether it is rational for him to prefer H_r to H_m; no rational principle of indifference is needed. He only needs to ask whether *actually* he has this preference. If he does not, that gives him a reason to alter his practical preferences.

In general, then, people's preferences are not entirely unconstrained by consistency, and the requirement of consistency may have an influence even over their practical preferences. On the basis of their nonpractical preferences, consistency may help to determine the pattern of their practical preferences. So the moderate Humean has a position that is still distinct from the extreme one. That is her argument.

5. The nature and epistemology of preferences

I shall try to show that this argument is unsuccessful. A moderate Humean requires practical preferences to be determined or influenced by reasoning based on nonpractical preferences. One possible response would be to deny that nonpractical preferences even exist: If you cannot have a choice, one might say, you cannot have a preference either. If that were so, the moderate Humean would obviously have no leg to stand on. But I think this response goes too far; I think people do, indeed, have nonpractical preferences. My own response, put roughly, will be that, although nonpractical preferences exist, they do not have enough independent substance to serve the moderate Humean's purposes. We are not able to reason from them to determine practical preferences in the way the moderate Humean requires.

What, exactly, *is* it for someone to have a nonpractical preference? If someone prefers *A* to *B*, where *A* and *B* are such that she could not have a choice between them, what does this amount to? We shall see that nonpractical preferences raise special difficulties. But let us start by asking the same question about preferences in general. What is it for a person to have a preference?

The notion of preference is a flexible one, and several different concepts may be collected under the same name. But for our purposes we can restrict the concept by at least two conditions that preferences must satisfy. The first is that a person must be able to know what his preferences are. Conceivably, we may have some concept of preference (a Freudian one, perhaps) such that we cannot know what our preferences are. But if so, this is not the concept a moderate Humean has in mind. A moderate Humean requires a person to be able to reason on the basis of his preferences to determine what other preferences he should have. Consequently, since preferences play a part in the person's reasoning, he must be able to know what they are. Our account of preferences must therefore supply a satisfactory explanation of how a person can come to know his preferences. This condition, I think, provides the best approach to the concept of preference. By asking, How can we know what our preferences are? we can discover what our concept of preference is.

The second condition we require preferences to meet is this. It must genuinely be a condition of rationality that a person's preferences should conform to the consistency requirements of decision theory – transitivity in particular. We must understand preferences in such a way that this is so. I think this condition provides a serious constraint on the notion of preferences, because if preferences are conceived in some popular ways (as feelings, for instance) it is very hard to see why rationality should require them to be transitive. I suspect this condition could contribute extra support to the conclusions of this essay. However, I shall actually make no use of it. The reason is that I could not use it without first settling what are the grounds of the consistency conditions, and I do not want to do that. This essay, as I said earlier, is not about the grounds of the moderate Humean's position. It is about whether the moderate Humean has a distinct position at all. So I shall rely on the first condition only.

Some sort of functionalist account of preference seems very natural – an account like this: A person prefers *A* to *B* if and only if she is in a state that typically has the following functional role . . . [14] Then the typical functional role has to be specified. For practical preferences, this is not difficult. At least a major part of the typical functional role of practical preference is to dispose the person to choose the preferred alternative, if she has a choice.

This account provides a ready explanation of how we can know our own practical preferences and other people's. There is a canonical test of a person's preferences: to see what she chooses when she has a choice.[15] In principle, a person can apply this test to herself, to discover her own preferences. In practice, however, the canonical test is often not available, because the subject never faces the appropriate choice. And in any case, even when it is available, it is often not the most natural test for a person to apply to herself. But I shall not discuss alternative tests now; it will be most convenient to postpone that discussion to Section 8.

A functionalist account may be available for nonpractical preferences too. But for a nonpractical preference, a disposition to choose A over B can be no part of its functional role, because the person cannot have a choice between A and B.[16] So what is the functional role of a nonpractical preference? More generally: what is it to have a nonpractical preference? To answer, let us examine the ways we may come to know what our nonpractical preferences are.

6. Knowing preferences by perception

How does a person come to know her nonpractical preferences? I can think of three answers that might be given.

First of all, preferences might be directly perceptible in some way. Start with practical preferences. These can be independently identified by their tendency to determine choices. But suppose they can also be perceived directly. Suppose, for instance, that if I scratch statements expressing two propositions in the dust around my feet, and then stand between them, I generally find myself leaning toward the one I prefer. Or suppose that, when I call to mind two propositions, I generally feel drawn to the one I prefer. Then we might take it as part of the functional role of a preference to bring about these leanings or feelings. We should certainly do so if the leanings or feelings themselves played a causal role in my choices. Suppose that when I am faced with a choice, I contemplate the alternatives, feel drawn to one of them, and as a result of that, make my choice. Then bringing about the feeling would undoubtedly count as one of the functional roles that identify a preference.

And now suppose I have these leanings or feelings even between alternatives that I could not have a choice between. Then the leanings or feelings might well be enough to determine that I have a preference

tween the alternatives, and what my preference is. This would be a
npractical preference. I would have a nonpractical preference be-
veen *A* and *B,* then, if and only if I am in a state that typically brings
about that I lean toward *A* when I stand between expressions of *A*
id *B* scratched in the dust, or I feel drawn toward *A* when I contemplate
and *B.* So this could be what it is for me to have a nonpractical
reference. And it would explain how I can come to know my non-
ractical preferences. I have only to observe my leanings or feelings.

If human nature was like this, the moderate Humean's argument
ould be sound. Maurice would be able to consult his leanings or feelings
determine whether or not he prefers H_r to H_m, or M_h to M_r, or R_m
R_h. If he finds he does not, rationality would require him to make
adjustment in his preferences.

We could draw the same conclusion if a person had perceptible de-
ees of desire, rather than perceptible preferences. In this case the
gument happens to be more complicated, but the complication makes
o significant difference. Suppose I could call an alternative to mind,
id by an inward glance determine how much I desire it. Suppose this
orks in such a way that, of two alternatives, I prefer the one an inward
ance reveals I desire more. (So for practical preferences, which can
e independently identified functionally, my inward glances reveal my
isposition to choose.) Then I could determine my preferences by inward
lances. The complication is this. If, for each proposition, there is a
egree to which I desire it, then my preferences are *necessarily* transitive.
the degree to which I desire *A* is greater than the degree to which I
esire *B,* and the degree to which I desire *B* is greater than the degree
which I desire *C,* then necessarily the degree to which I desire *A* is
reater than the degree to which I desire *C.* So, if I prefer *A* to *B,* and
prefer *B* to *C,* then necessarily I prefer *A* to *C.* Consequently, there
an be no conflict on grounds of transitivity between my practical pref-
rences and my nonpractical preferences. If Maurice has the practical
references I described for him, then *it follows* that he prefers H_r to
I_m, or M_h to M_r, or R_m to R_h. Transitivity is automatically satisfied; it
not a rational constraint on preferences. Nevertheless, there will still
e *other* rational constraints on preferences: namely, the other consist-
ncy axioms of decision theory. It will still be possible for practical and
onpractical preferences to conflict through these other axioms. The
oderate Humean's position will still be intact, therefore; rationality
ay still constrain practical preferences.

The situation I have been describing is possible. It is possible that
onpractical preferences (or degrees of desire) might have been directly
erceptible, by means of a feeling or in some other way. Certainly, it

is not possible that a preference might have *been* a feeling.[17] But no
practical preferences might have been *perceptible* by feelings, in the wa
I have described. If this had been so, the moderate Humean's positio
would have been distinct from the extreme Humean's. But, although
might have been so, actually it is not. So my case against the modera
Humean is only a contingent one. She would have been right if huma
nature had been different from how it actually is. But, as it happen
she is wrong.

As it happens, nonpractical preferences are not perceptible by fee
ings. The only evidence I have for this claim is common experience. N
doubt there are some feelings associated with preference. Some desire
at least, are accompanied by feelings, such as the violent passion c
resentment mentioned by Hume.[18] Perhaps a person can sometime
perceive his preferences between two simple objects of desire by noticin
which he feels drawn to. But we are talking about nonpractical pre
erences. These are inevitably between complex alternatives, which
requires some intellectual effort to understand. It is implausible that
preference between such things could be detected by a feeling. I sha
later be suggesting it could be detected by a process that might b
mistaken for this one: by weighing up the considerations in favor of th
two alternatives. A person who is weighing up considerations cou
believe herself to be judging which alternative she feels drawn to. Th
processes are actually quite different, because one is a rational proces
and the other is not. But they may be superficially similar, and that ma
help to conceal the implausibility of the view that nonpractical prefe
ences are perceived by feelings.

But in any case, I do not think much evidence is needed for my clain
It is widely accepted, even by Humeans.[19] Hume himself accepted tha
many desires cannot be perceived by feelings. Desires, he thought, ar
often *calm* passions "which, tho' they be real passions, produce littl
emotion in the mind, and are more known by their effects than by th
immediate feeling or sensation."[20]

7. Knowing preferences by their effects

That was the first way a person might come to know her nonpractic̆
preferences. In the remark of his I quoted just now, Hume suggests
second way: She might come to know them by their effects. He mean
their outward effects, as opposed to the feelings they generate.

What are these effects? The primary outward effect of a *practic̆
preference is to dispose a person to make a particular choice. A nor
practical preference is more remote from choice, but we can identify a

outward effect nonetheless. If a person has a particular nonpractical preference, that limits the practical preferences it is rational for her to have. Since people are typically rational, it therefore typically limits the practical preferences a person will have. Consequently, a person's nonpractical preferences can be identified through her practical preferences. From Maurice's practical preferences as I described them, we can tell something about his nonpractical preferences. At least if he is rational, either he prefers H_r to H_m, or R_m to R_h, or M_h to M_r.

This way of identifying a person's nonpractical preferences is available to other people besides the person. For someone else to identify my nonpractical preferences by this method, she must first identify my practical preferences by somehow discovering my dispositions to choose, and then work back from there. But Hume had in mind that I would come to know my *own* preferences in this way: from their effects. So I, too, would work back from my own dispositions to choose. How would I know what I am disposed to choose? Here it seems I have an advantage over other people. I can simply present myself with the choice in my imagination, and see what I decide.

Applying Hume's idea to nonpractical preferences raises a difficulty, though. The idea is that a person's practical preferences are causally affected by her nonpractical preferences, and the effects identify these nonpractical preferences. This gives us a functionalist conception of nonpractical preferences: I have a particular nonpractical preference if and only if I am in a state that typically brings it about that my practical preferences have such-and-such a pattern. But why should we believe that there is such a state? Why should we think that practical preferences are in any way affected by a separate range of preferences, the nonpractical ones? Usually, when we identify a mental state by means of its causal functions, we have separate grounds for thinking there is some causal process, of the appropriate sort, at work. A practical preference, for instance, is that mental state, whatever it is, that causes a person to make the choices she makes. And we have grounds for thinking that *some* mental state causes her choices. Consequently, although a practical preference is *identified* by the person's dispositions to choose, we have grounds for thinking it *is* actually something distinct from the disposition. But if a nonpractical preference is to be identified on the basis of practical preferences, we have no grounds for thinking that the state of having a nonpractical preference will be anything different from the state of having practical preferences of a particular form.

A moderate Humean needs a person to be able to reason from her nonpractical preferences to determine, on grounds of consistency, what her practical preferences should be. For this to be possible, her non-

practical preferences must be distinct from her practical preference
Yet I have just said that, if she identifies her nonpractical preferenc
by Hume's method, there is no reason to think they will be distinc
Furthermore, even if they are distinct, they will have been identifie
from her practical preferences on the assumption that her practical pre
erences are consistent with her nonpractical ones. So they could n
possibly give her a reason, on grounds of consistency, for having practic
preferences that are different from the ones she actually has.

This difficulty is only the reflection of a much more fundament
objection: a general objection to Hume's suggestion that a passion migl
be known by its effects. Hume, given the part he assigned to passio
in rationality, ought never to have made this suggestion. He clear
meant that a person might know of one of *her own* passions by its effect
And the effects he had in mind were, evidently, the person's acting
accordance with the passion – doing things that satisfy it. But accordi
to his own theory, these effects are mostly produced by the applicatio
of reason to the passion. We cast our view on every side, he though
and discover by reasoning whatever objects are connected to the origin
object of our passion by the relation of cause and effect. So "accordir
as our reasoning varies, our actions receive a subsequent variation."
The effects of a passion on action, then, are mediated by reason. .
person, however, cannot apply reason in this way unless she alread
knows what her passion is. Therefore, she cannot know her passion b
its effects.

The moderate Humean is *particularly* concerned to explain how rea
son can guide action. Consequently, she particularly cannot use th
account of how we come to know our preferences.

8. Knowing preferences by evaluation

Now the third answer to the question of how a person can come to kno
her nonpractical preferences. This is the one I favor. Suppose A and
are a pair of alternatives that a person could not have a choice betweer
so her preference between them is nonpractical. I suggest that she fin
out which she prefers by estimating the relative goodness of A and B
I suggest that she prefers A to B if and only if she estimates the goodne
of A higher than she estimates the goodness of B.

This is expressed a little awkwardly. It would be easier to say: a persc
prefers A to B if and only if she believes A to be better than B. B
David Lewis has shown that cannot be correct.[22] Lewis believes that h
demonstration refutes the opinions of an anti-Humean. In another pa
per, however, I have argued it does less than that.[23] It shows only tha

an anti-Humean (and everyone else, too) has to be careful about how she expresses her opinions. Preferences do not go by *beliefs* in degrees of good, but by *expectations* of good, and expectations cannot be identified with beliefs. My proposal about the nature of nonpractical preferences, set out more strictly, is that a person prefers A to B (where this preference is nonpractical) if and only if A has, according to her probabilities, the greater expectation of good. But the details of the formulation make no difference to this essay. And although an expectation is not a belief, it is compounded out of beliefs. It is in the same ballpark as a belief.

So the epistemology of nonpractical preferences, on my account, is like the epistemology of beliefs. The process of finding out what one's preferences are is like the process of finding out what one's beliefs are. In particular, it is like other matters of estimation: Would you say this plate or that teacup is the older? Would you estimate the standard of living to be higher in Germany or Sweden? To answer such questions, you consider the evidence and arguments available to you, and weigh them up as best you can. Maurice, similarly, must ask himself: Is H_r really better than H_m? This will require him to consider whether or not H_m really involves cowardice, whether cowardice is really bad, or whether perhaps the two alternatives are equally good, and so on. All of this is a matter of rational evaluation.

I described this process of evaluation as a process of finding out what one's preference is. But sometimes it may be a process of acquiring a new preference. I doubt there is a definite line between these things. It depends how long and complicated the process is. If it is quick and obvious, it will count as finding out; otherwise as acquisition. But even if it is acquisition, it is finding out too. At the same time as you acquire your new preference, you will come to know what it is. Either way, evaluation brings one to a knowledge of one's preference.

There is an obvious objection to my proposal. Suppose a person estimates the goodness of A higher than the goodness of B. Then she ought to prefer A to B; reason requires her to prefer A to B. I am proposing, also, that actually she does prefer A to B. So I am eliding the distinction between having a preference and its being the case that one ought to have a preference. Obviously, though, there is a genuine distinction here. Suppose a person estimates the goodness of not smoking higher than the goodness of smoking. Then she ought to prefer not to smoke. But she may actually prefer to smoke. That is plainly a possibility.

But I am not denying the distinction in general. I am only denying it for nonpractical preferences. I have said already that a practical preference, such as a preference for smoking, can be identified by its typical functional role, which is to bring about a disposition to choose. Typically, a person who is disposed to smoke prefers to smoke. And it is plain how she, and the rest of us, know what her preference is; the epistemology of this type of preference is clear. Then, separately, it may also happen that she estimates the goodness of not smoking above the goodness of smoking. That can clearly happen with a practical preference. But with a nonpractical preference, the difference is that we have no plausible epistemology that can bring a person to know what her preference is between alternatives, independently of how she estimates the goodness of the alternatives.

That is the argument I offer for my proposal. Estimating goodness is, so far as I can see, the only way we have of coming to know our nonpractical preferences. I have considered two alternatives theories. Each, if it had been successful, would have supported a different concept of preference from the one I am proposing. But neither is successful. Consequently, we have to conclude that to have a nonpractical preference for A over B is nothing other than to estimate A as better than B.

There is something more to say about smoking. To be sure, a person who is disposed to smoke prefers to smoke. But if she estimates the goodness of not smoking above the goodness of smoking, it would also be natural to say she prefers not to smoke. She prefers not to smoke but, because of weakness of will, she smokes. Evidently we have two different senses of 'prefer' here. We have at least two concepts of preference. According to one – call it the evaluative concept – a person prefers A to B if and only if she estimates the goodness of A above the goodness of B. According to the other – functionalist – concept, she prefers A to B if and only if she is in a state that typically leads her to choose A rather than B. The functionalist concept applies only to practical preferences. But the evaluative concept applies to both practical and nonpractical preferences. That is to say, the concept I propose for nonpractical preferences can be applied to practical preferences too.

Furthermore, the epistemology of the functionalist concept is problematic even for practical preferences. Its canonical test is to see what a person chooses when she has a choice. This test can be carried out for smoking, but for many of her practical preferences a person will not actually have a choice. What can be done then? There is the possibility I discussed earlier that a preference can be perceived, by a feeling or in some other way. But even for most practical preferences, that is not generally plausible. In practice, the best test for other people to use is generally to ask the person herself what she prefers. And the best test for her is to present herself with a choice in imagination, and see what she chooses. Now, how does that work? Normally, by her running through the deliberation she would run through if faced with the choice, and forming an estimate of the goodness of the alternatives. She can then conclude she prefers the one she estimates higher.

As a way of finding out what the person is disposed to choose, this test is unreliable. If she were actually to have the choice, she might choose the alternative that comes lower in her estimation, because of weakness of will. If she understands her own psychology well, she might be able to allow for her own weakness in making the imaginative test. But that allowance may well seem inappropriate to her if she is trying to find out her own preference. The process I have described, without the allowance, is an unreliable test for the functionalist concept of preference, but it is a perfectly reliable test for the evaluative concept. And when it comes to a preference that is remote from choice, the latter seems the more natural concept to apply. So I think that, because of epistemological difficulties, we very often apply the evaluative concept rather than the functionalist one, even for practical preferences.

Compare the conclusions of this section with Mark Johnston's comments, in "Dispositional Theories of Value," on David Lewis's paper with the same title.[24] Lewis considers how a person can come to know whether a thing is valuable. His proposal is that the person should place herself in a position of full imaginative acquaintance with that thing, and see whether she values it. By this he means: whether she desires to desire it. Lewis's dispositional theory of value implies that, if she does, the thing is indeed valuable. Reason plays a part in the process Lewis describes: It is involved in bringing the person into full imaginative acquaintance with the object. But once she has achieved this position, it is simply a causal matter – nothing to do with reason – whether or not she finds herself valuing the object.[25] Johnston, however, argues that it is unreasonable to exclude reason at this point. I am, in effect, adding an argument to Johnston's. How is the person to know that she values, or desires to desire, the object? I can think of no plausible answer if this state of desiring to desire is one that simply imposes itself on the person causally, as Lewis supposes. Most plausibly, a person will find out whether she desires to desire something by considering whether she has reason to desire to desire it. This is a matter of estimating its goodness, and it is a rational process. If she judges it good, that both makes it the case that she desires to desire it, and gives her the knowledge that she does so. Indeed, it makes it the case that she desires it, in the evaluative sense of "desire." So desiring to desire is no different from desiring in this sense.

9. Conclusion

In Section 4, I suggested that reason might guide Maurice like this. He can ask himself whether it is rational for him to prefer H_r to H_m. He might conclude it is not, because some rational principle requires him to be indifferent between these two alternatives. If so, he ought to change his practical preferences, because they are inconsistent with indifference between H_r and H_m. But this story does not suit a moderate Humean. According to a moderate Humean, Maurice has only to ask himself whether he *does* prefer H_r to H_m. He need not ask whether it is rational for him to do so. If he does not have this preference, then he ought to change his preferences in some way, and he may be brought to change his practical ones. Rationality guides him that way.

But I have now argued in Section 8, on epistemological grounds, that Maurice cannot really distinguish the question of whether he does have the preference from the question of whether it is rational for him to have it. To discover whether he has the preference, he will have to estimate the relative goodness of H_r and H_m, and this is the same process as considering whether it is rational to prefer H_r to H_m. Maurice cannot avoid considering the rationality of this preference. Unless he does, rationality can give him no guidance at all.

This by itself may not worry a moderate Humean. A moderate Humean, unlike an extreme Humean, accepts that preferences can be irrational. So she may be willing to concede that Maurice will have to consider whether it is rational to prefer H_r to H_m. But she must insist that, if a preference is irrational, that can only be because it is inconsistent with other preferences. I said that Maurice, in considering whether it is rational to prefer H_r to H_m, will have to consider the relative goodness of H_r and H_m. The moderate Humean need have no objection to that. But, she will have to say, the goodness of the alternatives, from Maurice's point of view, must itself be determined by Maurice's preferences. When Maurice is deciding whether H_r is better than H_m, I said he would have to consider, among other things, whether cowardice is really bad. But the moderate Humean will say he only has to consider whether he prefers not to be cowardly. If he does, then, for him, H_r is better than H_m.

But now the moderate Humean has come around in a circle. Her suggestion is that nonpractical preferences can be derived by principles of consistency from other preferences. These other preferences might themselves be nonpractical in the first instance. But in the end, nonpractical preferences will have to be derived from practical ones if we are to avoid the epistemological problem I have described. So the moderate Humean's suggestion is that nonpractical preferences are determined by consistency conditions from practical preferences. However, she started off (in Section 4) with the idea that practical preferences might be constrained, through the consistency conditions, by nonpractical preferences. This requires nonpractical preferences to be determined independently, and she has just concluded they are not. We have known since Section 2 that practical preferences are not constrained, through consistency, simply by other practical preferences. Consistency permits any pattern of practical preferences whatsoever.

I conclude that the moderate Humean cannot sustain her position. She must either become extreme or cease to be a Humean.

Notes

1 Actually, not all the axioms of decision theory are conditions of consistency. For instance, one axiom is *completeness:* For any pair of alternatives *A* and *B,* either *A* is preferred to *B,* or *B* to *A,* or the two are indifferent. This is not required by consistency.

2 There is a careful survey of money pump and Dutch book arguments in Mark J. Machina, "Dynamic Consistency and Non-expected Utility Models of Choice under Uncertainty," in Michael Bacharach and Susan Hurley, eds., *Essays in the Foundations of Decision Theory* (Oxford: Basil Blackwell, 1990).

3 "On Interpersonal Utility Theory," *Journal of Philosophy* 68 (1971):647–56.

4 There are weaker consistency axioms, but not defined on preferences. See Amartya K. Sen, *Collective Choice and Social Welfare* (San Francisco: Holden-Day, 1970), p. 17.

5 They are not "context-free," to use Edward McClennen's terminology in *Rationality and Dynamic Choice* (Cambridge: Cambridge University Press, 1990), p. 29.

6 In commenting on a previous discussion of mine – in Gay Meeks, ed., *Thoughtful Economic Man* (Cambridge: Cambridge University Press, 1991) – about the same example, McClennen (*Rationality and Dynamic Choice,* p. 67) suggests I simply took it for granted that a preference ordering must be context-free. This criticism is not perfectly just. The whole point of the example is that Maurice's preferences *do* depend on what McClennen calls the "context": on what choice is on offer. Nevertheless, by the device of individuating alternatives finely, Maurice is able to arrange all his preferences in a coherent, constant order. He is able to make them satisfy both transitivity and McClennen's condition of context-freeness. I did not *assume* Maurice's preferences were context-free; I showed how context-dependent preferences can be converted into context-free ones by fine individuation.

7 Provided her preferences are *complete,* that is: For any pair of alternatives,

either she prefers one to the other or she is indifferent between them. Then, if she does not prefer B_c to B_a, either she prefers B_a to B_c or she is indifferent between them. Consequently, since she prefers A_b to B_a, she prefers A_b to B_c. Similarly, if she does not prefer C_a to C_b, she prefers B_c to C_a, and if she does not prefer A_b to A_c, she prefers C_a to A_b. So she prefers A_b to B_c, B_c to C_a, and C_a to A_b. This is an intransitivity.

8 Leonard J. Savage, *The Foundations of Statistics,* 2d ed. (New York: Dover, 1972).

9 First by Maurice Allais, "The Foundations of a Positive Theory of Choice Involving Risk and a Criticism of the Postulates and Axioms of the American School," in Maurice Allais and Ole Hagen, eds., *Expected Utility Hypothesis and the Allais Paradox* (Dordrecht: Reidel, 1979), pp. 27–145. See also, for example, Edward C. McClennen, "Sure-thing doubts," in B. P. Stigum and F. Wenstøp, eds., *Foundations of Utility and Risk Theory with Applications* (Dordrecht: Reidel, 1983), pp. 117–36.

10 See Paul A. Samuelson, "Probability, Utility and the Independence Axiom," *Econometrica* 20 (1952): 670–8.

11 I have gone into them in my *Weighing Goods* (Oxford: Basil Blackwell, 1991), ch. 5.

12 The following alternative, tighter principle seems implausible: that it is not rational to have a preference between two alternatives that are equally good. Suppose one alternative is better for one person, and the other for someone else. These two considerations might exactly balance, so that the alternatives are equally good. Even so, it seems rational for one of these people to prefer the alternative that is better for herself.

13 I am not concerned with the question of "radical interpretation" discussed by Donald Davidson (*Inquiries Into Truth and Interpretation* [Oxford: Clarendon Press, 1984]) and David Lewis ("Radical interpretation," *Synthèse* 23 [1974]: 331–44), among others. This question is about how a person's preferences can come to be understood by an observer from the outside. My question is about how rationality can guide a person from the inside. The answers to the two questions have many points of contact, and the questions are treated together by Susan Hurley in *Natural Reasons* (Oxford: Clarendon Press, 1989), esp. ch. 5. But the answers also diverge at many points. For one thing, intelligibility, which is the aim of interpretation, differs from rationality; a person may be intelligible without being rational. For instance, a person (indeed everyone) might regularly attach too much importance in decision making to small probabilities of loss. This is intelligible but irrational. No doubt, as Davidson would point out, it is only intelligible against an extensive background of rationality. But it means that the axioms of conventional decision theory, which represent the requirements of rationality, do not represent the requirements of intelligibility. Conventional decision theory is therefore not the right instrument for the task of interpretation.

14 I take this version of functionalism from David Lewis, "An Argument for

the Identity Theory," *Journal of Philosophy* 63 (1966): 17–25, reprinted with additions in his *Philosophical Papers,* vol. 1 (Oxford: Clarendon Press, 1983), pp. 99–107.

15 The test is not infallible, because we have to allow for the possibility that offering the person a choice between *A* and *B* may alter her preference between *A* and *B*. A particular preference, that is to say, may be "finkish." See David Lewis, "Dispositional Theories of Value," *Proceedings of the Aristotelian Society,* Supplementary Volume 63 (1989): 113–37, 117 n. 6. A finkish preference is not context-free (see note 5). As note 6 explains, under fine individuation Maurice's preferences are context-free, and so not finkish.

16 Perhaps one might make sense of the counterfactual "if the person were, *per impossible,* to have a choice between *A* and *B* . . . ," and define a functional role in these terms. But doing that would give us no help with the epistemology of nonpractical preferences. There would be no canonical test of the sort I have described. Knowledge of nonpractical preferences would have to be acquired in one of the ways I am about to consider.

17 Some arguments for this point (at least, for the point that a desire cannot be a feeling) are to be found in Michael Smith, "The Humean Theory of Motivation," *Mind* 96 (1987): 36–61. Smith's main argument is that a desire has "propositional content" and a feeling does not. As it stands, I think this argument is inadequate. A desire might be an attitude *to* a proposition, just as fear is an attitude *to* a bull. The fear does not contain the bull, and the desire need not contain the proposition. As the fear is a feeling, so might the desire be. But Philip Pettit has pointed out to me (see Frank Jackson and Philip Pettit, "Functionalism and Broad Content," *Mind* 97 [1988]: 381–400) that if a desire for *P* is *necessarily* a desire for *P* rather than for some other proposition (and this seems plausible) then Smith is right. No feeling could be necessarily directed toward *P* rather than toward some other proposition.

18 David Hume, *A Treatise of Human Nature,* book 2, part 3, sec. 3.

19 By Michael Smith, for instance, in "Humean Theory of Motivation."

20 Hume, *Treatise,* book 2, part 3, sec. 3.

21 Ibid.

22 David Lewis, "Desire as Belief," *Mind* 97 (1988): 323–32.

23 John Broome, "Desire, Belief, and Expectation," *Mind* 100 (1991): 265–7.

24 Both in *Proceedings of the Aristotelian Society,* Supplementary Volume 63 (1989).

25 Lewis, "Dispositional Theories of Value," p. 121.

5

Welfare, preference, and rationality

L. W. SUMNER

My title situates preference in the position it has come to occupy during this century: as the putative link between individual welfare on the one hand and practical rationality on the other. This mediating role, connecting one of the principal evaluative notions in ethics and the central normative notion in rational choice theory, is an impressive accomplishment for what seems at first glance a rather homely little item in our folk psychology. It has managed to elevate itself to this status, at least within the empiricist tradition, by reaching separate alliances with its two companions. Empiricists have tended to be subjectivists about welfare and instrumentalists about rationality. On the side of welfare, the eclipse of hedonism left the preference theory alone in the field as a plausible subjective account of the nature of well-being. Thus the Welfare–Preference Connection:

> WP: An individual's welfare consists in the satisfaction of her preferences.

On the side of rationality, meanwhile, instrumentalism entailed that reasons for action can be given only by items internal to the agent's motivational set. Thus the Preference–Rationality Connection:

> PR: Rationality requires the individual agent to maximize the satisfaction of her preferences.

Since each of these connections is well established in its own sphere, the mediating role for preference seems secure. At the same time, however, something has clearly gone wrong. When we conjoin these two theses, the result is the Welfare–Rationality Connection:

> WR: Rationality requires the individual agent to maximize her own welfare.

But in that case WP and PR jointly yield a quick and easy "proof" of normative egoism, which enables us to demonstrate the irrationality of all choices motivated by anything other than self-interest. Normative egoism is not quite as absurd as psychological egoism, which treats disinterested choices not as irrational but as impossible. But it is still absurd.

So what has gone wrong? Since the argument from WP and PR to WR looks valid, it seems that the problem must lie with one or the other of the premises. But in that case we must question the role of preference either in our currently dominant theory of welfare or in our currently dominant theory of rationality, or both. I aim to question both.

1. The ambiguity of preference

We begin by interrogating the principal suspect. Quick and easy "proofs" of absurd propositions often equivocate on key notions. The key notion in this argument – preference – lends itself particularly well to equivocation, since in the hands of philosophers it tends to be given two quite distinct interpretations. What the two interpretations share is the formal structure of the concept: Preference is a two-place ordering relation holding between states of affairs, which is transitive, asymmetrical, and nonreflexive. These formal features do not, of course, distinguish preference from a vast number of other ordering relations. A substantive interpretation must therefore determine the range of orderings that preference is intended to comprehend (the semantics of the notion, as opposed to its syntax). Here the two main accounts in play part company.

In order to fix the distinction between them it is best to invoke the notion of an individual's interests – meaning by this not her welfare but rather the things in which she is interested. Being interested in something, in this sense, is the same as caring about it, or being concerned about it, or minding it – or, alternatively, the thing mattering to one in some way. It is a fundamental feature of interests or concerns that they admit of a positive–negative polarity: I can like something or dislike it, approve of it or disapprove of it, favor it or disfavor it, and so on. More to our present purpose, I can also like, approve of, or favor this more or less than that, or I can be indifferent between them. In this way my interests determine an ordering of states of the world.

The abstract notion of an interest or concern is broad enough to cover a wide range of modalities, including tastes, wants, desires, needs, aims, projects, values, ideals, commitments, affections, convictions, and principles. Which of these are we to count as preferences? It is the answer to this question that distinguishes the two philosophical interpretations of preference. On the broad interpretation every case of my favoring one thing over another counts as a preference on my part, regardless of its modality. My tastes in music and movies, my personal goals and ideals, my attachments and loyalties, my moral and political convictions – all these are indifferently to be reckoned among my preferences. On this interpretation there can obviously be no conflict between my preferences, on the one hand, and what I think I should or must do, on the other; any practical judgment of this latter sort simply reflects a rival preference. Weakness of will aside, therefore, choice reliably reveals preference: what I choose must be what, all things considered, I prefer.

On the narrow interpretation, by contrast, my preferences include only some of my interests: roughly speaking, my likes and dislikes, or wants and desires, as distinct from my commitments or convictions. The distinguishing feature of preferences, on this account, is quasi-hedonistic: To like something, or to want or desire it, requires finding it agreeable, or being attracted to it, or enjoying it, or something of the like. On this interpretation, therefore, my preferences may easily conflict with my practical judgments: I may want to do, or like doing, what I think I should or must not do. Furthermore, because preference, on the narrow interpretation, is not the sole determinant of choice, choice is not a reliable indicator of preference.

The vernacular notion of preference leans more toward the narrow sense. Because we tend to think of preferences as lightweight and subjective, we tend to confine the notion to the realm of taste (likes and dislikes) and resist its application to our more important values or commitments or convictions (these, we say, are not "mere" preferences). But ordinary usage does little to settle the issue between the two philosophical interpretations. It may be that we need some term to cover all of the modalities under which we rank states of the world and, if so, it may also be that 'preference' is as good a choice as any. If we decide to use the notion in this comprehensive way, we are not making a semantic mistake; we need only be careful not to confuse the broad notion with its equally legitimate narrow counterpart.

However, we are not always careful. Out of the ambiguity of preference we can construct a hypothesis capable of explaining how the seemingly plausible WP and PR can yield the utterly implausible WR. If the premises employ different interpretations of preference then they might both be true, while the inference to WR would be invalid. Let us therefore look more closely at the two connections.

2. Welfare and preference

The basic idea here is that something can benefit a person (directly or intrinsically) if and only if it satisfies some preference on the person's part. This kind of account now stands as the orthodox view of the nature of welfare, at least in the Anglo-American philosophical world. Its prominent recent defenders include John Rawls, R. M. Hare, James Griffin, and Joseph Raz.[1]

It is not difficult to see why welfare and preference should be thought to be intimately connected. It seems a very plausible idea that my life is going well for me when I am achieving my aims or getting what I want. It also seems a plausible hypothesis that the subjective point of view, from which my welfare is to be assessed, is given by the set of my preferences, and that the relative importance of the many goods that enrich my life is determined by their position in the hierarchical structure of these preferences. The preference account also yields the pleasing result that welfare is unified in its nature, however multiform it may be in its sources. Since it can readily acknowledge the role played in our well-being by idiosyncratic tastes and interests, the account has no difficulty explaining why you who love thrills find the quality of your life enhanced by sky-diving, while I who value tranquility realize the same gains by reading quietly under a tree. At the same time, however, if there are states of affairs for which everyone strives, or which are the indispensable means for the achievement of any aims, then these will count as (either intrinsic or instrumental) common goods.

In addition to these very considerable merits, the preference theory also seems in tune with the liberal spirit of the modern age, which tends to see human agents as pursuers of autonomously chosen projects.[2] Unlike objective theories, on which the sources of our well-being seem to be largely dictated by unalterable aspects of our biological nature, the preference account offers us the more flattering picture of ourselves as shapers of our own destinies, determiners of our own good. In this way it internalizes within the very nature of welfare the principal liberal virtues of self-direction and self-determination. Once this link has been established it is a simple matter to construct a welfarist defense of political liberty. It is little cause for wonder, therefore, that all of the principal recent advocates of the desire theory have also been political liberals.

But can welfare be equated with the satisfaction of preference? Not, it seems, if preference is interpreted in the broad sense. There is considerable plausibility in the idea that I am benefited by doing what I want or desire (i.e., what I prefer in the narrow sense), but none whatever in the idea that benefits will necessarily flow to me from my doing what I think is right or obligatory. Can welfare then be equated with the satisfaction of preference in the narrow sense? Not, it seems, if preferences are here understood merely as wants or desires. The currently dominant subjective theories all identify welfare with the achieve-

ment of aims or the satisfaction of desires. But these theories face
insuperable problems stemming from two essential features of aims or
desires, which I shall call their "intentionality" and their "prospectivity."

To say that preferences are intentional is to say that they are directed
upon objects whose existence they do not guarantee. That preferences
have objects is, of course, scarcely news; this much is ensured by the fact
that every want or desire is *for* something or other. In the surface gram-
mar of desire, these objects are often literally things, as when I want this
book or that car. Sometimes, however, they are activities (I want to go to
France) or states of affairs (I want the weather to be good for our picnic).
It is a simple trick to homogenize all these ostensibly different kinds of objects into states of affairs: To want the book is to want to own it or read it,
and to want to do something is to want the state of affairs that consists of
your doing it. It is then a further simple trick to turn these states of affairs
into propositions: To want the state of affairs that consists of your owning
the book is to want the proposition 'I own this book' to be true. By this
process of transformation, every desire comes to take some proposition
as its intentional object. And of course the fact that you want a proposition to be true does not guarantee its truth.

What the transformation highlights is the similarity between desires
and beliefs. Like beliefs, desires are attitudes whose intentional objects
are states of affairs or propositions. Just as beliefs can be verified or
falsified, desires can be satisfied or frustrated. A belief is verified by the
occurrence of the state of affairs (or the truth of the proposition) that
constitutes its intentional object. Likewise, a desire is satisfied by the
occurrence of the state of affairs (or the truth of the proposition) that
constitutes *its* intentional object.[3] Again like beliefs, desires can take as
their objects states of the world that are spatially or temporally remote
from their holders. This implies that my desire for something can be
satisfied without my being aware of it. All that is required in order for
my desire to be satisfied is that whatever I want actually happen. Carl
Sagan wants us to establish contact with extraterrestrial beings. Suppose
that twenty thousand years from now, some intelligent alien civilization
encounters one of our probes in deep space and deciphers the messages
that it carries. Sagan's desire will then have been satisfied, though he
will know nothing of it. By contrast, I cannot be (occurrently) liking or
enjoying something without being aware of this fact. My enjoyments
must therefore enter into my experience in a way that need not be true
of the satisfaction of my desires.

For the purposes of building a theory of welfare, intentionality is a
very awkward feature of desire or preference. According to the preference theory, something makes me better off when it satisfies some

desire on my part. Since my desires can range over spatially and temporally remote states of affairs, it follows that the satisfaction of many of them will occur at times or places too distant from me to have any (other) effect on me. In such cases it is difficult to see how having my desire or preference satisfied could possibly make my life go better.

Sometimes the absence of feedback into my life is due to contingent circumstances. Suppose that my brother suffers from some debilitating disease which I very much want to be cured. Having unsuccessfully sought medical treatment at home, he moves to Papua New Guinea where a promising new therapy is available. After his arrival he breaks off contact with me, and I receive no further news of his fate. Two years later the treatment succeeds and his disorder is completely cured. At this time my desire that he be cured (which I continue to hold) has been satisfied. Because I care deeply about his well-being, if I knew of this I would be greatly cheered. Since I never know of it, how can the cure make me better off?

All of us have many desires that, unbeknownst to us, will come to be satisfied during our lifetime. Like Carl Sagan, we also have many desires that will be satisfied, if ever, only after we are dead and gone. Sometimes the posthumous satisfaction of a desire is itself due to contingent circumstances, as when I want my daughter eventually to attend university but die before she is able to do so. In this case it is just unlucky for me that my desire is satisfied only after my demise. In other cases this outcome is ensured by the temporal location of the desired state of affairs. Nearly everyone now living wants the ecosystem of the planet to be in a healthy state two centuries from now, but no one now living will be living then. In still other cases, such as your wish to be remembered by your lover after your demise, if the desire is ever satisfied then this must (logically) occur posthumously. In any of these cases, if the desired state of affairs eventually comes about does it make our lives go better? If so, *when* do they go better? When the desire is satisfied? But how can the quality of our lives be improved after they have ended? Retroactively, at the time we held the desire? But how can what happens then affect us for better or worse now?

Sometimes it can seem to. James Griffin gives the following example:

It would not have been at all absurd for Bertrand Russell to have thought that if his work for nuclear disarmament had, after his death, actually reduced the risk of nuclear war, his last years would have been more worthwhile, and his life altogether more valuable, than if it all proved futile. True, if Russell had indeed succeeded, his life clearly would have been more valuable to others. But Russell could also have considered it more valuable from the point of view of his own self-interest.

However, when we look more closely at claims of posthumous benefits we find that they always seem to rest on conflating different modes of value. If Russell's work had turned out to contribute to eventual nuclear disarmament then this would of course have shown, retrospectively, that his life had enormous instrumental value; but this, as Griffin recognizes, is not the question at issue. Somewhat closer to the mark, if achievement is a perfectionist value, as it might well be, then posthumous success will also augment the perfection of a life, making it a better specimen of its kind. Perfectionist value seems clearly capable of retroactive improvement, and Russell might well have considered his life more valuable from that point of view. But from the standpoint of his own self-interest? That certainly does not follow, and seems much less plausible. It also seems an unlikely interpretation of Russell's own (imagined) evaluation. He can think that a more successful life is a better life without thinking that it must therefore have a higher payoff for him.

The issue of whether posthumously satisfied preferences can benefit their erstwhile holders is a hotly debated one. Some people find it just obvious that one of the few advantages of death is that it puts us beyond the possibility of further harm (I confess that I belong to this group), while others find it equally obvious that lives are capable of retroactive fluctuations in well-being.[4] In this polarized atmosphere, their implications for posthumous cases are probably insufficient by themselves to condemn desire theories of welfare. However, the posthumous cases are merely the most dramatic instances in which the satisfaction of a preference fails to benefit us because it fails to have any impact, direct or indirect, on our experience. The obvious remedy is to impose on the desire theory what Griffin has called an "experience requirement."[5] Such a requirement would stipulate that a state of affairs can make me better off only if it somehow enters my experience. It seems to me that a desire or preference theory can be a contender only if it incorporates an experience requirement, since only then will it be insulated against highly counterintuitive results flowing from the intentionality of desire, and especially from its capacity to settle on spatially or temporally distant objects. When desire theorists resist this requirement, this is probably because they suspect that once experience is admitted into their accounts as an added ingredient it will eventually displace desire altogether. They must therefore hold the line, lest a desire theory with an experience component mutate into an experience theory with no desire component. This suspicion is well grounded, as we see when we turn from intentionality to the second essential feature of desire, namely its prospectivity.

In explicating this feature, the analogy between desire and belief will once again be instructive. Suppose I now believe that it will snow next Christmas. My belief has two temporal indices, one for the time at which I hold the belief (now) and the other for the state of affairs that constitutes the intentional object of the belief (next Christmas). Where beliefs are concerned, these two indices can be ordered in any way whatever: I can hold beliefs at a particular time about earlier, contemporaneous, or later times. Likewise, every desire both is held at some particular time and directed upon a temporally indexed state of affairs. However, in the case of a desire the two indices must observe a particular order: I can desire now only that something occur later. Desires are always directed on the future, never on the past or present.[6] In being future-directed in this way, wanting once again contrasts with enjoying. I can (occurrently) enjoy only what I already have, while I can want only what I have not yet got.

Because a desire is always for some future state of affairs, at best it represents our *ex ante* expectation that the state will benefit us. (Even this much will not hold for disinterested desires.) This expectation, however, may be disconfirmed by our *ex post* experience of the state: We are all familiar with such disappointments. Since our desires always represent our *ex ante* expectations, there is always room for these expectations to be mistaken. But in that case the satisfaction of our desires does not guarantee that our lives will go well; only our *ex post* experience will do that.

Since it is the prospectivity of desire that creates this problem, it is tempting to try to put matters right by closing the gap between the way things are expected to go and the way they actually turn out. Thus it is common for desire accounts to stipulate that the only desires that count are those that are rational or considered or informed.[7] The standard of rationality appealed to may be either minimal, requiring no more than consistency within one's overall set of preferences, or rather more stringent, requiring that one's desires be capable of surviving "cognitive psychotherapy."[8] Informational demands likewise may vary, depending on what is counted as relevant information, and on how much of this is reckoned to be sufficient. Whatever the idealizing conditions adopted, their effect will be to screen out some of our actual desires.[9] Only the satisfaction of the surviving subset of desires will count as enhancing our well-being.

We need not concern ourselves with the precise formulation of these idealizing conditions, since, however they are formulated, their role within a desire theory is inherently puzzling. Consider the requirement that a desire be appropriately informed. This condition is imposed in order to eliminate mistakes about the objects of our desires. But it appears that the condition is either redundant within a desire theory or inconsistent with it. Suppose that the satisfaction of one of my desires has left me worse off. There seem to be two possible explanations of how this could have come about. One is that satisfying the desire made me to that extent better off, but it also frustrated other, more important desires, so that on balance I ended up worse off. I take an eagerly anticipated vacation in the Caribbean and find myself in the path of a hurricane; had I known of the danger in advance I would have gone somewhere else instead. My desire not to encounter a hurricane is stronger than my desire to vacation at just that resort; in satisfying the latter I frustrate the former and so end up worse off on the whole than if I had stayed home. The desire theory is perfectly capable of explaining all this without the requirement that my desires be informed. All that it needs to do is bring into play the full structure of those desires, including my priorities among them. In the light of all my actual desires I have suffered a net loss. Whenever this is the appropriate explanation of my plight, therefore, an information requirement will be redundant.

But there are, in addition, cases in which no further desires are involved and I am still worse off. I take up chess in the expectation that I will find its intricacy fascinating, only to discover that it bores me to death. Here we cannot appeal to any additional desires in order to explain how things have gone badly for me. (I did not have two desires, one to play chess and the other to enjoy playing it.) Furthermore, the expectation on which I acted can be as rational, considered, and informed as you like. All of the information I collected in advance about chess turned out to be correct; I made no mistakes, except in thinking that I would like it. That mistake was just the gap between my *ex ante* expectation and my *ex post* experience. The possibility of such a gap is guaranteed by the prospectivity of desire: My preferences about the future always represent my view *now* of how things will go *then*. Because the gap results from the very nature of desire, it cannot be closed merely by requiring that desires be rational or considered or informed.

The gap could be closed by stipulating that a desire does not count as informed – and thus its satisfaction does not count as making us better off – whenever the desired state of affairs turns out upon later experience to be disappointing or unrewarding. However, to take this step would be to confirm the desire theorist's suspicion that once our experience of states of the world is admitted as relevant then whether or not these states satisfy antecedent desires on our part is on the way to becoming irrelevant. For it would be tantamount to conceding that what matters, so far as our well-being is concerned, is our satisfaction and not merely the satisfaction of our desires. If an information requirement has any genuine work to do within a desire theory, therefore, it will be inconsistent with the basic rationale of the theory.

The argument to this point has focused on two essential properties of desires – their intentionality and their prospectivity – each of which opens up a logical gap between desire satisfaction and well-being. All of the difficulties for the desire theory that we have so far canvassed have a common logical form. Desires whose satisfaction never enters our experience at all and desires whose satisfaction proves disappointing in our subsequent experience – these are both families of cases in which preference satisfaction need not make us better off. What they demonstrate is that when a desire is satisfied it is a logically open question whether the welfare of its holder has thereby been enhanced. However, they do not exhaust the problems for the preference theory. If preference satisfaction is not logically sufficient for well-being, it is not logically necessary either. Once again, the root of the problem lies in the very nature of desire. As we have already noted, because desires are future-directed, at best they represent the anticipation of benefit. But just as we can be disappointed when we get what we expected or aimed for, so we can be pleasantly surprised when we encounter something we did not expect or aim for.

There are two points here, which need to be distinguished. As we have seen, the expansiveness of desire, its capacity to be directed on a virtually limitless range of (future) states of the world, causes problems for the preference theory. It is tempting, therefore, to narrow the theory by focusing exclusively on those desires that are also aims, by virtue of being incorporated into some hierarchy of intention.[10] If this restriction is introduced then the desire theory essentially equates welfare with success in achieving our aims or goals. But it is obvious that any such account would exclude too much.[11] Broadly speaking, the quality of our lives is enhanced both by what we do and by what happens to us. The fact that some benefits we enjoy are the result of good fortune rather than achievement on our part does not make them any less real. There is in this nothing intrinsically threatening for the desire theory. What chances to come our way with no effort on our part may still be something for which we had an antecedent desire. The problem here is the one we have already identified: how to circumscribe the set of eligible desires so as to close the logical gap between desire satisfaction and welfare.

The further difficulty stems from the fact that the welfare payoff of both achievements and windfalls often exceeds any antecedent expectations on our part. The most striking cases are those in which our expectations are either nonexistent or negative. Having never heard bluegrass, I chance on a band playing in the park and find that I like it. Having nursed a longstanding suspicion of the Mediterranean, I am persuaded against my better judgment to holiday there and have a wonderful time. In neither case did I have an antecedent desire for the state of affairs that, as it turns out, enhances my well-being. But then, just as the satisfaction of a desire on my part is not logically sufficient for an increase in the quality of my life, it is not logically necessary either.[12]

The equation of welfare with desire satisfaction therefore seems simultaneously too broad and too narrow: too broad because it admits desires whose satisfaction produces no benefits, too narrow because it excludes benefits that presuppose no antecedent desires. This is not, of course, a proof of the inadequacy of the theory. The problems of scope can be regarded as invitations to qualify the theory so as to contour desire satisfaction better to well-being,[13] and I can see no way of demonstrating in advance the fruitlessness of this enterprise. Furthermore, since the desire theory is still our best-developed account of the nature of welfare, it may well be premature to give up on it without trying out a few possible remedies.

However, I am persuaded that the theory suffers from more than a problem of scope. It also operates at the wrong level for an adequate theory of welfare. A theory must not identify welfare itself with any of its sources. One generally reliable source of well-being consists in the attainment of something antecedently wanted or aimed at. Our discussion has shown both that this source is only generally reliable, and that other sources, such as delightful surprises, matter too. The distinctive move of the desire theory is to treat desire satisfaction not as one (very general) welfare source among others but as the condition that anything must satisfy in order to count as such a source. Thus it purports to be a formal theory about the nature of welfare rather than a substantive inventory of its sources.[14] But if the satisfaction of our desires is merely one way in which our good can be advanced, then despite this claim of formality, the desire theory is operating at the wrong logical level.

3. Preference and rationality

If WP is plausible only on the narrow interpretation of preference, then PR plainly requires the broad sense. Since the dominant theory interprets rationality purely instrumentally, it provides no resources for the rational scrutiny of our chosen ends.[15] It follows that it must be agnostic about the content of those ends: Whatever they may be, practical reason requires only their efficient pursuit.[16] But then there can be no justification for restricting the range of preferences to those that are self-interested; if I boycott South African wine out of political conviction though I would really rather drink it, then I may do what is worse for me, but I do not thereby behave irrationally.

The fact that WP and PR require different conceptions of preference puts paid to the supposed derivation of normative egoism from their conjunction. However, although the "argument" to WR is plainly fallacious, the temptation to commit the fallacy is seemingly irresistible, at least to economists and rational choice theorists. All of the central results of general equilibrium theory are derivable as long as the market choices of consumers are assumed to manifest certain basic forms of consistency; it is not necessary to assume that in these choices consumers are seeking to maximize welfare or any other particular magnitude.[17] Given this fact, the conclusion that should have been drawn is that the concept of welfare is irrelevant to positive economic theory. As long as consumers' choices display the consistency required to generate utility functions, who cares what they are motivated by? The assumption of egoism seems to do no useful work here.[18] There may (or may not) be interesting empirical connections between market choices and economic welfare, but the two are logically distinct.[19] If utility is given a technical definition as that which is maximized in consistent choice,[20] then the equation of utility and welfare has been effectively abandoned. In that case it is utility that is indispensable to demand theory, not welfare.

Had this conclusion been drawn, then the concept of welfare would have been expelled altogether from positive economics.[21] But that is not what happened. Instead, the metric of individual welfare gains and losses was retained in locutions such as 'Pareto improvement' and 'Pareto optimum'. These welfarist notions are, strictly speaking, unnecessary to the purely formal results of general equilibrium theory. They appear instead in the interpretation of these results, as, for instance, when it is said that under conditions of perfect competition no one can be made better off without someone else being made worse off. Strictly speaking, all that 'makes *A* better/worse off' can mean here is "moves *A* to a higher/lower point in *A*'s preference ranking" (in the broad sense of preference). Nonetheless, the equation of utility and welfare survives as a kind of unthinking reflex.[22] By no means, therefore, has the concept of welfare ceased to play an important rhetorical role in positive economic theory. Its continuing presence in normative theory, on the other hand, is attested to by the very label 'welfare economics'. It must be emphasized that none of the (alleged) welfarist results in either domain depends on any assumed empirical correlation between utility and welfare. Instead, these results, or at any rate their standard interpretation, depend on an implicit equation of the two.[23]

In the rational choice literature, the more circumspect draw a clear distinction between instrumental rationality and normative egoism. David Gauthier puts the point nicely: "On the maximizing conception it is not interests in the self, that take oneself as object, but interests of the self, held by oneself as subject, that provide the basis for rational choice and action."[24] In our terms: The theory of rational choice requires preferences to be interpreted in the broadest and most comprehensive way, so as to include anything that could count, under the appropriate circumstances, as a rational ground of action. Having interpreted preferences in this way, the theory then offers a single criterion for practical rationality: A choice counts as rational just in case it maximizes satisfaction of the agent's preferences.

It is easy to see why the maximization of preference satisfaction should be thought to be central to an account of practical rationality, since it appears to be central to our notion of agency. Just as we are semantic creatures, capable of representing states of the world as objects of belief, so we are also deliberative creatures, capable of representing states of the world as objectives to be pursued in action. Both our beliefs and our actions form complex wholes whose interpretation requires the adoption of a principle of charity. On the cognitive side, this principle requires interpreting an individual's pattern of beliefs in such a way as to maximize consistency. Since inconsistency appears to be a form of irrationality, in this way a regulative ideal of cognitive rationality comes to be built into our very picture of a cognitive subject. Likewise, on the practical side, charity requires interpreting a pattern of behavior in such a way as to maximize its consistency, thus building an ideal of practical rationality into our very notion of agency.

On this view instrumentalism must tell at least part of the story about the nature of practical rationality. It seems clear, however, that this story will be very limited.[25] Rationality provides us with a norm, or ideal, which in any particular instance we may or may not manage to satisfy. The problem with the foregoing account is that irrational choice becomes virtually impossible. Whenever any choice of mine seems inconsistent with my preferences we will try to reinterpret the latter so as to save (or restore) consistency. Only when we cannot find a way to do this (and when will that be?) will we reluctantly conclude that my choice has been counterpreferential. The result is that weakness of will becomes the only intelligible deviation from the rational norm. The principle of charity captures the important truth that our behavior cannot be typically ır standardly irrational. But as the foundation of a theory of practical ationality, it is far too charitable.

Does instrumentalism tell the whole story about practical rationality? The dominant theory says it does. Practical rationality is purely a matter of the consistency of our preferences among themselves, and of our hoices with those preferences. Assuming this internal standard to be met, there are no further questions to be raised about the rationality ither of our preferences or of our choices. But this restriction to the nternal point of view is puzzling and seemingly arbitrary. Where cognitive functions are concerned, coherence does not appear to exhaust he demands of reason. Besides the internal standard of consistency ımong our beliefs, we also bring to bear an external standard of adequacy resting on notions of evidence and, ultimately, truth. After all, vith enough psychic effort even paranoiacs may be able to make their ıverall belief systems coherent. Despite its consistency with the rest of ny beliefs, my conviction that I am Genghis Khan remains irrational, ınce it is so massively at odds with evidence to the contrary that any easonable person would acknowledge and accept. The same external tandard of adequacy is failed by many more common beliefs that we abel not irrational but unreasonable – sexist or racist convictions about he inferiority of a specified target group furnish familiar examples. 3eliefs can therefore be contrary to reason either internally, by being nconsistent, or externally, by being stubbornly immune to counter evidence. Why should there be no parallel external standard for ends or ıreferences?

Can my ends be irrational? Suppose my obsession with personal cleanliness leads me to wage an unceasing war against dirt, to the neglect of everything else in my life – my family, my friends, my job, even my ıealth. When asked why it is so important to me to live in spotless and disinfected surroundings, my answer is that dirt is an evil whose eradication is worth any sacrifice on my part. Wouldn't you think it irrational of me to hold this as an overriding aim? And doesn't the irrationality :onsist in exaggerating the value of cleanliness relative to the other goods am prepared to give up for its sake? Hygiene has its place, we want o say, but it just doesn't have the degree of urgency that I am attaching o it.

As in the case of beliefs, ends that are downright irrational are relitively rare. But irrationality is only the extreme case of a preference or a belief) being contrary to reason. Unreasonable preferences are nuch more common. Your neighbor in the next apartment who keeps you awake all night by playing heavy metal rock at peak volume may aot be behaving irrationally, but he is being unreasonable. Of course, it is possible that the fault lies in his beliefs; perhaps he doesn't realize how much of the sound comes through your wall. But after you have complained a few times, and he persists, this explanation is no longer available. If we continue to think him unreasonable, which we do, it is because he is insufficiently sensitive to your well-being; he would make your life a misery in order to secure a relatively minor enhancement of his own listening pleasure. The problem with his preference ranking is that it fails to reflect the relative importance of the values at stake; he prefers the manifestly lesser good simply because it is his.

Unreasonable preferences, like unreasonable beliefs, appear to presuppose some objective order about which we may be culpably mistaken. In requiring that our preferences track value, common sense imposes on them an external standard analogous to the demand that our beliefs track truth. By construing practical rationality as merely instrumental, the dominant theory rejects any such standard. Friends of the theory typically take this defensive position because they resist the idea of a realm of objective values to supplement the realm of objective facts.[26] However, it is hard to see why we should treat this resistance as more than an undefended dogma.[27]

We can go further. Practical rationality is avowedly a normative matter: To show that a choice is rational, or reasonable, is to justify it in one particular way or from one particular point of view. In this respect, the rational is analogous to (or a species of) the right. We are entitled to ask of both notions how they acquire their normative force. Why does rationality matter? Why is irrationality a defect, or a fault? Any answer to these questions that takes us only to ends, or preferences, seems incomplete, for it invites the further question: Why does the satisfaction of preferences matter? Here is one possible answer. It matters when, and only when, the object of the preference has some form of independent value. In that case satisfying the preference will itself have value, and it is this that generates a reason with the power to justify choice. On this account the normative force of reasons, and thus of rationality, is derived from an antecedent set of objective values. Even narrow, limited instrumental rationality presupposes such values; in their absence we would have no ground for condemning irrational choices. In this respect, then, the good is prior not only to the right but also to the rational.

The foregoing is not a developed account of practical rationality; it is scarcely even a sketch of such an account. But suppose that something like it turns out to be the best story we can tell. How would this affect the role of preference in the theory of rational choice? Since consistency would continue to be one aspect of practical rationality, and since pref rences (in the broad sense) appear to be the appropriate bearers of consistency in the practical domain, then some connection between preference and rationality seems assured. Furthermore, even if it turns out that preferences, like beliefs, can be contrary to reason by some external standard, it will still be true that practical rationality has to do with preferences, just as cognitive rationality has to do with beliefs. In that sense, preference will remain central to rationality. These results, however, are relatively uninteresting. We must remember that in the broad sense preference comprehends all items capable of serving as reasons or action. It is a trivial thesis that reasons are the currency of practical rationality, which is not much less trivial when reasons have been re-labeled as preferences.

The more interesting result is that PR will have to be discarded. If preferences can themselves be unreasonable or irrational, then reason may not always counsel maximizing the satisfaction of whatever preferences we happen to have. Just as a complete theory of rational belief needs to make room for the concept of truth, so a complete theory of rational action will need to make room for the concept of (objective) value. But any such expansion of the theory will be a demotion for the concept of preference.

4. Conclusions

nce WP requires the narrow sense of preference, while PR requires e broad sense, the argument from them to WR is fallacious. Since 'R is so patently false, this is not a startling conclusion. What is more teresting is to ask what the role of preference would be in the best eories about welfare and rationality.

Here we derive somewhat asymmetrical results. The best theory of elfare will assign no constitutive role to preference (in the narrow nse of desire) at all; it will interpret welfare as a matter not of getting aat we want but of liking what we get. The best theory of practical ionality, on the other hand, may continue to find a place for preference (in the broad sense). However, if rationality in action is more an instrumental, that place may not be central. However this turns t, it is already clear that the notion of preference has been greatly erworked of late, at least in ethics and possibly also in the theory of ional choice. The time has come to give it a rest.

Notes

See John Rawls, *A Theory of Justice* (Cambridge, Mass.: Harvard University Press, 1971), ch. 7; R. M. Hare, *Moral Thinking: Its Levels, Method, and*

Point (Oxford: Clarendon Press, 1981), ch. 5; James Griffin, *Well-Being* (Oxford: Clarendon Press, 1986), chs. 1, 2; Joseph Raz, *The Morality of Freedom* (Oxford: Clarendon Press, 1986), ch. 12.

2 For a recent manifestation of this ethos, see Loren Lomasky, *Persons, Rights, and the Moral Community* (New York: Oxford University Press, 1987), ch. 2.

3 Griffin offers a different, but equally apt, analogy: "A desire is 'fulfilled' in the sense in which a clause in a contract is fulfilled: namely, what was agreed (desired) comes about." *Well-Being*, p. 14.

4 Ernest Partridge defends the first view in "Posthumous Interests and Posthumous Respect," *Ethics* 91, no. 2 (1981); Joel Feinberg defends the second in *Harm to Others* (New York: Oxford University Press, 1984), pp. 83–9. With his characteristic judiciousness, Aristotle argues both sides of the question (*Nicomachean Ethics* 1:10–11), finally settling for the conclusion that, while posthumous events can affect us for better or worse, the effects are relatively minor. Griffin has also felt the pull of both sides; see *Well-Being*, pp. 317–19n.

5 *Well-Being*, p. 13.

6 I can, of course, wish that past events had been otherwise. I can also have hopes about such events, if I don't know how things turned out. The first time I read Homer I hoped the Trojans would win; now I wish they had.

7 See, for instance, Rawls, *Theory of Justice*, ch. 7; Griffin, *Well-Being*, chs. 1–2.

8 For the latter requirement see R. B. Brandt, *A Theory of the Good and the Right* (Oxford: Clarendon Press, 1979), ch. 6. Gauthier employs a weaker standard in *Morals by Agreement* (Oxford: Clarendon Press, 1986), ch. 2. It should be noted, however, that neither Brandt nor Gauthier identifies welfare with the satisfaction of rational desire.

9 Could they also sweep in desires we don't actually have, but would have if the conditions were satisfied? Rawls's appeal to hypothetical choice seems to entail this: "In brief, our good is determined by the plan of life that we would adopt with full deliberative rationality if the future were accurately foreseen and adequately realized in the imagination. . . . Here it is worth stressing that a rational plan is one that would be selected if certain conditions were fulfilled. The criterion of the good is hypothetical in a way similar to the criterion of justice." *Theory of Justice*, p. 421. Griffin, on the other hand, requires that a desire be actual when satisfied (*Well-Being*, p. 11). It is not clear, however, how this latter requirement is consistent with his inclusion of posthumously satisfied desires.

10 This seems clearly to be what Rawls has in mind when he speaks of executing a rational plan of life. In his account of well-being, Joseph Raz also focuses on the pursuit of goals, thus on the success or failure of a life (*Morality of Freedom*, pp. 288–99). It should be noted, however, that well-being is not the whole story for Raz; what he calls self-interest is a matter of the satisfaction of "biologically determined needs and desires."

11 As Griffin recognizes (*Well-Being*, p. 22). An exclusive focus on project pursuit also seems to manifest a masculine bias. It applies only with great strain to close personal relationships, such as friendship and love.

12 In recognition of these problems, Griffin says that he is working with an "extended sense of desire": "The relevant sort of desire does not have to be held antecedently to its fulfilment (a human can enjoy something, want to have it continue or return, that he never knew he would enjoy, or even knew existed)." *Well-Being*, p. 315n. Prospectivity, however, is one of the features that distinguishes wanting from other positive attitudes, such as enjoying. If this feature is dropped, so as to include enjoying, then "wanting" effectively becomes coextensive with "having a positive attitude toward" or "having an interest in." But in that case the desire theory is no longer a determinate species of subjective theory.

13 Which is the way Griffin regards them; see *Well-Being*, pp. 16–23.

14 See ibid., pp. 31–4.

15 Except, perhaps, that these ends be coherent and considered; see Gauthier, *Morals by Agreement*, ch. 2.

16 Gauthier again: "in identifying rationality with the maximization of a measure of preference, the theory of rational choice disclaims all concern with the ends of action. Ends may be inferred from individual preferences; if the relationships among these preferences, and the manner in which they are held, satisfy the conditions of rational choice, then the theory accepts whatever ends they imply." Ibid., p. 26.

17 See Paul A. Samuelson, "A Note on the Pure Theory of Consumers' Behavior," *Economica*, new series 5 (1938); Samuelson, *Foundations of Economic Analysis* (Cambridge, Mass.: Harvard University Press, 1947), ch. 5; and Samuelson, "Consumption Theory in Terms of Revealed Preference," *Economica*, new series 15 (1948).

18 A weaker assumption, that of nontuism, may be necessary, since it ensures the independence of utility functions. See Philip H. Wicksteed, *The Common Sense of Political Economy and Selected Papers and Reviews on Economic Theory* (London: Routledge, 1933), pp. 179–81; and Gauthier, *Morals by Agreement*, p. 87.

19 As is suggested in I.M.D. Little, *Critique of Welfare Economics*, 2d ed. (Oxford: Clarendon Press, 1957), pp. 42ff.

20 "We assume that individuals attempt to maximize utility, and define utility as that which the individual attempts to maximize." D.M. Winch, *Analytical Welfare Economics* (Harmondsworth, England: Penguin Books, 1971), p. 25.

21 Sometimes, it seems, this conclusion is being drawn, as when Paul Samuelson tells us that "the consumer's market behavior is explained in terms of preferences, which are in turn defined only by behavior. The result can very easily be circular, and in many formulations undoubtedly is. Often nothing more is stated than the conclusion that people behave as they behave, a theorem which has no empirical implications, since it contains no hypotheses

and is consistent with all conceivable behavior, while refutable by none." *Foundations of Economic Analysis,* pp. 91–2. Cf. R. Duncan Luce and Howard Raiffa, *Games and Decisions: Introduction and Critical Survey* (New York: John Wiley, 1957), p. 50.

22 "[A]n individual shall be considered better off if he is in a chosen position. This assumption relates the Paretian value judgement directly to the utility function. Since we define utility as that which the individual attempts to maximize, it follows that he will choose more rather than less utility. An increase in his utility can then be regarded as synonymous with his being better off." Winch, *Analytical Welfare Economics,* p. 33.

23 The equation has not gone unchallenged in the economic literature; see, for instance, John Broome, "Choice and Value in Economics," *Oxford Economic Papers* 30, no. 3 (1978); and Amartya Sen, *Choice, Welfare and Measurement* (Oxford: Basil Blackwell, 1982), chs. 2, 4.

24 Gauthier, *Morals by Agreement,* p. 7.

25 I owe the ideas in this paragraph to Arthur Ripstein, who is not, however, to be held responsible for the way in which I have formulated them.

26 See, for instance, Gauthier, *Morals by Agreement,* ch. 2.

27 See L. W. Sumner, "Justice Contracted," *Dialogue* 26, no. 3 (1987):523–48.

6

Preference

ARTHUR RIPSTEIN

The concept of preference plays a central role in much recent moral and political philosophy. Partly because of its pedigree in such widely admired disciplines as economics and decision theory, its status seems secure. Preferences are taken by various philosophers to provide everything from a starting point for moral inquiry to the sole factor elected officials should take into account.[1] My aim in this essay is to call that status into question. I shall argue that the concept of preference cannot bear the theoretical weight in normative inquiry that it has been asked to support. The argument has two parts. The first examines the place of actual or "revealed" preference in moral argument, and shows how it fails to meet even minimal standards as an account of practical reason. The second part considers more sophisticated accounts of ideal or considered preferences, arguing that although they have enough structure to function in accounts of practical reason, their employment presupposes independent standards. This needn't be a damning criticism, except for the manner in which advocates of preference-based accounts maintain that those accounts do not incorporate any controversial normative claims. Much of the appeal of preference-based accounts of practical reason stems from their promise of providing a normative account of practical reason using minimal formal constraints of consistency and the prior motivations of the agent in question.

My strategy will be to establish and exploit parallels between the role of preference in contemporary moral philosophy and the role of perception in classical empiricism. Empiricist epistemology and utilitarian and contractarian moral philosophy have a common ancestry. They also share a common weakness. Each attempts to give an account of what

Material included in this essay was presented at the Canadian Philosophical Association Annual Congress at Université Laval, at Bowling Green State University, at the University of North Carolina at Chapel Hill, and at Columbia University. I am grateful to those audiences and to Cheryl Misak, Christopher Morris, Jan Narveson, Wayne Sumner, Cass Sunstein, and Mark Thornton for comments and discussion. Douglas Butler also made many helpful suggestions, and I dedicate this essay to his memory.

is taken to be a problematic concept – physical objects and knowledge on the one hand, a person's good or what she has reason to do on the other – and explain it as a construct out of what is taken to be an unproblematic concept – sensation on the one hand, preference on the other. Each retreats to what appears to be an individualistic and subjective account of the concept in question. Empiricist epistemology responds to skepticism about the existence of an external world by retreating to individual sensation as the building block of knowledge; empiricist ethics responds to controversy about practical reason and the good by retreating to subjective preference. The failures of classical empiricism are by now widely recognized. My aim is to extend antiempiricist arguments to preference-based accounts of ethics. I shall argue that, like the empiricist retreat, the retreat to preference is either so complete as to provide no account of practical reason or the good, or that the retreat is an illusion, and presupposes an independent account of the concept it was supposed to analyze.

For the sake of clarity, I must put to one side two sets of distinctions that can be drawn among preference-based accounts of the sorts outlined above. First, appeals to preference have been offered in two distinct guises. Sometimes they are presented as an account of an agent's good, on the supposition that an agent's good is to be identified with what he or she has chosen, or would choose. On other occasions, preferences figure in an account of what an agent has a reason to do. The two types of argument are plainly distinct, for someone may well have reason to do things that are in no sense part of his or her well-being.[2] But these differences turn on an additional question that need not concern us here, regarding the relation between a person's reasons for acting and his or her good. I shall focus on reasons for action, for it is here that preference-based accounts have both intuitive appeal and a distinguished pedigree.

In turn, on either construal, accounts of reason or the good have been offered as answering three different questions. First, they have been offered as conceptual accounts of the meaning of claims about what someone has reason to do. Second, they have been offered as ontological accounts of what it is for someone to have a reason to do something. Third, they have been offered as an account about how claims about what someone has reason to do can be justified, and thereby used to underwrite specific claims. I shall speak of justification; those supposing that such accounts are conceptual or ontological will be addressed in passing.

The appeal of preference-based accounts of practical reason is easy to see. Preference is a concept with a well-established explanatory role – typically people behave as they do in order to get what they want.

But preference can do more than allow views about practical reason to ride on the coattails of explanatory success. It is also possible to explain a person's action in light of what he or she had reason to do. A single concept provides the link between two disparate tasks.

1. Actual preference

A standard view of rationality identifies it with the successful pursuit of one's preferences. Such an account, in turn, requires certain constraints on eligible preferences. Though some candidate constraints are debated, at a minimum are two requirements of consistency. First, preferences must be transitively ordered: If I prefer A to B, and B to C, then I must also prefer A to C. Second, a preference ordering must be complete in that any two outcomes must be comparable. Without satisfying these constraints, it is impossible for a person to pursue her preferences consistently, because there is no room for a contrasting concept of inconsistency. Further constraints make it possible to measure success in that pursuit, including the avoidance of strategies sure to lead to losses, and failures to take likelihoods into account.[3] In order for formal constraints on preference to do any work, the content of those preferences must be determined. Consistency must be applied to something systematically identifiable.

I begin by considering attempts to base accounts of practical reasoning on actual preferences. Such accounts in turn divide into two groups, those that favor the preferences revealed in a person's behavior, and those that emphasize the preferences expressed by him or her.[4] Revealed preferences have recently been the subject of a considerable philosophical literature. Donald Davidson has argued that in order to make sense of an agent's behavior, one must suppose her to be rational, that is, to be acting in such a way as to optimally satisfy her preferences, given her beliefs about how to get what she wants. Davidson argues that without such an assumption of rationality, we have no hope of finding any sort of systematic relation between the person and her situation. The argument is straightforward.

From a formal point of view, the situation is analogous to fundamental measurement in physics, say of length, temperature, or mass. The assignment of numbers to any of these measures assumes that a very tight set of conditions holds. And I think that we can treat the cases as parallel in the following respect. Just as the satisfaction conditions for measuring length of mass may be viewed as constitutive of the range of application of the sciences that employ these measures, so the satisfaction of the conditions of consistency and coherence must be viewed as constitutive of the range of application of such concepts as those

of belief, desire, intention and action. . . . My point is that if we are to intelligibl
attribute attitudes and beliefs, or usefully describe motions as behavior, the
we are committed to finding, in the pattern of behavior, belief, and desire,
large degree of rationality and consistency.[5]

Some have supposed that this argument shows that a preference-base
account of practical reason is inescapable.[6] We seem to have no choic
but to view persons as on the whole doing what they have reason to do.
    But if Davidson's argument is successful, it points in the opposit
direction, showing that revealed preference is too weak to underwrit
a normative account of practical reason. If rationality is really a con
straint on interpretation, then the sense in which people do what the
have reasons to do is different from the question that theories of practica
reason look like they are trying to answer. An account of practical reaso
must, at a minimum, make possible the attribution of irrationality. Stan
dard cases include throwing good money after bad – for example, re
placing a muffler on an old car because one has just replaced the battery
– overinsuring, and in general acting in ways that are self-defeating ir
the long run. Other cases are more controversial, such as failing to use
one's abilities or indifference to the fate of others. But any account mus
make it possible for agents to succumb systematically to some of them.
If a constraint on the attribution of preference is that the agent ac
systematically so as to get what she prefers, there is no further questior
of rationality to be asked. One cannot ask whether she is choosing he
actions appropriately because that very appropriateness is built into the
notion of preference. If she appears irrational, or her behavior self-
defeating, "charity" requires that we attribute a different set of pref
erences to her. Davidson's own (brief) career as an experimental psy-
chologist illustrates this. Davidson sought to test whether people in
general were capable of satisfying standard axioms of rational choice.
He discovered that experimental subjects are very good – perhaps too
good – at satisfying them, because in the long run they turned out always
to act consistently toward satisfying *some* set of preferences.[7] The source
of the difficulty here should be clear: the content of a person's preferences is fixed entirely by the need to find her rational. Plainly a more
structured notion of preference is required.
    Expressed preferences, which manifest themselves in what a person
says she wants, seem like plausible candidates.[8] They have more structure than revealed preferences, because explicit avowals can depart from
rational behavior. But when we focus on the agent's express preferences,
supposing she has reason to do what she says she prefers to do, parallel
difficulties arise. There does seem to be room for the criticism of behavior, since someone may fail to do what she claims to want to do. I

Jane claims to prefer apples to oranges, yet chooses an orange on some occasion, she might seem to have failed to do what she has reason to do. But of course she can always claim either to have preferred an orange on this occasion or to have inadvertently picked up the wrong piece of fruit. That is, her expressed preferences, like her revealed preferences, can be reattributed in such a way as to make her come out rational. Now one might suppose that to do so would be illegitimate, supposing that there is a fact of the matter about what Jane prefers, quite apart from any special pleading that she or some interpreter might do, which determines whether or not she is rational. But if there is such a fact, we need more than expressed preferences to work with. Like revealed preferences, expressed preferences are too easily adjusted to guarantee rationality. In order to make preferences more determinate, their content cannot be exhausted by an assumption of rationality. For such a determination, more structure is needed.

2. Corrected preference

Both expressed and revealed preferences, taken at face value, fail to make sense of the extent to which rationality, and even consistency, must be thought of as an achievement rather than something to be assumed. The appeal to actual choice or desire does not allow the minimal amount of structure needed to make sense of that achievement. The formal apparatus cannot be made to act as a constraint at all unless the circumstances of choice or declared preference are specified. Otherwise, some set of preferences will always be satisfied.

One possible strategy, recently suggested by S. L. Hurley and John Broome,[9] requires importing additional distinctions between eligible combinations of preferences. Hurley and Broome each argue that if preferences are to be attributed to an agent, the attributor must assume that the agent has some reason for preferring one outcome to another. Broome illustrates with the case of Maurice, who prefers going to Rome to going mountaineering, prefers staying home to going to Rome, and prefers going mountaineering to staying home. Maurice seems irrational; his preferences are intransitive, indeed cyclical. But Broome points out that Maurice can legitimately get himself off the hook if he has a reason for preferring one to the other. Thus he might hate climbing, because he fears it, and so prefer Rome. Yet he might also prefer home to Rome because he tires of sightseeing, but, when given the choice between home and mountaineering, Maurice might well suppose that to stay home would be cowardly. Thus he is able to rationalize his preferences and restore his own rationality. Broome points out that not just any rationale will do; had Maurice claimed that his preferences reflected the fact that it was Thursday, we would convict him of irrationality.

Whatever its other strengths and weaknesses, it is clear that this strategy will not save preference-based accounts of rationality. It imports an independent account of rationality in order to give preferences a job to do. If whether or not a particular distinction is "eligible" constrains possible preferences, preference depends on an account of rationality rather than providing one.

An alternative and more popular strategy is to let some specification of the choice situation constrain the agent's preferences. By holding the situation of choice fixed, we avoid the easy rationalization that caused problems for expressed and revealed preferences. An agent has reason to do not whatever she actually does, but what she would do in appropriately idealized circumstances.

The easiest way to see this is to focus on the parallel structure of accounts of practical reason in terms of hypothetical choice and empiricist accounts of color and shape in terms of hypothetical perception. Just as claims about what an agent has reason to do are supposed to be defended by appeal to what he or she would choose under appropriate circumstances, so classical empiricism sought to treat perceptual properties and physical objects as constructed out of (because justified in terms of) the way things would look to a person under normal perceptual circumstances. Just as fatigue, misinformation, or emotional agitation can interfere with choice, so too can bad lighting interfere with perception. In each case there is a need to correct for unusual circumstances, but both normal perception and undistorted choice are supposed to be essential components.

Claims about physical objects cannot be justified in terms of actual sense contents alone for two reasons. First of all, counterfactual sense contents allow us to make sense of the possibility of error. If we want to claim that the world of medium-sized physical goods is constructed out of (i.e., justified in terms of) the world of sense, we need to be able to explain how the two can ever diverge. Nonstandard lighting conditions can make a tie that normally looks red look orange; a round coin appears oval from most angles. The phenomenalist can only say as much by talking about how the tie would look under normal conditions. But this is just the tip of the much larger iceberg that provides the second reason: It won't do simply to talk about the tie having changed color because to do so would leave no way of individuating and reidentifying the "constructed" physical objects.

The language of physical objects is a language of regularities involving enduring objects that retain some of their features. Although a dime may look round from one angle, elliptical from another, and flat from a third, it is essential to describing it as a single enduring coin to be able to relate those appearances to one another. Talk about actual sense contents only provides what Wilfrid Sellars calls "autobiographical regularities"[10] with no basis for assigning priority to any particular configuration of objects. Blinks, head angles, the pattern of the wallpaper, and more substantial empirical regularities are all on a par, as are the various ways a coin looks from different angles. The obvious way around this problem is to specify sensations in terms of head angles, locations, and perceptual conditions. But to do so is transparently circular, because head angles, locations, and perceptual conditions must be specified in nonsensory terms. Thus nonsensory terms enter into their own definition and justification. Counterfactual sensations – how things would look – seem a more plausible solution to this problem because they make it possible to relate sense contents to one another by talking about how they *would* be related independent of accidental circumstances.[11]

The situation with hypothetical preference is strictly parallel. Actual choice is not sufficient for a pair of reasons, strictly paralleling those that drove the epistemic phenomenalist to hypothetical perception. First is the possibility of error: An account of practical reason must allow for the possibility that a person has made an irrational choice. If we hope to construct the notion of rationality out of the notion of choice, we can't make them merely equivalent on pain of being unable to say that something was a bad choice even relative to the agent's other ends. Yet people often do make choices under duress, when misinformed, tired, or upset, that can't plausibly be treated as providing authoritative reasons for action. Just as talk about physical objects must satisfy the requirement that a single object endure even if it is misidentified, so must the idea of what is rational for a person to do satisfy the requirement that it be rational even if it is not chosen in some particular case. To account for overall consistency while allowing for inconsistent particular choices, there must be some way of distinguishing those choices that are definitive from those that are not.

Once again, this is the tip of a much larger iceberg. Like perceptual episodes, choices cannot be merely serially arranged, on pain of losing the distinction between choosing something one didn't want and changing one's mind back and forth. In order to maintain that distinction, one must appeal to what the agent would choose under suitable conditions.

Hypothetical choice has an additional wrinkle. Unlike perception of a public world of enduring objects, the content of rational choice may well vary across similarly situated individuals, as may the choices that they would make. Thus hypothetical preference must always be relativized to a particular individual.

3. Two kinds of procedure

The difficulty with accounts of hypothetical preferences can be laid out in terms of John Rawls's distinction between pure and imperfect procedures. Both pure and imperfect procedures are supposed to justify their outcomes by showing that they were generated in an appropriate manner. But the appropriateness of the procedures differs considerably. The outcome of a pure procedure is justified entirely in terms of the procedure that generates it. Rawls gives the example of a fair lottery: The winner just is whoever's number is drawn. An imperfect procedure, in contrast, justifies its consequences because it is a reliable indicator of a result that can be specified independently, but cannot be identified. Rawls offers two examples. The first is the familiar practice of dividing a cake equally by having the person who cuts it get the last choice of pieces. The other is a criminal trial, which seeks to convict all and only those who are guilty. In each case, the desired result can be specified apart from the process, while the process is a reliable means of generating it. In contrast, the result of a pure procedure cannot be specified except by reference to the procedure itself.[12]

In Rawls's terms, the notion of hypothetical choice is ambiguous between a pure procedure and an imperfect one. If it is an imperfect procedure, then there must be some independent specification of the rationality, in which case choice is not definitive of rationality.

The suggestion that hypothetical choice is a pure procedure fares no better. Because the choice is never actually made, a sophisticated specification of the conditions of choice is needed in order for it to determine what a person has reason to do. But to do so in any detail is to rig the choice in favor of a specified outcome. Hypothetical choice becomes merely an expository device. But if the conditions of choice aren't specified, then the hypothetical choice ceases to be an expository device because it turns out to be no device at all.[13]

I examine these possibilities in turn.

4. Moral phenomenalism

The parallel between hypothetical perception and hypothetical choice reveals the deep motivation for appealing to hypothetical rather than actual preferences. But it also reveals its fatal flaw – which is once again clear in the more familiar case of perception. Hypothetical perception is also ambiguous between a pure procedure and an imperfect one.

The difficulty with supposing that hypothetical perception constitutes an imperfect procedure should be clear: If physical objects exist whether or not they are perceived, and perception is merely a "reliable indicator" of their existence, they cannot be justified in terms of actual or hypothetical perception. At best, particular claims about what would be perceived depend on independently accepted claims about the way things are. Perception is ineliminable, but no longer constitutive.

But hypothetical perception cannot be a pure procedure either. The heart of the phenomenalist's claim is that the physical world is "constructed out of" actual and hypothetical sense contents, insofar as claims about it are justified solely in terms of them.[14] Phenomenalism runs into difficulty in providing a noncircular account of that construction. The appeal to hypothetical sense contents was introduced to make it possible to avoid the patently circular move of describing sense contents in terms of such physical features as head angles and the like. But this merely widens the circle without essentially changing it. Once we are committed to the existence of counterfactual sense contents, it turns out that they cannot be specified except by reference to the physical objects they are sensations of. The reason is simple: To talk about what something would look like under normal conditions is to appeal to an account of normal conditions. But 'normal conditions' must be specified in terms of physical objects. To specify what is normal in terms of what would be perceived leads to a regress of hypothetical perception. The alternative is to recognize that some account of the veridicality of normal conditions is required in order for hypothetical perception to figure in an account of the physical world.

As Sellars puts it, "We thus see that

x is red $= x$ looks red to standard observers in standard conditions

is a necessary truth *not* because the right-hand side is a definition of 'x is red,' but because 'standard conditions' means conditions in which things look what they are."[15]

Thus, Sellars suggests, talk about how things seem depend on how things (normally) are, rather than vice versa. Although it is couched in terms of meaning, Sellars's argument is best understood in terms of the role of hypothetical perception in justifying claims about how things are: Claims about how things would appear only justify claims about how things are because they depend on yet other claims about how things are. The claim is not that sensory experience is not possible without public concepts and an account of normal conditions, but that perceptual judgments about the way things are depend on accepting the truth of claims about normal conditions. Unless some specification of normal conditions is accepted, the two sides of the "definition" are not related; talk about how things look cannot be used to justify claims about how things are. But to accept an account of normal conditions is to go *outside* the vocabulary of sense out of which claims about the physical world were supposed to be justified.

I want to suggest that the situation is parallel in the case of hypothetical choice: Insofar as it is illuminating at all, talk about what would be chosen in appropriate circumstances is parasitic on some prior account of what the agent in question has reason to choose.

Modifying the Sellarsian formula accordingly, we get

x is rational (for Y) = x would be chosen (by Y) in ideal conditions

is a necessary truth *not* because the right-hand side is a definition of 'x is rational (for Y)', but because 'ideal conditions' means conditions in which people choose what is rational for them.

Recast in terms of justification rather than meaning, the claim is that talk about what would be chosen only counts as a justification against a background of an account of conditions of choice.

Why suppose that the parallel holds? A careful examination of the role of ideal conditions provides the key. Why do people choose what they do in ideal circumstances? Again, there are two possibilities. Ideal choice either serves as an imperfect procedure for determining a rational course of action, or else it is a pure procedure. The difficulty with claiming that it is an imperfect procedure should by now be clear: To claim it is an imperfect procedure is to require that some prior specification of the result it aims at be possible. To talk about a specified result in hypothetical terms is to add nothing to that prior specification.

What of the suggestion that it is a pure procedure? Phenomenalism about physical objects ran into difficulties because it turned out not to be a pure procedure. Can moral phenomenalism do any better?

The difficulty is to provide an account of the conditions under which a choice is to be made that is sufficiently determinate without begging any questions. Claims about what would ideally be chosen are empty unless some account of the ideal conditions is provided. Yet the idealization must be somehow justified. The trick is to do so without presupposing an account of what someone has reason to do.

If no account of the basis of choice is specified, the hypothetical choice is indeterminate. We are told only that such choices diverge from actual choices, without any account of which possible choices are authoritative. There are too many circumstances and too many ways in which the agent might work his or her existing preferences into some coherent order. To identify what the person has reason to do with one of those choices, without saying which one, is to offer no account at all. The notion of rationality is tied to choice in the same way that truth is tied to inquiry in a caricature of Peirce's convergent realism: We know that truth is whatever an ideal community of inquirers would eventually agree on, while having no idea of which practices or communities count as ideal.

This indeterminacy is not simply a matter of not knowing in advance what the agent will choose. The problem goes deeper, because there must be some way of adjudicating between alternative idealizations. If some determinate account is provided, the question arises of how it in particular is to be justified, except by recourse to considerations about what the agent has reason to do. To do so, though, is to fall into the very sort of circularity that created problems for phenomenalism.[16]

5. A way out?

Perhaps the dilemma is too stark. Why not slip between the horns by limiting the degree of idealization? Bishop Butler spoke of a "cool hour" of choice, in which various influences recognized as disturbing proper choice were eliminated, thus clearing the mind and allowing choice to proceed. Thus anger, weakness of will, temptation, fatigue, and other forms of duress are readily discounted, just as legal contracts made under duress are thought to be void.

This apparent middle ground turns out not to be a middle ground at all. The dilemma recurs in a more acute form: How specific are normal circumstances? How are the circumstances of the cool hour themselves to be specified?

Consider the seemingly straightforward case of the requirement that an agent be well informed.[17] In deliberating about how best to satisfy my ends, extra information is always useful, subject only to time constraints. Yet if that is all that information is doing, it would seem that I must already know what is good for me, and only be concerned about how to get it. In contrast, if I am reflecting about what ends matter to me, the role of extra information is less clear. The problem is not that it would take too long to learn of the alternatives (for hypothetical time is no time at all), but that it is hard to see what role the information plays. If one is choosing means toward some end, the advantage of additional information is obvious. If information is not supposed to concern how to adapt means to ends, it is not obvious what role it plays, nor why decisions made in the presence of information count as well informed. Might one not be driven to despair by knowing too much?[18]

Similar difficulties multiply. Does it include the absence of all emotions, or only short-lived ones? To exclude all is to make emotional attachments irrelevant to rationality; yet to specify which are to be excluded is not a simple matter. Do moods count? Are choices made when bored, lonely, or elated significant? Does exposure to advertising linking beer with hard work or chewing gum with sexuality undermine choice? Does working at a tedious job or taking orders undermine the capacity to choose? What about attitudes toward risk, or general levels of insecurity? How many alternatives should the agent be familiar with?

I mention these examples not to belittle them, nor even to show that describing a "cool hour" is impossible. Indeed, most of them are common in debates between defenders of ideal preference, who disagree about which conditions are ideal. My aim is to show that to justify some particular description of ideal conditions requires a tacit appeal to some independently motivated account of what the agent has reason to do. That is what makes questions about the effects of various constraints seem appropriate. Otherwise we are left with no way of deciding between alternative ways in which an agent's preferences might be filtered. Unless such questions are answered, the notion of undistorted reason remains empty, and hypothetical choice remains entirely open-ended. But the only way to justify answering them in a specific way is to look at the probable results of such choices – in other words to rig the choice, and render it impure.

Even if an uncontroversial account of distorting influences could be supplied, a further difficulty emerges when we consider what they are being distorted *from*. It is often reasonable to talk about what would happen if circumstances were normal – the canoe would ride better if there were less weight in the bow, the soap would lather if the water were softer – because the distorting influence is distorting what is taken to be a normal course of events. Normally (i.e., when properly trimmed) canoes ride bow up; soap normally lathers in water. Even in the case of perception, "normal" conditions are specifiable, provided one has an independent account of veridical perception. Likewise, the concept of duress in contract law is parasitic on an independent assumption that people are normally capable of making responsible choices. Talk about hypothetical choice has no such background to rely on.

Once again, the parallel with phenomenalism is instructive. Phenomenalism grows out of a set of reasonable assumptions about the circumstances in which perception fails to be veridical: A rectangular tower looks round from far away; a blue tie looks green under yellow light. Under such circumstances, perceptual experience fails to be a reliable indicator of physical properties and events. Suitably corrected, its reliability is restored. But the appropriate corrections can only be made in terms of an independent specification of the conditions of successful perception. A suitably corrected imperfect procedure does not become a pure one.

By the same token, moral phenomenalism starts with plausible assumptions about conditions that interfere with an agent choosing rationally. If someone is tired, upset, or excited, she may choose badly. Under such circumstances, choice fails to be a reliable procedure for determining what an agent has reason to do. Suitably corrected, it is such a procedure. But once again, the appropriate corrections can only be justified in light of an independent specification of what is rational. A suitably corrected imperfect procedure does not become a pure one.

This is not to say that were a person to be in suitable circumstances, his choices would not provide reasons for action, any more than the difficulties with phenomenalism show that looking at something in normal lighting does not show its color. Rather, the point is that the connection between preference and rationality depends on an independently established account of the latter.[19]

6. Two versions of hypothetical choice

Questions about what someone would do or want in hypothetical circumstances admit of two very different construals. These can be brought out by considering second-person queries about a person's behavior in imaginary situations. Such questions have the form "What would you do if . . . ?" If someone offered a bribe? If your best friend was being considered for a position for which you supposed there were better-qualified candidates? If you were caught arguing inconsistently? Such questions admit of two construals. One may be asking for something like a *prediction:* Based on what you know about yourself, how do you think you would react in such circumstances? Such questions are often asked in the context of a sort of unmasking – don't be so critical, you probably wouldn't be able to act any differently. Alternatively, one might be asking for *advice:* What do you think someone ought to do in such circumstances? The two construals invite different answers: A person might deny he would accept a bribe while conceding that he might well be enticed; or predict that she would favor a friend while hoping for the strength not to; or hope he would change his views on the basis of argument, while suspecting based on past experience that he would be dogmatic. In each case, talk about what one would do is not an appeal to any regular course of events, but an opaque way of capturing what one ought to do.[20] To be sure, there are cases in which the two

construals collapse into one: An instrumentally rational agent concerned
only with advancing her ends will predictably do what she ought to do
in order to advance those ends. But the two construals diverge in all
those cases where what someone judges best is not what she will predictably do.[21,22]

7. Choice, reflection, and hypothetical choice

The idea of basing practical reason on preference has two further sources
of plausibility. The first is the view that a person's life is his to live in
light of a conception of the good he has chosen. Not only is much political
rhetoric couched in terms of choice; political culture more generally is
informed by a presumption of a burden of proof according to which
every issue must be treated as a matter of individual choice unless there
is some reason to interfere with it. But this is a substantive political
claim, and the concept of rationality cannot be rigged to presuppose it.

The second is the importance of reflection in such choices. A choice
made in a cool hour is more likely to reflect one's deepest aspirations
than one made in haste, under pressure, or in conformity with one's
social situation. Moral reflection is also intimately connected to notions
of autonomy and seems to make choices worthy of respect. But hypothetical reflection is no reflection at all; the importance of reflection is
that it take place, not the particular result it achieves. That is, if reflection
is a "pure procedure" it needs to take place to justify its outcome. Just
as a fair lottery is fair because it has actually taken place, so too is a
reflective choice legitimate because it has. To talk about what would
have been chosen is like justifying some distribution of wealth by saying
it could have been the outcome of a series of fair bets. Reflection that
never actually takes place provides no justification at all, because the
process itself carries the moral value. Hypothetical choices do not require constitutional protection.

Still, the difficulties with ideal-choice accounts of rationality do not
depend entirely on the fact that the choices are nonactual. An account
that only applies if the agent actually has gone through the process of
reflective choice subject to some set of constraints,[23] avoids the problems
that result from the fact that the choice was never actually made. But
it still faces the central problem: It collapses an imperfect procedure
into a pure procedure. Whether or not the process of deliberation is
actually carried out, some justification must be given for employing some
particular set of constraints on that process. Given the multiplicity of
possible constraints, there is no way to choose between them without

taking into account the results they issue. To do so, though, involves an independent standard of practical reason.

8. Conclusion

I conclude with a modest positive proposal. In the first appendix to *An Enquiry Concerning the Principles of Morals,* Hume says

Ask a man why he uses exercise, he will answer, *because he desires to keep his health.* If you then enquire, *why he desires health,* he will readily reply *because sickness is painful.* If you push your enquiries further, and desire a reason *why he hates pain,* it is impossible that he can give any. This is an ultimate end, and is never referred to any other object. . . . Something must be [un]desireable on its own account, and this because of its immediate accord or agreement with human sentiment and affection.[24]

The view that Hume seems to be expressing here rests on a confusion. The reason that we take a person's dislike for pain as a final step in justification is not that "agreement with human sentiment" automatically provides reasons for action, any more than perception on its own provides reasons for belief.

Hume is concerned with the fact that the process of giving reasons seems to come to an end once a person appeals to his or her preferences. Hume's suggestion seems to be that preferences just *are* reasons. I wish to offer a different diagnosis. Appeal to preference works in two quite different ways, parallel to appeal to perception. Sometimes one expresses a preference as a way of revealing that reasons have failed to move one's will, just as one confesses that things still look a certain way after being convinced that they aren't so. This is a parasitic sense, for one is not offering reasons so much as withdrawing from the giving of them. More often, one states a preference as a way of giving a reason, in part as a way of saying that this is a private matter, and nobody else has any business telling me what to do. That is, one appeals to preferences to justify behavior in what one takes to be circumstances in which such appeal is appropriate. The latter is the interesting case. Its analysis depends on a more complete account of what the analogue in practical reason of "normal" perceptual conditions might turn out to be. Whether a preference provides a reason for action depends on whether those conditions are satisfied; apart from them, no answer is possible. Thus, to use a favorite example of philosophers, in choosing flavors of ice cream, my preference provides me with all the reason I need, because of the context. But my dislike of members of some minority does not give me any reason whatsoever in carrying out the tasks of some public office. Again, a compulsive desire to wash my hands provides no reason; whether or not a whim provides a reason depends on the context.[25] A full spelling out of those conditions awaits two lines of development. On one side, an account of individual circumstances of choice is needed. From another, the very sorts of developments in political philosophy that preference-based accounts sought to provide, including perhaps an articulation and defense of a distinction between public and private matters, may be needed. Those matters must wait for another occasion.

Notes

1 In connection with starting points for moral inquiry, see, for example, Derek Parfit, *Reasons and Persons* (Oxford: Oxford University Press, 1984); John Mackie, *Ethics: Inventing Right and Wrong* (Harmondsworth, England: Penguin Books, 1978); David Gauthier, *Morals by Agreement* (Oxford: Clarendon Press, 1986); G. H. von Wright, *Varieties of Goodness* (London: Routledge and Kegan Paul, 1963); James Griffin, *Well-Being* (Oxford: Clarendon Press, 1986); John Rawls, *A Theory of Justice* (Cambridge, Mass.: Harvard University Press, 1971); John Harsanyi, *Essays on Ethics, Social Behavior, and Scientific Explanation* (Dordrecht: Reidel, 1976); Richard Brandt, *A Theory of the Good and Right* (Oxford: Clarendon Press, 1978); and David Lewis, "Dispositional Theories of Value," *Proceedings of the Aristotelian Society,* Supplementary Volume 63 (1989).

The entire "public choice" literature presumes that preferences are the appropriate inputs to governmental decision making. Seminal works include James Buchanan and Gordon Tullock, *The Calculus of Consent* (Ann Arbor: University of Michigan Press, 1962); and Kenneth Arrow, *Social Choice and Individual Values*, 2d ed. (New Haven: Yale University Press, 1963). For a critique, see Cass Sunstein, "Preferences and Politics," *Philosophy and Public Affairs* 20, no. 3 (winter 1991):3–34.

2 The literature on this subject divides roughly equally between accounts of reason and accounts of the good. In their works cited in note 1, Derek Parfit, John Mackie, and David Gauthier seek to derive preference-based accounts of the requirements of practical reason. In their cited works, G.H. von Wright, James Griffin, and John Rawls all defend accounts of the good that appeal to choice. In the nineteenth century, accounts of good were offered by J. S. Mill in *Utilitarianism* and Henry Sidgwick in *The Methods of Ethics.* John Harsanyi (*Essays on Ethics*) defends choice-based accounts of both, in different places, as does Richard Brandt (*Theory of the Good and Right*). David Lewis ("Dispositional Theories of Value") offers a preference-based account of "value" that appears to be generic between the two.

3 Of course, the details of these constraints are controversial in ways that need not concern us here. For standard treatments, see Richard Jeffrey, *The Logic of Decision,* 2d ed. (University of Chicago Press, Chicago, 1983); R. D.

Luce and H. Raiffa; *Games and Decisions* (New York: John Wiley, 1957); and Gauthier, *Morals by Agreement*.

4 A third possibility, though immediately tempting, quickly proves hopeless: the view that preferences are experienced conscious states. This view, associated both with traditional empiricism and more recently with "Austrian economics," is put forward by Eugene von Böhm-Bawerk, *Karl Marx and the Close of His System* (New York: Augustus M. Kelley, 1949; translation of *Zum Abschluss des Marxchen Systems,* Berlin, 1896), and developed by Ludwig von Mises in *Human Action* (Chicago: University of Chicago Press, 1949). Its difficulty arises from its claim that preferences are both present to consciousness and apply to indefinitely many possible cases. For reasons made familiar by Wittgenstein, such an account works no better for preference than for rule following. See *Philosophical Investigations,* paragraph 70.

5 Donald Davidson, "Psychology as Philosophy," in his *Essays on Actions and Events* (Oxford: Clarendon Press, 1980), p. 237.

6 Including Davidson: See his "A New Basis for Decision Theory," in *Theory and Decision* (1986).

7 Davidson, "Psychology as Philosophy," in *Essays on Actions and Events.*

8 Davidson's view does not include a sharp line between expressed and revealed preferences. Speech behavior is treated as simply more behavior, on the basis of which preferences can be attributed, given an assumption of overall rationality.

9 See S. L. Hurley, *Natural Reasons* (Oxford: Clarendon Press, 1989); John Broome, "Rationality and the Sure Thing Principle," in Gay Meeks, ed., *Thoughtful Economic Man* (Cambridge: Cambridge University Press, 1991); and Broome, *Weighing Choices* (Oxford: Basil Blackwell, 1991).

10 Wilfrid Sellars, "Phenomenalism," in *Science, Perception, and Reality* (London: Routledge and Kegan Paul, 1964).

11 Berkeley provides an alternative way out of this problem: He claims that to be is to be actually perceived by God. As a result, all things are always actually perceived, so no counterfactuals need to be introduced. Subsequent phenomenalists have been unwilling to embrace Berkeley's solution.

12 Rawls, *Theory of Justice,* p. 85. It is not clear that there are any procedures that are entirely pure in Rawls's sense. Even a lottery produces a result specificable as random. Still, it must actually take place in order for there to be a winner. The same may be true of cake cutting – there are infinitely many equal divisions, though cutting is required to produce a specific one.

13 Although it is hard to resist the temptation to say that an agent ought to do what she would decide to do if she knew everything, it is not at all obvious why this should be so. It may be that if I knew everything I would offer people unsolicited advice; it does not follow that I should do so now.

14 Rudolf Carnap, *The Logical Structure of the World and Pseudo-problems in Philosophy,* translated by Rolf George (Berkeley: University of California

Press, 1967), pp. 5–10, 148–51. See also J. S. Mill, *An Examination of Sir William Hamilton's Philosophy,* Appendix.

15 Wilfrid Sellars, "Empiricism and the Philosophy of Mind," in *Science, Perception and Reality* (London: Routledge and Kegan Paul, 1964), p. 147.

16 In *Well-Being,* James Griffin offers another (heroic) compromise, claiming that under ideal circumstances, people will in fact choose just those goods that are independently known to be valuable. The role of choice in Griffin's account remains obscure, except insofar as it leaves room for a state to actively promote those goods without being coercive.

17 This construal is offered as an account of what is good for a person by, among others, Rawls, Brandt, and Sidgwick, and (with a minor modification incorporating "experience" rather than full information) by Lewis as an account of value.

18 This point has been made in various ways by Mark Johnston, "Dispositional Theories of Value," *Proceedings of the Aristotelian Society,* Supplementary Volume 63 (1989); J. David Velleman, "Brandt's Definition of 'Good,' " *Philosophical Review* 97, no. 3 (July 1988): 353–71; and Allan Gibbard, *Wise Choices, Apt Feelings* (Cambridge, Mass.: Harvard University Press, 1990).

19 Sellars's own account of color treats it as a feature of perceivers rather than of objects. Perhaps an account of choice can be constructed in parallel fashion. The account I have given of hypothetical choice need not take a stand on this question. Phenomenalism's parallel structure, and Sellars's account of it, applies to shapes as well as colors. The issue concerns the need for a nonperceptual account of perceivable properties, not their mind-independence.

20 Stanley Cavell makes a related point in discussing what he calls "Projective Imagination." See *The Claim of Reason* (Oxford: Oxford University Press, 1979).

21 In experiments studying obedience to authority, Stanley Milgram found that most subjects were willing to inflict what they believed to be painful and even lethal electrical shocks when pressured to do so by experimenters. But of course most people, when asked what they would do, denied that they would be so obedient. Plainly the evaluative and predictive senses of "would" have come apart in these cases. See Stanley Milgram, *Obedience to Authority* (New York: Harper and Row, 1974).

22 Annette Baier has proposed that the worthiness of particular cases of trust can be assessed by considering whether it would survive knowledge of its basis. Baier's suggestion employs the normative sense of 'would' involved here. Psychological mechanisms of various sorts may reinforce bad trust as they reinforce bad faith. The test has content because it relies on assessing whether one could justify continuing the trust, rather than whether one could psychologically pull it off. See "Trust and Antitrust," *Ethics* 96 (1986): 231–60.

23 See, for example, Gauthier, *Morals by Agreement,* ch. 2, which supposes

that preferences are rational only if revealed and expressed preferences coincide.

24 David Hume, *An Enquiry Concerning the Principles of Morals,* in L. A. Selby-Bigge, ed., *Enquiries concerning Human Understanding and concerning the Principles of Morals* (Oxford: Clarendon Press, 1975), p. 293.

25 Empiricist philosophers sometimes suggest that sensory inputs provide *prima facie,* but defeasible, grounds for belief. Whatever its merits in the case of perception, such an account can only be readily extended to preferences with care. Compulsive urges, and perhaps morally unacceptable ones as well, do not provide reasons that are simply outweighed; they are defeated entirely.

7

Reason and needs

DAVID COPP

There is a conception of rational self-grounded deliberation and choice. It is a conception of self-grounded choice in that, when we have it in play, we view a person as rational if she aims to realize the good from her own standpoint. And we view a person's actions as rational when they contribute to realizing the good from her own standpoint. The conception is morally neutral in the sense that, with it in play, we do not judge the rationality of people or of their actions on the basis of our own moral views. This conception supports, for example, our judgment that it is coherent to ask for reasons to be moral, and that a morally appalling tyrant could conceivably be entirely rational in the choices he makes. Machiavelli's *Prince* provides a convincing account of rational statecraft even though Machiavelli's ruler does not act on moral reasons. I do not believe there is room to doubt that we have a conception of self-grounded rationality. But there is of course room for disagreement about what to count as the good "from an agent's own standpoint," especially since this is to some extent a term of art. I shall make a few remarks about this before I state my goals for this essay.

It would be a mistake to equate the good "from an agent's standpoint"

This essay is based on my manuscript *Morality, Skepticism and Society.* I am grateful for the useful comments of the students who read versions of the manuscript in seminars I gave at the University of Illinois at Chicago in 1987 and the University of California, Davis, in 1989. I presented versions of the essay to the Department of Philosophy at the University of Oklahoma in February 1990 and to the conference on "Value, Welfare, and Morality" at Bowling Green State University in April 1990, and I am grateful for the helpful discussion on both occasions. I am also indebted to John Broome, Gilbert Harman, and Garrett Thomson for useful discussions and comments. My research was assisted by the generous support of several institutions. During the year 1983–4, I held a Research Grant and Research Time Stipend (410-82-0640) from the Social Sciences and Humanities Research Council of Canada. During the spring of 1986, I benefited from a Short Research Leave that was awarded me by the Campus Research Board of the University of Illinois at Chicago. Most recently, the generosity of the Research Triangle Foundation enabled me to spend the year 1988–9 at the National Humanities Center, North Carolina. Simon Fraser University granted me the leaves of absence I required in order to take advantage of these opportunities.

with what would be good for the agent. For example, an altruistic goal may be good from my standpoint, and therefore be rational for me to pursue, quite independently of whether achieving it would also contribute to my own good. Moreover, certain things might arguably be good for me without being good from my standpoint. Some would argue, for example, that it would be good for me to develop and exercise my talents in a way that would call forth the maximum level of complexity in skills required for their exercise. Yet this may not be good from my standpoint, for I may value and enjoy exercising less subtle talents in a less complex way. Hence, the conception of self-grounded rational choice is not the conception of choice aimed at realizing the agent's *own* good.

It would more obviously be a mistake to equate the good from the agent's standpoint with the good *simpliciter*. For example, democracy is something most of us would agree to be good, but it would not be good from the standpoint of Machiavelli's prince. A certain strategically motivated policy of deceiving the population might be good from the standpoint of the prince, but it would not be good *simpliciter*. Nor is the prince likely to think that it would be good *simpliciter*. It would be a mistake to equate the good from the agent's standpoint with what the agent would judge to be good *simpliciter*. It seems at least conceivable, for example, that Machiavelli's prince would agree with us that democracy would be good *simpliciter* even though he does not value it and he would not be rational to pursue it, since it would not be good from his standpoint.

The conception of self-grounded rational choice is the conception of choice that does well at realizing the good from the agent's standpoint. It is not the conception of choice that does well at realizing what the agent *takes* to be good from her standpoint. People can be mistaken in what they take to be good from their standpoint. They can be confused, deceived, or manipulated. We can aim to improve people's ability to recognize the good from their standpoint, just as Machiavelli aimed to explain what is good from the standpoint of a prince.

All of these points about the good from an agent's standpoint are accepted in the standard theories of deliberative rationality, which I call "preference theories." Preference theories treat the good from an agent's standpoint as a function of his "preferences," where the term 'preference' is used to refer to any of his pro-attitudes, including his desires, hopes, and so on. Theories of this kind can be analyzed as the conjunction of two claims: a claim to the effect that the rationally required action for an agent in a circumstance is the action that would maximize the good from his standpoint, and an account of the good from an agent's standpoint as a function of his preferences.

As I formulate them, each theory of rational deliberation proposes a norm that we can use to evaluate people's choices as rationally required, rationally prohibited, or as merely rational, in the sense of rationally permitted. A norm of self-grounded rationality would relate actions to something that could plausibly be regarded as good from the standpoint of the agent. There must be something about the agent that determines what counts as good from her standpoint. For example, a simple preference theory proposes a norm to the effect that the rationally required action for an agent in a situation is the action that would maximize the expected degree to which her preferences will be satisfied. Such a theory has implications about what counts as a reason for an action. The simple preference theory implies, for example, that reasons are nothing but facts about the tendency of actions to satisfy the agent's preferences. In general, a theory counts the fact that S's action a would have property p as a reason for S to do a just in case, given the theory's account of the good from the standpoint of S, the fact that S's doing a would have property p entails that S's doing a would contribute to the good from S's standpoint.

I shall argue that preference theories are too simple. To be sure, one's preferences are a source of reasons in ordinary circumstances, but they are not always a source of reasons. Moreover, meeting one's basic needs is central to achieving the good from one's own standpoint. And what a person basically needs is not determined by her preferences, nor is the rationality of her seeking to meet her needs dependent on her preferences. I shall defend three theses about needs. First, people have certain basic needs and what a person basically needs is not determined by her preferences or other psychological states. I shall call this the "objectivity-of-needs thesis." Second, if a person has a basic need for something, then she has a reason to secure it for herself, or to keep it if she already has it. I shall call this the "weak reason-and-needs thesis." Third, if doing a certain thing would prevent a person from meeting her basic needs, then she is not rationally required to do it. This is the "strong reason-and-needs thesis."

I shall argue that an adequate theory of self-grounded rationality would have to take into account more than simply the agent's preferences; it would also have to take into account her needs and values. I shall propose what I call the "principle of needs-and-values rationality," or the "needs-and-values principle," a standard of rational choice that judges actions in light of the agent's needs, values, and preferences.

1. Needs and preference theories

I begin with The Case of the Sudden Urge. Suppose I have a sudden very strong urge to taste cyanide. I am fully informed about cyanide. I know what it does to human bodies and I have vividly pictured to myself what it does. Yet I now confront a bottle of the stuff and I find myself with this macabre urge – a "preference" – to taste it. It is clear that, given that tasting the cyanide would kill me, I have a reason not to taste it. In fact, given what cyanide does, my having the urge to taste it gives me a reason to avoid cyanide entirely; it does not give me any reason at all to taste it. No investigation of my psychology is required in order to show this. Furthermore, given that tasting the cyanide would prevent me from realizing my basic needs, including my need to survive and my need for physical integrity, I am not rationally *required* to taste the cyanide no matter what else might be true of me. No investigation of my psychology is required in order to show this either. There are two key claims here: first, the urge is no reason to taste, and second, I am not rationally required to taste since I can otherwise meet my needs.

Let me now consider a new case, The Case of the Rational Suicide. In the previous case, I am assailed by the urge to taste the cyanide even though my prospects are quite rosy. But in the new case, I have decided to end my life by taking some cyanide. I have evaluated my life by my own standards and I have decided that I would prefer not to exist. I have decided that my life is not worth living. And let us assume that this decision would survive careful reevaluation. It is not that I would change my assessment were I to look at things more calmly or carefully. I have decided to take the cyanide, but suppose that I balk at the last moment. It seems to me that I am not irrational to balk, even though my future prospects are sufficiently bleak, from the standpoint of my own preferences and values, that I also would not have been irrational to go ahead and end my life. The key claim here is, again, that I am not rationally required to end my life by tasting the cyanide provided that I could carry on and at least meet my basic needs.

If we assume the objectivity of basic needs, which I shall assume until the next section of the essay, then my two key claims about the examples are supported by the strong thesis about reasons and needs. The weak thesis implies that since tasting the cyanide would kill me, and thereby deprive me of what I need in order to survive, I have a reason not to taste it. It also implies that my urge to taste cyanide is a reason for me to avoid possessing any. The strong thesis allows, in the case of the rational suicide, that I would be "rational" to commit suicide, in that I would be rationally *permitted* to commit suicide. And it allows the possibility of a person's being rationally required to commit suicide if he is not in a position to meet his basic needs. But in the case of the sudden urge, I am able to meet my needs. Given this, and given that tasting the cyanide would prevent me from meeting my needs, the strong thesis implies that my urge is no reason to taste the cyanide. For if it were, then in some possible case of this kind, my urge presumably could tip the balance and ensure that I would be rationally required to taste the cyanide. Yet the strong thesis implies that I am not rationally required to taste it in any possible circumstance where I am able to meet my needs.

I shall now argue that if the objectivity-of-needs thesis is correct, then no preference theory can support our intuitions about the examples. To begin, consider the simple theory I mentioned above. It implies that I would be rationally required to taste the cyanide if my preferences lined up appropriately with the world. It is obvious, of course, that tasting the cyanide would frustrate any desires I have for my future as well as desires I would otherwise have in the future. But if my desires for the future are sufficiently ambitious or if the future would be sufficiently bleak, as in the case of the rational suicide, then it may turn out that I will maximize the satisfaction of my desires by taking the cyanide. If so, then the simple theory implies that I am rationally required to take the cyanide even though taking it clearly would prevent me from meeting my needs. Any preference theory would entail that if I had an appropriate psychology, I would be rationally required to taste the cyanide. Moreover, a preference theory would imply that whether or not I have a reason *not* to taste the cyanide depends on the state of my psychology. This is enough to show that preference theories conflict with our intuitions in the examples. For we want to say that the fact that the cyanide would kill me is sufficient to give me a reason not to taste it and is sufficient to show that I am not rationally required to taste it as long as I am in a position to meet my basic needs.

Indeed, the simple theory faces even more embarrassment. For it implies that the fact that tasting the cyanide would satisfy my urge is a reason for me to taste it. Yet our intuition in The Case of the Sudden Urge is that, given that I can meet my needs, and given what cyanide will do to me, the fact that I have this urge gives me a reason to avoid cyanide, not a reason to taste it. An advocate of the simple theory might reply that the urge gives me at least a very weak reason to taste the cyanide, although the reason is overridden by the fact that taking the cyanide would kill me and thereby prevent me from realizing any of my other preferences.[1] But consider now a series of examples, in each one of which my urge is stronger and more stubborn than in the last. The simple theory would presumably have to say that the stronger or more stubborn my urge, the better or stronger the reason it gives me to taste the cyanide. And it would have to say that the stronger my reason, the less decisively it is overridden by my other preferences, other things being equal. But I want to say that I have no reason to taste the cyanide in any of the sudden urge cases, and that a stronger urge would give me a stronger reason to avoid cyanide, not a stronger reason to taste it.

No doubt it will be objected that a well-designed preference theory could escape these charges. For example, a theory might incorporate a condition restricting the desires, the satisfaction of which counts as a reason, to those that would survive reflection and deliberation of a particularly challenging kind.[2] Or a theory might incorporate a test restricting the preferences that count as reason-giving to those that the agent has endorsed, in that she at least does not desire not to have them.[3] Or a theory could combine these two tests and hold that a desire is a rational consideration just in case it would both persist and be endorsed by the agent after reflection and deliberation. It could then be argued that a desire to taste cyanide would not ordinarily survive in an agent who had properly reflected and deliberated, and it would not ordinarily be endorsed by the agent, for unless a person desired to kill himself, he would ordinarily desire to be rid of the urge to taste cyanide.

Perhaps it is correct in the case of the sudden urge that my urge to taste cyanide would fail tests of these kinds, especially the combined test. If I reflected adequately on the fact that tasting the cyanide would be fatal, my urge might disappear and it is unlikely that I would endorse it. But there is no guarantee that the urge would either disappear or fail to be endorsed by me. It could be stubborn enough that it would survive reflection and deliberation, and I could be so taken with curiosity that I would endorse it, wanting to satisfy it. However, if my urge were this strong and persistent, and if I were this curious, we would be all the more convinced that the urge gives me a reason to avoid cyanide. We would not intuitively count it as giving me a reason to taste the cyanide.[4] The problem is that a preference theory treats the rationality of tasting the cyanide as depending on the actual workings of my psychology. Hence, assuming that the theory is neither *ad hoc* nor question-begging, a preference theory will leave it a contingent matter whether my urge to taste the cyanide would qualify as giving me a reason to taste it, even though tasting it would kill me, and even though I would otherwise be able to meet my needs.

To be sure, a preference theory could simply rule out urges and whims by fiat. For although a preference theory holds that the good for an agent is determined by facts about his pro-attitudes, it does not have to say that all pro-attitudes are sources of reasons. Yet some urges do give us reason to choose one way rather than another. My urge to smell a rose ordinarily gives me a reason to smell a rose, for example. Of course, a theory might attempt to rule out exactly the problematic urges and whims by some very refined device, as I try to do in the needs-and-values principle, but doing so would be *ad hoc* unless some rationale could be given for the device that did not involve an implicit concession that there are reasons that are not grounded in one's preferences. I am willing to make this concession explicitly.

Some preference theories take a longer and more reflective view of the agent's life. Consider, for example, the idea, which is suggested by remarks of John Rawls, that rationality consists in maximizing the satisfaction of the coherent life plan that one has at the time of choice, or that one would acquire as a result of deliberation and reflection at that time.[5] David Gauthier suggests a view of this kind in saying that a fully reasoned action would express a single coherent integrated set of reflectively endorsed concerns.[6] Life-plan views of this kind offer several ways to neutralize the problem about the sudden urge to taste cyanide. For the urge would be unlikely to fit into a single coherent and integrated life plan. Tasting the cyanide would prevent me from satisfying virtually any life plan.

Unfortunately, matters are not so simple. One kind of theory would evaluate the rationality of my taking the cyanide in relation to the life plan I would adopt as a result of deliberation at the time that I have the urge. But if I am sufficiently overtaken by the urge, it could be that that plan would give pride of place to tasting cyanide. The underlying idea of a life-plan view is presumably to assess the rationality of a person's actions in light of their impact on her life as a whole. Perhaps then we should evaluate actions on the basis of their expected impact on a life plan that reflects the agent's lasting concerns and interests rather than the concerns she merely happens to have at the time of action. Unfortunately, a person's concerns and interests normally change as she lives her life, and the result can be that the life plan a person would adopt at one time may be quite different from the plan that she would adopt at another time. And it may be quite unclear how to integrate into a coherent and lasting lifetime plan all of a person's concerns through the whole of her life, including perhaps concerns she would have had under certain counterfactual circumstances. For these reasons, it simply is not realistic to make the rationality of a person and of her actions depend on her being someone who would or could formulate a lasting plan for her life as a whole.

Leaving these problems aside, however, the chief problem with life-plan theories in the present context is that mere urges are sometimes sources of reasons even if they would lead a person to depart from his plans. For instance, it might be quite rational to indulge a whim by traveling abroad for a year even if one of the costs would be to delay graduation from college. Again, although indulging a whim to do something unplanned would interfere with any plan, this does not mean that doing so would always be irrational. Hence, the mere fact that satisfying my urge to taste the cyanide would interfere with my life plan is not sufficient to show that it gives me no reason to taste the cyanide. A more complex story must be told.[7] And since life-plan theories do not take directly into account the impact of a person's plans and preferences on his ability to satisfy his basic needs, they cannot accommodate our intuitions about the urge to taste cyanide. For our intuition is that the fact that tasting the cyanide would prevent me from meeting my basic needs is sufficient by itself to mean that I have a reason not to taste the cyanide. And it is sufficient to mean that I am not rationally required to taste the cyanide as long as I am able to satisfy my basic needs. Life-plan theories cannot ensure these results and do not recognize the significance of the fact about needs.

Attempts to deal with our intuitions about the cyanide examples within a preference theory can all be short-circuited by a simple argument. For if my three theses about needs are accepted, there is a fundamental problem with preference theories that cannot be repaired. According to the reason-and-needs theses, the rationality of a choice can depend directly on how it relates to the basic needs of the agent. I have a reason to seek the things that I need and I am never rationally required to do something that would undermine my ability to meet my needs. If the objectivity-of-needs thesis is correct, moreover, then what a person basically needs is not determined by facts about the preferences a person happens to have. It follows therefore from the conjunction of my three theses about needs that the rationality of an action is not determined solely by facts about the preferences the agent happens to have. And this means that no preference theory can accommodate the theses about reason and needs.

One caveat is required in order to cinch the argument. A preference theory allows that the rationality of a choice depends on whether it would in fact contribute to the realization of the good from the agent's own standpoint. And, of course, in ordinary circumstances, meeting one's basic needs would contribute to the realization of one's good. According to a preference theory, however, whether one is rational to meet one's needs depends on the facts about one's pro-attitudes which, according to the theory, determine what counts as good from one's standpoint. If I would prefer overall to kill myself, then I may have no reason, according to a preference theory, to secure for myself certain things that I need in order to live. And I may be rationally required to deprive myself of something that I need in order to live. These results are inconsistent with the reason and needs theses.

To summarize: The mere urge to taste the cyanide seems intuitively to be no reason at all. I submit that it is disqualified as a reason by the fact that tasting it would ensure that I fail to meet my most basic needs. Any adequate theory of rationality must account for the case of the sudden urge, and I claim that no preference theory can do so. For the importance to an agent's good of his meeting his needs is not fully accounted for by facts about the preferences he happens to have.

2. Needs, basic needs, and reasons

Some of the things we need are needed only in light of other things we want, prefer, or value. For example, if I want to write to a friend right now, I may need a pen and paper. In this case, I need the pen and paper only because I want to write to my friend, and the status of the pen as something I need depends on this fact about my psychology. I will call needs of this sort "occasional needs." Some needs are more fundamental. For example, I need food and water, light, shelter, health, a source of heat in cold weather, friends, companions, and a sense of self-respect, among other things. These are needs I have in common with every other person. Their status as needs does not depend on peculiarities of my preferences. These are things that are ordinarily essential to every person's good. I shall call needs of this sort "basic needs."[8] David Braybrooke calls them "course-of-life needs."[9] It is basic or course-of-life needs that enter my account of rationality.

The notion of a basic need is controversial and difficult, but Braybrooke contends that anyone with the concept would agree that certain things are matters of need, such as periodic rest, including sleep, and freedom from harassment, including freedom from being continually frightened.[10] Of course, he points out, a need can be met in different ways, by different "forms of provision," and it can be met to different degrees, even though there may be a "minimum standard of provision" appropriate to each person under each heading of need. For example, we believe there is a need for sleep, but we are not committed to thinking that everyone needs the same amount of sleep and in the same kind of bed and so on. The minimum amount that would meet one person's need might be different from the minimum amount that would meet another's need.[11]

A basic need gives rise to derivative needs for the things required in order to meet it. For example, if light is a basic need, and if I am trapped down a mine, then I need a source of artificial light. Since there is not a presumption that everyone in the human population needs a source of artificial light, we do not classify it as a matter of basic need. But a source of artificial light is a "form of provision" that may be required in certain circumstances in order to meet the need for light. Things that are in this way required for meeting a basic need may be called "required forms of provision." The distinction between such things and matters of basic need is dependent on background circumstances, since if everyone were trapped in a mine we might come to classify a source of artificial light as a matter of basic need. But this does not gainsay the usefulness of the distinction.

When it is claimed that a person needs something, it is in order to ask what she needs it for. I shall speak of the "ground" of a need, in referring to the thing a matter of need is needed for. A person needs something when she requires it in order to realize something that she desires, prefers, or values, but if this is the only ground of the need, the need is merely occasional. In order to understand basic needs, we need to identify the ground(s) of the basic matters of need. We need to understand why it is that a basic need can be grounded in things a person may not even desire or value and why it is that other things cannot ground a need unless they are desired or valued. For example, people need food and air in order to survive, and they need food and air even if they do not want to survive. This is what makes them basic needs. But I need a pen and paper right now only because I want to write to my friend right now. I might not otherwise need the pen and paper. I must explain this, and I require a general account that will apply to all of the matters of basic need.

According to the weak reason-and-needs thesis, if I have a basic need for something, then I have a reason to secure it for myself, or to keep it if I already have it. I take this thesis to be noncontroversial, although it does need to be blended into a comprehensive account of rational choice, as I shall explain. It is a substantive thesis about practical reason rather than a conceptual point, for the very idea that something has a need does not entail that it has a reason. Plants have needs without having reasons. It is easy to understand why occasional needs are a source of reasons, provided we assume that a person ordinarily has a reason to secure what is required in order to realize his desires, preferences, and values. But it is more difficult to understand why I have reason to try to secure for myself a minimum standard of provision of matters of basic need, for the status of something as a matter of basic need does not depend on my wanting it. Hence, whatever it is that grounds matters of basic need must be such that there is a presumption that every person has a reason to try to achieve it or keep it for herself, independently of her desires, preferences, or values.

Two ideas seem central to the idea of a basic need. First, a person must meet her basic needs in order to avoid harm.[12] David Wiggins suggests that to be deprived of a matter of basic need is to be harmed or to be subjected to a nonnegligible probability of harm, given the "laws of nature, unalterable and invariable environmental facts, or facts about human constitution."[13] And Garrett Thomson suggests that if a person has a basic need for something, then his life would be "blighted or seriously harmed without it."[14] If, then, the matters of basic need are things that we require in the nature of things in order to avoid a blighted or harmed life, we can see a connection between meeting basic needs and acting rationally. For there is a presumption that every person has a reason to avoid a blighted or harmed life, independently of her desires, preferences, or values.

The second central idea is that basic needs are the requirements of a "normal" life. Hence, Braybrooke says that basic needs are the things that are "essential to living or to functioning normally."[15] This idea is slippery. The notion of a "normal" human life is subject to interpretation in light of different ideas people may have in different circumstances about what is to be expected in human life. But in the present context, a viable conception of normal life would have to be connected with the idea that the basic needs are required to avoid a blighted and harmed life. Both of these ideas come into play when we consider the basic needs of other living things. For example, in order to avoid certain obvious harms, a plant needs an appropriate amount of water, namely an amount that will enable it to develop in a manner normal for its kind. The connection between the ideas of harm and normality in the case of a human is that a person's life is blighted and harmed if he is deprived of the things that he would need in the nature of things in order to lead a normal life, for he would then be unable to choose a normal life. That is, our theory must make the following connection: What it counts as normal life in this context must be such that a person who is deprived of (the ability to live) a normal life is *ipso facto* leading a blighted and harmed life.

This means that a statistical conception of normality is not what we need in this context. In certain historical contexts, for example, a statistically normal life would be a life of illiteracy, and yet a person who "deprived" of the "opportunity" to be illiterate, by being taught to read, is not thereby harmed. The weak reason-and-needs thesis implies that "normality" is to be read in such a way that *anyone* can be presumed to have a reason to want what is required for a 'normal' life. The present project requires "normal life" to be construed as a form of life deprivation of which would constitute a harm in any context.[16]

Braybrooke attempts to render more precise the notion of a normal life by explaining it as a certain kind of life in a society. He suggests that basic needs are things that, at some time in the course of the life of every member of the population, are "[presumptively] indispensable to mind or body in performing [without derangement] the tasks assigned them] under a combination of basic social roles, namely, the roles of parent, householder, worker and citizen."[17] But it would be a mistake to think that a person's life must count as blighted if he is not serving in a combination of these social roles. A person who has freely chosen a nonstandard life may nevertheless be leading a nonblighted life. And this means that the basic needs are not the requirements for a standard life of the sort Braybrooke describes. Yet a person's life *would* seem blighted if she were unable to choose a standard life even if she wanted such a life. Perhaps, then, the basic needs are the requirements for being able to choose what kind of life to live, whether it be a standard life or a nonstandard life. My proposal about the basic needs builds on this idea.

The kind of life that is the ground of the basic needs must be one that every person can be presumed to have a reason to try to secure for himself and to keep, and it must be such that any life that failed to be of this kind would count as harmed or blighted. Now it seems to me that every agent can be presumed to have a reason to seek to be, in a certain sense, a "rational and autonomous agent"; to seek to be an agent who, at a minimum, has the ability to choose how he shall live his life on the basis of values he has formed, values that he has the capacity to evaluate and to pursue. I therefore propose that the "normal" kind of life that grounds the basic needs is life as a rational and autonomous agent. The basic needs are the things that, at some time in the course of life, are indispensable to a rational and autonomous life for a human, given the "laws of nature, unalterable and invariable environmental facts, or facts about human constitution." That is, they are essential either to maintaining the capability of pursuing one's values or to ensuring that one develops and continues to have the capacity to develop and evaluate a set of values. To be deprived of these capabilities and capacities, as I shall explain in the next section, is to suffer a significant loss. Matters of basic need are the things required to avoid this loss.

The things standardly taken to be basic needs can be accounted for on the basis of their being requirements for a human to have and pursue values. A human agent requires bodily and psychological integrity in order to have values and the capability of pursuing her values. Hence my account implies that bodily and psychological integrity are funda mental matters of need for humans. Physical survival is a basic need because survival is essential if one is to pursue one's values. And in ordinary circumstances, one would not develop values without an ed ucation, at least of a basic sort. Friendships give a person the psycho logical security and the help he would typically require in order to flourish in pursuing his values. Without basic security, a person could neither develop nor pursue values. And, for a final example, human ordinarily require sleep in order to preserve their psychological integrity To be sure, the forms of provision for the basic needs will vary with one's circumstances and one's nature. But the matters of basic need are the invariable empirical requirements of rational and autonomous life

I cannot here fill in all the details of my account of the basic need or attempt to deal with objections.[18] There are details that I have not yet worked out. But the key point is that if I am correct about the ground of basic needs, then every agent can be presumed to have a reason to seek to satisfy his basic needs. The idea that there is a pre sumption of this does not rule out the possibility that in extraordinar circumstances someone may have good reasons to choose otherwise But before we attempt to imagine such circumstances, we must be clea what a life without values and the capability of pursuing them would be like.

3. Values

In order to support the ideas of the last section, I need to make clea what it is for an agent to have values. I propose identifying a person' values with his stable and at least minimally endorsed preferences abou the course of his life. Preferences about the course of one's life inforr a person's answers to questions such as, How do you want to live you life? and Thinking about your life as a whole, what do you want it t be like? People normally do have such preferences, I think. For example someone might prefer a life of excitement to a life of comfort. A person' values would shape the course of her life if she lived up to them. The are not merely transitory course-of-life preferences, or passing desire but have a significant stability. And a person identifies with the cours of-life preferences that are her values. She is content to have them an she would not be content to anticipate losing one of them, and thes ttitudes toward them must themselves have a significant stability. My claim is not that a person must explicitly endorse her values, for she may not have given them much thought. But she must be content to have them in that, for example, she does not explicitly regret them, and he would not regret them if she considered them, and this lack of regret must itself be stable. I do not think it would be plausible to count preferences that a person regrets as among her values.

I therefore propose the following account, which I call the "conative account" of a person's values:

> One's values at time t are preferences one has at t about the course of one's life (a) that are stable over a period in one's life that includes t, and (b) that one is at t content to have, and (c) that one would not be content at t to anticipate losing, where (d) the attitudes indicated in (b) and (c) are themselves stable.

use the term 'preference' to refer to any pro-attitude, including desires, hopes, and so on.[19]

One might object that a person who values excitement could be quite content to realize that he will eventually prefer comfort.[20] But such a person does not sufficiently identify with a life of excitement. It may be that he values living in accord with his relatively stable course-of-life preferences, which now include a desire for excitement, and which he realizes will eventually include a desire for a life of comfort, but I do not think that he values excitement as much. One might also object to my restricting the object of a person's values to the course of his own life. According to my account, even a person's moral values are among his stable and endorsed course-of-life preferences, such as the desire to live a life of strict moral duty or the desire to make a contribution to the good of society. But we often take a person's values to extend to evaluations of other people's lives.[21] If this is correct, then I should not offer my theory as a theory of values *simpliciter*. Of course, I do not deny that we can have stable and endorsed preferences about lives in general as well as about our own lives. But I believe it is more plausible to say that a person would be living a blighted life if he lacked stable and endorsed preferences about his own life than to say that a person would be leading a blighted life if he lacked preferences about lives in general. I prefer my account for this reason, even if it is somewhat manipulative.

There are alternatives to the conative account, including especially "cognitive accounts," according to which a person's values are her *beliefs* about what course of life for her would be intrinsically good or valuable. I will call such beliefs "cognitive values." The principle of needs-and-

values rationality could be developed with a cognitive account rathe
than my conative account. But I shall argue that the conative accour
is intuitively more plausible as an account of what it is to value some
thing. And more important, it fits better in my theory of basic needs
because it makes better sense of the idea that a person's life would b
harmed or blighted if she lacked values. It also does better at makin
plausible the principle of needs-and-values rationality, which I will ex
plain in the next section.

Consider, for example, a painter who is deeply content to be an artist
He prefers the life he is living to any other he can imagine, and the
preference has been stable and preferred. Yet suppose that he has bee
so influenced by the prevailing ideology of his society that he believe
life as a businessman would be intrinsically best for him. He would offe
the conventional reasons for this view, if he were challenged to explai
why he believes it. I submit that what he values is the artistic life he i
living rather than the life of a businessman, even though he would den
that the artistic life is intrinsically good. This example shows that
person may have values even if she does not believe that the life sh
deeply prefers would be intrinsically valuable, and even if she does no
have any cognitive values at all. For a person's values are fundamenta
attitudes toward her life that shape her choices of how to live. Whe
things go well, they explain her basic stances toward her life. Cognitiv
values seem not to explain a person's basic choices in the way conativ
values do, as the example makes clear. For the conative account ties
person's values directly to considerations that can explain her choice
about her life. Imagine now an unsophisticated potter in a primitiv
society who is deeply content with his life but seems to lack the concep
of the intrinsically good. It would be implausible to take his simpl
enduring contentment with his life as evidence that he has the concep
of the good, and it would also be implausible to take his lack of thi
concept to undermine the claim that he values the life he is living. Bu
the cognitive account would imply that the potter has no values. For i
order to have a belief, one must have the relevant concepts, and thi
means that the cognitive account implies that in order to have values
person must have the concept of the intrinsically good. The cognitiv
account would also have difficulty attributing values to a skeptic abou
intrinsic goods no matter what attitude she takes to her life. But th
conative account has no problem with cases of these kinds.

More important, the conative account makes better sense of my ide
that a person's life would be harmed or blighted if she lacked value:
The unsophisticated potter lacks cognitive values but he does have col

ative values. This is enough to show that his life has direction, and we would surely not want to say that his life must count as blighted simply because he lacks the concept of the intrinsically good. Yet consider what it would mean for a person to lack any conative values.

A person without conative values might still have preferences about his life, but there would be little stability to them. Or, if he does have stable course-of-life preferences, he does not identify with them; he is not content with the preferences he has, or he would be content to anticipate their loss. His life lacks any substantive and lasting direction with which he can identify. In a life that is given texture by a set of values, a whim to have an ice cream cone would offer a preferred and happy diversion from the direction given by one's values. But in the life of a person without values, a mere preference would not be a reliable indicator of the direction of the good from his standpoint. One's values determine what we may think of as the *direction* of one's good; a person without values is without an "orientation" in life. There is not a good that he can discern, for he does not even value satisfying his needs or his preferences.

A person without values has no compelling reason to pursue anything except the prerequisites of her good, including centrally a sense of direction or of value in life, which requires that she acquire values. She has reason to seek a set of stable attitudes toward her life. Values provide the direction to life that a rational person pursues. If a person had no values, the satisfaction of her less fundamental basic needs would still leave her without direction, even though it would provide her with the resources to proceed in some direction or other. To be sure, the pursuit of value in one's life may involve exploring one's preferences, for values can develop out of our mere preferences through experience. Hence, one's need to find value would ground a reason to satisfy one's preferences. However, mere preferences by themselves cannot provide one with direction, for preferences without values would be like the shifting wind, where one must settle on a destination in order to give direction to one's choices. If there is one fundamental human need, it is to possess a set of values, and I think it fair to presume of every agent that she has a reason to seek to have values.

Of course, even though the unsophisticated potter has values, his life may still seem blighted if he lacks the capacity to appraise reflectively his own values or if he lacks the capacity to pursue any set of values different from his actual set.[22] Having values provides one with something to choose – a course of life for which one has a stable preference, and which one prefers to prefer and to continue to prefer. It provides direction. But it is equally important to have the capacity to choose one's direction, and, having chosen, it is important that one have the capability of moving in that direction.

To summarize, I have claimed that the ground of basic needs is a rational and autonomous life. This is what the matters of basic need are required for. I claimed that such a life is at a minimum a life in which one has values and the capacity to appraise and pursue one's values. I also defended a conative conception of values as stable and preferred preferences about the course of one's life. In order to defend these claims, I attempted to show that the things ordinarily viewed as matters of basic need are requirements for having and pursuing values, at least for humans in the typical circumstances of human life. And I attempted to make plausible the idea that any agent can be presumed to have a reason to seek to have and to keep the requirements of a rational and autonomous life, namely, the requirements for having, appraising, and pursuing values. This is what makes sense of basic needs as rational considerations.

It also explains why the reasons given us by our basic needs deserve a place in a complete account of self-grounded rational deliberation. To be sure, an agent may not herself judge that it would be good for her to meet her own needs; she may be deeply self-destructive. Nevertheless, it surely ought to be counted as good from a person's own standpoint that she endeavor to meet her basic needs. For basic needs are the requirements for having and pursuing any values at all, and having and pursuing values is essential to rational and autonomous agency. Hence, any rational agent has a reason for meeting needs that is grounded in something fundamental to her life as a rational agent.

4. Competition among values, preferences, and needs

I shall argue, in effect, that there are three different sources of self-grounded reasons: basic needs, values, and mere preferences. Needs and values are equally important, and they have strict priority over preferences in a sense I shall explain. Needs and values are related to one another, yet they can conflict, and something must be said about what rationality requires when they do conflict.

The conative account of values is more appropriate than the cognitive account to a theory of self-grounded rationality. For a person who believes that a given life would be best for him may have no reason to pursue it unless he also or thereby prefers it in the sense given by my account, having a stable and endorsed preference for it. Recall, for example, the case of the contented painter. His belief that life as a businessman would be intrinsically best for him gives him no reason to go to business school, especially since he values (conatively) his life as an artist. In general, I submit, beliefs about the good life are a source of self-grounded reasons only when they are integrated into a person's preferences, ideally in a way that is stable and endorsed by the person.

A person's conative values do not give him reasons, it seems to me, unless they would survive a process of reflection and deliberation. Suppose, for example, that the unsophisticated potter's values would change if he were to reflect on them, taking into account what is known about the empirical world and making no errors of reasoning or of logic. He would cease to value his potting and desire to leave his society. In this case, his values are mistaken from his own standpoint in a sense, and we would not want to say that he would be irrational not to pursue his potting.

Let me begin with cases of conflict between values and basic needs. The firefighters and other cleanup workers who entered the area of the stricken nuclear power plant at Chernobyl faced obvious risks to their health, but if they were volunteers, they may have faced the risk in order to contribute to the safety of the population at large, something they must have valued. Surely, it will be said, someone can rationally choose to pursue something of immense value to her, even if the cost is a substantial risk or even a loss of a matter of basic need. Surely the firefighters were rational to do what they did. Again, in order to pursue his art, Bernard Williams's Gauguin may turn away from some of his basic needs, such as his need for friendship, and he is not necessarily irrational to do so.[23] A mountain climber puts at risk her ability to satisfy her needs and she need not be irrational in doing so. A person working among the victims of an epidemic may put his ability to satisfy his needs at risk, and have good reason to do so, given what he values. A person's values may give him reason to put his needs at risk in order to serve the needs of others. In general, a person may rationally pursue the course of life that he values while neglecting or putting at risk his ability to satisfy his needs.

It remains true, of course, that the firefighters had a reason to avoid risks to their health. I constructed the examples to show that it could be rational to risk a matter of basic need in order to further a course of life that the agent values. But the same examples can be used to show that it could be rational to forgo something the agent values in order to protect a matter of basic need. For a firefighter would have been rational to decide not to enter the area of Chernobyl. Perhaps it will be said that in so choosing, the firefighter would reveal that she values less contributing to the safety of the population at large than she would have revealed, had she chosen to participate in the attempt to extinguish the fire. Yet this is not clear. She may have been torn by the decision, worrying about her health on the one hand, but feeling the push of her moral values on the other. The example illustrates a conflict between a person's values and her basic needs. It seems clear that, on the one hand, it would not be irrational to refuse to fight the fire, for the fire-fighter would thereby be securing a matter of basic need, and on the other hand, it would not be irrational to fight the fire, even at risk to her health, for the firefighter would thereby be pursuing something of great value to her. From the perspective of her values, it would be best for her to fight the fire, but from the perspective of her needs, it would be best for her to refuse. Either choice would be rationally permitted.

Let me now state the position I wish to propose. A rational person tries to achieve the satisfaction of his needs over the long run, at least to an appropriate minimum standard of provision, and he seeks to act in conformity with his values for the course of his life and to promote his values when he can. Conflict between these objectives can be re-solved either way. That is, if each of one's options is in conflict either with serving one's needs on balance or with serving one's values on balance, as in the case of a Gauguin who must decide between friend-ships and painting, then it is indeterminate how best to serve one's good. One is free to choose either way. However, when a rational person faces a choice among options none of which is in conflict either with his needs or with his values, as in the case of choosing a flavor of ice cream, then he chooses as he prefers. These reflections suggest the following principle of choice, which I call the principle of needs-and-values rationality:

> An agent is rationally required to choose option x rather than y at a time t if and only if, either (a) option x would at t best serve on balance both his basic needs and his living in accord with his values at t, or (b) he prefers x at t and it is not the case that y would better serve either his basic needs or his living in accord with his values at t, where (c) values and preferences that he has are taken into account in applying (a) and (b) if and only if they would survive at t a process of reflection and deliberation in which he considered them carefully in the light of what is known empir-ically and made no epistemic errors and no errors of logic. In other cases, an agent is rationally permitted to choose either way.[24]

The principle implies that a person is never rationally required to do otherwise than best serve her basic needs. And a person is never ra-tionally required to do otherwise than best serve her values. If there is not a conflict between her needs and her values, then she is required

o choose the option that would best serve both her needs overall and
her values overall, to a sufficiently good approximation. If several op-
ions are essentially indistinguishable with respect to how well they
would serve her values and needs, she is required to choose the one
that she prefers. Yet when her values and her needs are in conflict,
reason does not determine which way she ought to choose.

The needs-and-values principle is an idealization that is not adequate
to certain examples. In the rest of this section I shall clarify it and test
it against examples that may seem problematic.

A person is rationally required to serve his needs only to an appropriate minimum standard of provision. For example, in ordinary circumstances, a preference for chocolate ice cream gives a person a reason
to choose chocolate even if strawberry has slightly more nutritional
value. A person satisfies her basic nutritional needs by achieving the
relevant minimum intakes of relevant substances; she has no reason to
seek more, unless there is a significant risk of shortages in the future.
In any event, the needs-and-values principle should be understood in
this light. Serving our needs means in context serving them to the relevant minimum standard of provision.

In complex situations, especially if several needs are in conflict with
one another, it may be quite unclear how to choose in order to maximize
the ability to fulfill one's needs overall and on balance, and I do not
have a formula to offer. This illustrates one way in which my account
is an idealization. It is also possible for one's values to be in conflict,
and in such cases, it can be unclear how to choose in order to maximize
the fulfillment of one's values overall and on balance. A person may
not be able to integrate all of her values into a coherent ordering.

The needs-and-values principle implies that a person's needs do not
override her values nor do her values override her needs. Reason does
not require serving one's needs at a cost to one's values nor does it
require serving one's values at a cost to one's needs; it permits either.
Yet it may be objected that certain of a person's values will be relatively
trivial and certain needs are extremely important; the choice between
a trivial value and a pressing need is not arbitrary from a rational point
of view, for a rational person would surely satisfy the important need
rather than the trivial value. For example, painting is not a trivial value
in Gauguin's life, and he may be rational to choose to pursue his art at
the expense of certain of his basic needs, but painting for an occasional
weekend artist is much less significant, and it perhaps would not be
sensible for the weekender to give up his friendships in order to pursue
his hobby. It is also the case, on the other hand, that certain matters
of need are relatively minor and that certain of our values are of immense

importance to us. For example, the need for just the right amount c
potassium in one's diet, if there is such a need, may seem trivial b
comparison with the value of philosophy, and if there were a conflic
between the pursuit of philosophy and the pursuit of enough potassiun
reason arguably would support the philosophy rather than the pota:
sium. In reply to these objections, I should stress that the principle c
choice I offered is meant to make reference to what will best contribut
on balance to one's meeting one's needs and to what will best contribut
on balance to one's living in accord with one's values. Although th
mountain climber does put great value in climbing, it is all of his needs
on balance, that argue against climbing, not just, say, the need fo
potassium in his diet. It is when needs on balance conflict with value
on balance that reason gives one a free choice.

Preferences that are not values are "mere preferences." They ar
often sources of reasons. For example, my preference for chocolate ic
cream is a reason to choose chocolate ice cream provided that so choos
ing is compatible with my needs and my values, as it normally woul
be. But given the strict priority of serving needs and values over mer
preferences, our mere preferences, such as our transitory preference
and whims, are not always sources of reasons. For example, since m
desire to taste the cyanide in the case of the sudden urge is a mere whin
and does not reflect my values, and since tasting the cyanide woul
undermine my needs, the urge does not give me a reason to taste th
cyanide. Clearly I would not be rationally required to taste the cyanide
Preferences that are not values give us reasons only when they do no
conflict with our values or our needs.

The restriction I have just stated on the reasons given us by mer
preferences is in fact fairly weak. It permits that a desire to smoke :
cigarette may give one a reason to smoke a cigarette. For even if smokin;
conflicts with reasons given by one's need to secure one's health, smok
ing this cigarette does not. In addition, the restriction permits that :
whim may give one a reason, for whims may be entirely compatible witl
serving one's needs and values. Yet many whims would not give u.
reasons. For example, a whim to crawl on the lawn and eat grass is n
reason to do so, when acting in this way would undermine one's self
respect. But in the context of a game, it could well be a reason.

My principle gives quite different treatment to values and to mer
preferences and this certainly is an idealization, given that the differenc
between values and preferences is at least partly a matter of degree
Consider, for example, the differences between the attitudes of a Gau
guin toward his art and the attitudes of a typical hobbyist. A hobbyis
might be entirely content to think of himself in five years with a new

hobby, but not content to think of himself without hobbies. He values his hobbies but not his painting per se. A Gauguin values his painting, and not just as a result of valuing having some occupation or other. For a Gauguin would take steps to prevent himself from losing his desire to paint, or, at least, he would regret this anticipated loss. Mere preferences are different. I have liked chocolate ice cream for a long time, but I am entirely content to think of myself preferring a different flavor in five years.

Mere preferences are either less stable or less long-lived than one's values, or they may not be the object of stable contentment, or they may not be preferences about the course of one's life as a whole. A merely transitory whim differs greatly on all relevant dimensions from a value that is central to a person's personality, and so a rational person would not give them the same kind of role in her deliberation. She would let her value take precedence over her whim. She would not sacrifice her life's work in order to indulge an urge to taste cyanide. But some "mere" preferences can be quite similar to some values. For example, the hobbyist's attitude toward his painting may come close to qualifying as among his values. A rational person would treat her values and her near-values in nearly the same way, other things being equal, and this is not adequately reflected in the principle I stated.

The account I am urging represents a compromise between a lifetime and a present-time theory of practical reason. On the one hand, one's basic needs are things that are essential to one's good over the course of one's lifetime. A rational person takes into account his needs over his entire life. Moreover, a person's values are preferences regarding the course of his life. On the other hand, the values that a rational person serves are the values he has at the time of choice and the mere preferences that give him reasons are those he has at the time of choice. I have no reason to worry about my whims at other times, unless I have a preference to do so. Similarly, the fact that I used to have certain values, or that I will have certain values in the future, is no reason to serve those values now unless either I now value satisfying the values I have at other times or I have a basic need to ensure this ability in the future. But basic needs are different. For example, my need for nourishment gives me a reason to seek nourishment at regular intervals during my life, and to ensure that I will be able to nourish myself in the future, regardless of the desires I have now or will have in the future.

I shall leave a number of questions unanswered, the most important of which concern moral reasons: How does the needs-and-values principle mesh with the idea that there are moral reasons? Are moral reasons overriding? These are difficult questions, and I shall limit myself to the reminder that the needs-and-values principle is a principle of self-grounded deliberative rationality. If I have moral values among my course-of-life preferences, then the needs-and-values principle takes them into account. But moral reasons as such are not self-grounded; hence, it is coherent to ask for self-grounded reasons to take moral reasons seriously. The precise relation between moral reasons and self-grounded reasons is of course one of the central issues of moral philosophy.

5. Conclusion

I have had the following objectives in this essay. First, I wanted to defend the idea that the rationality of our choices can depend on how they affect our ability to meet our basic needs. I defended a weak and a strong reason-and-needs thesis. The weak thesis asserts that if a person has a basic need for something, then she has a reason to secure it or to keep it. The strong thesis asserts that if doing a certain thing would prevent a person from meeting her basic needs, then she is not rationally required to do it.

My second goal was to support the objectivity of basic needs. What a person needs is not determined by her preferences or other psychological states. I attempted to defend this thesis by presenting a theory of basic needs. I proposed that the ground of our basic needs is life as a rational and autonomous agent. The basic matters of need are the fundamental requirements for having values and for appraising and pursuing them.

Given the objectivity of basic needs and the two reason-and-needs theses, no preference theory of rational choice can be correct. My third objective was to support this claim. If I am correct, then no theory that construes rationality as a matter of the maximization of expected preference satisfaction, or that proposes any other purely preference-based criterion of rationality, can be correct. An adequate conception would have to treat basic needs as a source of reasons.

Finally, I proposed a criterion of rational choice that I called the needs-and-values principle. The criterion is an oversimplification in various ways that I attempted to explain. But it does at least show the significance that I believe attaches to the meeting of needs in the life of a rational person.

Notes

1 Garrett Thomson urged me to discuss this objection here.
2 David Gauthier and Richard Brandt offer views of this sort. See R. B.

Brandt, *A Theory of the Good and the Right* (Oxford: Oxford University Press, 1979); and David Gauthier, *Morals by Agreement* (Oxford: Clarendon Press, 1986). Gauthier speaks of the agreement between "behavioural" preference expressed in choice and "attitudinal" preference expressed in speech (pp. 27–8). He says that rationality consists in the endeavor to maximize the fulfillment of considered preferences, where "Preferences are considered if and only if there is no conflict between their behavioral and attitudinal dimensions and they are stable under experience and reflection" (pp. 32–3).

3 David Gauthier offers a test of this kind in "Value, Reasons, and the Sense of Justice," Chapter 10 of this volume. In *Morals by Agreement,* however, Gauthier seems not to attach any significance to whether a desire is endorsed by the agent. See the next note.

4 The desire to smoke is a familiar example of a desire that many people continue to have, and even to endorse, despite knowing the effect of smoking on their health, one of their basic needs. In *Morals by Agreement,* Gauthier discusses a person who both prefers to smoke and prefers to prefer not to smoke. He says the strength of the person's preferences, and the effect that smoking is likely to have on their fulfillment, determines whether it is rational for her to smoke. We may suppose that the person acknowledges that she has an interest in not smoking, but Gauthier says that that would be simply to suppose her to express another preference, a preference not to smoke (pp. 32–3). But since smoking is injurious to health and a person needs health, I say the person in Gauthier's example would have a reason not to smoke even if she were reflectively to endorse her desire to smoke and even if she denied an interest in not smoking and lacked any desire not to smoke. Smoking this cigarette may not be harmful, however, so I would allow that the desire to smoke this cigarette may give one a reason to smoke it even though the desire to taste cyanide does not give one a reason to taste cyanide. The needs-and-values principle that I advocate permits me to take this position, as I explain below.

5 John Rawls says, for instance, that "the rational plan for a person is the one . . . which he would choose with deliberative rationality. It is the plan that would be decided upon as the outcome of careful reflection in which the agent reviewed, in the light of all the relevant facts, what it would be like to carry out these plans and thereby ascertained the course of action that would best realize his more fundamental desires." See his *A Theory of Justice* (Cambridge, Mass.: Harvard University Press, 1971), p. 417.

6 Gauthier suggests that a rational agent would seek to maximize her utility, where utility is the fulfillment of her reflectively endorsed intentional states, including desires and beliefs, which she has integrated into a single coherent view. "Value, Reasons, and the Sense of Justice," Chapter 10 of this volume.

7 Michael Bratman has developed a complex position about the rationality of plans and intentions that, it may seem, can blunt the problem of the sudden

urge. See his *Intention, Plans, and Practical Reason* (Cambridge, Mass. Harvard University Press, 1987). Bratman argues in effect that once an agent makes a plan or forms an intention, rationality may require that the plan or intention remain stable, and that the agent act on it, even in circumstances in which the agent would rationally decide to act otherwise if she were to consider doing so (pp. 60–106). In the case at hand, he might say, I would not be rational to reconsider my life plan in the face of a sudden urge to taste cyanide, for reasonable habits of reconsideration would not lead me to reconsider (p. 66). Moreover, intentions provide "framework reasons," which constrain the admissibility of options (pp. 32–5). In the case of the sudden urge, the framework reasons provided by a rational life plan would exclude as irrational the option of tasting the cyanide. In this sense, my urge would provide me with no reason to taste the cyanide. I do not believe, however, that Bratman's theory deals fully with my worry. First, his theory is not a (standard) preference theory. At any rate, Bratman argues that intentions are different in kind from ordinary pro-attitudes (pp. 10, 15–18). Moreover, second, Bratman allows for what he calls the "external" evaluation of actions, which abstracts from the framework reasons provided by the agent's prior plans and intentions (pp. 42–9). My argument in the text takes up this external point of view, so framework reasons do not directly address the problem raised by the sudden urge. Finally, Bratman simply assumes for the sake of argument that some form of preference theory accounts for the rationality of plans and intentions and for the rationality of actions when they are evaluated from the external point of view (pp. 20–3). I am arguing to the contrary.

8 The distinction is drawn by many writers, including, for example, James Griffin. See his *Well-Being: Its Meaning, Measurement, and Moral Importance* (Oxford: Clarendon Press, 1986), p. 41.

9 David Braybrooke, *Meeting Needs* (Princeton: Princeton University Press, 1987), p. 29. I have taken many of my examples of needs and my basic approach to the theory of needs from Braybrooke.

10 Ibid., p. 36.

11 Ibid., pp. 38–47.

12 This idea supports the plausibility of Braybrooke's view that needs have *moral* priority over preferences (ibid., pp. 60–75). I agree, of course, that this idea has plausibility as a substantive moral or political principle. It is not plausible, however, to hold that the moral priority of needs over preferences is entailed by the *concept* of a need, for a moral skeptic could admit without contradiction that humans need water.

13 David Wiggins, "Claims of Need," *Needs, Values, Truth* (Oxford: Basil Blackwell, 1987), p. 15, also p. 10. See also Joel Feinberg, *Social Philosophy* (Englewood Cliffs, N.J.: Prentice-Hall, 1973), p. 111; D. W. Stampe, "Need," *Australasian Journal of Philosophy* 66 (1988): 135.

14 Garrett Thomson, *Needs* (London: Routledge and Kegan Paul, 1987), p. 8.

15 See Braybrooke, *Meeting Needs*, p. 31. Griffin proposes that the basic needs

are the things required in order to realize "the normal ends of human life." *Well-Being*, p. 42.

16 There is inevitable vagueness here, because the notion of harm is vague. This means that, on my view, an account of reasons for action will be vague to the extent that the allied notions of harm and of normal life are vague. But some degree of vagueness is surely to be expected. We hold, for example, that anyone has a reason to believe a proposition that is "supported" by sufficiently "weighty" evidence. This thesis about reasons to believe is also vague, and I don't think we have a happily precise account either of evidence or of the weight of evidence, yet we still believe the thesis. Vagueness in the notion of a need is no reason to deny the reasons-and-needs thesis.

17 Braybrooke, *Meeting Needs*, p. 48.

18 I offer a bit more detail in my paper "The Right to an Adequate Standard of Living: Justice, Autonomy, and the Basic Needs," *Social Philosophy and Policy* 9(1992): 231–61.

19 Gilbert Harman criticizes this account in his "Desired Desires," Chapter 8 of this volume. I reformulated clause (a) in an attempt to meet one of his objections.

20 This objection is due to Garrett Thomson. For similar examples, see Derek Parfit, *Reasons and Persons* (Oxford: Clarendon Press, 1984).

21 This objection is due to Gilbert Harman.

22 I am not arguing that a person's life would be blighted if he did not actually reflectively appraise his own values. I believe this, but I am merely arguing for the importance of having the capacity to appraise one's values.

23 Bernard Williams uses his somewhat imaginary Gauguin to illustrate a different point. See *Moral Luck* (Cambridge: Cambridge University Press, 1981), pp. 22–6.

24 For simplicity, I have not attempted to take account of uncertainty and risk. The needs-and-values principle ought ideally to speak of the "expected contribution" of actions to the agent's meeting his needs and serving his values.

8

Desired desires

GILBERT HARMAN

A number of philosophers have appealed to "second-order desires" (desires about desires) in order to explain basic moral notions. Harry Frankfurt has suggested that freedom of the will might be identified with the ability to satisfy a certain sort of second-order desire[1] and Richard Jeffrey has made a similar proposal.[2] Gary Watson has objected that the resulting account of freedom of the will does not work and that the appeals made to second-order desires should be replaced with references to what an agent *values*.[3]

Watson's view can be reconciled with Frankfurt's if valuing is identified with a kind of second-order desire. David Lewis has offered such an identification[4] and David Copp has recently suggested that we might identify a person's values with preferences for which the person has a certain second-order preference.[5]

However, these appeals to second-order desires in order to explain freedom of the will, valuing, or values are all unsuccessful.

In arguing for this negative conclusion, I defend a number of subsidiary points: (1) Positive intentions are reflexive or self-referential. (2) Intrinsic desires are not just noninstrumental desires. (3) To value something is in part to want it. (4) There is sometimes a difference between believing that something is good and valuing it. (5) There is a difference between valuing something and having it as one of your values.

1. Frankfurt on freedom of the will

Frankfurt motivates his view by criticizing Strawson's account of the concept of a person. Strawson holds that the concept of a person is "the concept of a type of entity such that *both* predicates ascribing states of consciousness *and* predicates ascribing corporeal characteristics . . . are

In preparing the present version of this essay I am indebted to discussions with David Lewis, Harry Frankfurt, Alfred Mele, and David Copp, although we all remain in disagreement. Its preparation was supported in part by a research grant to Princeton University from the James S. McDonnell Foundation.

equally applicable to a single individual of that single type."[6] Frankfurt points out that Strawson's suggestion fails to distinguish people from many other animate beings and announces his own view that "one essential difference between persons and other creatures is to be found in the structure of a person's will. . . . [Persons] are able to form what I shall call 'second-order desires' or 'desires of the second order.' " "No animal other than man . . . appears to have the capacity for reflective self-evaluation that is manifested in the formation of second-order desires." Frankfurt explains that he means 'desire' loosely to include anything a person can be said "to want," where this covers "a rather broad range of possibilities."[7]

Frankfurt says, "it is having second-order volitions, and not having second-order desires generally, that I regard as essential to being a person," where a second-order volition is wanting a certain desire to be one's will, that is, wanting a certain desire to be "effective in action." He uses

the term 'wanton' to refer to agents who have first-order desires but who are not persons because, whether or not they have desires of the second order, they have no second-order volitions. . . . The class of wantons includes all nonhuman animals that have desires and all very young children. Perhaps it also includes some adult human beings as well. In any case, adult humans may be more or less wanton; they may act wantonly, in response to first-order desires concerning which they have no volitions of the second order, more or less frequently.[8]

To illustrate his thesis, Frankfurt distinguishes between two kinds of drug addict: an unwilling addict, who wants his desire for the drug not to be effective, and a wanton, who is not "concerned whether the desires that move him to act are desires by which he wants to be moved to act." Frankfurt claims that the wanton addict may deliberate and make plans to obtain the drug he desires. "But it never occurs to him to consider whether he wants the relations among his desires to result in his having the will he has."[9]

Frankfurt connects the capacity for forming second-order volitions and the capacity "both of enjoying and of lacking freedom of the will," where freedom of the will is not just "freedom of action." He says:

freedom of action is (roughly, at least) the freedom to do what one wants to do. Analogously, then, the statement that a person enjoys freedom of the will means (also roughly) that he is free to want what he wants to want. More precisely, it means that he is free to will what he wants to will, or to have the will he wants. . . . It is in securing the conformity of his will to his second-order volitions, then, that a person exercises freedom of the will.[10]

Wanting someone to do something for you. One way to begin to explore Frankfurt's proposals is to consider the different ways in which you might want someone to do something for you. In one case, you want someone to do something for you because that person knows that you want it. For example, you want a friend to bring you flowers as a result of your friend's recognition that you want flowers. In a different case, you want someone to do something but not because of your desire. For example, you want a doctor to say you are going to recover because he thinks you are going to recover, not merely because he realizes you want him to say that you are going to recover.[11]

Often when you want someone P to do something for you, your hope is that P will recognize your desire and be motivated by that recognition to do what you want. In such cases, you have a second-order desire that your first-order desire will be effective in getting you what you want, via its recognition by P.

Second-order desires also figure in H. P. Grice's theory of communicative meaning. According to Grice, a speaker S communicating with an audience *A* means that *M* only if S intends *A* to think that *M* by virtue of *A*'s recognition of S's intention that *A* should think that *M*.[12] Now, intentions count as desires for Frankfurt because, if you intend to do something, there is a sense in which that is what you want to do (even if there are other respects in which you do not want to do it). So, wherever Grice's analysis of communicative intentions applies, such communication will involve a second-order desire that a first-order desire should be effective.

To have such a second-order desire is not yet to have a second-order "volition" in Frankfurt's sense, because it is not the same as having the second-order desire that your first-order desire to do something should be effective in action. To have the second-order desire that your first-order desire for flowers will be effective in getting you what you want via your friend's recognition of that desire is not quite the same, for example, as having the second-order desire that your first-order desire to say, "I'd love some flowers," should be effective in leading you to say, "I'd love some flowers."

Everyone, or almost everyone, has second-order nonvolitional desires, because everyone, or almost everyone, has communicative intentions. In particular, almost any actual human addict will have communicative intentions in trying to purchase the needed drug. Almost any addict will be capable of wanting a friend to provide some of the drug on recognizing the addict's desire for it. Furthermore, it is likely that some animals can have communicative intentions.[13]

Positive intentions. As I have argued elsewhere, intentions are typically self-referential and therefore are not only first-order, but second-order and every higher-order as well. In particular, an intention is typically the intention that that very intention will result in your doing what you intend to do.[14] John Searle has independently defended a similar conclusion by way of a different argument.[15]

By a 'positive intention' I mean an intention to do something that you suppose you will do in consequence of your adopting that intention. For example, consider the intention to clean up your room. Normally, this would be a positive intention, because when you form such an intention you suppose that you will clean up your room only if your having that intention leads to your doing so. Positive intentions contrast with negative intentions, as for example when you decide not to clean up your room, where you suppose that what you intend, namely that you not clean up your room, will be so whether or not you form the negative intention not to clean up your room, as long as you do not form the positive intention to clean up your room. There are also conditional intentions, like the intention to clean up your room if asked to do so, where you do not unconditionally suppose that the intention will lead to success but suppose only that it will have an effect if you are asked to clean up your room.[16]

There is a sense of 'doing something' in which cleaning up your room is doing something and not cleaning up your room is not doing something. The positive intention to clean up your room is an intention to do something. The negative intention not to clean up your room is not an intention to do something in this sense. (The distinction is not merely a grammatical distinction. The intention to stay home can be a negative intention that is not an intention to do something in the relevant sense even though the intention is not negatively expressed.)

Doing something is active, an action. What makes an event your action in this sense is in part that it is controlled or "guided"[17] by your intentions. To intend to do something that is an action is therefore to intend that there be an event of a certain sort that is controlled or guided by your intentions. So, a positive intention is an intention that something will happen in a way that is controlled or guided by your intentions. In particular, your intention is that something will happen that is controlled or guided by that very intention. So, a positive intention is reflexive or self-referential – it refers to itself.

The practical reasoning that culminates in a positive intention has to be sensitive to whether the conclusion of the reasoning will make a relevant difference and lead to your doing what you intend to do.

Negative and conditional intentions aside, you can't rationally decide to do something if you believe that your decision will make no difference. It is not enough to suppose that what you propose to do will make a difference; you must also suppose that your decision will make a difference. If you fall off a cliff and realize that you will continue to fall whatever your intentions are, then you cannot rationally decide to stop falling. What you would propose to do, namely, to stop falling, would make a difference to what happens: Things would work out differently if you could stop falling. The trouble is that a decision to stop falling won't make a difference. A decision to stop falling can be a reasonable practical conclusion only if you can suppose that your practical conclusion can influence what happens. If you can't conclude that your intention will lead to your doing what you intend, then you can't reach that conclusion as the result of practical reasoning. And that is just what would be expected if the intention (that is, the conclusion of your practical reasoning) includes the thought that it leads (in a more or less specific way) to an intended result. Furthermore, I can't think of any other natural way to capture this point without appeal to self-referential intentions.

You can rationally form a positive intention to do something only if you can see how your intention might lead you to do it. You do not have to have all the details worked out if your plan is that you will work out the details later, as needed. But you do need to be able to suppose that whether you do it or not might depend on whether you have the intention to do it, at least in the sense that your intention might contribute to your doing it. If you cannot see your intention as a possible means, you have no reason to form the intention. So, in forming that intention, you have to intend that your intention will contribute to the intended effect. Your full plan is that your intention will lead in a certain (more or less clearly specified) way to your acting in the way you intend.

There are two arguments here for the conclusion that positive intentions are self-referential.

> First argument: When an intention is the result of practical reasoning, the intention is the conclusion of that reasoning. You can rationally reach a positive intention through practical reasoning only if you can conclude (C) that the intention will make a difference by leading to your doing as you intend. The conclusion (C) that your intention will lead to your doing as you intend has to be part of your practical conclusion.[18] So, the conclusion (C) that your intention will lead to your doing as you intend has to be part of your intention.

Second argument: If an intention to do *A* is a positive intention, you suppose you will do *A* only if you intend to do *A* and you suppose that intending to do *A* promises to lead to your doing *A*. To make such suppositions about your intention is to view your intention as part of your means for doing *A*. If you form the intention of doing *A*, supposing that *M* will be part of your means for doing *A*, then your intention to do *A* includes an intention to do *A* by virtue of *M*. So, your positive intention to do *A* is in part the intention to do *A* by virtue of having that intention.

Ends and means. Frankfurt offers the following objection:

[O]ne usually selects a means in the light of an end one has adopted; but since the formation of an intention is itself the adoption of an end, how can it also be the selection or provision of a means to that end? It would be as though every end automatically came provided with one useful means to attaining it – namely, the intention to attain it! . . .

In deciding upon what means to use in seeking a certain end, I will have reasons for regarding *M* as an appropriate means or for selecting it over other possible means. My reasons for forming an intention are not like that. They are simply my reasons for adopting the end; they are not reasons, given that the end has been adopted, for using certain means to achieve it. It is true that I cannot rationally adopt an end unless I believe that I might be able to achieve it. But that is not the same as believing that my intention to achieve it might lead me to achieve it.[19]

My response is that we must distinguish the narrow notion of intention from the wider notion of desire. All intentions are desires, in Frankfurt's wide sense of 'desire', but not all desires are intentions. So we have to distinguish intended ends from merely desired and not intended ends. One can desire an end without any idea of how it might be obtained; but one cannot *intend* to obtain an end without some idea of how it might be obtained.

I agree that one usually selects a means in the light of an end one has adopted. But that does not mean one must first select an end and only then select a means to that end. My claim is that, if selecting an end is forming a positive intention, one can select that end only if one has some idea of how to achieve it. Such an idea is an idea of what one might do to achieve that end. But an idea of what one might do is an idea of one or more events that are controlled or guided by one's intention. So one can select an end only if one has a conception of how one's intention might lead to or guide or control one's achieving that end. In accepting that end, what one accepts is a plan that includes an account of how one's acceptance of that plan leads to one's achieving that end. So I am arguing that every such end does come "provided with one useful means to attaining it – namely the intention to attain it!"

One's reasons for forming an intention are not just one's reasons for adopting the intended end rather than some other end, since one's reasons for forming an intention also include one's reasons for forming an intention as opposed to merely desiring or hoping for that end.

One's acceptance of a given end or goal is part of a larger practical conclusion. The reasons why some parts of that larger conclusion are there are not the same as the reasons why other parts are there. One's reasons for including a given end or goal are not the same as one's reasons for including a particular means to that goal. One selects the means in order to achieve the goal, not the other way round. But one's whole practical conclusion is what one intends. One intends the whole plan, not just the final end. One's plan is that one's intention will lead in a certain way to a certain result. In other words, one's whole practical conclusion involves as a part the thought that that whole conclusion will lead in a certain way to a certain result.

The relevant sense in which you cannot rationally adopt an end unless you believe you might be able to achieve it is this: You cannot rationally adopt an end as part of a positive intention unless at the same time you can rationally conclude (as part of your plan) that your having that intention will lead to your achieving that end. Whether or not you *believe* that your intention will lead you to achieve it, your plan must be that your having that intention will lead you to achieve it.[20]

Infinite regress. "If positive intentions are self-referential, isn't a bad infinite regress generated?" To have a positive intention to do *D* is then to have an intention that your intention will lead you to do *D*. "So do you not also have an intention concerning your intention that your intention will lead you to do *D*? And so forth?"[21]

My reply is that the regress is not a "bad infinite regress." There is only a single intention that refers to itself. It is the intention that that very intention will lead in such and such a more or less specified way to such and such a result. In words: My acceptance of this very conclusion will lead to such and such a result.

I have discussed issues raised by self-reference elsewhere.[22]

A baby's intentions. Alfred Mele objects that his eight-month-old daughter can intend to crawl toward him without having any concept of intention and, he argues, if she does not have the concept of an intention, her intention in crawling toward him cannot be in part that ıer intention will lead her to get to him. He concludes that we must ·eject the thesis that positive intentions are always self-referential.[23] I reply that the baby does not need a full-fledged concept of intention ın order to have self-referential intentions. The question is whether she ıcts as she does because of a complex planning procedure that is sensitive ·o whether and how the conclusion of this procedure might affect what ıappens. It is irrelevant whether the baby has a concept of intention ›eyond that. For example, the baby does not need to have the concept ›f a state of intention that others might be in. It is also irrelevant whether :he baby has an explicit mental representation of its intention.[24] John Perry has observed that a child can have the thought that "it is raining" .vithout having any concepts of places or times and without any inner nental representations of particular places and times, even though the :ontent of the child's thought concerns rain at a particular place and a ›articular time.[25] The child can have thoughts that are about particular ›laces and times without having concepts or representations of those ›laces and times. Similarly, the content of a child's intention can be in ›art about that intention without the child having any distinctive concept ›r mental representation of that intention.

Furthermore, it is important to distinguish purely verbal questions ıbout how we use the word "intention" from more substantive questions :oncerning what goes on in full-fledged practical reasoning leading to Jecisions and plans. As Mele observes, it is an empirical question what eads his eight-month-old daughter to crawl toward him as she does.[26] ıt may very well be true that his daughter acts as she does because of ı complex internal planning procedure that is highly sensitive to whether ınd how the conclusion of this procedure might affect what happens. Or it may be true that there is no such procedure going on when his Jaughter crawls toward him.

The purely verbal issue is whether it would be correct to describe his daughter as "intending" to crawl toward him on the assumption that there was no such inner procedure. Suppose for example that she .vas simply disposed to crawl in the direction in which she saw him, whether or not there was an obstacle, with no planning at all concerning how to get to him. If so, would it be correct to describe her as 'intending" to crawl toward her father? Mele himself may want to say this. Then such "intentions" are (presumably) not about :hemselves.

But this does not touch the substantive point that positive intentions :hat are the conclusions of full-fledged practical reasoning have to be ıbout themselves, since full-fledged practical reasoning is sensitive to :he effects of accepting the practical conclusions to which it leads.

Autonomy and second-order volitions. Recall Frankfurt's proposal: The difference between an autonomous agent and a wanton is that an autonomous agent but not a wanton has second-order volitions, where a second-order volition is a second-order desire that a first-order desire should be effective in action.

Frankfurt uses the term 'desire' loosely to include any case in which a person might be said to "want" to do something. Therefore, intention count as desires for Frankfurt. So any positive intention is a second order volition of the relevant sort. A positive intention is in part the intention (desire) that one's intention (desire) should be effective. This implies that any creature with positive intentions is an autonomous agent and not a mere wanton.

But then Frankfurt must be wrong about animals being non autonomous wantons. Animals are capable of avoiding obstacles and of sufficient (even if limited) planning, which means that they must be capable of the sort of practical reasoning that is sensitive to which practical conclusions might be effective in action. So animals must have second-order volitions in Frankfurt's sense.

Consider also Frankfurt's distinction between the willing addict, the wanton, and the unwilling addict. Frankfurt says that all three addicts want to take the drug. The unwilling addict desires not to desire to take the drug and desires that his desire to take the drug not be effective But his first-order desire to take the drug is stronger than his desire that the first-order desire not be effective. So he is unfree. He acts against his will even though he does what he wants. By contrast, the willing addict is quite happy that his desire for the drug should be effective and the wanton has no desire one way or the other as to whether his desire for the drug should be effective, according to Frankfurt.

The trouble is that both the unwilling addict and the alleged wanton intend to take the drug. This intention is a positive intention, namely the intention that that very intention will lead him to take the drug. Given Frankfurt's loose sense of 'desire', this counts as a second-order volition in Frankfurt's sense. So, Frankfurt has to count all three addicts as autonomous agents with free will.

I conclude that Frankfurt's appeal to second-order volitions is not the key to distinguishing autonomy from nonautonomy and does not allow an account of freedom of the will.

2. Lewis on valuing

I now turn to David Lewis's proposal to identify valuing something with desiring to desire it. Lewis's stated reasons for this identification are perfunctory; he is mainly concerned to argue for a dispositional theory of value, a theory with which I will not be concerned.

Lewis motivates his account of valuing as follows. He first suggests that valuing something "might be a feeling, or a belief, or a desire. Or a combination of these; or something that is two or three of them at once; or some fourth thing. But let us set these hypotheses aside, and hope to get by with something simpler."[27] Notice, by the way, that Lewis must here be using the term 'desire' broadly, in the way Frankfurt does, to include anything a person might be said to want. Otherwise Lewis's threefold classification would not be plausible. So, in particular, Lewis too must count an intention as a desire.

After ruling out the hypothesis that valuing is just a feeling or just a belief, Lewis is left with the conclusion that valuing is a desire. "But," he adds,

we'd better not say that valuing something is just the same as desiring it. That may do for some of us: those who manage, by strength of will or by good luck, to desire exactly as they desire to desire. But not all of us are so fortunate. The thoughtful addict may desire his euphoric daze, but not value it. Even apart from all the costs and risks, he may hate himself for desiring something he values not at all. It is a desire he wants very much to get rid of. He desires his high, but he does not desire to desire it, and in fact he desires not to desire it. He does not desire an unaltered, mundane state of consciousness, but he does desire to desire it. We conclude that he does not value what he desires, but rather he values what he desires to desire.[28]

After saying that it is hard to imagine more complicated cases involving desires of higher order and also that we have to allow for "someone who desires to value differently than he does," Lewis "hesitantly" concludes, "we do better to stop on the second rung: valuing is just desiring to desire."[29]

However, there is an important footnote:

It is comparatively easy to imagine *instrumental* third-order desires. Maybe our addict wishes he could like himself better than he does; and not by doing away with his addiction, which he takes to be impossible, but by becoming reconciled to it and accepting himself as he is. Or maybe he just fears that his second-order desire not to be addicted will someday lead him to suffer the pains of withdrawal. Either way, he wants to be rid of his second-order desire not to be addicted, but he wants it not for itself but as a means to some end. This is irrelevant: presumably it is intrinsic, not instrumental desiring that is relevant to what someone values.

This footnote is puzzling. You can value something instrumentally. For example, you may value someone's opinion without having an in-

trinsic desire to know that person's opinion and without having an intrinsic second-order desire to want to know that opinion. Why then does
Lewis presume that only intrinsic desiring is relevant to what someone
values?

Perhaps he means that his theory only works for valuing something
intrinsically. If so, Lewis's view is, more specifically, that to value something intrinsically is to have an intrinsic desire that you have an (intrinsic)
desire for it.[30]

Communicative intentions and values. One way to motivate Lewis's
footnoted restriction to intrinsic value and intrinsic desires is to recall
our earlier discussion of communicative intentions and second-order
desires that first-order desires should be effective in getting you what
you want.

Consider what the theory would look like without this restriction and,
in particular, consider the following scenario.

You want flowers, you want John to recognize that you want flowers, and you want this to lead John to give you flowers. You want
to do something that will indicate to John that you want flowers.
You want to say to John, "I would love to have some flowers."
So, you want to form the intention of saying it.

Here you want to have the intention of saying, "I would love to have
some flowers." Since an intention counts as a desire for Lewis, you have
a desire for a certain sort of desire that you say this. So Lewis's theory
without any restriction to intrinsic desires would imply that you value
saying this. But normally in this situation this would not be something
you value.

By restricting the relevant desires to intrinsic desires, Lewis avoids
the conclusion that you value saying "I would love to have some
flowers." In the scenario given, only the flowers are wanted intrinsically.
Your desire to say, "I would love to have some flowers," is an instrumental desire, since you want to say it because of hoped-for results of
saying it. Furthermore, you have only an instrumental desire to intend
to say it, because of results you expect from having that intention.

But, at this point, we need to say more about the distinction between
intrinsic and other sorts of desires.

Instrumental and intrinsic desires. Your desire for D is instrumental if
you desire D because you think getting D will get you something else
E that you desire. You see D as a means to E.

It might be proposed that we define intrinsic desires by contrast with
instrumental desires. If you desire D but not as a means to anything

else, then your desire for *D* would be an intrinsic desire, according to his criterion.

But, consider a desire to hear good news – for example, the desire to hear the doctor say you will recover. This is not an instrumental desire; you do not suppose that the doctor's saying this would promote any end of yours. So it would be an intrinsic desire, by the proposed criterion. You might believe that your having a certain desire is good news in this sense. For example, you might believe that a certain bodily condition makes you resistant to cancer and also causes you to have an intrinsic desire to exercise. An intrinsic desire to exercise would be a sign that you have that bodily condition. Reflecting on this leads you to desire that you have an intrinsic desire to exercise. This latter second-order desire would count as intrinsic, by the suggested criterion, because it is not an instrumental desire. It is not that you want the effects of a desire to exercise; you want to desire to exercise, because that would be a sign of your having a desirable bodily condition.[31]

On the assumption that a desire is intrinsic to the extent that it is not instrumental, Lewis's account of valuing would imply incorrectly that to have this intrinsic desire to have an intrinsic desire to exercise would be to value exercise. The implication would be incorrect, because you can have such a second-order intrinsic desire without valuing exercise at all.

The best way to avoid this unwelcome result is to define what is to count as an intrinsic desire in such a way that this particular second-order desire does not count. For example, we might stipulate that your desire for *D* is not an intrinsic desire to the extent that you desire *D* only because you desire something else *E* and you believe that having *D* would make it more likely that you have *E,* either because *D* might bring about *E* or because *D* might be a sign of *E.*

Now consider the following case. Someone tells you that the experience of listening to Mozart is intrinsically desirable. You believe this. Since you want to do things that are intrinsically desirable, you come to desire that experience. Is this last desire to have the experience of listening to Mozart an intrinsic desire? No, because it depends on your desire to do things that are intrinsically desirable.[32]

One moral is that to want something only because you think it is good is not to want it intrinsically.[33]

Valuing and believing valuable. Notice that, quite apart from considerations of intrinsic desire and intrinsic value, you can believe that something is valuable without valuing it.

In the Mozart example just given, you think it would be valuable to listen to Mozart, although you do not yet value listening to Mozart.

There are instances in which you take something to be valuable tha you once valued but out of weariness no longer value, as Michael Stocke has pointed out.

Through spiritual or physical tiredness, through accidie, through weakness o body, through illness, through general apathy, through despair, through inability to concentrate, through a feeling of uselessness or futility, and so on, one may feel less and less motivated to seek what is good. One's lessened desire need not signal, much less be the product of, the fact that, or one's belief that, there is less good to be obtained or produced, as in the case of a universal Weltshmertz. Indeed, a frequent added defect of being in such "depressions" is that one see all the good to be won or saved and one lacks the will, interest, desire o strength.[34]

In these examples, one "sees all the good to be won," so, as in the Mozart example, one believes that something is of value, but withou valuing it.

Commenting on this passage from Stocker, Michael Smith wrongly takes it to show that "we may value something without desiring it."[35] But the examples given are examples in which a person has an evaluative belief without valuing what he takes to be good. We may think tha something is good without desiring it, but we cannot value something without desiring it.[36]

Valuing and desiring. I now want to describe some apparen counterexamples to David Lewis's proposal that to value something intrinsically is to have a second-order intrinsic desire to have an intrinsic desire. First, I describe a case in which you have the relevant second order desire without valuing the thing in question. Second I describe a case in which someone values something without having the relevan second-order desire.

Consider, first, what is involved in valuing listening to Mozart. Simply desiring to desire listening to Mozart is clearly insufficient. You may wish you did desire to listen to Mozart, because it would make your life more pleasant to have such a desire, given all the Mozart concerts you have to attend. In that case, your desire to desire listening to Mozar would be an instrumental desire for an intrinsic desire. Clearly in such a case you still do not value listening to Mozart.

Furthermore, it is not enough that you should also acquire an intrinsic second-order desire to want to listen to Mozart, if you continue to lack any first-order desire to listen to Mozart. To me, this is as clear as the case in which you have merely an instrumental desire to want to lister to Mozart. If you do not yet want to listen to Mozart, then you do no yet value listening to Mozart.

Furthermore, someone who likes to listen to Mozart can value tening to Mozart without having any second-order desire to have (or continue to have) that first-order desire. A person can value listening Mozart and be quite neutral in his attitude about his desire to listen Mozart. He might realize that his musical interests are easily changed. or all he knows he might at any point stop being interested in listening Mozart, and come to be interested in listening to Mahler instead. He alizes that he might stop valuing listening to Mozart and instead start luing listening to Mahler. This person might have no desire at all that is not happen – no desire at all that he should continue to want to ten to Mozart. He can value listening to Mozart without wanting to ant it.

I find it difficult to imagine an actual case in which a person would quire an intrinsic second-order desire to desire to listen to Mozart. It ould not be enough for the person to have a second-order desire to ant to listen to Mozart that arises out of the belief that it is an trinsically good thing to desire to listen to Mozart. As we have seen, e resulting desire would not be an intrinsic desire, since it would pend on the existence of the person's desire to have intrinsically sirable desires.

By the way, although it seems to me to be generally true that, when person values something, the person does not have an intrinsic second-der desire of the relevant sort, it is not always easy to show this. onsider valuing such things as (1) being an honest person, (2) complishing something significant in your life, and (3) the well-being particular people, especially members of your family. I am inclined believe that, although I have second-order desires to have first-order sires for these things, my second-order desires are almost certainly ot intrinsic desires. My desire to desire the well-being of members of y family, for example, seems to me to be an instrumental desire, arising part from the thought that my desiring this will promote their well- ing. Similarly for the other values mentioned.

I concede that my having instrumental reasons for such second-order sires does not guarantee my not also having intrinsic second-order sires of this sort. Furthermore, I find it unclear how to test for the ossibility that these desires might be at least partly intrinsic. But I see reason to suppose that these second-order desires of mine are at ast partly intrinsic.

Suppose I were to be placed in a situation in which I could no longer ve any effect on the welfare of members of my family. I would be stressed at the further prospect of no longer caring about them. Does at show that I have an intrinsic desire to (continue to) care about

them? No, because I don't want to be the sort of person who does n
care for his family. My distress would be due at least in part to n
instrumental second-order desire to continue to care about my fami
so as not to become the sort of person who does not care about h
family.

Also I would view not caring about my family as "bad news
indicating that I was a bad kind of person, so I still have
noninstrumental nonintrinsic reason to want to care about my fami
even if I am no longer able to do anything for them.

I conclude that I do not have an intrinsic desire to care about n
family. My reasons for this conclusion are (1) that I don't feel as if
have any such intrinsic desire over and above the nonintrinsic desires
have in this regard, and (2) I don't see what there is about my patte
of desiring that needs to be explained by an intrinsic second-order desir

The unwilling addict revisited. Recall Lewis's version of Frankfurt
unwilling addict.

He desires his high, but he does not desire to desire it, and in fact he desir
not to desire it. He does not desire an unaltered, mundane state of consciousnes
but he does desire to desire it. We conclude that he does not value what h
desires, but rather he values what he desires to desire.[37]

Two points. First, it seems to me to be absolutely clear that th
unwilling addict does desire an "unaltered, mundane state of consciou
ness." The problem is that this desire is overcome by the addict's oth
desire, to take the drug.

Second, Lewis's theory requires more than that the unwilling addi
should have a second-order desire to desire an "unaltered, mundan
state of consciousness," if the addict is to be said to value such a stat
The theory also requires that the unwilling addict should have an *intrins
second-order desire of this sort. But Lewis does not argue (or eve
claim) there is such an intrinsic second-order desire in this case and
seems clear to me that the addict would not normally have an intrins
second-order desire of this sort. Clearly, the addict has an instrument
second-order desire – he wants to have a stronger first-order desire fo
an "unaltered, mundane state of consciousness" as a means of ove
coming his other first-order desire for the altered state of consciousne
induced by the drug. But there is no reason to attribute to the addi
any additional intrinsic desire of the relevant sort.

3. Copp's analysis of values

avid Copp has suggested the following "conative account of values":

ne's "values" at a time are preferences one has at that time about the course
one's life (a) that have been stable and secure in the past, and (b) that one
at that time content to have, and (c) that one would not be content at that
ne to anticipate losing in the future, where (d) the latter preferences have
emselves been stable and secure.[38]

Clauses (b) and (c) refer to second-order preferences, so this account
sembles Lewis's account. But there are several differences.

One important difference is that Lewis's account is presented as an
count of what it is for a person to value something whereas Copp's
count is presented as an account of what a person's values are. The
fference is that between 'value' as a verb and 'value' as a noun, in
ne sense of the noun 'value'. (Copp is not concerned with a person's
lues in the sense of things that are valuable about the person.)[39]

It might seem at first that a person's values in the relevant sense are
e same as what the person values, but this is not so. Jack can value
ne's opinion of him without one of Jack's values being Jane's opinion
' him. Jack can value listening to Mozart without it being true that
ne of his values in the relevant sense is listening to Mozart.

'Jack values honesty' does seem to be equivalent to 'One of Jack's
lues is honesty' (where this is not to be interpreted as saying that one
Jack's good qualities is honesty). On the other hand, although it
early makes sense to say, "Jack values happiness," it does not clearly
ake sense to say, "One of Jack's values is happiness."

The noun 'value' in this sense is not closely related to the verb. The
un is similar in meaning to 'principle'. For example, it makes sense
say, "One of Jack's values is that a person should always tell the
uth," which is close to saying, "One of Jack's principles is that a person
ould always tell the truth." On the other hand, we would not normally
y, "One of Jack's values is the principle that a person should always
ll the truth," whereas we might say, "Jack values the principle that a
rson should always tell the truth."[40]

In any event, the differences in our use of the noun and the verb
uld mean that Copp and Lewis are not discussing the same concept.
we might consider whether Copp's and Lewis's respective analyses
e plausible either for a person's valuing something or for a person's
lues in the relevant sense.

One difference between Copp and Lewis is that Copp identifies a

person's values with first-order preferences that satisfy certain furth
conditions (including conditions involving second-order desire
whereas Lewis identifies a person's valuings with certain second-or
desires. This means that Copp is not subject to one of my objections
Lewis, namely, that (contrary to what Lewis claims) a person does
value something unless he already wants it.

On the other hand, Copp is subject to the opposite objection:
person might fail to desire X even though X is one of that perso
values. Michael Stocker's despairing person "sees all the good to
won or saved" but "lacks the will, interest, desire or strength." One
this person's values might be to promote the cause of human justic
even though he no longer values promoting human justice, no long
has any desire to do so, and lacks any desire to have a desire to do

Copp requires that the relevant first-order preferences have a cert
content: They are preferences about the course of one's life. Lewis h
no restriction of this sort on content. Copp's restriction doesn't wo
for certain cases of valuing, such as Jack's valuing Jane's opinion
him. That is a case of instrumental valuing, of course. It also seems
fail for certain cases of intrinsic valuing, such as Jack's valuing t
happiness of his children.

Copp's restriction also seems to fail for a person's values in the r
evant sense, since a person's values in this sense are not restricted
preferences about that person's life. A person can have values co
cerning how people in general should live their lives. For example,
one of Jack's values is honesty, that is not just a preference about t
course of Jack's life.

Another of Copp's restrictions not found in Lewis is that the pr
erences in question have been stable and secure in the past. This i
plausibly rules out new values or new valuing.

The second-order aspect of Copp's analysis is contained in his
quirement that one be content to have the preferences in question a
not content to anticipate losing those preference in the future. I ha
already argued that this fails for certain cases of valuing: A person w
values listening to Mozart might be quite complacent about the prospe
of coming to value listening to Mahler instead. It is more plausible
a requirement on a person's values. I can't think of any counterexample
If your values include honesty, I would expect you not to be content
anticipate losing your preference for honesty.

There are counterexamples in the other direction, however. A pe
son's preference can satisfy Copp's definition without the thing preferr
being one of the person's values or one of the things that the pers
values. For example, Jack may prefer to part his hair on the left, whe

this preference is a preference (a) that has been stable and secure in the past, (b) that Jack is content to have, (c) and that Jack, because of a certain rigidity, would not be content to anticipate losing in the future, and (d) where the latter preferences are stable and secure. These conditions can all be satisfied without Jack's values including his parting his hair on the left and without it being true that he values parting his hair on the left.

Valuing. What is it, then, to value something? It seems to me that valuing something involves desiring it – a first-order desire. It seems clear to me that if you don't have a first-order desire for something, you do not value it.[41] Furthermore, as I have argued, you can value something without having a second-order desire to have a first-order desire for it. On the other hand, not all desiring is valuing. You can want to go to the movies tonight without valuing going to the movies tonight. I conclude that valuing is a particular kind of desiring, but I am unable to say more about what kind.

As for a person's values, I find that an even more perplexing notion.

4. Conclusion

I have looked at Frankfurt's account of freedom of the will, Lewis's account of valuing, and Copp's account of a person's values. All three accounts appeal to second-order desires in somewhat different ways. Each faces specific counterexamples. In considering the fate of these accounts, it looks unlikely to me that any appeal to second-order desires can provide the key to an adequate philosophical account of freedom of the will or of what it is to value something.

Notes

1 Harry Frankfurt, "Freedom of the Will and the Concept of a Person," *Journal of Philosophy* 68 (1971):5–20, reprinted in Harry Frankfurt, *The Importance of What We Care About* (Cambridge: Cambridge University Press, 1988), pp. 11–25.
2 Richard Jeffrey, "Preferences among Preferences," *Journal of Philosophy* 71 (1974):377–91.
3 Gary Watson, "Free Agency," *Journal of Philosophy* 72 (1975):205–20
4 David Lewis, "Dispositional Theories of Value," *Proceedings of the Aristotelian Society,* Supplementary Volume 63 (1989):113–37.
5 David Copp, "Reason and Needs," Chapter 7 of this volume.
6 P. F. Strawson, *Individuals* (London: Methuen, 1959), pp. 101–2.
7 Frankfurt, "Freedom of the Will," pp. 6, 7, 12–13.

8 Ibid., pp. 10, 11.

9 Ibid., p. 12.

10 Ibid., pp. 14, 15.

11 Claudia Mills drew this distinction in a paper written for a seminar at Princeton University in about 1979.

12 H. P. Grice, "Meaning," *Philosophical Review* 66 (1957):777–88.

13 David Premack, *Gavagai! or the Future History of the Animal Language Controversy* (Cambridge, Mass.: MIT Press, 1986).

14 Gilbert Harman, "Practical Reasoning," *Review of Metaphysics* 29 (1976):431–63; Harman, *Change in View: Principles of Reasoning* (Cambridge, Mass.: MIT Press/Bradford Books, 1986), ch. 8.

15 John Searle, *Intentionality, an Essay in the Philosophy of Mind* (Cambridge: Cambridge University Press, 1983), ch. 3.

16 The distinction between these three sorts of intention is further elaborated in Harman, "Practical Reasoning," and in *Change in View*, pp. 80–2.

17 The term 'guided' is suggested by Harry Frankfurt, who writes about an agent guiding an action in "The Problem of Action," *American Philosophical Quarterly* 15 (1978), reprinted in Frankfurt, *Importance of What We Care About*, pp. 69–79. Alfred R. Mele takes an action to be guided by an intention or plan in "Are Intentions Self-Referential?" *Philosophical Studies* 52 (1987):309–29. Frankfurt points out that guidance need not involve an actual causal relation; a hypothetical causal relation is sometimes enough. It may be that usually a plan guides an action by virtue of causing aspects of the action, but there are also cases in which there is merely a conditional dependence between plan and action, a readiness to intervene if things go off track. A positive intention to run someone down blends into a merely conditional intention to turn the wheel if needed to adjust the aim of your car.

18 C cannot follow your practical conclusion (P) because P can be reached only if C has already been reached. C cannot precede P either, since C has to be a conclusion about that particular P: C makes sense only if P exists.

19 Personal communication (1990).

20 George Wilson interprets this as the claim that you have to continue to have the intention until you achieve your end. *The Intentionality of Human Action*, rev. ed. (Stanford: Stanford University Press, 1989), pp. 278–80. That is too strong. You don't always need to suppose that your intention will persist until your aim is accomplished. Your plan is that your now having that intention will lead in some more or less specified way to your accomplishing what you intend. Sometimes your plan involves your continuing to have that intention and sometimes it does not.

21 Frankfurt, personal communication (1990).

22 Harman, *Change in View*, pp. 87–8.

23 Alfred R. Mele, "Are Intentions Self-Referential?" *Philosophical Studies* 52 (1987):309–29.

24 George Wilson expresses skepticism about such explicit mental representation in *Intentionality of Human Action*, pp. 277–8.

25 John Perry's Hempel lectures at Princeton, spring 1990.

26 Or did. This was several years ago.

27 Lewis, "Dispositional Theories of Value," p. 114.

28 Ibid., p. 115. Lewis makes footnote reference to the articles by Harry Frankfurt and Richard Jeffrey previously mentioned.

29 Ibid.

30 I have included the words "intrinsic" and "intrinsically" three times here, once in parentheses. Lewis's footnote does not make it absolutely clear whether all three occurrences are needed.

31 This is the sort of example that is mentioned in the causal decision theory literature. David Lewis, "Causal Decision Theory," *Australasian Journal of Philosophy* 59 (1981):9; R. C. Jeffrey, *The Logic of Decision,* 2d ed. (Chicago: University of Chicago Press, 1983), p. 15.

32 David Lewis pointed this out to me in a discussion of these issues.

33 This bears on Warren Quinn's essay "Putting Rationality in its Place," Chapter 3 of this volume. Quinn argues that desire is always based on the thought that something is good. His view would seem to have the implausible consequence that there are no intrinsic desires.

34 Michael Stocker, "Desiring the Bad: An Essay in Moral Psychology," *Journal of Philosophy* 76 (1979):744.

35 Michael Smith, "Valuing: Desiring or Believing," in David Charles and Kathleen Lennon, eds., *Reductionism and Anti-Reductionism* (Oxford: Clarendon Press, forthcoming).

36 Just as it is important to distinguish believing that something is good from valuing it, it is also important to distinguish the belief that something is good from the belief that it is valuable. A good baseball bat need not be a valuable baseball bat, a good discussion is not necessarily the same thing as a valuable discussion, a good life is not the same thing as a valuable life, and honesty is good whether or not it is also valuable.

37 Lewis, "Dispositional Theories of Value," p. 115.

38 David Copp, "Reason and Needs," quoting from a handout distributed at the April 1990 Bowling Green conference.

39 It is possible to conflate these two senses of the word 'value'. The otherwise acute Michael Smith does so and also wrongly identifies having value with valuing something. This occurs in a critique of some remarks of Gauthier's in Smith, "Valuing: Desiring or Believing?" Gauthier is concerned with whether satisfaction of certain preferences is of value. Smith conflates this question with the question whether having such preferences is to have values in the sense with which we are concerned here; Smith also conflates that question with the question whether having such preferences is to value the things preferred.

40 Here I am indebted to Katherine Miller and Christiane Fellbaum.

41 I am indebted to Alfred Mele for pointing out to me that exception must be made for the case in which the something in question itself involves your having a desire. Valuing that sort of something involves desiring it, and such a desire is by definition not a first-order desire.

9

On the winding road from good to right

JAMES GRIFFIN

Many of us travel the road from good to right. We move from premises about well-being (which is how I am using the word 'good') to conclusions about what morally we ought to do. That may not be the only way we reach moral conclusions. And we may not all take the straight line between the two that some utilitarians do. And we may sometimes travel in the opposite direction too. In fact, I find the road hard to make out and the flow of traffic bemusing. Hence, my choice of subject.

1. Constraints on the route

There seem to me to be several constraints on the route from good to right.

The nature of individual flourishing. One constraint comes out of prudential values. I use 'prudence' not in the ordinary sense of a due concern for one's future, but in the philosopher's broad sense of whatever has to do with one's interests. I have written about this subject elsewhere[1] and anyway have space only to sketch a view rather than to argue for it.

Prudential deliberation leads, I think, to some such list of values as this:

1. Enjoyment.
2. The components of a characteristically human existence (that is, the components of agency: autonomy, minimum material provision, liberty).
3. Understanding (at least on certain basic personal and metaphysical matters).
4. Accomplishment (that is, the sort of achievements in one's life that give it weight or substance).
5. Deep personal relations.

ou may not entirely agree with that list, but you may agree with enough
out it to accept what I have to say. A striking feature of many items on the list is their long-term, life-
ructuring character. In that respect, they are quite unlike the one value
classical utilitarianism, which on the dominant interpretation is a
ental state, an experience, and so much more short-term. So even if
u disagree with my list but at least agree that some prudential values
e of this life-structuring sort, then that is enough for the moment. To
ve deep attachments to particular persons is to acquire motives that
ape much of one's life and carry on through most of it. To accomplish
mething with one's life requires dedication to particular projects that
pically narrow and absorb one's attention. Many prudential values
volve commitments – to particular persons, institutions, causes, and
ojects. One cannot live a prudentially good life, one cannot fully
urish, without becoming in large measure partial. That partiality then
comes part of one; it is not something that one can psychologically
ter into and exit from at will. It involves becoming a certain kind of
rson. Even short-term pleasures have finally to be judged in a fairly
ng-term, character-fixing way, because a person has to decide how
uch place to give to living for day-to-day pleasures seen up against
her forms of life.

We know that consequentialist thought, to which many of us give
me place in our moral deliberation, can be applied either directly to
ts by assessing their consequences or only indirectly to acts by assessing
stead consequences of living by a set of rules or of having certain sorts
dispositions, and so on. And we assume that any prudential value
eory (hedonism, say, or my list of values) can be plugged into any of
ese different forms of consequentialism. But that may not be so. A
nsequentialist's outlook has to take in more than just acts, one by
ne. Commitments do not leave one able, occasion by occasion, having
viewed all actions in some sense within human capacity before dis-
ositions are formed, to choose the best. Some commitments will not
ave one with time to see chances for doing more good; other com-
itments, especially to other persons, will not leave one able to take
em even if one saw them. Of course, an act-consequentialist can in-
ude among his options becoming a person of commitments, but to opt
at way would be for him subversive: It would change the source of
s action and the distinctive form of his deliberation.

On the prudential theory that I am proposing, one should become
eply partial. On any plausible morality, one should be impartial –
erhaps even as strongly impartial as utilitarians believe, counting every-

body for one. There is a tension between prudence and morality that myself can see no way totally to dispel.

One must not exaggerate the tension. There are also ways in whi prudence and morality are in harmony. For one thing, it is impossib to make a sharp cut between prudential and moral values. Morali penetrates prudence: One can get no full account of a prudentially goc life without introducing morality. One prudential value is understandin and one key piece of understanding is what is of value, which will incluc the value of other persons, and what kind of life is consonant with th knowledge. Another is accomplishment – that is, bringing off somethin that has the weight and value that makes one's life fulfilled. And tl sorts of values that have that potent status give prominent place to wh it is for others to flourish. Again, even if you disagree with my list, yc may agree at least that morality penetrates prudence.

And I think that Sidgwick was wrong to find contradiction betwee or a dualism of, prudence and morality in practical reason itself.[2] Tl fact that there are prudential reasons for action and moral reasons wi no overarching super-reasons to mediate between them is no more wo rying than that there are irreducibly different prudential values with r super-value. As with value, all that we need for comparability is to l able to rank reasons as stronger, less strong, and equally strong. M own view is that on an adequate account of prudential reasons, the force as reasons is not restricted to the prudential domain. I understar that I have a (prudential) reason to accomplish something with my lif because accomplishment is something that makes a life – not *my* li especially – better. To see a prudential value correctly is to see it a valuable in any life. So my reason for accepting a small cost now for large benefit later in my own life spills over into a reason for me t accept a small cost to me for a large benefit to you. I must, on pain c losing grip on the notion of a reason for action itself, see reasons sprea ing beyond the bounds of my own life. Contrary to a long tradition i philosophy, there is no gap between egoistic and altruistic rationality t be bridged.

Still, even if prudence and morality penetrate one another, a tensic between them persists. What causes it is not touched by these elemen of harmony. The stubborn fact is that flourishing points to partialit and morality points away from it. This tension runs very deep. On might think that it could be reduced if we would, as perhaps we shoulc make impartial benevolence our central project; then one could accon plish something with one's life (prudential value) by behaving impartiall (moral value). But this would merely be to realize one prudential valu at the expense of many others – at the expense, say, of deep person:

relations, of many forms of enjoyment, and, if this project takes much of one's time, of a lot of understanding. The tension even arises inside the aim of impartially maximizing the good, on its own. The world in which everyone's life is as good as possible would be a world in which people were full of commitments. The impartial ideal, then, would be a world populated by agents incapable of promoting the impartial ideal. And what one comes to see as one's own individual form of flourishing becomes a large part of what one is; it combines many of the strands of one's personal identity. One's concern for one's own flourishing is not separate from one's concern for the survival of one's individual self. That is why Bernard Williams sees in the demands of impartial maximization of good a threat to a person's "integrity," which if the person lets go far becomes tantamount to "suicide." And it is why John Updike says in his autobiography, "We are social creatures but, unlike ants and bees, not just that; there is something intrinsically and individually vital which must be defended against the claims even of virtue."[3]

If the term 'ethics' is used broadly, so as to encompass both prudence and morality, then there is an inevitable tension between the ethical demands of impartiality and the ethical demands of individual flourishing. Somehow these two parts of ethics must be made, if not harmonious, at least combinable in one normative point of view, and in one personality.

The personal circumstances of decision. This is a line of thought that we owe to Richard Hare.[4] The personal circumstances of moral choice vary. Typically, we are short of time, facts, and fellow feeling. But on rare occasions we find ourselves with time to think things through, not badly informed, and fairly dispassionate. It is unlikely that our thought ought to proceed in the same way in these different circumstances. Then there is the closely connected matter of moral education. Since the seventeenth century, philosophers have by and large ignored moral education (J. S. Mill, with his discussion of "internal sanctions," is a rare and not very happy exception). But the way we are taught in childhood sets us on a moral path pretty much for life. Moral dispositions, to be effective, have to be deep, and going against them will be difficult. And the whole complicated weave of training, sanctions, policies, principles, habits, dispositions, and feelings has to be shaped for the usual case, not the odd one. So a morally well-trained person will have motives that are, for good reason, to some degree insensitive to exceptions. These considerations lead Hare to distinguish two levels of moral thinking. We have, he suggests, an *intuitive* level on which we decide what to do by appealing to well-entrenched principles made for the standard case. But these principles can conflict, or can fit an odd case badly, or can need finer tuning; so we must also be able to function on a *critical* level on which we can reason about particular cases and about the adequacy of our intuitive principles. The case for some such distinction seems to me very strong, and strong independently of one's normative views – independent, for instance, of Hare's own broadly utilitarian views. Every substantive ethics will have to find place for different levels or sets of norms, and that imposes constraints on the move from good to right.

The limits of the will. 'Ought' implies 'can'. And 'practical reason' implies 'can'. That is, we should not say that a person has a "reason" to do what clearly is beyond his capacity. If I see a young girl teetering on a cliff far above me, I might wish that I could fly to her, Superman-like, and snatch her from death. It would be desirable to do it, but I should resist any claim that I had a reason to do it. Let me leave aside whether my resistance would arise from the senselessness or merely the pointlessness of saying that I had a reason. There is no sharp line between those two. It is enough that we will not say it. Now, our limits are not only physical but also psychological. Beliefs about the limits of the will have largely shaped commonsense morality. Any morality must meet what might be called the requirement of psychological realism. Moral rules must mesh with natural human motivation. One cannot ask for what the human frame cannot deliver. One certainly may ask someone to get his trousers wet in order to save a drowning child, but not to sacrifice his life to do it. That explains the line that common sense draws between duty and what is beyond the call of duty.

This brings moral philosophers up against an empirical question on which much of what they say turns but which they largely ignore: What are the limits of human motivation?

We know that evolution has entrenched in us both self-interest and limited altruism. We, like other species, defend ourselves with a tenacity that we do not display over many others. Our form of consciousness itself reflects the primacy of self-interest: Our perceptions of our own pleasure and pain have a unique vividness to our minds and a privileged link to our motivation;[5] our own everyday concerns fill our field of attention, the concerns of others appearing faintly at the periphery. And there is genetic bonding to a few others. Many species, humans among them, are capable of great self-sacrifice, especially to protect offspring. Even outside the circle of blood relations, we sometimes, though only rarely, form ties of love that still our self-interest.

How can we expect being like that, ferociously self-interested and of very limited altruism, to be capable of impartiality? One answer is that beings like that can overcome the lack of natural vividness in their consciousness of others.[6] We can learn more about them; we can use our imagination to fill out the picture; we can even actually go and see. We know how one photograph of a starving child can make thousands reach for their checkbooks.

But is the problem only one of shortage of knowledge, or knowledge that lacks vividness? I doubt it. Well-intentioned famine relief workers, who have the starving victims filling their field of vision, no doubt make great sacrifices to help them but do not generally sacrifice themselves right to the point where their marginal loss equals the others' marginal gain. And the explanation cannot just be that anyone who helps others must keep healthy or wealthy enough to go on helping. It is true that there are often good impartial-maximizing reasons for those aiding to have more than those aided. But relief workers generally do not sacrifice themselves up to that point either. And I find it hard to think that it is because their knowledge is still somehow incomplete or faint. To see the problem as simply one about knowledge does not take the full measure of its difficulty.

Though that seems to me right, there are reasons to hesitate. In time of war, hundreds of thousands of ordinary people go off to defend their country at the risk of their lives. If military training can motivate them to go into battle, could not a well-conducted moral training do something comparable for us? But I suspect that an important element in the motivation of soldiers is the belief that they will not be the ones to die. Going into battle does not have the certainty of sacrifice, great though the potential sacrifice be. And when soldiers are sent on missions with an especially high risk of death, there is often a shift from command to request: Volunteers are called for. Still, there is no denying that soldiers can be brought to accept great potential danger. In most cases they do, I suspect, out of fear of the sergeant or a court-martial, or shame at the prospect of letting their comrades down. This suggests that we could surround the moral life with comparable institutions and sanctions: We could have a kind of neighborhood Red Guard to keep us up to the moral mark. It would be a terrible price to pay, and we are willing to pay a comparable price in an emergency such as war because of the exceptional importance of what is at stake. But perhaps we ought to think that what is at stake in morality is equally important. I think that there may be something to be said for our moving a bit in this direction, but I doubt that the full Brave New World apparatus could be justified. The cost in bleakness and tension would be huge, and though battles come only occasionally in a soldier's life, moral battles, especially on the impartial-maximizing conception, occur all the time. And to produce moral action by fear denies an agent autonomy, and loss of autonomy is a loss of both an important prudential value and an essential component of morality, at least as most of us now conceive of morality. It is true that some soldiers (and sports competitors and mothers when their children are threatened) can raise themselves to such emotional intensity, even without Brave New World pressures, that they acquire powers that they do not normally have. But I doubt that we can use what people are capable of at the pitch of excitement as evidence of what they are capable of day in and day out, which is what morality needs. We do, nonetheless, expect great sacrifices if the alternative is dire enough: I ought, I think, to accept my own death to stop the madman from getting at the nuclear button. That may be because the threat is so appalling that we expect motivation more naturally to follow. It is perhaps also because the event is exceptional: It is a demand that would finish me off but not the sort of incessant demand that would come from impartial maximization and would undermine my life, and others' lives, at every point.

To my mind, the evidence goes against the epistemological answer. But there is a second answer: Instead of increasing knowledge, we should revolutionize the will. Instead of just enhancing information, we should be concerned with finding an inspiring conception of what morality is. This, I think, is Iris Murdoch's answer.[7] Modern moral philosophy, she thinks, is unambitious. It sets modest goals; it assumes that our psychological capacities are puny. But goals and capacities are connected. Truly noble aims inspire action that would otherwise be beyond us. They can turn egoism into something approaching altruism. I do not know how far she thinks this transformation can go, but perhaps it can, in the end, turn ordinary people into saints and heroes – or a good approximation of them. The good, she says, is "what makes a man act unselfishly in a concentration camp." She sees the aim of morality, as does one Christian tradition, as not stopping short of perfection:

What of the command, "Be ye therefore perfect"? Would it not be more sensible to say: "Be ye therefore slightly improved"? Some psychologists warn us that if our standards are too high we shall become neurotic. It seems to me that the idea of love arises necessarily in this context. The idea of perfection moves and possibly changes us because it inspires love in the part of us that is more worthy. One cannot feel unmixed love for a mediocre moral standard any more than one can for the work of a mediocre artist.[8]

Are there any such transforming goals? If I thought that I was created by God, that my bodily life was an illusory passage to eternal bliss, that my flourishing consisted in the extinction of my own ego, and if I had the psychological support of a community of believers living the same sort of life, then perhaps I could make sacrifices that I cannot now make. But such a metaphysics would have replaced my present conception of my own flourishing with a very different one. But I do not, nor do many religious believers, have such metaphysical beliefs, nor see any reason to adopt them. My and their conception of human flourishing is nothing like that. Murdoch's own view of the goal of moral life is something like Plato's Form of the Good, and she sees it as having a magnetic power akin to many religious conceptions.[9] I myself have trouble understanding what she means by the powerful "sovereignty" of good. Certainly some moral goals, even demanding ones, can inspire, while others dispirit. The best I can do in understanding the "sovereignty" of good, however, is to see it as something not unlike the impartial maximization of the good. But that goal, though inspiring, is not inspiring enough to transform motivation in the necessary way (at least, that is what I concluded a moment ago). The goals that might transform it we see no reason to adopt; the goals that we see reason to adopt do not transform it.

I may, of course, exaggerate what is needed. We may not need a goal capable of inspiring us actually to realize it. Perhaps it will do to have a goal toward which we can make a little progress. When Jesus said, "Be ye therefore perfect," he must have known that we should always remain largely imperfect but that we might still find point in trying for perfection. But 'trying' implies 'thinking that one has a chance of doing'. Since we have no reason to think that we can be perfect, Jesus' injunction comes down to the one Iris Murdoch guys: If not quite "Be ye therefore slightly improved," then "Be ye therefore as good as you can." Putting this into action-guiding form, it might be: "Come as close to maximizing impartially as you can." But this line of thought, I think, also fails to take the full measure of the problem. Should we even want to be saints (if I may secularize the term by using it of the utterly impartial maximizer)? Such saintliness is not the ideal form of human life. One can raise one's capacity for selflessness and generalized love of humanity only by reducing one's commitments to particular persons and projects. The impartial maximizer of good lives a much less good life himself. A society of such maximizers would be much less good than one with love of and commitment to individuals. To adopt saintliness as a goal would be a dreadful denial of human flourishing. And it is no reply that rational maximizers, for just that reason, would stop short of abandoning commitments to individuals. To do that would be instead to abandon the attempt to come as close to saintliness (in this secularized sense) as one can. It might still be that on grounds of impartial maximization of good, one or two persons should sacrifice themselves to saintliness in order **t** save hundreds of others who could then live proper unsaintly lives. B**u** what saintliness cannot be is the general goal toward which we all oug**h** to strive.

The importance of groups. I suggested earlier that the nature **o** prudential values leads us away from looking at consequences act b**y** act. So do the facts of social life.

As a group we have to solve coordination problems. Often we wa**n** the same things, but we will not get them unless we harmonize o**u**r actions. We cannot repel the attack if we all rush to man the same pos**t.** Then we also have to solve the more taxing cooperation problems. The**r**e are cases where each of us has an aim that he can bring off on his ow**n** but he would be better off if he did it with others. Each of us wants t**o** prosper, but would prosper more by cooperating with the rest. But **i**n such cases what each of us puts in and takes out can vary from perso**n** to person a lot, so solutions are typically not as easy as with coordinatio**n** problems. A famous example of a cooperation problem is the Prisoner**'s** Dilemma.[10] When two persons find themselves in a situation with th**e** form of a Prisoner's Dilemma, or a form close to it, they have to avo**id** landing in the third-best outcome for each. The most to be hoped fo**r** from any device that both parties would accept willingly is one that lead**s** to the best of the symmetrical results, mutual silence, so we nee**d** something to ensure the second-best outcome for each. Even if one **o**f the parties to the Dilemma is impartially benevolent and so willing t**o** sacrifice himself, what he would most want would still be the secon**d** best outcome for each, mutual silence, because that is best overall. S**o** given human nature, individuals need help to bring this outcome abou**t.** And in some real-life Prisoner's Dilemmas, or in situations formall**y** close to them, there are several possible equally good solutions. The**n** we need to be not only prodded down a promising path but also prodde**d** down the same promising path. Some cooperation problems contai**n** coordination problems.

So morality must take account of group actions. Part of the solutio**n** to Prisoner's Dilemmas is for one to look not at one's own acts occasio**n** by occasion, but at what groups do – to think strategically, not tacticall**y.** The strategic outlook would tell us to do what is necessary – agreements**,** conventions, institutions, education, persuasion, penalties – to hit o**n** and sustain beneficial cooperation.[11] Merely by shifting to a strategi**c** outlook a consequentialist might sometimes agree to what is called **a** political solution to a Prisoner's Dilemma. We might all, for instance**,** agree on an inescapable system of taxation, or one with drastic penaltie**s** for cheaters. Still, it is well known that detection often cannot be assured nor sanctions be made fully effective, and so political solutions are not always enough. Then we need to supplement them with what is called a psychological solution. We might raise children to have strong moral inhibitions. But this, too, is not always enough. Sometimes education is unsuccessful. Anyway, as we have seen, even if everyone were impartially benevolent and thinking strategically, we should often need to coordinate action and to find reassurance that enough others are going to cooperate in some way for cooperation actually to have the best results, and also that not so many will cooperate that it would be better if some of us struck out on independent beneficial action of our own.

There is more to human nature than strategic moral outlooks, and much of it comes to our aid in making cooperation likely and so rational. Many institutions and attitudes existed well before humans rose to the level of self-consciousness that allows moral reflection. The origins of the institution of property may go as deep as to a genetically based human correlate of animal territoriality. The origins certainly also include the natural tendency to see ourselves in what we labor over, in the hardly fully conscious movement of thought: "It's my doing; I am now in it; it's mine." This is as much sentiment as thought, and it gets articulated in philosophy as the labor theory of property. Facts about the limits of human motivation also shape the institution. We are people of limited altruism; we will work to benefit ourselves and those close to us but not to benefit just anybody. And we just find ourselves in certain social and economic relations. We are not a tribe; we are not linked hierarchically by personal ties. We are in a huge industrial society of strangers, and that makes some distributive rules relevant and others irrelevant. As a result, many of our social institutions are already in place; moral philosophers do not, out of their own materials, have to provide all the reasons and motives that go into constructing them. They have, rather, to provide answers to such questions as: Why join in beneficial cooperation? Why encourage its development? What in our institutions needs changing?

Many social institutions are obligation-generating. You promised, so you should do it. Since you are the parent, you ought to look after the child. It is her property, so hands off. At times we operate with principles internal to the institutions; at other times, since there is no saying that the institutions are in perfect order, we step outside and assess them, for which we have to have different principles.

We live our lives within a setting of morally essential social institutions, conventions, and practices on the one hand and of prudentially essential personal commitments and involvements on the other. Together they constitute a complex structure of obligations and rights. These social institutions (and personal commitments too) are obligation-generating and rights-bestowing. Now, these obligations and rights give an agent reasons to do things for persons in his society that he does not have to those in the world at large, and to those in his particular cooperative enterprises that he does not have to those outside them, and to those in his family that he does not have to his society at large. As a result, there will be many obligations to those close that do not exist to those distant. And they will be obligations of great weight, because the institutions generating them are responsible for most of the major goods of our life. Unless we have reason to think that these social institutions are seriously defective, we have good reason to accept these obligations.

The limits of knowledge. I said earlier, in talking about what I called "the personal circumstances of decision," that we are characteristically short of facts. I had in mind then a class of facts of which we are usually short but every now and then are not. What I now want to remark on are the sorts of facts that are permanently beyond our reach – many of them right at the heart of what determines our obligations. For instance, certain social institutions, such as an institution of property, are so vastly complex that we cannot really hope to tell how beneficial certain particular forms of the institution are. That kind of utility calculation is simply beyond us. It is not that there is any problem in principle with it; it is, rather, that we do not have, and cannot find, and probably could not adequately get our minds around all the important evidence. We can sometimes assess this or that feature; we can, therefore, with some hope of success, change this or that part of the institution. But in general we just live within the institutions that we are born into. These institutions are natural growths, with roots well below the level of human consciousness and choice. We might be able to see at least that we are better off inside the institution than outside, even though we may not be best off and could not tell if we were. There are many forms that an institution of property can take, but we quickly reach a point where, even though the alternatives may not be equally beneficial, we cannot rank them. Then, what justifies the claim that we are obliged is not (that is, not entirely) the general good but the bare fact that this is the institution into which we happen to have been born.

Let me give one more example. The limits of our obligation are fixed by, among other things, the limits of our will. But where are they? That is an empirical question of immense complexity. We do not now know the answer, and I doubt that we ever shall, except in terms that will leave the limits still largely indeterminate. But despite our ignorance, we go on to form a picture of what a normal human agent can manage, which in turn determines our conception of what a moral agent must do. The picture has a large element of arbitrariness to it, and so too does the corresponding conception of moral obligation. We should like to think that moral obligations are not arbitrary, but since the limits of knowledge are inescapable, so too is the arbitrariness. To what extent can I deny myself and my family in order to help the world's starving? Our large measure of ignorance about that, along with our ignorance about the value of various institutions and practices, will mean that we have simply to choose a policy for ourselves (say, to contribute 2 percent of gross income to famine relief) and then stick to it. The limits of knowledge leave arbitrariness and contingencies a large role in determining moral obligations – for instance, the arbitrariness of the actual percentage we fix on for contributions to famine relief, and the deep and complex social forces that have shaped our particular institution of property.

2. Clusters of norms

Those, then, are five facts of moral life. Each of them imposes certain constraints on the route we may take from good to right. But before I come to the constraints, let me go on for a while with facts about moral life – although the facts that I now want to turn to contain a yet more generous amount of interpretation than before.

It seems to me that our norms of action break up, roughly, into sets or clusters. There is, clearly enough, a cluster of prudential norms. I said earlier that, to my mind, there is an inevitable tension between a moral norm of impartiality and the prudential norms of individual flourishing. It may seem that what I then went on to say about the limits of the will relaxes that tension. Morality cannot demand a degree of impartiality that the will cannot deliver. But our ignorance about what the will can deliver leaves us with the job of deciding, and up to a point just stipulating, limits of the will, and the tension arises again, acutely, in that freedom of decision. This conflict between prudence and morality cannot be entirely resolved even if one accepts that moral norms are overriding. The conflict that I have in mind crops up at the early stage of our fixing the boundaries of the moral, so morality's trumping prudence does not regulate prudence's fixing morality.

Then there are moral norms. There is the moral code dominant in one's community, a code that is widely taught, forms many of our expectations about how others will act, is cited publicly to justify or criticize. The community through which this code extends may be small or large (in any case, the criteria of identity for a code are vague, and the more content one attributes to the code the less wide its jurisdiction is likely to be). But there being a fairly extensive code, both in content and application, confers obvious benefits on a community, so the wider the jurisdiction the better. But if the norms are to serve their purpose, there are certain pressures on them. They cannot be too demanding (otherwise they will not be observed), nor too complex (otherwise they will not be understood), and so on. They have to be rather like the Ten Commandments: a bit crude, planted early and deep, widely respected.

Then most of us adapt the public code, perhaps a lot, to suit our own case. We develop a personal code. Why should I who am capable of a little more effort and attention and of keeping a few more exceptions in mind than the average person, determine in my own private life what I should do by appeal to rules designed for a different sort of person? The limits of human motivation mean that one should not ask too much, but there is no reason to ask too little. There are pressures too on this everyday personal code. I, like everyone else, am characteristically short of time, facts, and fellow feeling. So a certain simplicity, a certain shaping for the usual rather than the exceptional case, a certain bias toward others (so long as it does not go beyond psychological limits) to counteract my natural bias toward myself is likely to appear. Moral dispositions, to be effective, have to be deep, and going against them will be rare and difficult.

We should probably also distinguish a cluster of social norms, though they might also be regarded as a sub-cluster within the two previous clusters. These are the norms relevant not to decisions about somewhat detached individual action but to collective decisions within a community. For instance, relations and motivation in a family are so different from those in a large, impersonal cooperative economic enterprise that a principle of fair distribution in the one may well differ from that in the other. We have evolved, often not especially consciously, social rules about who puts in what and who takes out what in cooperative enterprises from which we all benefit more than we should by going it alone. Many pressures are at work here that do not appear in families. The sheer size of most societies is bound to affect the content of the norms. For one thing, the extent of my knowledge of the persons involved varies enormously. I know a lot about my children. I do not, nor does anyone, nor can anyone easily, have even roughly comparable knowledge about all the citizens of a state. I am able, therefore, to fine-tune distributions between my children; I might know, for instance, that one of them would just joylessly squander any money I gave him. But a government cannot do much fine-tuning of social distributions; it just does not know enough. So we are forced to a kind of egalitarianism on the social level that we are not on the individual. Moreover, lives can be lived in very different ways and be equally good. While I can know fairly well what would make my children's lives better, I cannot hope to know this of all citizens. So there are pressures toward neutrality on the social scale, at least between all respectable conceptions of the good life, that do not appear on the individual scale. Then there is the important consideration that a society needs to command assent, to reconcile its citizens to decisions that sometimes will severely damage their own interests. Citizens will not easily be reconciled to decisions emerging from a conception of the good that they hotly dispute, and this too is a force for neutrality. So, norms for social choice will work with a relatively narrow, neutral conception of well-being, whereas norms for individual choice will use a comprehensive conception that has place for a person's own tastes and aspirations.[12] Also, social norms may include egalitarian requirements absent in norms for private life. In short, there are norms that we see applying to us as members of, and as together constituting, large groups.

Then there will be a cluster of critical norms, the norms that we fall back on in reflection when the norms in the other clusters conflict with one another or do not fit a special case or begin to look suspect. Some philosophers have recently suggested that our moral thought has a two-level or a multilevel structure, and they must, in some sense, be right.[13] The norms that we ordinarily use to guide our action must themselves be open to criticism, and the norms that appear in critical reflection have to be somewhat different from our everyday action-guiding norms, though what the critical norms are, and how they relate to the everyday norms, is not at all obvious.

I should acknowledge that, as I see it, the division of norms into five clusters that I have just roughly sketched is neither sharp nor exhaustive. Our norms are unlikely to have grown in a way that would make them a system; they have grown, by fits and starts, in response to pressing, heterogeneous practical needs. They have taken their shape partly from the kinds of circumstances we found ourselves in, from the sorts of problems that we faced. Since the problems were different – sometimes large-scale political, sometimes small-scale personal, sometimes about dispositions for facing moral life generally, sometimes about the way to decide out-of-the-way cases – it would not be surprising for different clusters of norms to have emerged. But the kinds of problems we face, and the norms we devise to solve them, are not sharply distinct. Bor-

derline cases are likely to abound. Even after we have corrected and
systematized our principles as much as we can, we are unlikely to find
sharp lines. And further clusters of norms, besides the five I have men
tioned, can be distinguished on the same basis. For instance, the prin
ciples for behavior between nations are distinct from what I have been
calling social norms. In the case of social norms ownership, fidelity to
agreements, fair participation, and cooperation are central. But the
principles that apply between rich nations and poor are quite different
There is no single cooperative enterprise (even in the loose sense that
there is in one country); rules of participation lose relevance; with the
failure of the Lockean Proviso of "as much and as good" a lot of the
backing for property rights disappears; and so on.[14]

Still, the important point is that we are faced by a rather bewildering
variety of clusters of norms, norms that often point in opposite direc
tions. But that, you may think, is the purpose of moral theory. The
forces that I listed in the last section are the forces that, as I see it, have
actually shaped our moral norms. What these forces leave us with is our
messy commonsense morality. And it is a natural thought that the job
of moral philosophy is to come on the scene to replace this mess with
something simpler or at least more systematic. But can it?

3. How systematic can we make the clusters?

What do these observations show about the move from good to right'
I think that they push the good far into the background of our thought
about what is morally right. But the good might still, though in the
background, exert a simplifying and systematizing influence over the
clusters of norms. However, the forces that I have mentioned as shaping
our norms are, I think, largely inescapable. They are either inescapable
limits to moral life or pressures that arise in the course of solving its
inescapable problems. So the numerous and often reduplicating norm
that have actually grown up do not form a messy garden that the moral
philosopher, with ruthless weeding, tidies up. Some tidying is, I am sure
possible, but the degree of system that we can introduce into this thicket
of clusters is limited.

Let me take the example of our norms of property. The state of
presystematic, commonsense morality is roughly this. There are norms
of property in the moral code dominant in our society: Don't steal
Don't trespass. There are norms of property in our personal codes
perhaps qualifying or adding exceptions to the social norms. Then there
is a legal system, which defines rights of acquisition, retention, and
transfer of property. It will define, among other things, what taxes

ociety may impose on one's private property beyond the costs of main-
aining it. The norms generated by the legal system are also, sometimes
•r to some extent, regarded as moral norms. Then, crucially, there are
he critical norms that we fall back on in our assessment and amendment
•f these other norms.

What are these critical norms and how much authority have they got?
\lan Ryan, at the end of his book on property, suggests that two traditions have dominated the scene over the last two centuries.[15] The
3ritish utilitarian tradition assesses property in instrumental terms: Does
. particular form of property have good results such as security, incen-
ive, and check on government power? The Continental tradition as-
esses it in terms of the flourishing of the self: Do traditional forms of
•rivate property enhance self-realization, as Hegel thought, or do they
hwart it, as Marx thought? But at a deeper level these two traditions
nerge. They both accept that property is to be assessed by appeal to
he quality of life. That seems to me right. The obvious principle to
.ppeal to in critical reflection about property is the promotion of well-
•eing. That appeal, I should say, has two strands: a maximizing (or at
.ny rate an augmentative) strand and a distributive strand. I want to
:oncentrate on the effects of the first: If that is one of our critical
:onsiderations, how much system will it introduce?

There is an obvious answer. On its own, without the complication of
•ther (for instance, distributive) critical considerations, it could deliver
he systematic structure of indirect utilitarianism. The norms of property
n our social and personal codes and in our legal system would then be
een as having moral standing in virtue of their content's being deter-
nined, or structured, by impartial benevolence. But I doubt that things
.re so simple.

The correct account of well-being, as we have seen, pushes its im-
•artial promotion well into the background. We live by our life-
.tructuring attachments, commitments, and aims. That is what a good
ife is like, and when that picture of a good life is joined to, among
•ther things, a plausible account of the limits of the will, moral norms
nay well result: I ought to look after *my* children; I may focus my
:oncerns on *my* projects. And social institutions have much the same
:ffect. If we want life to go well, we join with others in accepting
olutions to coordination and cooperation problems, and the institutions
hat constitute those solutions contain their own standards for right and
vrong. I think that there is much in Geoffrey Warnock's and John
√fackie's belief that norms meant to promote a broadly utilitarian aim
ad better not be utilitarian in content,[16] though I think that they ex-
.ggerate the amount of insulation needed. There is no reason to think,

contrary to what they say, that impartial benevolence should not b allowed to appear in these other clusters in a subprinciple of limite operation. Still, the important point is that we live our lives necessari within a framework of social rules and of personal aims. Between then those rules and aims provide most of the grounds we use to decide th rightness and wrongness of our actions.

Many utilitarians agree. What they agree with, though, is that im partial benevolence is not the moral decision procedure, that it is no the mode of thought that we should generally engage in to decide wha to do. They regard it, rather, as the criterion of moral right and wron as what in the end makes acts the one or the other. But I suspect tha impartial benevolence cannot have even that status. There seems to b too much else also making acts right or wrong for impartial benevolenc to have the uniqueness that the criterion of right and wrong would need

I think that we tend to come to ethics with a false assumption. W expect the content of morality to derive from one kind of source namely, from principles of one sort or another. We expect it to deriv from the good, or from the right, or from fairly normative standards c rationality. The reality seems to me quite different. When we understan the forces shaping moral norms of property, say, we see how hetere geneous the forces are. The norms are not shaped by some single foundational value, such as impartial benevolence. They are also shape by convention and arbitrary decision. They are shaped by the institutio of property that happens to have evolved in our society. And wha happens to evolve is determined partly by the picture of the human wi that we work with. And that picture is formed by a combination c empirical and evaluative decision. We have to decide what in fact th limits of the will are. But that decision has an evaluative componen What humans can be motivated to do turns partly on what they fin worth doing. One has to strike a balance between our desire for ind vidual flourishing and our attraction to impartial benevolence. Withi a large range, there is nothing available to us to determine where t strike the balance. So, in this way, what is morally required is, up to point, invented or chosen. The principle of impartial benevolence ma animate the content of morality, but so indirectly and so incompletel that it is, I think, better to regard it merely as an important influenc and not as the criterion of right and wrong.

Our system of property is one, but only one, solution to a larg cooperation problem. It generates obligations: Each of us must kee hands off the other's property. Some people think that they can asse whole complex social institutions, such as property, as to how benefici they are, but most of us do not. It is not that there is any problem i principle with doing so; it is, rather, that we do not have, and cannot find, and probably could not adequately get our mind around all the important evidence. We can, we think, assess this or that feature; we can, therefore, with some hope of success change this or that part of the institution. But in general we just live within the institutions that we are born into. These institutions are usually natural growths, with roots below the level of human consciousness, and they continue to grow around us during our lifetimes. We might be able to see at least that we are better off inside them than outside, even though we may not be best off and could not tell whether we were. What is sanctioned by impartial benevolence is not just *our* institution of property and *its* set of norms; various institutions and other sets are also sanctioned, and there quickly comes a point beyond which we cannot rank more finely. For that reason, we are bound to work within the norms of an institution that, so far as we can tell, is working tolerably well. And if norms from two different clusters conflict – say, that I should promote my children's well-being and that I should respect your property – I suspect that the norm of impartial maximization will often not be up to providing a resolution. What we shall find, I think, is that, except in extreme cases when the conflicting values are very different in weight, we cannot even make reasonable estimates of probable benefits and harms in the consequences.

Suppose that I can benefit my children by a fiddle of my firm's books. And suppose that, to resolve the conflict, I appeal to the fact that the benefit exceeds the harm. But, as we have seen, the norms of property are not shaped by some single foundational value, say impartial benevolence. Even the permission to favor one's own children is not shaped so simply: Its boundaries are to some degree unfixed and, to the extent that they are fixed, are the result, among other things, of guesses about the limits of the will and of fiat. So there is no common currency behind all moral norms to which we can always resort for resolution of conflict. On the contrary, we often find an obligation emerging from one indispensable cluster of norms and another from another, when the mixture of the shaping forces is so complex that there is no common denominator. The complexity of the forces shaping norms will sometimes deny impartial benevolence its mediating role. So I doubt that we shall find system in ethics in this sense: Principles in various clusters will conflict with one another, and what system the clusters have will be too slight always to provide resolution.

Now, utilitarians might concede my point. There are many forces shaping norms, they might allow, impartial benevolence being only one of them. They might, though, resist the conclusion I draw from it. They might insist that only one shaping force, namely impartial benevolence, gives a norm, now not its content, but its status as a norm of morally right or wrong action. Impartial benevolence is, they might still insist, the sole criterion of moral right and wrong, in this sense: It alone gives acts moral significance. But they would still be trying to defend a higher degree of system than is, I think, plausible. The most that they could claim is that impartial benevolence is what we might call an "ideal" criterion of right and wrong, the word 'ideal' marking its remoteness from most decision and action. But then there would also be place for talk of an "actual" criterion of right and wrong. The "ideal" criterion would be simply what gives acts standing as moral rights or wrongs. And utilitarians might also hold that the norm of impartial benevolence has at least the following connection to the norms of all other clusters: that if, say, a feature of our institution of property produced less utility than some alternative, then without special reasons it would not generate a moral norm. Whether accepting that connection gives utilitarians all that they should regard as essential I shall leave aside. But besides this "ideal" criterion, we should also want an "actual" criterion of right and wrong. Various pieces of knowledge are just permanently out of reach, even out of the reach of our estimates of probability. One particular institution of property might be inferior in utility to another but that fact be among those permanently out of reach. Since there are such inaccessible facts, something other than utility levels, or their probabilities, come into play, for us in our actual situation, to make an act right or wrong. This is not to confuse what I just distinguished – namely, the criterion of right and wrong and the mode of thought to use in choosing how to act. It is, instead, to preserve a sense of the criterion of right and wrong relevant to people like us, with many utility levels beyond our ken. What comes into play in the "actual" criterion is the shape of the institution of property that *we* happen to have and that, with perhaps the exception of this or that feature, we have no reason to challenge. Two persons in different societies might find themselves faced with different property-generated obligations, though otherwise in the same circumstances. And they might each be willing to acknowledge that they do not and cannot know how to rank their two institutions against each other as to utility. But nonetheless, each of them can say, "What makes this act right is that it is required by *my* institution." And I doubt that there is enough in impartial benevolence's being the "ideal" criterion of right and wrong, as opposed to the "actual" one, to introduce the degree of system into the clusters of norms that I doubted earlier.

We have to give up the hope (those of us who have harbored it) that we can actually arrive at moral norms shaped solely by moral reasons for action, in contrast to the norms shaped, in no small degree, by convention and arbitrary decision that we have now. Moral philosophy can provide grounds for criticizing our present norms. But when we have gone as far as criticism will, for the moment, carry us, we shall still not have eliminated all elements of convention and arbitrariness. Since life with these less than ideal norms is the only moral life we are ever going to have, we must get on with it.

It may seem that my line of thought leads to an unattractive conservatism: We must often, I say, simply live within the institutions that we are born into. But it need not have conservative consequences. That moral criticism has its limits is compatible with its having plenty of scope still in the present world. When one thinks about the starving, for instance, one sees, I believe, that the problem is not natural disasters, nor even shortage of food in the afflicted countries (and often not even in the afflicted regions within them), nor overpopulation, but rigid property rights that allow those owning the food available in the afflicted country (or region) to hold onto it while tens of thousands of their fellow citizens die. The real solution to starvation is not external aid but internal reform in many Third World countries, especially reform of their system of property. But when property laws are changed enough to allow a minimum social provision – when in parts of Latin America the few families that control most of the arable land are made to turn much of it over to the landless peasants, for example – one will eventually reach the sort of institution of property that I have had in mind. Then, though there will no doubt still be scope for criticism, we shall be getting close to its limits.

4. On the road

My subject is the movement of thought from premises about the good to conclusions about the right. That subject raises the doubt, Are the good and the right independent enough from one another for one of them to be logically prior to the other? Though two great traditions in moral philosophy, teleology and deontology, accept that they are, there is much to be said on the other side. Still, that is not my subject. And I think that the good and the right are at least independent enough for my subject to be worthwhile.

There are various considerations that push the good well into the background of our moral thought. What they leave in the foreground are several clusters of norms, not always pointing in the same direction. The clusters prompt us to wonder how systematic we can make them. One possibility is that, although the good is pushed well into the background, it plays a key systematizing role from there. But the good is not the only figure in the background, not the only important force shaping our norms. Even confining ourselves to a fairly utilitarian dimension of moral thought, as I have done, the amount of system that we can introduce is limited.

I have confined my attention not only to a fairly utilitarian dimension but also to just one example: the moral norms of property. But there are other norms about which we can say much the same. It is an open question how widespread the system-defeating elements of conventionality and arbitrariness are.

Notes

1 James Griffin, *Well-Being* (Oxford: Clarendon Press, 1986), part 1.

2 Henry Sidgwick, *The Methods of Ethics,* 7th ed. (London: Macmillan, 1907), pp. 404, 506–9.

3 Bernard Williams, "Persons, Character and Morality" and "Utilitarianism and Self-Indulgence," in his *Moral Luck* (Cambridge: Cambridge University Press, 1981); also Williams, "A Critique of Utilitarianism," in J. Smart and B. Williams, *Utilitarianism: For and Against* (Cambridge: Cambridge University Press, 1973), secs. 3, 5. There is much that Williams says about integrity with which I disagree, but this, his central point, seems to me right. T. L. S. Sprigge develops the same theme illuminatingly in *The Rational Foundations of Ethics* (London: Routledge, 1988), pp. 181ff. John Updike, *Self-Consciousness* (London: Penguin Books, 1990), p.201.

4 For a full recent statement of it, see R. M. Hare, *Moral Thinking* (Oxford: Clarendon Press, 1981), ch. 2, sec. 1 and ch. 3. For earlier statements, see his "Principles," *Proceedings of the Aristotelian Society* 73 (1972–3); "Ethical Theory and Utilitarianism," in H. D. Lewis, ed., *Contemporary British Philosophy,* 4th series (London: Allen and Unwin, 1976); and "Moral Philosophy", in B. Magee, ed., *Men of Ideas* (London: B.B.C. Publications, 1978).

5 See Sprigge, *Rational Foundations of Ethics,* pp. 181–2.

6 This is Shelly Kagan's answer in *The Limits of Morality* (Oxford: Clarendon Press, 1989), ch. 8. I argue against this answer in much the same terms as here in my review of Kagan's book, *Mind* 99 (1990).

7 For her chief statement, see Iris Murdoch, *The Sovereignty of Good* (London: Routledge and Kegan Paul, 1970). But see also a profile of her in *The Independent* (London), 29 April 1989.

8 Iris Murdoch, quoted in "Profile," *The Independent* (London), 29 April 1989.

9 Murdoch, *Sovereignty of Good,* esp. pp. 92–4.

10 I give my own views more fully in *Well-Being,* ch. 10.

11 But we should not carry this line of thought back so far that it is seen as the reason for moving from the state of nature to society. If there were no

norms, standards, conventions, or institutions, human life would not be worse than it could be. It would not be recognizable as human life. The picture of a normless state of nature is (close to?) incoherent. If there were no conventions and associated norms, there would be no language, which is essentially normative. If there were no language, there would be no articulable reasons. We start already inside society; we do not find reasons to move to it, even if the move were regarded as purely hypothetical. Political philosophy's besetting sin is overintellectualizing, overrationalizing society and its norms. Society and many of its key norms are a natural growth, a setting within which, and only within which, we can debate the pros and cons of features of our social life.

12 I believe that this understates the case. We may need not two but several conceptions of well-being, differing in richness of content, for use in different social contexts. See my paper "A Case for a Substantive Account of the Quality of Life," in A. Sen and M. C. Nussbaum, eds., *The Quality of Life* (Oxford: Clarendon Press, 1992).

13 For a description of a two-level structure, see Hare, *Moral Thinking,* chs. 2 and 3; and of a multilevel structure, see my *Well-Being,* chs. 10, 11, 13. See also T. M. Scanlon, "Levels of Moral Thinking," in D. Seanor and N. Fotion, eds., *Hare and Critics* (Oxford: Clarendon Press, 1988).

14 For further discussion, see my *Well-Being,* pp. 304–7.

15 Alan Ryan, *Property and Political Theory* (Oxford: Basil Blackwell, 1984), esp. pp. 161–2.

16 G. J. Warnock, *The Object of Morality* (London: Methuen, 1971), chs. 3 and 4; J. L. Mackie, *Ethics* (Harmondsworth, England: Penguin Books, 1977), ch. 5. Mackie, for instance, characterizes the view that he adopted earlier in his book as "utilitarian in the very broad sense that it took general human well-being as in some way the foundation of morality."

10

Value, reasons, and the sense of justice

DAVID GAUTHIER

1. Introduction

In this essay I want to sketch some features of moral dispositions and their relation to values and reasons for acting that I have either ignored or oversimplified in previous work. In *Morals by Agreement* I treated morality primarily as an artifice that enables rational agents to reach agreement with their fellows about the distribution of the fruits of their interaction and to adhere to these agreements against considerations of present advantage.[1] I outlined a very crude derivation of moral dispositions from the demands of practical rationality, understood in a variant of the maximizing way that has become orthodox in economics and the theory of rational choice.[2] But one might also and quite properly consider morality not as an artifice but as a set of natural dispositions. Although I introduced such an idea in *Morals by Agreement*,[3] it played no part in the central arguments of my book. Here I begin from the idea of a natural morality, and consider its place in rational agency conceived somewhat more broadly than in rational choice. To focus and limit my account I shall treat the sense of justice as characteristic of moral dispositions, and examine its role in moral deliberation and evaluation. Much of what I have to say is very rough, omitting refinements and qualifications that if pursued might prove to undermine some of the positions that I shall endorse. One would of course like to say nothing that did not have the ring of eternal truth, but the history of philosophy does not make me confident of such success.

2. Kantian naturalism

The framework within which I shall construct my account might be labeled Kantian naturalism. Although I intend this label to indicate an affinity with Kant, and in particular with his account of the role of the understanding in the *Critique of Pure Reason,* I am not offering an interpretation of his views. Indeed my project here is linked to my earlier endeavor to subvert Kant's account of practical reason by appealing to his views on speculative reason.[4]

I shall sketch the main features of Kantian naturalism very briefly. Human beings share, certainly with some other mammals, perhaps with some other vertebrates and cephalopods, the capacity for a rich variety of intentional states – beliefs, desires, emotions, and feelings – that enter centrally into the explanation of their behavior. But human beings also possess a linguistic capacity that enables them to represent their own intentional states and thereby to include those states among the objects of their awareness, and in particular to place those states within a single awareness, which is the self. The manifold of intentional states is thus unified, both at a time and over time, into a single experience, and this task of unification is the work of reason. To be sure, this task is never completed; the ideas of a single experience and a coherent self are heuristic ideals.

In representing intentional states linguistically and making them objects of awareness, human beings not only move in the direction of a unified experience and a unifying self, but also gain a reflective and critical distance from their beliefs, desires, and feelings. I do not mean by this merely that the act of representation itself imposes a distance between an agent and what is represented. My point is not that all human intentional states are objects of awareness; they are not. We frequently impute desires to an individual in explaining her behavior whether or not these desires are consciously acknowledged by her. Rather my point is that insofar as intentional states come to be objects of awareness, an agent is able to distance herself from her representations and address them reflectively and critically, considering, to take the most obvious case, whether she has reason to believe or desire or feel what she has represented as a belief or desire or emotion.

This reflective distance brings with it a motivational distance. The agent considers not only what to think but also what to do. This distance is not always present; a person lashes out in anger or flees in terror. But it is necessary to reasoned action, which results from deliberation and evaluation. A fully reasoned action would express the agent's overall consideration of her intentional states. The account of human action that treats choice simply as the product of belief and desire provides a Procrustean bed for reasoned behavior. The model may be best adapted to accounts of behavior that express the intentionality found in apes, dogs, elephants, and other animals, who lack the reflexive and reflective awareness characteristic of language users. Of course this is not to say that human beings do not relate their choices to their beliefs and desires, but rather to claim that the way in which this relation occurs, mediated

by the representation of intentional states and the partial unification c
those represented states in the direction of a single experience, is nc
adequately conveyed by the simple belief/desire account.

But there is a further crucial respect in which the belief/desire accoun
fails to accommodate human action. One of its core features is that a
motivational force is to be understood in terms of desire, belief bein
itself motivationally inert. There must be a clear distinction among in
tentional states, separating those that are from those that are not mc
tivating. But our accounts of reasoned behavior reveal no suc
distinction. We understand reasoned choice in terms of an agent's overal
intentional stance toward the world, a stance that includes both epistemi
and conative aspects, but not demarcated in the clear way required b
the simple belief/desire account. Furthermore we have no ground fc
supposing that in all cases the conative aspects of the agent's intentiona
stance can be ultimately traced to an initially given set of desires tha
have been subjected to representation and reflection. In explaining hu
man behavior we cannot take as primitively given a set of element
corresponding to what we identify as desires in accounting for the be
havior of an animal capable of intentional states but without linguisti
capacity, such as a dog, and then trace their motivational force throug
a process of reflection until we reach actual choices. To the extent tha
the belief/desire account would lead us to expect to be able to offer suc
an explanation, it is not merely inadequate but mistaken.

To put my point very simply, what is represented as conatively sig
nificant need not have an ascertainable basis in desire. The reasonin
agent is not necessarily restricted in his deliberations by what he ca
identify as his desires, much less by what he might consider the presen
motivational force of those desires. A dog's behavior must reflect it
desires and reflect them in their present strengths; our theory of canin
behavior affords us no mode of explanation that would relate desire t
action in an alternative way. But our theory of human behavior afford
us just such an alternative, in relating human action to the reflectiv
and unifying processes that I have identified with reason. Althoug
rational capacities distinguish human beings from other animals, the
are of course to be explained within the same evolutionary framewor
and to be related to the same animal physiology as all other capacities
Thus I speak of Kantian *naturalism*.

A central feature of Kantian naturalism as I have characterized it i
the place it gives to language in making possible the awareness of in
tentional states that underlies both experience and self-awareness. I
one were to agree with those philosophers who interpret and endors
Wittgenstein's critique of private language as insisting that languag

must be a social phenomenon, one would then see the self as a socially constituted entity. This is no part of my account, although it is not incompatible with it. But whether or not language can be private, it makes possible the sense that each individual human being possesses of herself as an experiencing and acting subject, and this is a sense of individual privacy. In unifying her intentional states the individual creates an essentially private inner space, with its own epistemic and conative landscape. Possessing such a space, she has the capacity to distinguish and defend her beliefs, concerns, and attitudes in the face of quite different and even opposed beliefs, concerns, and attitudes that she ascribes to others.

3. The sense of justice

I turn now to the sense of justice. For the moment the framework that I have outlined will recede into the background, but its relevance should become clear as I proceed. The sense of justice, like all moral dispositions, is a normative capacity. A normative capacity is characterized by a standard or measure defined on some domain, so that in exercising the capacity one applies the standard or measure to a member or members of the domain, and takes oneself to have a reason to favor and promote what meets the standard or most fulfills the measure. Thus a normative capacity manifests itself both affectively in evaluation and conatively or practically in deliberation and action. And these are essential; the capacity is not exhibited merely in the ability to apply its standard independently of evaluation and action. Thus a person who learns to distinguish actions or persons or institutions in terms of the standard of justice, but who sees no reason to favor or encourage or perform just actions, does not possess a sense of justice. We might say that he possesses a sense of what is just, but that is a very different thing – not a sense or a moral disposition at all, but a (mere) understanding.

One might suppose that although a sense of justice involves more than an understanding of what is just, nevertheless its discriminative role in determining what is just may be sharply separated from its affective and practical roles. In other words, one might suppose that a sense of justice embraces a range of evaluative and conative responses to certain characteristics of actions and persons that may be identified quite independently of these responses. If this were so, then someone possessing a sense of justice and someone lacking such a sense would share a common cognitive apprehension of persons and actions and institutions – an apprehension of what is just and unjust – but would

differ in the feelings and concerns directed to this apprehension. Again
this is the view of normative capacities that I attribute to John McDowe
which entails that only from the perspective of the concerns that cha
acterize a sense of justice can one apprehend what is and is not jus
On this view the sense of justice is not constituted by a set of affecti
and practical responses to what is independently apprehended, as ju
or unjust, but rather by a set of concerns on the basis of which v
discriminate among persons and actions in ways that are evaluative
and conatively significant.

McDowell does not deny that in each particular context, if an actio
or person is just then there must be some nonevaluative characterist
or feature in virtue of which it is just. It might seem that in acceptin
this supervenience, McDowell would be committed to the view th
quite independently of our possessing a sense of justice, we could a
prehend these just-making characteristics. And if this were the cas
then it would be natural to suppose that the sense of justice was itse
entirely constituted by affective and conative responses to these ind
pendently apprehended just-making characteristics. But McDowell ir
sists that

> Supervenience requires only that one be able to find differences expressible
> terms of the level supervened upon [i.e., the nonevaluative] whenever one wan
> to make different judgements in terms of the supervening level [i.e., the eva
> uative]. It does not follow from the satisfaction of this requirement that the s
> of items to which a supervening term is correctly applied need constitute a kir
> recognizable as such at the level supervened upon.[6]

In each instance of just action there are nonevaluative features of th
action that make it just. But the just-making features in one instanc
need not be related to the just-making features in other instances i
some way that may be characterized independently of the concern
expressed in our sense of justice. It is only from the perspective give
by these concerns that we can grasp the relationship among differer
instances of just action. If justice focuses on interaction among persor
and the way in which the benefits and costs of interaction are to t
distributed, then a person who failed to grasp our concern with th
manner of distribution would be unable to relate the various action
and outcomes we classify as just, even though in each instance he woul
recognize those characteristics that we should point to as our basis fc
calling that particular action or outcome just. There are no natur:
nonnormative characteristics of actions that we can apprehend as uni
versally just-making.

I want to endorse this denial and the claim that to ascertain th presence or absence of some evaluative characteristic such as justice, one must understand the relevant affective and practical concerns – in this case, those that are expressed in our sense of justice. However, I want nevertheless to maintain that it is possible to ascertain what is just without thereby committing oneself to any positive or favorable evaluation of what is just, and without being in any way disposed to bring about or support what is just in one's actions. I want to reject McDowell's skepticism about "mastering the extension of a value concept from the external standpoint," if by 'external' he intends any standpoint that does not involve sharing the evaluator's concerns.[7] Although one must enter into the concerns that inform our sense of justice, one need not accept these concerns as one's own. A person who lacks a sense of justice can, at least in principle, discriminate what is just. She can grasp the justice of an action or person, and not merely the presence of some supposed just-making but nonnormative characteristic. She can understand the role justice plays in evaluation and deliberation. But lacking a sense of justice, she may be neither affectively nor conatively engaged by her understanding of this role or her grasp of what is just. My position is at this point thoroughly non-Platonistic; to know the just need not be to love it or to care for it at all.

The person who lacks a sense of justice and yet can discriminate what is just enters into the just person's point of view without sharing it. This need not be an easy task. But the general possibility of entering into an evaluative perspective without sharing it is surely a familiar one. It is essential to the task of the anthropologist who must grasp the evaluative and practical standpoint of the persons she is studying without thereby ceasing to embrace her own usually quite different standpoint. But it is also exhibited in such mundane activities as tea tasting; the professional tea taster needs to be able to recognize what typical tea drinkers want in tea whether or not his own palate, more trained and experienced, leads him to share their evaluation. He must learn to identify what others find to be tasty tea even if he does not consider it tasty, and even though there need be no set of nonevaluative characteristics of tea that he can learn to identify, such that possession of that set is correlated with eliciting the favorable responses of tea drinkers. In learning to be a tea taster, he learns to enter into the point of view of typical tea drinkers, and so to discriminate among teas from that point of view whether or not he comes to share it. Of course, very often we seek to enter into an evaluative perspective because we expect and hope to come to share it. Thus the neophyte oenophile develops her ability to discriminate among the various characteristics of wines because she expects her enjoyment of wine to be enhanced as her evaluations come to be based

in her new powers of discrimination. But she may be disappointed, an
find that her developed expertise in discriminating among wines is no
accompanied by her sharing the usual tastes of oenophiles.

One may know what is just yet neither love it nor be in any wa
moved by it. However, one could not know what is just if no one love
it. Only if some persons actually have the concerns expressed in ou
sense of justice, is there a point of view from which justice may b
discerned. Suppose that human beings were fully benevolent, caring a
much for their fellows as for themselves. Or suppose on the other han
that each human being alone could provide for all of his needs and ha
no interest in or care for his fellows.[8] In either of these circumstance
the concerns characteristic of justice would not exist, and there woul
be no basis for distinguishing actions or persons as just or unjust. Some
one might object that although no basis for justice would be recognized
yet given our concerns we have such a basis and could distinguish justic
and injustice where these beings were unaware of it. But this would b
mistaken. If there were a race of purely solitary beings, and one of the
were to take for her use what another had expended his labor to produce
there would be no more injustice than if one lion were to gorge on th
antelope that another had killed. And this would not be because of
lack of normative understanding. We need not suppose that these sol
itary beings, like lions, lack the reflective awareness of their concern
that enables them to evaluate their behavior. In denying that there i
any basis for identifying their actions as just or unjust, we need not den
that were these beings to become familiar with us, they would be abl
to understand our basis for discerning justice in our actions and insti
tutions, although since they would not share it, they would not discer
justice in their own actions.

4. The reality of justice

If there would be no justice did no one love it, or at least have th
concerns characteristic of our sense of justice, must there be justice i
someone does love it or have these concerns? More generally, in orde
to identify an evaluative or normative characteristic in some thing, is i
both necessary and sufficient that it stand as a potential object of th
appropriate concern? To attempt to answer this question I shall conside
another supposed evaluative characteristic, piety. Like justice and in
justice, piety and impiety may be thought to characterize actions, per
sons, and institutions. And if we ask what are the concerns that giv
rise to the discernment of piety, we shall, I suppose, agree that th
answer is to be found among those concerns that relate to the gods, o

what is divine. Piety is surely an excellent illustration of those of cDowell's contentions that I have endorsed. What must seem to an tside observer as actions that share no distinguishing characteristics ll be identified by the believer as instances of piety, given her view "what the gods love."[9]

But there are no gods – or so I shall assume. The nonbeliever has no sis for discerning piety or impiety in his own actions. To be sure, if understands the perspective of the believer, he may be able to dis- guish in his own behavior what from that perspective would be called ous and what impious, but he will not suppose that therefore his own tions exhibit piety or impiety. And note that this is not simply because does not and indeed, given his unbelief, cannot intend his actions to pious or impious. For intent need not enter into the basis by which e believer discriminates; what the gods love may be certain forms of havior however intended. But furthermore the nonbeliever will also ny that the believer's actions are really pious or impious. And he will ny this without denying that the believer exhibits certain concerns on e basis of which she distinguishes piety from impiety. Indeed he will ny this even if he can enter into the believer's perspective sufficiently be able to discern what the believer takes to be piety, and of course discern it in terms of the believer's concerns. The nonbeliever insists at these concerns are not well-founded in that they reflect and express mistaken view of the world. And given this mistake, he will insist that hat the believer purports to discern given her concerns is unreal. If ere are no gods then nothing is or can be really pious or impious.

There are two quite different views that an outsider may take toward e evaluations and prescriptions of those whose concerns she does not are. On the one hand the outsider may regard the difference in con- rns as no more than that. She will not then deny the reality of the valuative or prescriptive characteristics that others discern, although e will insist that they have no application outside the context of their ncern, and so no application from her own point of view. But if she oes not share concerns because she believes that they express a mis- ken view of the world, then she will deny the reality of the evaluative haracteristics that others purport to discern given those concerns.

But these two views of alien concerns do not exhaust the possibilities. n many cases a person may regard concerns that she does not share, ot as merely different, but also not as resting on a fundamentally istaken worldview. Suppose for example that she encounters persons ho think it cowardly not to risk one's life to avenge the slightest offense. Iere she may suppose that they are mistaken, not in having concerns hat distinguish courageous from cowardly behavior, but in having the

particular concerns that determine their way of making the distinction
She does not deny that their way of discriminating courageous acts from
cowardly or foolhardy acts reflects their concerns, but she denies the
appropriateness of those concerns. But the standard of appropriatene
must itself be a normative consideration. If those who regard as coward
any failure to try to avenge an offense share her standard of appropria
concerns, and if that standard supports her own view of courage, then
they are guilty of some form of normative incoherence or inconsistenc
But quite likely they do not share their critic's standard of appropriate
ness. Must we suppose either that this is a mere difference, so tha
neither holding nor rejecting the standard involves any mistake, or tha
it rests on incompatible worldviews?

To pursue fully the question of appropriate standards would take m
beyond my present inquiry, which is limited to the sense of justice. Bt
it should be evident that troubling questions about the reality of justic
and injustice lurk in these reflections on piety and courage. Later in m
inquiry I shall defend the sense of justice against one argument tha
would treat it as ill-founded and so dismiss the distinction between ju
and unjust as chimerical.

5. Justice and the self

An account of the sense of justice is an account of a normative capacity
How may it proceed? If we were to take the deliverances of our sens
of justice straightforwardly as the facts that the account must accom
modate by providing their normative grounds, and against which it ma
be checked by determining that its principles do indeed give rise to thes
deliverances, then we should be guilty of assuming our sense of justic
to be in order as it is. Mention of piety and courage should put us o
guard against this. But there is in fact little danger of taking our sens
of justice to be fully in order, so long as we are concerned with it
deliverances for ourselves and our fellows. For in seeking the normativ
grounds of our own judgments of what is just and unjust, we cannot b
content merely with finding principles that would ground our existin
judgments. The principles must themselves be acceptable, and this ac
ceptability is not determined merely by considering whether they to
are deliverances of our sense of justice. To be sure, questions of cc
herence between principles and particular judgments may be raise
within the framework of one's sense of justice. But the interesting an
important questions go beyond it. We might find a coherent character
ization of our sense of justice but be unable to give it any furthe

ationale. And that would be enough to show our sense of justice to be
efective. A normative capacity, such as the sense of justice, does not
xist in isolation from our other concerns and beliefs. I began by sketch-
ıg a framework within which to inquire into the various specific ca-
acities and dispositions we possess. That framework focuses on the
nifying activity of reason in constructing both a coherent experience
nd a coherent experiencer, or self. What we seek is an account of our
ense of justice that may be integrated with our understanding of a
nified self.

Justice is the primary virtue of interaction. Human beings interact in
ays that require them to consider how the benefits that may be realized
y their interaction are to be distributed. Justice focuses on this distri-
ution. As Hume recognized, beings who for whatever reason did not
ıce distributive problems would lack the concerns that give rise to ideas
f justice and injustice.[10] An account of our sense of justice must there-
ore enable us to understand its role in resolving the distributive prob-
ems arising in our interpersonal relations. It will need to offer or to
ppeal to an account of the structure and circumstances of interaction.
ınd it will need to offer or to appeal to an account of agency.

Kantian naturalism provides the appropriate context for understand-
ıg agency. The agent is conceived as possessing a normative capacity
ɔr deliberation to which I have already alluded in the idea that a fully
easoned action would express her overall consideration of her inten-
ıonal states. The unifying activity of reason gives her, ideally, a single
oherent integrated set of reflectively endorsed concerns that provide
er with reasons for acting. These concerns are constitutive of her sense
f self, so that in seeking to realize them she gives practical expression
ɔ her sense of being an individual agent. I suggest that we may identify
he idea of acting to realize a fully integrated set of concerns with the
raditional conception of autonomy. And in so doing we should em-
hasize again the importance of the distancing effects of reason. The
ims expressed in fully reasoned action have received the agent's re-
ective endorsement, so that she is not and does not feel herself to be
npelled by desires that she must take as givens.

But what distinguishes justice is its relation to interaction. The indi-
idual possessing a sense of justice sees herself and her fellows as having
istinctive reasons of justice that carry independent weight in their de-
berations insofar as their actions may affect others. Justice requires
ome correspondence between the effects and the persons affected, so
hat in a more traditional terminology, each receives his due. And this
equirement is, if not necessarily overriding, yet not a mere corollary

of some more fundamental ground of action. *Fiat iustitia ruat caelu.*
may strike us as exaggerated, but also as expressive of the felt weigl
of the deliverances of the sense of justice.[11]

6. The circumstances of justice

Hume and Rawls have usefully examined the circumstances that ow
sense of justice addresses.[12] In *Morals by Agreement* I endeavored t
build on their accounts, claiming "that the fundamental circumstance
of justice ... are awareness of externalities in our environment, ar
awareness of self-bias in our character."[13] But that claim needs revisioi
To begin with the second, subjective component, self-bias, althoug
certainly typical of the circumstances of justice, does not seem to t
necessary. Rather the awareness that persons are independent agent
each with his own objectives that may or may not correspond to or mes
with the objectives of other persons, is the primary subjective featui
of the circumstances of justice. It might be said that each person
biased in favor of his own objectives, but we should resist saying thi
Central to Kantian naturalism is the recognition that each person, i
developing a sense of self, develops a basis for action, so that in seekir
to realize that basis he gives practical expression to his sense of beir
an individual agent. To say that an agent is self-biased, where this
understood as the endeavor to realize one's concerns (as opposed t
those of other agents), is therefore no more than to say that he is a
individual agent and that the concerns he expresses in his actions ai
the concerns of a self. These concerns need not be directed on or to c
for himself; typically many of them are so directed, but the idea o
individual agency is neutral with respect to what we might call the bia
of the agent's concerns. Self-bias specifies the direction of the agent
concerns, and in this sense it is not a necessary circumstance of justice
We should think of the sense of justice as concerned with interactio
among independent agents, each with his own basis of action, and avoi
using language that may suggest that these agents must be self-biase
in their objectives.

What of the objective component in the circumstances of justice
the awareness of externalities in the environment? Let us go back t
the idea of scarcity, and ask what invites the attention of justice. Th
simple fact that not all concerns can be realized is not in itself sufficien
I suggest that the kind of scarcity that humans face determines thre
features of what I shall call "realization," or the fulfillment of concern.
which are relevant to the sense of justice. First, realization is partiall
competitive, so that the fullest feasible realization of one person's cor

erns precludes the fullest realization of the concerns of at least some others. Second, realization is variable, so that to speak very roughly, the total extent of realization is not fixed; in seeking to realize our concerns we are not engaged in a zero-sum interaction with our fellows. And third, realization may be mutually enhanced, so that in some contexts each person may expect to realize her concerns through interaction with her fellows to an extent greater than she could hope to do in their absence.

The first of these features seems necessary to the development of a sense of justice. Were realization to be entirely noncompetitive, then either it could not be mutually enhanced, in which case each person would by choice be purely solitary and there would be no interaction, or it could be mutually enhanced, and interaction would reflect the natural harmony of those concerns that were affected. In neither case would the idea of justice manifest itself. What of the second feature? Here context is important. Whether interaction is seen as essentially zero-sum may depend on how its scope is determined. Thus someone might claim (however implausibly) that the interaction of all living beings is zero-sum, even though human interaction is not. Or that human interaction is zero-sum, although interaction among (only) men, and among (only) women, is not, so that all of the members of one sex may be able to gain but at a cost to the members of the other. Justice as we know it presupposes a non-zero-sum context of interaction, so that the normative capacities of beings who took their typical contexts of interaction to be zero-sum would be very different from ours. They would not possess what we should recognize as a sense of justice.

Consider now the third feature, that realization may be mutually enhanced so that interaction is or may be mutually advantageous in relation to a no-interaction base. Suppose several groups of persons to be crowding their environment (whether materially or in some other way), so that the members of each would prefer that the others were absent. Nevertheless it will not follow that each group is best advised to seek to eliminate its rivals; the resulting war might prove mutually costly. Realization is clearly competitive and variable but not mutually enhancing. We may be reminded of Hobbes's view of the relationships among men in the state of nature, although I do not think that Hobbes actually supposed that each would prefer solitude to the presence of at least some fellows.[14] Even in the Hobbesean state of nature some interaction can be mutually enhancing. But Hobbes's argument nevertheless suggests that mere avoidance of the costs of mutual hostility is sufficient rationale for some measure of justice.

But even if belief in the possibility of mutually enhancing interaction

is not necessary for a sense of justice, we may expect its deliverance
to be affected by estimating the prospects for such interaction among
persons for whom realization is competitive and variable. Justice among
those who are at the deepest level enemies, each wishing the absence
of the other, differs from justice among those who are at least po-
tentially friends, capable of finding welcome prospects for mutual
interaction. To be sure, persons who exhibit justice in their interaction
may come to appreciate prospects for mutual enhancement that would
otherwise remain unnoticed. Hobbes seems to have been aware of
this, without realizing that justice may then convert enmity into
friendship.[15]

What about externalities? In a perfect market in which externalities
are absent, realization is competitive, variable, and mutually enhancing.
In *Morals by Agreement* I argued that market arrangements are neither
just nor unjust, but these arrangements clearly fall within the scope of
the sense of justice if that scope is set by the competitive, variable
realization of individual objectives. Here I want to distinguish the concept of justice from the particular conception that I defend as appropriate to the context of rational choice. In that context the market will
render justice mute, as I argued in my book. But if we treat justice not
as a rational artifice but as a natural moral disposition, then we may
not simply assume that it is irrelevant to the market context of fully
voluntary agreement.

7. Motivation

Where interaction may be mutually enhancing – that is, advantageous
in relation to a no-interaction base – then it should be. Where no one
need lose, then all should gain. I take this to be a core deliverance of
our sense of justice, or indeed of our moral sensibility more generally.
Whatever may be a person's due, it cannot be to receive a lesser realization of her objectives from her interaction with her fellows than she
would have received in their absence, if they receive greater realization
of their own objectives than they would have received in her absence.
This is the idea that I expressed by the modified Lockean Proviso.[16] It
is wrong to better one's situation by worsening the situation of another
– that is, to realize one's concerns more fully than one would have done
in the absence of the other, by imposing a lesser realization on her than
she would have expected in one's own absence. But whereas in *Morals
by Agreement* I took the Lockean Proviso to be the strongest constraint
on natural interaction compatible with maximizing rationality, here I
take it rather as the weakest of the deliverances of our sense of justice.

t addresses only situations in which there is a prospect of mutual enhancement, and imposes only a minimal constraint on the behavior of
persons in those situations.

If the sense of justice were merely to require that where mutual
advantage is possible, it be realized, it would not address the distribution
of that advantage. Take what each person could realize for himself in
the absence of his fellows as base; call what can be realized above the
level of this base the surplus from interaction.[17] The sense of justice
addresses the distribution of this surplus, determining for each person
his share or due, and disposing each neither to seek nor to accept more
than his own due, and neither to participate nor to acquiesce in measures
that would deprive others of their due. In addition it disposes each to
seek and indeed to demand his own due, expecting others both to refrain
from measures that would deprive him of it, and at least in some circumstances, to give him the positive assistance necessary for him to
obtain it. And it disposes each to expect and to favor the similar demand
by others for their due.

If we think of society as the framework within which persons interact,
then the core demand that justice makes on society is that it be, in
Rawls's useful phrase, "a cooperative venture for mutual advantage"[18]
- a venture that assures to each participant a share of the surplus from
interaction.[19] We may then call the basis for the particular institutions
and practices of society the "terms of cooperation," and justice will
require that these ensure that each receives her due share of the net
social surplus, gaining appropriate benefits and paying a portion of necessary costs. (My use of 'due' at this point is simply as a placeholder,
to make clear that justice requires more than that each receive some
share of the surplus.) The sense of justice must then afford its possessor
strong affective support for maintaining and adhering to the terms of
cooperation, and create in her the desire and expectation that others
will show similar support. It motivates compliance with the terms of
cooperation.

This motivation seems crucial to the success of society as a cooperative venture. For despite the benefits that the venture offers, it is
unlikely to be sufficiently supported by the participants in the absence
of any motivation directly favoring compliance with the terms of cooperation. Although we should expect persons to show varying degrees
of concern for their fellows, based on ties of blood and affection, yet
we should not expect to find that generalized concern that would stably
uphold the curbs and constraints required by an overall venture affording mutual enhancement. Individuals may be expected to favor
their own concerns and those of friends and relatives. And this fa-

voritism may be most clearly manifested on those occasions, inevitable in any large-scale cooperative venture, that would allow individuals to free-ride on their fellows, benefiting from others' efforts while withholding their own. Thus apart from considerations of justice each person may be expected to pursue straightforwardly his own concerns with some deference to those of friends and relatives. The sense of justice must uphold the curbs and constraints that are needed if the outcome of social interaction is not to display favoritism or partiality or allow free-riding.

Furthermore, the knowledge that others are motivated by considerations of justice prevents the willingness of any person, himself motivated by considerations of justice to contribute to the production of the social surplus, from being inhibited by the suspicion or fear that he would not receive his due share of that surplus. Even when each is willing to do his own part in maintaining the terms of cooperation, this willingness is likely to be conditional on the expectation that others will similarly do their part. Indeed, the sense of justice supports this demand for assurance. For it directs each person to demand his own due, which he can reasonably expect only if others adhere to the terms of cooperation. Thus only if each person is just and expects his fellows to be just, may we expect that society will elicit each person's full support in contributing to the surplus from interaction, and so maximize its success as a cooperative venture.

The constraints upheld by justice are found in social institutions and practices, laws, customs, and moral principles. Thus the sense of justice motivates compliance with these social, moral, and legal requirements, at least insofar as they affect interpersonal relations. And it also motivates advocacy of similar compliance by others, so that persons take it as a reason (though not necessarily a sufficient reason) for performing an action that it would encourage or reward their fellows' compliance or discourage or punish their violation of social constraints. Prereflectively this compliance and advocacy may be relatively undiscriminating. Indeed, we may think of the sense of justice as in some respects a refinement on a more general disposition to conform to what is established, a disposition expressed in Nietzsche's "morality of mores,"[20] taking over its core motivation to compliance while discriminating among the claims to compliance made by various customs and practices, rules and institutions. If we continue to consider it *prima facie* just to conform to what is established, we may be primarily influenced by the recognition that insofar as persons form expectations on the basis of what is established, we must conform to give them what they consider their due.

8. Explaining and justifying

If the sense of justice develops from a prior, humanly primitive disposition to conform to whatever is established, then Kantian naturalism offers a plausible framework for understanding this development. For we may think of the sense of justice as reconciling the apparently conflicting demands posed by self-awareness and conformity. Conformity intrudes on the private inner space that each individual creates in unifying her intentional states. Now my interest is not in unconscious or subconscious mechanisms that serve to internalize the demand of conformity, representing it as emanating from within the agent, but rather in the simultaneous limitation and rationalization of conformity that is effected by the idea of justice. For the conformity required by justice recognizes, and indeed is based on, the idea of what is due the agent. Each agent claims her due against conformity, but she may expect recognition of that claim by her fellows only if she recognizes their corresponding claims, and so conforms to what guarantees those claims.

The argument here may seem familiar and fallacious, an attempt to bludgeon would-be amoral beings by arguing that they are rationally required to recognize claims of their fellows, in virtue of the claims they make themselves. Such an argument would fail because it does not show that an agent is rationally required to make any claims. But the argument here begins with each agent's awareness of a normative claim – that of conformity. The agent then responds with an opposed normative claim arising from her sense of self; this response requires the agent to recognize the parallel claims of her fellows, and so provides a new basis for conformity, not to whatever is established, but limited to those arrangements that uphold everyone's claim. Thus a sense of justice develops from an original disposition to conform. The argument is primarily explanatory rather than justificatory. Neither the original claim of conformity nor the agent's response is given any rational foundation.

But it may then be urged that even if this derivation of the sense of justice has some explanatory plausibility, the fully reflective agent should move beyond it. Why should she not simply dismiss the original claim of conformity as unfounded in her own concerns? And why should she not similarly dismiss the claims of justice? Although a sense of justice is advantageous to all in making it possible for them to enjoy the surplus from interaction, it is not advantageous to any individual. In introducing the role of the sense of justice in making social cooperation possible, I emphasized the need to prevent free-riding. But it is individually advantageous to be a free-rider. A person who lacks a sense of justice will have no internal brake to stop him taking advantage of his fellows'

compliance with the constraints of cooperation while ignoring thos-
constraints himself whenever he finds it possible and profitable to d-
so. His behavior may of course show a regard for his friends and relatives, and indeed more than a decent regard, so that he may endeavo-
to provide them with social benefits in excess of their due at the expens-
of strangers for whom he has no affective concern. But in all this he i-
simply manifesting the requirement of reason in giving overall consideration to his intentional states, and dismissing those putative evaluations and directives that do not reflect such consideration. He does no-
deny that many of his fellows have a sense of justice, but he takes th-
concerns that it expresses to be arbitrary and opposed to a proper sens-
of self, so that its deliverances are, like those of piety, chimerical.

This dismissal of justice is unsound. We must distinguish the effect
of acting on a sense of justice from the effects of possessing such a sense-
Insofar as a sense of justice leads one to moderate one's pursuit of one'-
own concerns, it motivates one to act in ways that would not be supported by one's other reasons for acting. Note that such ways of actin-
need not always be unwelcome, in that possession of a sense of justic-
disposes one to favor compliance with just constraints, so that a trul-
just person would not want to pursue her own benefit at another'-
expense, or take more than her due share and leave others with les-
than their due. Nevertheless what she wants may not be what would b-
in her interest or to her advantage, in the sense of best realizing thos-
of her concerns that are independent of her moral dispositions.

However, possession of a sense of justice may nevertheless be greatl-
to one's advantage even in realizing one's nonmoral concerns, becaus-
it contributes to making one a welcome participant in cooperative ven-
tures. No one wants a person who altogether lacks a sense of justice a-
a fellow cooperator, for such a person may not reasonably be expecte-
to be adequately disposed to uphold the terms on which interaction i-
mutually desirable. Even persons who would cooperate in order to vic-
timize others wish for fair dealing among themselves. Since social cooperation is necessary if human beings are to survive, reproduce, an-
flourish, we may suppose that each person will want her fellows to-
possess a sense of justice, will prefer to interact with others possessin-
such a sense rather than others lacking it, and will want herself to posses-
a sense of justice insofar as it increases their willingness to interact wit-
her and so affords her a fuller realization of her own concerns. And thi-
last consideration is crucial, for it suggests that the benefit of possessin-
a sense of justice, in terms of the effects on how one is regarded an-
treated by others, may reasonably be expected to outweigh any cos-

imposed by being just and so curbing one's pursuit of one's own concerns by a regard for what is due to one's fellows.

A community of persons each possessing a sense of justice may be expected to exhibit both greater stability and greater success in capturing the potential fruits of cooperation than a comparably sized group of persons lacking that sense. Competition between the two groups should favor the former. A sense of justice is thus functionally useful at the social level. Furthermore an individual's prospects are enhanced, *ceteris paribus*, by membership in a stable and successful community. But whether our interest is explanatory or justificatory, we should not appeal directly to these considerations in accounting for our sense of justice; to do so would be to fall prey to the functionalist error. In saying that an individual's prospects are enhanced by belonging to a community whose members share a sense of justice, we point to the benefits one receives from the justice of others. But in offering a rationale for the sense of justice, we look to its role in the realization of the concerns of the individual possessor. In saying that an individual's prospects are enhanced by being welcomed by one's fellows as a participant in the community's activities, we point to the benefits one receives from one's own disposition to justice. This is essential to any account that relates justice to the perspective of the individual agent.

9. Instrumental and intrinsic value

It may now seem that I have represented the sense of justice merely as an individually beneficial refinement on a natural, prereflective disposition to conform. But this would be to ignore its distinctive attitudinal structure, and to suggest, mistakenly and misleadingly, that the values with which justice is concerned are themselves merely instrumental. From the standpoint of justice each person views both herself and her fellows as having valid claims on the benefits of social cooperation. But she does not relate these claims to her own concerns, much less her own interests. Although possession of a sense of justice may be instrumentally valuable to an agent, this does not mean that from the perspective of justice she views either just social arrangements or the other persons participating in these arrangements merely as instrumentally valuable, letting her attitude toward them vary in whatever way would suit her concerns. A person who took this instrumental view would not be just because, as Hobbes says, "his Will is not framed by the Justice, but by the apparent benefit of what he is to do."[21] Rather, she views just social arrangements as morally valuable because they afford every person, and not merely herself, his due share of the fruits of social cooperation. In this way, she gives expression to the Kantian idea, embedded in the terms of cooperation, that persons are ends in themselves. And only insofar as she does this can she be said to possess a sense of justice.

To understand a moral disposition we must make a clear distinction between its value and the value or values it determines. An individual's reflectively endorsed concerns determine his values. Some of these concerns may be related more or less directly to his desires. But I have insisted that such a relationship is not necessary; among an individual's concerns will be some that have no ascertainable basis in desire. And these will include concerns that derive from, or perhaps better, constitute his moral dispositions. The sense of justice involves a concern with mutual realization distributed in accordance with what each person is due; this concern singles out justice as a value. If we ask why a person has justice among his values, we are answered by learning that he has a sense of justice – that is, a concern or range of concerns directed at the distribution of benefits and costs viewed as requirements for and products of social interaction. A person might of course have other concerns with some or all of the same things viewed quite differently. Those concerns, based on different intentional states, are not the direct province of justice, and do not explain why a person has justice among his values.

Is justice an intrinsic value? I have related justice to the idea of persons as ends in themselves; it might be thought that one values justice only because one values persons as ends, and so instrumentally. But valuing justice is valuing persons as ends. Just social relationships are those that relate persons as ends in themselves. Justice expresses an ideal of interaction; we should not think of this ideal in abstraction from the persons interacting, or as embodying a value distinct from the value of those persons. But to take justice as an intrinsic value is perfectly compatible with recognizing that the sense of justice may and indeed must itself be valued instrumentally, as contributing to the realization of our other concerns. This is exactly what I have maintained to combat the view that in concerning oneself with justice, one acts against a proper regard for one's self. There should be nothing surprising in finding that prudence recommends having a sense of justice. But this is not to find that justice is no more than a form of prudence.

A sense of justice may be of instrumental or incidental value in many ways. A person may find that by being just she acquires a reputation for justice that earns her honor among her fellows. Valuing honor, she values her sense of justice and the particular just acts it prompts her to perform, as means to it. But any value that accrues to justice or the sense of justice in such a way as this is purely incidental. And such incidental value, arising from particular concerns that an individual may or may not have, should not be equated with the instrumental value that, I have argued, accrues to the sense of justice because it makes us welcome partners in interaction with others. For in this way the sense of justice is instrumentally valuable, not because of some concern that we may chance to have, but because of the basic circumstances of human life. Individuals can survive and flourish, can realize their goals whatever those goals may be, only in association with their fellows. A characteristic, such as the sense of justice, that fits them for such association, is then of value whatever their particular aims and concerns. And it is because justice is of value in this way that it is a genuine moral disposition, and that the values it determines – the intrinsic values of justice and of persons as ends in themselves – are real and not, like the supposed value of piety, chimerical.

10. Necessary instrumental value

I have made two large claims, both of which need to be defended. The first is that the sense of justice is, as it were, of necessary instrumental value. The second is that only in being of necessary instrumental value does justice establish its credentials as a genuine moral disposition. The position I want to defend is, I think, very similar to one that Philippa Foot advanced and later rejected.[22] I think that she was right the first time.

In claiming that justice is a necessary instrumental value, I am not maintaining that a person lacking a sense of justice cannot survive, and even flourish in terms of the concerns he actually has. What I am maintaining is that from the perspective of any person's formative years, in which his moral character is largely determined, he could not expect to flourish without a sense of justice. Hobbes attempts a somewhat similar argument against the Foole's dismissal of justice, but unsuccessfully insofar as he addresses it to particular acts of injustice, arguing that a person who performs such acts does sometimes succeed, but may not reasonably expect to succeed.[23] This is surely wrong. But Hobbes also seems to recognize what is not wrong, that a person whose character is not disposed to justice may succeed, but *ex ante* may not reasonably expect to succeed. If one were able to choose one's character, then one would choose to have those dispositions that would best fit one for cooperative interaction with one's fellows. Note of course that such dispositions will not lead one simply to turn the other cheek, or to persist in seeking a fair and mutually advantageous distribution of the fruits of interaction in circumstances where, it may be all too clear, one's fellows are bent solely on maximizing their own shares. A sense of justice, I have insisted, leads one to demand one's own due as well as to recognize what is due others. It leads one to seek justice and not to acquiesce in injustice whether toward oneself or one's fellows.

A more radical defense of the instrumental value of a sense of justice might insist that it is necessary not only to the expectation of flourishing, but to actual flourishing, claiming that the lives of persons lacking a sense of justice are, in virtue of that lack, ultimately unsatisfactory and unsatisfying. I am inclined to think that such a defense is largely but not wholly correct. One cannot show that it must be correct simply by appealing, as my argument does, to the circumstances of human life. And surely there are persons who possess concerns that they can realize sufficiently to find genuinely satisfying, and yet lack any sense of justice. But such persons are lucky, albeit not in ways that others would wish for them!

Before turning to the second claim – that a sense of justice must be of necessary instrumental value to persons if its deliverances are not to be dismissed as chimerical – I should make one important qualification in my defense of the value of a sense of justice. We can imagine societies in which the members, although not lacking in moral dispositions, nevertheless possess a moral sensibility sufficiently different from our own that it would not include a sense of justice. Indeed there may well be such societies. Now in such social circumstances adding a sense of justice to one's moral sensibility might well not be expected to be of value to a person. My argument can accommodate this, provided we may reasonably hold that the worldview of the members of the society in question is deeply mistaken in ways that enable us to understand, while rejecting, their overall moral sensibility. If, for example, they see human interaction as essentially if not exclusively zero-sum, so that they fail to recognize as a normal possibility that interaction can mutually enhance the agents' realization of their concerns, then their moral sensibility will no doubt be very different from our own, and they may not possess anything akin to our sense of justice. And in their society someone who manifested what we should recognize as a sense of justice might do very badly indeed. But we may reasonably insist that they fail to recognize the real possibilities for mutual enhancement that human interaction can afford. Their moral sensibility rests on false assumptions, and so when its deliverances oppose our own moral views we may dismiss them as mistaken. And we should not suppose that the failure of a sense of justice to be of value among persons whose morality is thus flawed, is any objection to our defense of its necessary instrumental value.

11. Morality and instrumental value

Why should a genuine moral disposition be necessarily of instrumental value? Does this requirement not reduce morality to a mere instrument of the nonmoral? I have claimed that moral values such as justice are intrinsic and not instrumental. But if moral values depend on moral dispositions, which have merely instrumental value and must have this value if their deliverances are not to be rejected, then is not morality itself merely instrumental? Or if not merely instrumental, then is not its noninstrumental value accidental, arising only if persons happen to have affective concerns with their fellows? Perhaps this would hold were morality no more than a rational artifice, accepted by persons so that they might better realize their nonmoral concerns. I offered such a derivation of morality in *Morals by Agreement*. I began with agents lacking all moral concerns, and I showed, or claimed to show, that they would rationally introduce morality into their interactions in order better to achieve their nonmoral ends. Such agents would become moral but they would not be naturally moral.

Now I do not want to reject a distinction between moral and nonmoral concerns, although I do not suppose that there is a neat and exhaustive division between the exclusively moral and the exclusively nonmoral. But in thinking of persons as naturally possessing a sense of justice, I am embracing a quite different starting point from that in my book. Moral dispositions are as natural to human beings as nonmoral ones, so that in considering real persons we cannot distinguish a nonmoral base and a moral superstructure. And so in claiming that a sense of justice is necessarily of instrumental value to persons, I am not saying that it is of instrumental value simply to realize nonmoral ends. Rather my claim is that the concerns expressed in our sense of justice are integrally related to our capacity to realize, under normal conditions, any set of aims that could be adequate to human life. A person who refused to acknowledge a sense of justice as part of the overall set of reflectively endorsed intentional states that constitutes the self, on the ground that its concerns required her to curb the realization of other interests, would be depriving herself of one of the capacities that she must expect to need for her fullest self-realization. She may not and characteristically would not think of this self-realization as exclusively nonmoral in character. The sense of justice, and more generally our moral sensibility, is not a mere instrument for our nonmoral gratification.

My second claim is therefore that a genuine moral disposition must play an essential role in human self-realization. Only this role is sufficient if the individual agent is to endorse its deliverances as discerning what has intrinsic value and as providing compelling reasons for acting. If she were to regard her moral sensibilities as at least in principle dispensable, she could not reflectively treat them as having intrinsic significance. As claimants to discern intrinsic value and compelling reasons they would be revealed as impostors.

My account of the sense of justice links Platonic and Kantian elements. The link is established through the necessity of social cooperation to individual realization.[24] The regard that each has for her fellows as ends in themselves – the regard that ensures her adherence to and advocacy of the terms of cooperation – is grounded in her recognition that lacking such regard, she may not reasonably expect to be welcomed as a partner in those social arrangements that afford each participant the opportunity for greater self-realization than could otherwise be expected.

12. Practical reason

The sense of justice involves not only noninstrumental valuation but also noninstrumental practical reasons. As I said at the outset, the possessor of a normative capacity takes himself to have a reason to favor and promote what meets its standard or best fulfills its measure. Such a reason bears no direct relation to the fulfillment of his desires, or indeed to the realization of any of his concerns that are independent of his sense of justice. It is simply and straightforwardly a reason to be just, a reason that enters into the agent's deliberations and determines or at least influences his will by the justice of what he is to do, and not by some other measure of its desirability. But it may be argued that although someone with a sense of justice takes himself to have such a reason, yet he is mistaken. Real reasons for acting must be directly linked to the overall realization of his concerns, so that to act in a way that, although supported by considerations of justice, is contrary to this realization, is irrational.

This objection raises issues that I cannot pretend to treat fully in the present context. The construction of an adequate theory of practical reason I take to be one of the most pressing issues in current philosophical inquiry, and although I have very definite thoughts about some of the features required in such a theory, I can only sketch a few of the most important ideas here. The practical deliverances of any normative disposition, including any moral sensibility, present themselves to the possessor of the disposition as reasons for acting. Thus for example a person possessing a sense of piety must consider that she has a reason to perform any action available to her that she judges pious, and to refrain from any action that she judges impious. She may, of course, have, or consider herself to have, other reasons for or against performing these same actions, quite unrelated to her sense of piety. No particular disposition affords exclusive reasons for acting, although some may provide normally overriding reasons.

But the deliverances of a normative disposition provide genuine or real reasons for acting only if the disposition is rationally sustainable. Some dispositions fail to be rationally sustainable because they rest on irrational belief; others fail because possessing them and attending to their deliverances is contrary to the fullest realization of their possessor's overall concerns. There are complex issues here that I must ignore; for example, a disposition may prove to be rationally sustainable for an individual in particular circumstances, because of the false beliefs or unreasonable expectations of her fellows. Thus the disposition of a woman to defer to men's wishes without expecting reciprocal deference on their part, may be sustainable in circumstances in which marriage is essential to any woman's well-being and standing, and failure to exhibit deference would jeopardize her prospects of marrying or remaining married. But such a disposition would not be sustainable in general since in other circumstances it would inhibit a woman's fullest self-realization. In some circumstances, as I have already noted, a sense of justice would not be rationally sustainable; a person living in a society in which interaction was considered as typically zero-sum would find no reason to embrace anything that we should recognize as a sense of justice. We should beware of supposing that there must be a simple yes/no answer to the question whether dispositions that happen to be sustainable because of untoward circumstances, or fail to be sustainable because of such circumstances, provide genuine reasons for acting. But I must leave further exploration of these matters to some other occasion.

The underlying idea of the theory of rational choice, that a rational agent seeks to maximize his utility, where utility is a measure of preference fulfillment, seems to me basically sound, if we relate an agent's preferences to the reflectively endorsed intentional states that he has unified into a single experience. But this idea does not translate straightforwardly into an account of reasons for acting and rational choices in the way in which economists and other advocates of rational choice commonly suppose. Among an agent's reasons for acting may be some that have nothing directly to do with the maximization of his utility. An agent who acts at each moment to maximize his utility or (in the language that I have used here) to promote the fullest realization of his concerns may fail to realize those concerns as fully as he might have done. He may fail because his manner of acting may limit the extent of the opportunities he has to realize his concerns, and a directly or straightforwardly maximizing way of acting may be severely limiting. Moral dispositions typically provide an agent with reasons for acting that constrain straightforwardly maximizing behavior, and their value to their possessor lies in part in that very constraint, for it is the negative side of their role in motivating him to comply and to advocate compliance with the terms of cooperation, and so to be welcomed by his fellows as a member of society.

The theory of rational choice shares much of its weakness with the belief/desire account of human action. Both see choice and action as resulting directly from given discrete beliefs and desires. In the theory of rational choice, belief is represented by subjective probability and desire by utility; an agent's deliberation may then be represented reductively by a maximizing calculation. Now there are circumstances in which such a representation may have considerable heuristic value. But as a model of deliberation it is worse than an oversimplification. Insofar as it translates an individual's overall realization of his concerns, which of course sets a global-maximizing problem, into an endeavor to maximize at the level of each particular choice, it distorts our understanding of rational behavior. However, although the perspective of Kantian naturalism may help us to realize that we should not expect to find a direct maximizing explanation of, or rationale for, each particular rational act, it does not tell us clearly what we should expect to find or offer an account of rational action with anything comparable to the apparent conceptual precision of rational choice theory. And so the claim that the deliverances of the sense of justice constitute genuine reasons for acting must be left here without the deep embedding in a theory of practical reason that it needs.

13. Rational agreement

To this point my discussion has been deliberately coarse-grained. I have treated the sense of justice as concerned with what is due each person in social cooperation, and as motivating compliance with those institutions and practices that ensure that each receives her due, but the idea of what is due has done no determinate work. The production of a social surplus is compatible with a wide range of ways in which it may be distributed among the cooperating individuals. It might be supposed that persons would take the existing distribution for granted, and treat acceptance of the burdens and benefits it allots each as just, and rejection of these burdens and benefits as unjust. Hume may seem to suggest such a view.[25] But it would be mistaken.

A developed sense of justice motivates advocacy of and compliance with a selective range of social organizations, practices, and principles, both external such as laws, and internal such as moral standards. A practice is advocated when individuals take the fact that an action would help to create or sustain it as a reason for performing the action. They may, of course, have other reasons for and against performing actions that would sustain advocated practices; a sense of justice should not be assumed to override all other motivation. Advocacy and compliance are quite different; a person who lobbies or votes to introduce or retain a tax that he evades advocates it but does not comply with it; a person who pays a tax that she lobbies or votes to repeal complies with it but does not advocate it. Typically advocacy is more selective than compliance. Thus a person may be moved by her sense of justice to comply with those actual institutions and practices that seem necessary for social interaction so long as society is at least minimally cooperative in affording some benefit to each person, while advocating practices that meet some narrower standard. She may advocate legal reform but not practice civil disobedience.

A developed sense of justice discriminates among practices and institutions. The basis of discrimination is found in giving content to the idea that justice affords each person her due share of social benefits and costs. But the sense of justice alone is not sufficient to specify what is due. It must be related to some conception of human persons and their relation to the world. Historically this has yielded very different pronouncements about what is just and unjust. Now I suppose, with Jon Elster, that human beings develop by "intentional and deliberate adaptation."[26] To understand fully any of our normative capacities we must relate them to such adaptation. And here of course I endorse Elster's suggestion that what is centrally involved is "the generalized capacity for global maximization,"[27] which I have already taken to be at the core of rational agency. Human beings can exercise this capacity in order to focus their natural sense of justice in whatever way is most fully consonant with rational deliberation.

But we should not suppose that we may appeal to the idea of maximizing the realization of our concerns to determine what is just and unjust independently of our possession of a sense of justice. Thus in relation to my discussion of morality and the affections in *Morals by Agreement,* I am not treating the sense of justice merely as a capacity that affectively disposes us to favor whatever is independently established as moral, but rather as one that enters directly into establishing what is moral, as well as disposing us to favor it by compliance and advocacy.[28] But I continue to relate justice to the idea of rational agreement. The key point is that given the maximizing perspective, the sense of justice picks out the idea of rational agreement as determining each person's due and thereby discriminating between what is just and what is unjust. The natural sense of justice is focused by relating the requirements of justice to the agreement of persons conceived as choosing *ex ante* the terms and conditions of their prospective interaction. I need not expand on this idea here, since my account would be a straightforward application of the discussion of bargaining and justice in *Morals by Agreement,* leading to the claim that the principle of minimax relative concession is the basis of the deliverances of a fully developed and informed sense of justice.[29]

Of course I do not suppose that we can understand the actual deliverances of justice throughout human history in terms of rational agreement, much less in the more precise terms of minimax relative concession. The understanding of ourselves and our situation that leads us to relate justice to rational agreement is related to the emergence of a nonteleological and nontheistic worldview, and this is historically a recent occurrence. As we do not suppose that our ancestors had an adequate explanatory understanding of many aspects of their world, so we should not suppose that they had a fully adequate grasp of just practices and institutions. And lacking a fully adequate grasp, our ancestors took as reasons for acting deliverances of their sense of justice that we should now take to be mistaken, and so not truly reasons at all.

What I want to emphasize in the present context is that rational agreement not only provides a particular standard for the deliverances of justice, but also provides a procedure that is itself morally neutral, but serves to focus the morally evaluative perspective of justice. The just person views her fellows, not as instruments that she may use in advancing her own ends, but as partners in a cooperative enterprise, each of whom is due a share of its benefits. She determines what is due her partners by how she views them; seeing them as rational deliberators, she determines their due in interaction by appealing to what would be the outcome of their joint deliberation about the terms of interaction. In other words she supposes that what is due a rational deliberator from interaction is what he would agree to voluntarily but subject to his recognition that everyone involved in the interaction also agree. In this way she gives determinate content to the idea that from the standpoint of justice persons are valued as ends in themselves.

14. Conclusion

In *Morals by Agreement* I developed a theory of morality, and in particular of justice, as part of the theory of rational choice. A theory of the sense of justice is clearly no part of the theory of rational choice, even though it may use its ideas in considering the deliverances of justice. The sense of justice itself can no more be necessary to rationality than is the sense of sight. But as a person without the sense of sight must suffer an impoverished sensory experience, so a person without the sense of justice must suffer an impoverished affective experience. And as a rational person needs to learn what sight reveals in order to understand her world, so a rational person needs to learn what justice requires in order to act in her world. Did justice not exist, she would have to invent it.

Notes

1 David Gauthier, *Morals by Agreement* (Oxford: Clarendon Press, 1986).
2 The details of the variant concern the rationale for acting against considerations of present advantage; I shall not pursue them directly here but they relate to the discussion in Section 12 below.
3 Pp. 326–9, 337–9.
4 See David Gauthier, "The Unity of Reason: A Subversive Reinterpretation of Kant," *Ethics* 96 (1985):74–88. In what follows, I shall use reason to refer to the capacity that on my view plays a role parallel to that Kant assigns to the understanding. To replicate his terminology would be both complicating and misleading.
5 I take McDowell's view from his rejection of the disentangling argument in "Non-Cognitivism and Rule-Following," in Steven H. Holtzman and Christopher M. Leich, eds., *Wittgenstein: to Follow a Rule* (London: Routledge and Kegan Paul, 1981), pp. 141–62; the discussion appears on pp. 144–5.
6 Ibid., pp. 144–5.
7 Ibid., p. 155.
8 I take these suppositions from David Hume's discussion of the circumstances of justice; see *Enquiry Concerning the Principles of Morals*, part 1, sec. 3.
9 In relating piety to what the gods love I have in mind Plato's *Euthyphro*.
10 Hume, *Enquiry*, part 1, sec. 3.
11 The phrase quoted is found in a number of variants attributed to different sources.
12 See Hume, *Enquiry*, part 1, sec. 3; and John Rawls, *A Theory of Justice* (Cambridge, Mass.: Harvard University Press, 1971), pp. 126–30.
13 P. 116.
14 If this be doubted, consider Hobbes's account of the incommodities of war, most of which would also be incommodities of solitude. *Leviathan*, orig. ed. (London: Andrew Crooke, 1651), ch. 13, p. 61.
15 Hobbes's discussion of the incommodities of war indicates, by contrast, the prospects for mutual enhancement in society, but he nevertheless insists that "men have no pleasure . . . in keeping company, where there is no power

able to overawe them all." *Leviathan*, ch. 13, p. 61. Hobbes does not suggest that "Culture of the Earth ... commodious Building ... Knowledge of the face of the Earth ... Arts ... Letters ... Society" (p. 62) might be grounds for persons taking pleasure in the company of their fellows.

16 Gauthier, *Morals by Agreement*, esp. p. 205.

17 Note that this need not be the "cooperative surplus," as I define it in ibid., p. 141. The cooperative surplus represents in effect what can be realized above the base set by the initial bargaining position, which need not be the no-interaction point.

18 Rawls, *Theory of Justice*, p. 4.

19 I understand here by cooperation any interaction in which each accommodates her behavior to that of the others in ways that ensure greater expected realization for each than in the absence of any interaction. I distinguish cooperative interaction from noncooperative, in which each straightforwardly seeks the greatest realization of her concerns, adjusting her behavior given her expectations about her fellows, but not accommodating her behavior to ensure that all benefit. In *Morals by Agreement* I relate cooperation explicitly to a rational choice framework, but I am not presupposing such a framework here.

20 The phrase, in German *die Sittlichkeit der Sitte*, is introduced in *The Dawn*, sec. 9.

21 *Leviathan*, ch. 15, p. 74.

22 See "Moral Beliefs," in Philippa Foot, ed., *Theories of Ethics* (Oxford: Oxford University Press, 1967), pp. 96–100 and her "Introduction," pp. 8–9.

23 *Leviathan*, ch. 15, p. 73.

24 I interpret Plato's argument in the *Republic* as requiring that the disposition to justice be shown to be an intrinsic part of human self-realization. Of course I no more offer my account of justice as an interpretation of Plato than I offer Kantian naturalism as an interpretation of Kant.

25 See Hume, *A Treatise of Human Nature*, vol. 3, part 2, sec. 3.

26 Jon Elster, *Ulysses and the Sirens: Studies in Rationality and Irrationality* (Cambridge: Cambridge University Press, 1979), p. 16.

27 Ibid.

28 See Gauthier, *Morals by Agreement*, pp. 327–9.

29 Ibid., ch. 5; the principle is stated on p. 145.

11

Agent-relativity of value, deontic restraints, and self-ownership

ERIC MACK

In this essay, I sketch the main features of a doctrine of moral individualism, that is, a doctrine that takes the separate moral importance of individuals seriously enough.[1] This moral individualism displays two distinct but complexly related facets. The first of these facets – the core of moral individualism's theory of the good – is the agent-relativity of all value. The second of these facets – the core of moral individualism's theory of the right – is the existence of deontic restraints upon any agent's promotion of value, restraints that are correlative to each individual's natural moral jurisdiction over himself. In the present essay, I attempt to provide two levels of rationale for this moral individualism. On one level, this doctrine is offered as the sanctuary for those who thoroughly reject the sort of impartial consequentialism that is exemplified by standard utilitarianism. It is the natural refuge for such critics because it articulates and embraces the assumptions implicit within the most common criticisms of impartial consequentialism. On another and more foundational level, I seek to begin from a minimalist conception of practical rationality as individual value maximization, to proceed through a construal of value as agent-relative yet objective, and to arrive, by way of further arguments, at the reasonableness of the recognition of deontic restraints upon what persons may do to others in the course of their value-promoting activities. Even within this more foundational level of argument, my claim is not that everything rests on the independently sturdy shoulders of individual value maximization. Rather, the relative normative modesty and initial plausibility of this starting point acquires enhanced credibility as it is further articulated and situated within a complementary theory of moral side constraints.

This essay is highly compressed and programmatic. It lays out the bare outlines of the case for a doctrine of moral individualism. Numerous relevant issues are not addressed and most topics that are taken up are dealt with too briefly or too indirectly. That said, I turn to an account of the subject matter of each of the succeeding sections. In Section 1, I briefly recount the integrity objection and the justice objection against consequentialism. In Section 2, I defend the coherence of a system of agent-relative values within which value is essentially value for this or that specific agent who stands in some particular relation to the valuable state and who, through that relation, has reason to promote that state. In Section 3, I assert the existence of such values and argue that they are the only sort of values we have reason to affirm. In Section 4, I maintain that the rejection of agent-neutral values does not imply the subjectivity of values and I argue for the objectivity of agent-relative values. In Section 5, I provide arguments for construing deontic restraints and the correlative claims of each to moral authority over himself as complements to the agent-relativity of value within a rational normative system.

1. The integrity and justice objections

Impartial consequentialism has in recent years been subjected to a double-barreled barrage of criticisms.[2] One barrel, or the ammunition therein, consists of the integrity objection, which itself comes in both a substantive and a structural form. The substantive form of the objection is by far the simpler. This version focuses on the damage that agents will be required to do *to themselves* vis-à-vis nonfulfillment of their respective rational plans of life should they abide by the demands of consequentialism. Impartialist morality systematically demands that individuals make unreasonable sacrifices of their own personal values – of values that constitute their respective rational life plans. When due regard is paid to the separateness of persons and to the singular values that promise to be realized within their respective lives, the demands of impartial consequentialism are seen to be unduly stringent, to say the least.

The structural form of the integrity objection is more subtle. It maintains that the demands placed upon individuals by consequentialism are incompatible with individuals' developing coherently integrated lives through genuine commitment to their respective and particular life projects. This structural version focuses on the purported damage that agents will do to themselves as integrated selves, that is, to their capacity to have cohesive plans of life, if they are even to be disposed to accede to the external demands of consequentialism. This form of the objection is structural because it does not reject consequentialism in the name of the value of the particular life projects that individuals will have to forgo, should they abide by the specific dictates of that morality. Rather this version turns on the claim in moral psychology that belief in consequentialism undercuts the allegiance to particular life projects through which people constitute their respective lives. According to the structural integrity objection, there is a type of pragmatic contradiction within advocacy of consequentialism. On the one hand, this advocacy presumes the existence of agents with integrated lives; these are the agents it addresses and envisions as the beneficiaries of its prescriptions. On the other hand, genuine acceptance by those addressees of what is advocated undermines that integration. The two forms of the objection are connected by the general admonition against the sacrifice of the personal on the altar of the impersonal and the specific suggestion that personal integration is itself among or partially constitutive of each agent's separate good.

The second barrel of the double barrage against impartial consequentialism is loaded with the justice objection, according to which consequentialism sanctions, indeed mandates, unjust impositions of sacrifices upon individuals for the sake of the global good. This objection focuses on the wrongful damage that threatens an agent at the hands of other agents when those agents march under the consequentialist banner. The justice objection shares with the integrity objection a concern for individuals as beings with their own separate personal importance or standing. But whereas the integrity objection stems from a sense of the propriety of each person's incorporating the personal importance of her own interests, plans, and so on, within her own choices and activities, the justice objection stems from a sense that others also ought in some way to contour their actions toward that person in accordance with that person's separate personal importance or standing. This criticism appeals, then, to the theory of the right – for example, to principles of justice or rights that deontically bar at least certain fruitful, value-promoting impositions.

Like the integrity objection, the justice objection can take either of two forms: the antiaggregative form and the fully anticonsequentialist form. The antiaggregative version insists that what is wrong with certain versions of consequentialism is that they do not include the satisfaction of the antiaggregationist's favorite distributive norm in the ranking of alternative outcomes – or that these forms of consequentialism do not incorporate the favored distributional concern in a sufficiently deep, systematic, or principled way. For the antiaggregationist, the problem with these forms of consequentialism is that they are "unrestrained by distinct distributive principles."[3] For the antiaggregationist, justice requires and is satisfied by a principled sensitivity to the distribution of values, that is, by the adoption of a "distribution-sensitive" form of consequentialism.

The antiaggregationist remains a member of the impartial consequentialist camp. The basic structure of the position remains one in which an outcome is ranked as best and, hence, as most valuable, and this ranking is supposed to provide each individual with reason – indeed, a reason with the authority of justice – to promote that outcome. There are two key problems with this position. The first problem is that it requires an agent-neutral value ranking of alternative worlds the possibility of which, I believe, is radically undercut by the agent-relativity of values. The second problem is that distribution sensitivity is not adequate to capture the intuitive core of the justice objection. Under a distribution-sensitive ranking, rightness remains a matter of promoting the now more complexly defined most highly ranked world. The justice that the antiaggregationist demands will never forbid (or will never forbid in a sufficiently systematic or principled way) those incursions upon individuals that are required for the promotion of the world ranked best by his distribution-sensitive theory.

By definition, distribution-sensitive consequentialism will condemn only imposed sacrifices that are distributionally defective. Distribution sensitivity will affirm and account for the wrongfulness of Ann's imposing some loss on Betty only when that imposition yields a distribution of value that ranks lower, in terms of the favored allocative norm, than the distribution that is undone or precluded by Ann's action. Suppose then that we know that Ann has enslaved Betty or, at least, has unilaterally initiated and maintained a policy of long-term maximal expropriation of the fruits of Betty's talents and efforts. No distribution-sensitive consequentialism will allow us to condemn Ann's treatment of Betty simply on the basis of this information.[4] This is because, for all we know, Ann's treatment of Betty may yield a more highly ranked allocation of values than that treatment disrupts or precludes. It may yield a greater totality or a greater equality of utility, well-being, or wealth than would otherwise exist. Or it may engender a distribution of utility, well-being, or wealth that does better by the worst-off inhabitant of the Ann-Betty society than would any other available arrangement. Should Ann's action turn out to be distributionally meritorious – as gauged by the enshrined allocative norm – we will have to proclaim its justice (and the injustice of Betty's resistance to Ann's program). Thus, in two respects distribution sensitivity is inadequate for capturing the inviolability that justice ascribes to individuals. First, in particular instances it proclaims to be just treatments of individuals that encroach upon the inviolability of persons, if anything ever does. Second, it misidentifies the crucial defect in unjust impositions of losses. It construes the injustice of Ann's enslavement or exploitation of Betty as consisting in or being derivative from the (supposed) misallocation generated by

1at enslavement or exploitation. But the wrongfulness of Ann's be-
avior resides in the manner in which Ann treats Betty, in the trespass
pon Betty's person. Whether or not this trespass has valued or dis-
alued allocational effects is irrelevant to the primary question about
1e quality and justice of Ann's behavior.

The fully anticonsequentialist form of the justice objection recognizes
1at there are some means that are not justified by highly rated ends,
ven when the rating of ends is as duly distribution-sensitive as one
ould possibly want. In short, there can be moral reasons against certain
npositions of sacrifices upon individuals that are independent of both
1e personal and the impersonal disvalue of their outcomes. What are
resupposed by and needed for the sustenance of the fully anticonse-
uentialist form of the justice objection are deontic restraints. Moral
ide constraints gain plausibility in virtue of being presupposed by the
ally anticonsequentialist critique. But at the same time, a satisfactory
indication of that critique demands a significantly freestanding account
f deontic restraints on value-promoting actions and policies.

2. The coherence of the agent-relativity of values

n this section, I begin the exposition of the structural core of moral
1dividualism's theory of the good. I distinguish between agent-relative
nd agent-neutral values and reasons and rebut arguments against the
oherence of competing agent-relative values.

A given state of affairs, for example, a particular bit of sensory plea-
ure S_1, is valuable if and only if it provides a reason (of value) for
romoting it. It is valuable if and only if it provides a basis for ranking
world W_1 that contains S_1 higher than an otherwise identical world W_2
hat lacks that state of affairs. The ranking of W_1 over W_2 provides a
eason (of value) for promoting W_1 rather than W_2. Values and hence
ankings and reasons (of value) can be construed in either an agent-
elative or an agent-neutral fashion. State of affairs S_1 is valuable relative
> agent A_1 if and only if although S_1 provides A_1 with reason to promote
:, S_1 need not provide any other agent with reason to bring about S_1.
he prospect of S_1 or the associated ranking of W_1 over W_2 provides A_1
rith reason for promoting W_1. But these reasons, reflective as they are
'f value and ranking relative to A_1, tell us nothing about whether A_2
as any reason to promote S_1 or W_1. Indeed, the *absence* of S_1 may be
aluable relative to agent A_2 and this absence in W_2 may be a basis for
\.$_2$'s ranking W_2 over W_1. It is perfectly consistent with A_1's having
gent-relative reason to promote S_1 that A_2 have comparable reason to
romote what is incompatible with S_1 and hence to thwart A_1's doing

what he has reason to do. Since the value of S_1 arises within, and henc essentially depends upon, its relation to A_1 – in the case at hand, A_1 sensory pleasure is valuable as an experience of A_1 – its value is relativ to A_1. It provides A_1, who stands in the relation of being the prospectiv subject of S_1, with reason to promote S_1 that other agents do not have This agent-relative reason to advance S_1 "include[s] an essential refe ence to the person who has it"[5] precisely because the account of th value itself makes essential reference to the agent for whom the valu exists.

A value is agent-neutral value if and only if that value by its ver nature beckons to everyone – that is, if and only if by its very nature provides everyone with reason to advance or maintain it. Although . may exist within the experience or life of a particular agent, if its valu is agent-neutral, then its standing in some such relation to a particul: agent is inessential to its value. Hence, the summons issued by this valu is not addressed solely to some particular agent (or agents) within who relationship to S_2 the value of S_2 resides. If S_2 has agent-neutral valu its presence in W_2 is a basis for each agent to rank W_2 over an otherwis identical W_1; W_2 is better than W_1 *full stop*. This goes beyond W_2 bein better relative to agent A_1, better relative to A_2, . . . better relative A_n. W_2 is, of the alternatives under consideration, The World Th: Ought To Be Promoted, The World That Ought To Exist. Having th exalted status, it calls upon each agent to contribute to its promotio without consideration of whose experience or life (if anyone's) S_2 wi occur in. For many individuals that summons will simply require th: they accede to the actions of those agents who can promote W_2 wit the least agent-neutral opportunity cost – without consideration of i whose experience or life that cost will fall.[6]

There is a long tradition of objections to the very idea of the agen relativity of values or, at least, to the coherence of affirming agen relative values for agents who may find their respective values to be i competition. The most common target of these objections has bee ethical egoism, which paradigmatically maintains the agent-relativity (all value.[7] In defense of the coherence of the agent-relativity of value proceed indirectly by criticizing G. E. Moore's quasi-authoritative a guments against the coherence of that paradigm of agent-relative theor ethical egoism.[8] The first of three connected objections is that the goo ness of any state of affairs cannot have reference to some particul: individual as part of its essential description.

What, then, is meant by 'my own good'? In what sense can a thing be good *f* *me?* It is obvious, if we reflect, that the only thing which can belong to m which can be mine, is something which is good, and not the fact that it is good. When, therefore, I talk of anything I get as 'my own good', I must mean either that the thing I get is good, or that my possessing it is good. In both cases it is only the thing or the possession of it which is *mine,* and not the *goodness* of that thing or that possession.[9]

The core of Moore's argument seems to be the claim that the only intelligible function of the 'for me' in the assertion that 'S_1 is good for me' is to indicate that I am the person in possession of (or subject to) S_1. The 'for me' locates the good or its ownership. It indicates S_1's actual or potential receptacle; but it is incidental to S_1's being good. The goodness of S_1 is not a function of its location, of its standing in the relation to me of being possessed, enjoyed, desired, and so forth, by me. This, I take it, is also what Moore means by the claim that "it is only the thing or the possession of it which is *mine,* and not the *goodness* of that thing or that possession."

If there is any force at all to Moore's argument, it is a product of Moore's mischaracterization of the ethical egoist's position. Moore's language suggests that the egoist believes in a type of axiological Midas effect through which, by being touched by my possession, by being mine, S_1 acquires value. But according to the egoist, S_1's being "mine" signifies its standing to me in some further and more substantive relation, for example, its fulfilling my preference, its satisfying my desire, its being constitutive of my self-realization, in virtue of which *I* have reason to promote S_1. S_1's fulfilling, satisfying, or realizing my preference, desire, or self is what provides me, as the being whose fulfillment, satisfaction, or realization will be attained, with reason to produce S_1. Since the occurrence of S_1 need not also fulfill the preference, desire, and so on, of agent A_1, it need not provide A_1 with any reason for action whatsoever.

Moore's second argument asserts the incoherence of affirming the ultimacy of each agent's good. For this is said to imply that each agent's good is *the* supreme good. According to Moore:

If, therefore, it is true of any single man's "interest" or "happiness" that it ought to be his sole ultimate end, this can only mean that man's "interest" or "happiness" is *the sole good, the* Universal Good, and the only thing that anybody ought to aim at. What Egoism holds, therefore, is that *each* man's happiness is the sole good – that a number of different things are *each* of them the only good thing there is – an absolute contradiction![10]

But, clearly, no inference of the sort Moore expresses is justified. What ethical egoism holds is that each person's happiness (or whatever) is that person's sole ultimate good – that there are as many distinct ultimate

goods as there are persons, each being the ultimate good for the perso
whose happiness (or whatever) it is. Only if the first objection to th
relativizing of the good to individual agents were correct, which it i
not, would the damning inference of the sort Moore expresses b
justified.

The third common argument against ethical egoism as an instance c
the agent-relativity of value turns on the demand for the compossibilit
of all the actions that agents ought, all values considered, to perform
It is held to be a sign of irrationality for an ethical system to requir
both that A_1 do X and that A_2 do Y in some actual or even merel
conceivable situation such that it is impossible that both X and Y b
performed. An ethical system should tell people what ought to be done
However, ethical egoism fails to dictate what ought to be done – Shoul
it be X or should it be Y? Or, if it does prescribe what ought to b
done, it insists upon the impossible, namely, the joint performance c
X and Y. This latter charge will bear the weight of the argument if it i
maintained that every rational ethical system must include the rule: 1
X ought to be done and Y ought to be done, then X-and-Y ought to b
done.

Any such demand for the compossibility of all teleologically justifie
actions reflects the belief that there is a comprehensive metric of valu
the maximum promotion of which governs how each agent should act
Not only is the incommensurability of agent-relative values assume
away, but so is any incommensurability among agent-neutral values tha
might put justified-value pursuers at odds with one another. The pre
sumption is that as soldiers in pursuit of a common and fully ordere
cause, whatever it is that A_1 and A_2 should respectively do, those action
must be compossible. Yet this postulation of commensurability invoke
precisely the image of the world of values that the agent-relativist i
concerned to challenge. The agent-relativist refuses to pronounce upo
what ought to be done. Insofar as pronouncements of this form impl
transcendence of the perspective of particular agents, the agent-relativis
denies their valid application. When, all agent-relative values consid
ered, A_1 ought to do X and A_2 ought to do Y and X and Y are no
compossible, the agent-relativist is ... well, neutral *qua* moral theoris
between X and Y. He does not aspire to wield a morality that decree
whose interests or projects should be sacrificed to whom. Were th
agent-relativist to endorse the impersonal claims that X ought to b
done and that Y ought to be done, then he might indeed be committe
to the composite impersonal claim that X-and-Y ought to be done –
done by agents enrolled in the collective whose common cause bot
requires that X be done and that Y be done. The agent-relativist, how

:ver, only affirms prescriptions of the form "A_1 ought to do X" and he denies inferences from such claims to ones of the impersonal form "X ought to be done (by A_1, A_2, or A_n)."[11]

3. The exclusive existence of agent-relative values

I have argued for the coherence of affirming agent-relative values but only incidentally for the existence of such values. In this section, I more emphatically assert the existence of agent-relative values and argue that only such values exist, that is, that agent-neutral values do not exist. If people ever have reasons for action, the satisfaction of their own desires or the realization of their own purposes, commitments, or capacities must be among these reasons. The objects of such reason-based actions are values, albeit each object is valuable relative to the agent in whose life that object will occur. The existence of agent-relative values is, I take it, the presumption embodied in the conception of rationality in economics and decision theory. Some prospective outcomes are reasons for action; and in order for any particular prospective outcome to provide me with a reason for action it must enter into my utility function. Yet its so providing me with a reason for action, its being a value (for me), implies nothing at all about its providing others with reasons for action. Indeed, the presumption of economic rationality is that *all* value is agent-relative. As is often noted, it is the modesty of this conception of rationality that makes it an attractive minimalist starting place for moral theory.

The acceptance of the agent-relativity of at least some values seems required if one agrees that "the distinction between any one individual and any other is real and fundamental." For then, as Sidgwick put it:

'I' am concerned with the quality of my existence as an individual in a sense, fundamentally important, in which I am not concerned with the quality of the existence of other individuals: and this being so, I do not see how it can be proved that this distinction is not to be taken as fundamental in determining the ultimate end of rational action for the individual.[12]

The question is whether there is any end of action the value of which is *not* relative to the individual (or individuals) in whose particular life (or lives) that end will be a "quality of ... existence" and, hence, the value of which provides everyone with agent-neutral reason for its promotion. Rather than provide here a general argument against the existence of agent-neutral values, I propose instead to examine critically three forceful arguments for the agent-neutrality of some values that appear in Thomas Nagel's *The View from Nowhere*. The present case

against the existence of agent-neutral values rests on the failure of thes
arguments to persuade.

Focusing on the (dis)value of pain, Nagel's strategy is to promot
pain from agent-relative to agent-neutral badness.

[P]rimitive pleasures and pains provide at least agent-relative reasons for pursu
and avoidance – reasons that can be affirmed from an objective standpoint [i.e
reasons that "can be recognized . . . from outside"] and that do not merely de
scribe the actual motivation of the agent.[13]

But does pain provide agent-neutral reason for its avoidance? Nage
offers three somewhat discreet arguments for an affirmative answer. W
may label them: (A) the dissociation argument; (B) the concern by/fc
others argument; and (C) the impersonal hatefulness argument.

(A) Dissociation occurs, according to Nagel, if I do not assign agent
neutral badness to my pain. My objective self becomes dissociated fror
my subjective self because the latter has reason to end the sufferin
while the former, as objective spectator, only acknowledges that EM
the observed subjective self, has reason to want it to stop. My subjectiv
self, as my daughter at age four was wont to say, is "really really"
against this suffering; but my objective self is . . . well, objective, dis
interested. If only agent-relative badness is assigned to my pain, onl
the agent whose pain it is can take a substantive, contentful stand agains
the pain. The only judgment that the objective self can make is tha
this person, EM, whom the objective spectator is observing, has reason
to negate the suffering. My objective self, therefore, becomes as distan
from my subjective self as other reason-acknowledging agents are.

Now, if I had an objective self, if I were in part an objective self o
the sort Nagel is imagining, then I *might* be concerned about bein
dissociated from my subjective self. On the other hand, to the exten
that I am charmed by this dualist imagery, I will find value in dissociation
What's the point of having two selves unless the objective, rational
depersonalized, and disembodied self can free itself from, rise above
and view with detachment the concerns of the subjective and particu
laristic self? Invoking the imagery of two selves while also insisting upo
a structure for value that allows those two selves to live in harmony ma
be a matter of wanting both to have and to eat one's metaphysical cake
Furthermore, while my belief in the agent-neutral badness of EM'
suffering will tend to align my objective self with my subjective self, m
belief in the agent-neutral badness of *others'* suffering draws my two
selves apart. For the agent-relative badness of suffering tells my sub
jective self to focus on the reduction of EM's suffering while the agent
neutral badness of suffering at large tells my objective self to attend to

he reduction of suffering at large. In almost all circumstances, one of hese practices will have to be sacrificed to the other. If I dispose myself o respond to the agent-neutral values affirmed by my objective self, I vill usually have to suppress or at least dissociate from the counsel of ny subjective self and vice versa.

(B) The concern by/for others argument suggests that plausible accounts of others being moved by our suffering and our being moved by others' suffering invoke the agent-neutral badness of suffering. Nagel argues that

f . . . we limit ourselves to relative reasons, [the sufferer] will have to say that hough he has reason to want an analgesic, there is no reason for him to have one, or for anyone else who happens to be around to give him one.[14]

This is partially correct but mostly misleading. Clearly, if the badness of suffering is agent-relative, the sufferer cannot say that there is an agent-neutral reason for her to have the analgesic. But that is not to deny the existence of an agent-relative reason for her to have it. Nor is it to deny the existence of agent-relative reasons had by some of those who happen to be around her to provide her with an analgesic. A blissful cessation of her screams, or even her feeling better, may be among the states of affairs that are good for some or all of these agents. Nagel asks us to imagine a fellow sufferer who

professes to hope we both will be given morphine, but I [the first-person, agent-relativist sufferer] fail to understand this. I understand why he has reason to want morphine for himself, but what reason does he have to want *me* to get some? Does my groaning bother him?[15]

That may be it. My groaning may be drowning out the answers on Hollywood Squares. Or it may be that my groaning bothers him because my being in pain, in a way that is vivid and present to him, bothers him. Because I am near to him and he is a person of normal sympathies, his sympathy extends to me. So he has a reason to want it to stop – a reason that does not extend to the suffering of those whom, perhaps simply because of their distance from him, his sympathies do not embrace.

However, implicit in Nagel's final rhetorical question is another, more difficult question. Does the fellow patient's reason for wanting my suffering to cease rest merely on his aversion toward my groaning or on his disaffection for my suffering? As a "normative realist," Nagel holds about reasons for action that "we have to discover them instead of deriving them from our preexisting motives."[16] Thus, his suggested answer is that the fellow patient's reaction does not rest entirely on his ultimate distaste for my pain (behavior). At least in part it is responsive

to the discovered, objective badness of my suffering. I agree with Nagel'
belief in the objective disvalue of my pain. But does this imply the agen
neutrality of its disvalue? It does if and only if objective values – value
that are not simply a function of our affective states – must be agen
neutral values. I will reject this highly contentious claim in the nex
section. In the case at hand, it should be noted that the objectivity c
the badness of my pain may play a role in my fellow patient's havin
reason to lessen my pain without this indicating the agent-neutrality c
the badness of my pain. For that objectivity may function to engage m
fellow patient's sympathy toward those suffering objective evils.

(C) Nagel's impersonal hatefulness argument urges us to see a com
ponent of our rejection of pain as occurring on an impersonal plan
where objective self confronts agent-neutral value:

> [T]he pain, though it comes attached to a person and his individual perspective
> is just as clearly hateful to the objective self as to the subjective individual. Th
> pain can be detached in thought from the fact that it is mine without losing an
> of its dreadfulness. It has, so to speak, a life of its own.[17]

The force of this passage lies in the simple idea that pain is dreadfu
It is dreadful in itself so that the correct response to prospective pai
is dread; pain is the sort of thing that a rational person wants not t
exist. But, again, does this contention specifically point to the agen
neutral badness of pain? One can agree that the dreadfulness of pai
has "a life of its own" – so that anyone facing the prospect of pain ha
a reason to avoid it whatever his attitude toward pain – without agreein
that the objective awfulness of pain gives everyone reason to want
specific prospective pain not to exist. In recognizing the dreadfulness c
the pain faced by another, I do more than understand her motivatio
in avoiding it; I also see that she ought to want to escape it. But as a
objective spectator, I do not, thereby, have reason to prevent her pain

Nevertheless other passages within Nagel's impersonal hatefulnes
argument seem designed to block the idea that the awfulness of pai
may sustain only agent-relative reasons. This is how we may read th
following argument:

> The [sufferer's] desire to be rid of pain has only the pain as its object. . . . [I
> I lacked or lost the conception of myself as distinct from other possible or actua
> persons, I could still apprehend the badness of pain, immediately. . . . [T]he fac
> that it is mine – the concept of myself – doesn't come into my perception of th
> badness of my pain.[18]

Here we have come full circle to Moore's original claim that the minenes
of the pain is incidental to its badness. The pain I desire to get rid o
happens to be mine; but its being mine is not essential to its badness.

Now, it is true that I do not have to *register* the pain as mine in order to apprehend its badness. I don't have to say to myself, "This is the pain that *I* am undergoing," before I can recognize that it merits elimination. I simply indict pain as I immediately experience it. Yet the pain that I indict is the pain that is immediate to me – which is to say, my pain. "The immediate attitude of the subject" of the pain is simply that this current condition should cease. The subject does not, within that immediate indictment, address the issue of who has reason to eliminate this suffering. But if it is his suffering that he indicts and if he recognizes that others in parallel fashion indict the suffering immediate to them, the natural conclusion is that each has reason, assuming mutual disinterest, to eliminate his own suffering.[19]

One further point needs to be made about the reasons that others might have for relieving my suffering. Even the total absence of value-based reasons for others to alleviate my suffering would hardly entail the absence of *all* reasons; my doctor may have a duty to relieve my suffering whether she likes it or not, whether it advances her ends or not. And so might others. To say that all values are agent-relative and that, therefore, all value-based reasons for action are agent-relative, is fully compatible with maintaining the existence of other sorts of reasons for or against action, for example, deontic constraints on people's behavior.

4. The objectivity of agent-relative values

It is time to pursue further the distinction between the agent-relativity of values and the subjectivity of values and to defend the objectivity of agent-relative values. I have two main motives for doing so. The first is to insulate the case for the agent-relativity of values from arguments against the subjectivity of values. The second is to set the stage for appealing to the objectivity of values in the course of arguing for rights and deontic restraints in the final section of this essay.

Subjectivism is the view that "value is created or determined through preference. Values are the products of our affections."[20] Value comes into existence by being conferred upon otherwise valueless states of affairs and it is conferred by our preferences or desires or commitments. Subjectivism contrasts with objectivism, the view that affections can, at least sometimes, be evaluated as appropriate or not, as rational or not, depending upon whether their objects are worthy of our affections. Subjectivism is not automatically tied to the agent-relativity of value. It might be held that, by being the object of someone's desire, a state of affairs has agent-neutral value conferred upon it. It is this linkage of subjectivism with agent-neutrality, more than any illicit universalization that is at work within J. S. Mill's notorious inference from each person' happiness being a good (for that person) in virtue of being desired (b that person) to the general happiness being what all persons have reaso to promote.[21]

Still, there are plausible links between subjectivism and agent relativism. Subjectivism is a natural expression of the more genera agent-relativist idea that what is valuable is valuable in and through it relation to agents. Subjectivism specifies affective relations as those i and through which states of affairs have value. And the idea that valu exists as the bestowal of affection, in turn, supports the nonneutralit of value. This support derives from a sense that the power of any pref erence to confer value has a limited effective range. While my desir for S_1 may have the power to confer value on S_1 for me, it is difficu to see my desire for S_1 having the power to bestow upon S_1 an agent neutral value that summons all to its service. The value that my desir confers, the reason that my preference generates, seems at most t extend to the person whose desire or preference is at work.

(Nonperverse) subjectivists and objectivists agree that pleasure an other forms of felt satisfaction are good while pain and other forms o felt dissatisfaction are bad. But is the value of pleasure "created o determined through preference"? One route to a negative answer pro ceeds by imagining two individuals, A_3 and A_4, whose affections an disaffections are precisely alike except that A_3 has formed or has bee formed with an aversion to sensorial pleasure while A_4 has formed o has been formed with a normal affection for that mode of experience More precisely, their other desires are exactly alike except that th counterpart to A_3's second-order preference for the satisfaction of he desire to avoid pleasure is A_4's second-order preference for the satis faction of his desire for pleasure. A_3's aversion to pleasure does not i any way contribute to her actual or potential possession of commitment or projects that are of value to her and that are unavailable to A_4 becaus of his hankering for pleasure. Suppose also that A_3 and A_4 fulfill eac of their respective desires to the same degree. And imagine further tha A_3 would to that very same degree satisfy a desire for sensory pleasur were she to have that desire rather than an aversion toward it while A would fulfill to that same degree a desire to avoid pleasure were he t have that aversion.

Now here is a crucial and I think highly plausible judgment: A_4 i better off than A_3. There is a human good that obtains in A_4's life tha does not obtain in A_3's life (and there is no compensating good in A_3' life). And this extra good is not a matter of there being an *additiona* bject of A$_4$'s affections. For A$_3$ has an object of affection that A$_4$ lacks, namely, the absence of pleasure. What makes the difference between ow well off A$_3$ and A$_4$ are is the difference between *what* is desired by hem, not any difference in the number of desires or their strength or heir degree of satisfaction. However, if subjectivism were true, if value were the product of preference, it would not be true that A$_4$ is better off than A$_3$. It would not be true that *what* is desired itself matters. Thus, subjectivism must be false.

Parallel arguments can be offered if we concern ourselves not with a preference for sensory pleasure homogeneously conceived, but rather with much more particular appetites the objects of which are specific experiential states. Consider Loren Lomasky's example of a yen for (the aste of) a kosher dill pickle.[22] Does the existence of the desire itself provide a reason to favor the occurrence of the desired experience? Lomasky points out that a person subject to such an appetite can some-times respond in one of two ways. She can proceed to fulfill the appetite. Or she can proceed to extinguish it. If the existence of an appetite itself provides a reason to indulge it, then in such a case and on the basis of the facts already specified, the agent would be more rational to satisfy the appetite than to extinguish it. Well, does the agent, on the basis of those specified facts, have more reason to fulfill the appetite than to extinguish it? No.

This answer is startling only insofar as one has been assuming that the fulfillment of this agent's appetite for the (taste of the) kosher dill will satisfy the agent, that in particular it will provide her with that unique dill-pickle-tasting pleasure. It is quite natural, of course, to as-sume that the taste experience and the distinctive pleasure of the taste experience come together in a tightly wrapped package. But we can imagine and I have been imagining otherwise. We can suppose that our agent has recently lost her capacity actually to have the kosher-dill-pickle-tasting pleasure and yet, at least for a while, retains the yen for and the capacity to experience the taste. Then, although satisfaction in the sense of the occurrence of the object of her affection can be realized, *her* satisfaction is not in the cards. Our agent is subject to the felt dissatisfaction of having her secondary preference for fulfilling her yen frustrated. But this dissatisfaction can at least as well be avoided by extinguishing her primary desire as by fulfilling it. In this case – a case in which the normal linkage between the fulfillment of a preference and the satisfaction of the agent having that preference has been broken – it is clear that the preference for a certain state as such provides no reason for the agent to promote that state. The nonsatisfying fulfillment of the yen for the kosher dill has as such no value for this agent. But it

ought to if value is created or determined by one's preferences. Thu
again, subjectivism is false.

Subjectivism does not intend to restrict the good and the bad to typ
of experience. As Gauthier points out, "subjectivism concerns th
ground of value, not its object. There is no restriction on the nature o
those states of affairs that may be objects of preference, and so th
may be valued."[23] An agent may have as the object of her preference
a career as a computer programmer, ownership of a complete set o
braided-hair half-cent coins, the health of her children, or being th
author of the definitive case for classical liberalism. However, the mor
we move away from preferences that can be thought of as appetites
for example, the preference for sensory pleasure or for the distinctiv
taste of a good kosher dill – and toward those preferences that can b
described as commitments, projects, or plans, the more difficult it be
comes to take the preference at hand as grounding the value or eve
the agent's perception of value of the object of that preference. For th
sort of preference involved in a commitment, project, or plan is no
given as a type of yen, itching, or urge. One does not find oneself wit
projects in the way that one finds oneself with a hankering for a koshe
dill. It is through our loyalty to our special commitments and project
that we evaluate and regulate our appetites and the pursuit of the
fulfillment and marshal our psychic and physical resources in the creatio
of our separate lives. From where, then, do preferences of this sor
come? They come at least in part from judgments that the projects meri
being undertaken and are worthy of our accomplishment. Only firr
convictions about the value and importance of our commitments an
projects sustain their capacity to give direction and structure to our lives

These convictions cannot be based upon the value of the sensor
payoff that is tied to the fulfillment of projects. For unlike the satisfactio
of a yen, the fulfillment of a project does not typically involve an as
sociated *sensory* payoff. It does typically involve an associated felt sat
isfaction. But this glow of satisfaction – satisfaction in th
accomplishment of something worth doing and something to which on
has been devoted as a thing worth doing – also cannot be the basis fo
the agent's guiding convictions about the value and importance of he
projects. For that afterglow is a creature of the perceived worth of th
project. Absent an agent's perception of the value of the end pursued
– a value that resides in the end and not in its achievement being a
means to the agent's felt satisfaction – that end's achievement would
not bring felt satisfaction. Thus, even if the value of sensory and fel
satisfaction were "created or determined" by agents' affection for them
the occurrence of the latter would at least for the most part be made

possible by agents' belief that their commitments and projects have a value and importance that are not themselves created or determined by their affections.

In short: (1) When an agent takes herself to have reason to direct and contour her life for the sake of a long-term goal, she must ascribe value to that goal which she herself does not bestow on it; and (2) if it is not an illusion that agents do sometimes actually have reason to direct and contour their lives for the sake of long-term goals, then agents must sometimes be correct in their ascription of nonbestowed value to those goals (as they are correct in their ascription of value to pleasure and felt satisfaction). This is sufficient to meet Gauthier's challenge to the objectivist that he make a plausible case that "reference to objective value occurs in *the best explanation* we can provide for our actions and choices."[24]

The hallmark of an objectivist position is that certain experiences, states, activities, and so on, of an agent constitute components of his (prospective) good independent of their being desired by that agent.[25] It is good for an agent to live, to possess efficacy in his interaction with the world, to develop and exercise his world-interactive, cognitive, affective, and social capacities. The natural objectivist formula for an agent's good is the fullest feasible actualization of that individual's goal-oriented capacities and resources – including the realization of his orientation toward felt satisfactions. The components of each agent's prospective well-being stand to that person in the relation of being the prospective articulations or realizations of aspects of his constitution as the purposive being he is.

But is it possible that this rejection of subjectivism reopens the door to value-neutralism? It may appear that the invocation against the subjectivist of the good of pleasure, of felt satisfaction, of talents exercised, of knowledge, friendship, and so on, constitutes an appeal to agent-neutral values and, hence, a surrender of agent-relativity. Consider a person who devotes her life to ascertaining the true authorship of the Shakespearean plays. This goal is pursued with a sense that a correct historical understanding of these works is important and that this importance is nonidiosyncratic. The literary researcher thinks, "It's a good thing to know who wrote those plays," not "It's good to exercise my epistemic capacities." It seems that the worthiness that the researcher responds to is the nonrelativized, that is, agent-neutral, good of knowledge.

Nevertheless, if our researcher is not a fanatic, she will recognize that the worthiness possessed by her project does not as such call for others to support her endeavor. She will recognize that other agents may without fault or even misfortune be completely indifferent to this question of authorship. It may not at all engage their "desire to know."[26] Moreover, the nonidiosyncratic quality of our researcher's reasons can be understood without appeal to the agent-neutral value of discoveries about the play's authorship. When the researcher says, "It's a good thing to know who wrote those plays," she is not only indicating the agent-relative value (for her) of this knowledge. She is also pointing to a particular goal and to a type of goal the achievement of which, either directly or vicariously, may be valuable to others and in which she may be inviting them to share. She is placing her project in a broader explanatory pattern and is associating it with similar projects that both she and her listeners may value. She is presenting this knowledge or knowledge in general as offering permanent possibilities for the realization of (agent-relative) value.

5. Self-integration, recognition, and rights

There is a natural link between: (a) the agent-relativity of value and the concern for personal integration that motivates the integrity objections; and (b) deontic side constraints and the concern for personal inviolability that motivates the justice objection. I limit myself here to two arguments. The first of these ties the acceptance of deontic restraints and persons' correlative rights over themselves to the concerns that motivate the integrity objections. The second argument ascribes rights to persons on the basis of their *status* as sources and prospective subjects of agent-relative value and as bearers of agent-relative reasons for action.

(1) Although the focus of the integrity objections is the threat to an agent's personal value and integrity posed by his acceptance of consequentialism, it turns out that this threat is best blocked by the adoption of a moral theory that both affirms the personal value of agents' separate commitments and projects and the right of each agent to devote himself to the pursuit his own ends. Each agent's devotion to long-term self-defining commitments and projects has to be maintained in the face of: (i) competing demands placed upon his person, talents, and energy by others; (ii) others' assertion of the rectitude of these competing demands; and (iii) actual or threatened pressure to elicit his abandonment of his commitments and projects for the sake of these external demands. In the face of these factors, an agent's morally confident allegiance to those commitments and projects requires more than his belief that he has reasons of his own to devote his capacities and resources to his particular ends – while others, of course, may have reasons of their own of entirely comparable (agent-relative) force to thwart their advance-

ment. His morally confident allegiance requires that he believe that he is justified in his pursuit of personal value. For him to believe that he is justified in this endeavor he must believe that there is a moral asymmetry between his devotion of his person to his ends and others' devotion of him to their purposes. He has to believe that some interpersonally sound moral principle favors his choice about the disposition of his person and powers over the multitude of competing choices about his person and powers that are favored by others.

However, the moral asymmetry that vindicates him in his devotion of his personal capacities and resources in pursuit of his valued ends cannot be a matter of the greater agent-neutral value of these ends compared to the ends that others would have him serve. It cannot be a matter of his choice having priority because of its greater commensurable value. It must, instead, be a matter of his choice being favored because it is *his,* that is, of his having the authority to decide which of these competing ends *he* is to serve. An agent must, I contend, see himself as having this moral sovereignty over himself if, in the face of all those competing demands, he is to be steadfast in his commitments and projects to the degree generally required for self-definition and self-integration. An agent cannot have the requisite degree of commitment and motivation toward his own ends without rejecting, at least implicitly, the image of himself as a means or resource morally available to others for the pursuit of their respective ends. "Having rights enables us to 'stand up like men,' to look others in the eye, and to feel in some fundamental way the equal of everyone";[27] and standing up like a man is crucial for the achievement of the values constituting one's personal life plan and one's self-integration. A coherent moral doctrine that is intended to take seriously the integrity objections against consequentialism must, in order to vindicate each individual's sense of being justified in his pursuit of his own separate ends, affirm not only the special value to each individual of his particular goals and projects but also each individual's rightful command over himself in the pursuit of those ends.

(2) The second argument focuses on the *status* of individuals as bearers of agent-relative reasons and as sources and prospective subjects of agent-relative value. It involves two claims. The first is that the affirmation of others as beings with rational ends of their own with equal, albeit incommensurable, ultimacy must have some practical significance for one's own behavior. The second claim is that the appropriate practical response to the existence of others as beings with rational ends of their own is constraint on the treatment of those beings as means to one's own ends.

The affirmation of the agent-relativity of values is the affirmation o
each agent as the possessor of rational ends of her own and of reason
for devoting herself to the pursuit and attainment of those ends. It i
the attestation of the propriety of each agent's devotion to her rationa
life plan. This affirmation places each of us within a "world of reasons
including [one's] own, [that] does not exist only from [one's] own poin
of view." The acknowledgment of this normative reality – which is no
a mere abstract, philosophical affirmation, but takes the form of ac
knowledging the existence of particular fellow creatures with their sep
arate ultimate goods – places rational demands upon our behavior. The
rejection of normative solipsism requires "a practical analogue of the
rejection of [theoretical] solipsism."[28] Some difference in one's action
must be called for when one moves from the solipsistic conviction tha
the only real values in the universe are the values of one's unique sel
to belief in the equal reality of value-for-others. It would be bizarre fo
such an enormous shift in one's conception of the normative landscape
– a shift from an egotistic subjectivism to the inclusion of others a
beings comparably oriented to value – to have no implications for one'
views about how one ought to act.

The practical recognition of others as equal coinhabitants of the mora
universe cannot, however, take the form of mandatory additions to the
set of one's rational goals. The additional values one will have come to
recognize are values relative to others that one need in no way share.[2]
Indeed, one may recognize that the realization of certain of those value
conflicts with one's own. Thus, the general form that practical recog
nition of one's coinhabitants in the moral universe must take is constrain
on the manner in which one pursues one's own goals. The practica
analogue of the rejection of solipsism is not an alteration of one's ends
but rather a restriction on one's means of attaining them. The mark o
the nonpsychopathic recognition of another's existence as a being with
rational ends of her own is a disposition not to treat that person as a
natural resource available for one's use and exploitation.

To make matters more concrete and vivid, imagine that you have had
the belief that your coinhabitants of the world are humanoid androids
– beings without values, purposes, or reasons for action, but complexly
programmed to act and react as genuine human beings would. Because
of their subtle reactive powers, your relationship with these beings is
strategic. Your choices take account of their anticipated responses to
your choices and so on. Suppose further you have discovered in yourself
an appetite for the sight of spurting red liquids – a sight you can most
cost-effectively enjoy by sneaking up on and decapitating your coinhabitants. The resulting lovely spray of blood-colored fluid is seen by

you as perfectly analogous to the pleasing little tune played by your computer when you win some highly interactive video game.

Now suppose that (somehow) you come to realize that your coinhabitants are humans, that they are not merely programmed entities but beings having their own (agent-relative) values and reasons for the promotion of those values. By hypothesis, in terms of strategic action aimed at maximizing your valued outcomes, this recognition calls for no change in your behavior. For this discovery does not change your expectations about how your fellow beings will act and react. Yet should not this recognition of the reality of others as value pursuers and bearers of reasons for their pursuits have some effect on your behavior? Should it not have some effect even if you have no sympathetic participation with these newly discovered values-for-others and, hence, even if you do not acquire by sympathetic engagement an (agent-relative) reason for maintaining or promoting their values? If it seems as though it should (and doesn't it?), if your failure to modify your behavior would reasonably be taken as evidence of your failure genuinely to recognize this reality (and wouldn't it?), then this practical recognition must take the form of restraints upon your treatment of these other persons in the course of your pursuit of your own valued ends.

However, the plausibility of the claim that the recognition of others with ultimate values of their own makes demands on one's own behavior seems to depend upon the degree or sort of reality possessed by those values. One of my reasons for advancing an objectivist account of (agent-relative) values and rejecting a subjectivist account is the suspicion that the latter grants too little reality to others' values to sustain the present argument. I suspect that those who see little force in this argument do so because they perceive it in terms of a subjectivist vision of values. I said that to affirm the ultimacy of the each person's agent-relative values is to attest to the propriety of each person's devotion to his own rational life plan. This propriety in no way requires that one agent's valuable ends be promoted by any other agent. Nor does persons-acting-in-the-service-of-their-own-ends become a higher-order agent-neutral good that each is called upon to serve. Rather, the propriety of person A_2's devotion to his own rational life plan is duly recognized by A_1 if, but only if, A_1 eschews treating A_2 as grist for A_1's mill. But does this propriety of A_2's devotion to his valued ends obtain independently of A_2's preferences or is this propriety "created or determined" by A_2's preferences? It seems that the latter will be the case if A_2's ends have their value in virtue of A_2's affection for them. But in that case this value and the propriety of A_2's promoting it merely exists *in mente* – in A_2's *mente!* – and not *in re*.

Given a subjectivist account of A_2's values, A_1 may understandably ask, what is it to me that within and from the point of view of A_2's affective condition certain states are valuable for A_2 and A_2 has reason to promote them? Such subjectively based value, reason, and propriety does not confront A_1 as an objective normative reality to which it would be reasonable to respond in some way. The subjectivist account does not actually affirm a common "world of reasons" but only a plurality of worlds of (subjective) reasons. Although it may (barely) escape normative solipsism, it attains no more than a type of normative monadology in which each unit, sealed within its affective self, makes no normative contact with any other. In contrast, on the objectivist account, the value of A_2's valuable ends and the propriety of his pursuing them obtain *in re* and not merely *in mente*. They are part of the reality that confronts A_1. This is a reality that, I have suggested, cannot genuinely be recognized by A_1 without A_1's eschewing treating A_2 as a morally available means to A_1's ends, that is, without A_1's recognizing A_2's moral jurisdiction over himself.

The fully anticonsequentialist form of the justice objection maintains that justice cannot be a matter of the generation of even a duly distribution-sensitive social outcome. For construing justice in this way will not capture our sense of persons' moral inviolability, and the actual pursuit of (supposedly) agent-neutrally best social outcomes will in fact sometimes require encroaching upon persons' inviolable spheres. A theory of justice will avoid these problems only if, at its core, it is a doctrine of moral side constraints. But on what can such constraints ultimately rest if not the (supposed) agent-neutral value of compliance with them? Two answers have been suggested here: (1) the need for a moral theory to endorse persons' rights over themselves if that theory is to embrace and protect personal value including the personal value of self-integration; and (2) the need to give practical recognition to the normative reality that each person has ultimate ends of her own to which she rationally and with propriety devotes herself – a practical recognition that takes the form of acknowledging each person's moral authority over herself.

This claim to self-ownership offers each agent protection against the demands that others may make in the name of their enlightened or misguided ends or in the name of spurious conceptions of transcendent value. It sanctifies each agent's pursuit of her own ends on the condition that her pursuits not transgress upon others' like rights. It provides the core of moral individualism's theory of the right, which complements the agent-relativity of value, which forms the nub of moral individualism's theory of the good.

Notes

1 An earlier version of this moral individualism appears in my "Moral Individualism: Agent-Relativity and Deontic Restraints," *Social Philosophy and Policy* 7, no.1 (autumn 1989): 81–111.

2 On the integrity and justice objections, see Samuel Scheffler, *The Rejection of Consequentialism* (Oxford: Clarendon Press, 1982).

3 H. L. A. Hart, "Utilitarianism and Natural Rights," *Tulane Law Review* 53, no.3 (April 1979): 663–80.

4 The one apparent exception to this is the Paretian norm that precludes any alteration that leaves anyone worse off than that party would be under the status quo – which is to say, precludes any genuine redistribution. This norm can immunize from alteration *any* profile of utilities or packets of wealth, etc., whatever its shape. So perhaps it should not count as "distribution-sensitive."

5 See Thomas Nagel, *The View from Nowhere* (New York: Oxford University Press, 1986), pp. 152–3. Nagel, however, would deny the particular claim that the value of sensory pleasure is agent-relative.

6 In describing W_2 as being identical to W_1 except for the inclusion of S_2, we unrealistically assume that (restricting our focus to these two worlds) there is no opportunity cost in promoting W_2.

7 For a survey and critique of these objections see Jesse Kalin, "Two Types of Moral Reasoning: Egoism as A Moral Theory," *Canadian Journal of Philosophy* 4, no.2 (November 1975): 323–56; and Eric Mack, "Egoism and Rights," *The Personalist* 54, no.1 (winter 1973): 5–33.

8 G. E. Moore, *Principia Ethica* (Cambridge: Cambridge University Press, 1960).

9 Ibid., p.98.

10 Ibid., p. 99.

11 See Kalin, "Two Types of Moral Reasoning," pp. 340–4.

12 Henry Sidgwick, *The Methods of Ethics* (Chicago: University of Chicago Press, 1962), p.498.

13 Nagel, *View from Nowhere,* p.158. In the uncut version of what appears within the brackets, Nagel (p.150) speaks more portentously of reasons that "can be recognized and *accepted* from the outside."

14 Ibid., p.160.

15 Ibid.

16 Ibid., p.139.

17 Ibid., p.160

18 Ibid., p.161.

19 Moreover, it is implausible to imagine, as Nagel does, that an agent who lacked or lost the conception of himself would form the sophisticated judgment, "*This experience* ought not to go on, *whoever* is having it." Ibid., p.161.

20 David Gauthier, *Morals by Agreement* (Oxford: Clarendon Press, 1986), p.47.

21 J. S. Mill, *Utilitarianism* (Indianapolis: Bobbs-Merrill, 1957), pp.44–5.

22 Loren Lomasky, *Persons, Rights and the Moral Community* (New York: Oxford University Press, 1987), p.231. The argument in this and the next several paragraphs and, especially, the idea of a choice between satisfying and extinguishing desires, draws on ibid., pp.229–37. See also Lomasky's unpublished "Rational Choice, Rational Choosers" (Bowling Green State University, 1990).

23 Gauthier, *Morals by Agreement*, p.47. It would probably be better for Gauthier to speak of "final" or "ultimate" value than of "intrinsic" value.

24 Gauthier, *Morals by Agreement*, p.56.

25 A pervasive correlation between the objects of an agent's core affections and components of his good may, nevertheless, exist because agents may desire what they sense to be their good and a given agent's incapacity to desire some end disqualifies it from being among that agent's goods.

26 Another possibility, not to be explored here, is that value is agent-neutral (or, at least, not agent-relative) while reasons of value for action remain agent-relative. Knowledge is good; knowledge as such is not an agent-relative value. But only those achievements of knowledge that realize the powers and/or aspirations of A_1 provide A_1 with reason to act.

27 Joel Feinberg, "The Nature and Value of Rights," *Journal of Value Inquiry* 4 (1970): 252.

28 Nagel, *View from Nowhere*, p.140.

29 Of course, the departure from solipsism will lead to the discovery or the formation of particular shared values with certain other individuals.

12

Agent-relativity – the very idea

JONATHAN DANCY

What exactly is being asserted by those who claim (and denied by those who deny) that there are agent-relative reasons? I motivate the idea of an agent-relative reason in the following way. I have a personal project, which is to write a good book on ethics. This is very important to me; it informs and gives sense to a central decade of my life. But I know that in some sense it does not matter much whether I succeed or fail. The world will not be much the richer for my success, nor much the poorer for my failure. It is hard to express this point uncontentiously, but there is enormous pressure to say something like "it doesn't *really* matter" or "it doesn't *objectively* matter" whether I succeed or fail. But it matters very much to me. We might try to say there is great value for me if I succeed, but it is not really important whether I succeed or not. Now the point here is that I know both these things. I know that it matters to me very much and that it doesn't really matter as much as it matters to me. Neither of these things is hidden from me. I have a perfectly clear idea of how much it really matters, and another perfectly clear idea of how much it matters to me. Neither idea is a distortion of the other. I am not engaged here in special pleading or in cooking the books to suit myself. Of course, there is a tension in my position. But it is not the tension associated with contradiction. I am not making the mistake of thinking that my success matters a lot and only a little. I simply recognize that my success does not matter as much as it matters to me. (So 'matters to me' is not to be understood as 'believed by me to matter'.) In a way this is merely a consequence of the recognition that *I* don't matter much.[1] But we shouldn't therefore assume that I am somehow wrong to find success in my project important.

I think everyone who has a personal project will feel this tension. What is more, it is a tension that remains even when I recognize that it does matter ("objectively," "really") whether those who have projects succeed in them. Each such success is of value, but its value is as nothing compared to the value to the person whose project it is. So even if I

add the value of someone (me in this case) succeeding in a centra
personal project to that of the publication of a good book on ethics (i
this case, mine), I don't escape the tension between that limited valu
and the value there is to me. But this tension is one that I can live with
It doesn't undermine the wholeness or integrity of my life, in the sens
that I can cope with it and not be torn apart by it. It does demand car
in the juggling of demands on my time and energy and my right to ignor
those demands on occasion to pursue my own project.

This sense that there can be a tension in the situation that does no
derive from self-contradiction or from confusion is, I think, the leadin
thought in the construction of agent-relative value.[2] We are to use th
notion of agent-relative value to describe that situation as a tensio
between agent-relative and agent-neutral value, both of which are clearl
present to the agent and to others. It is to preserve this thought that
have been trying to stress the importance of not assuming from th
outset that agent-relative value is at best a distortion of agent-neutra
value – a justified distortion, perhaps, but still a distortion. If we d
start with that assumption we have simply begged the question agains
the picture that in my view drives the conception of agent-relativity.

I have been making this initial case in favor of agent-relativity b
appeal to only one class of potential agent-relative reasons, those o
autonomy (i.e., those stemming from my right to pursue personal proj
ects and in general build my own life). We can, however, immediatel
see that the point is not restricted to those. Reasons of supererogatio
(i.e., those which justify my failing to make a sacrifice that would involv
great personal cost) seem likely to fit the pattern as well.[3] I may b
perfectly well aware that the cost to myself does not matter as much a
it matters to me, without thinking of either of these thoughts a
misconceived.

I take this as my starting point in trying to build up a philosophica
account of the agent-relative.

What is it for a reason to be agent-relative? This is Nagel's account

If a reason can be given a general form which does not include an essentia
reference to the person who has it, it is an *agent-neutral* reason. For example
if it is a reason for anyone to do or want something that it would reduce th
amount of wretchedness in the world, then that is an agent-neutral reason. I
on the other hand the general form of a reason does include an essential referenc
to the person who has it, it is an *agent-relative* reason. For example, if it is
reason for anyone to do or want something that it would be in *his* interest, the
that is a relative reason.[4]

I have four comments to make on this definition of the agent-relative
First, there is a danger that on Nagel's account all Humean reason

(i.e., all complete reasons for action that consist of Humean combinations of beliefs and desires, conceived as Hume conceives them) will be agent-relative. This would mean that for Nagel the question whether there are any agent-neutral reasons would revolve around the truth or falsehood of a Humean theory of motivation. However, this is perhaps only a threat for an extreme version of Humeanism that asserts that *all* reasons are or include desires. A weaker version might hold that some beliefs are reasons too; they *become* reasons when associated with a suitable desire. And if some beliefs are reasons, Humeans can perhaps accept the existence of agent-neutral reasons, namely the beliefs. Humeans can do this if they allow that the fact that I believe it to be sunny need not be among my reasons for putting on my hat when I put it on because of the sun; it is *its being sunny* (i.e., *what* I believe, not my believing it) that is my reason. A desire is an agent-relative reason because it is *my desire not to get burnt* that is (another part of my complete) reason for putting on the hat. This latter reason does contain an essential reference to me in the way that the belief-reason does not.

One might say, then, that some forms of Humeanism can find room for both agent-relative and agent-neutral reasons. Or one might (more plausibly, in my view) deny this on the grounds that to suppose a mere fact can be a reason is to move away from Humean theories altogether. But whichever view one takes on this point, it is surely very odd to find Nagel holding that it is the agent-relative reasons that are most securely in place, and that we are having to work hard to establish even the possibility of agent-neutral ones.[5] It is true that Nagel's view that there are non-Humean forms of motivation puts him in a position to say there are agent-neutral reasons. But we have surely already moved miles away from the topic we were originally intending to discuss. The question whether some beliefs are reasons and if so whether they count as agent-neutral ones is nowhere near questions about the implicit tension between the agent-relative and the agent-neutral that Nagel is really wanting to talk about. This leads me to suspect that his official characterization of the agent-relative leaves something to be desired; it has led us off on a tangent.

Second, that characterization begs an important question, namely whether one can have an agent-relative reason for promoting a state of affairs that is not specified essentially by reference to oneself. This matters because not all personal projects are ones whose success conditions are bound up with one's own contribution. For instance, my project might be that a cure for AIDS be found, not particularly that I find it or that my efforts contribute to its being found. Of course, my having this project means that I work toward the finding of a cure, either in the lab or by raising funds or whatever. But it does not mean that I shall be disappointed (at least not with respect to my project) if someone else finds the cure in a way to which my own efforts did not in fact contribute at all. Of course, this project is in another sense impersonal, since the project is not defined with reference to myself. But it may still be a personal project in the sense we are discussing here, since it is one that is central to and gives point to much of my life.

Admittedly, I could have had the project of finding the cure or at least of being involved in the finding of the cure. But in my view that would just have been a different project, and impersonal personal projects of the sort I think possible are ones we should find room for. They are certainly more selfless than other projects. But that they are distinct is surely shown by the fact that a life that revolves around the search for a cure for AIDS may be considered well spent by the searcher, while a person whose central project in life is not that she search for a cure but that a cure be found may wonder whether her efforts were well spent if she dies when the cure is still unknown. And Nagel's account of agent-relativity rules these out by definition. This is a second defect.

It would be wrong to reply here that reasons that stem from personal projects are agent-relative because, even where my project is not defined by reference to myself, the reasons that it generates will be. One might think this because one feels that my basic reason for spending time and energy on seeking a cure for AIDS is *that this is my project,* a reason that clearly contains essential reference to myself. So although I might spend money on attending a conference on AIDS in Reykjavik that could be "better" spent on famine relief, the reason that justifies this, if any does, will be an agent-relative one in Nagel's sense. I want to suggest, however, that this move introduces "one thought too many," to use Bernard Williams's helpful phrase. My reason for attending the conference is that this makes it more probable that I (or maybe someone else) will find the cure for AIDS. This could only be a nonconsequentialist reason for me if I have a personal project of the relevant sort, but this does not mean that my having that project is here playing the role of a reason – it merely allows something else to stand as a reason.

The last point I want to make about Nagel's approach is dependent on a later remark of his:

Ethics is concerned not only with what should happen, but also independently with what people should or may *do.* Neutral reasons underlie the former; but relative reasons can affect the latter.[6]

First, it is odd to say that ethics is concerned with what should happen almost as if there are events that ought to take place, it being wrong or them not to. There are no such events, as Nagel himself suggests elsewhere.[7] Ethics is concerned with actions and agents; these are the only objects capable of bearing moral properties. Second, it cannot be right to say that neutral reasons concern what should happen in any sense in which that can be contrasted with what people should do. We can with some strain make sense of this in some of the cases that Nagel discusses, for instance my ascribing more value to my caring for my children than to their being cared for. But elsewhere the tension between reasons that demand me to make a sacrifice (the agent-neutral ones) and those that may ground an option to refrain (the agent-relative) is not usefully conceived as a tension between events that ought to happen and actions that we are or are not permitted to do.

As is often the case with Nagel's work, then, I applaud the intention but feel that things have gone wrong somewhere. Now the defects I discern in his specific account of the difference between agent-relative and agent-neutral reasons should be put in the context of his account of objectivity. And I want to argue briefly that his conception of objectivity actually makes it harder for him to give a convincing defense of agent-relativity (which is, after all, what is needed). He takes it that agent-neutral reasons are more objective than agent-relative ones, and by this he means that their force is visible from points of view that have less in common with our own, that share fewer of our specific peculiarities.[8] This approach generates three thoughts, all of which are in my view probably wrong.

The first is that the right criterion of objectivity is whether the force of a reason can be recognized by creatures relevantly different from ourselves – the more different the creatures, the more objective the reason. I concede that this is a criterion that one *could* apply to reasons, though of course it is a test that eventually all reasons will fail. But in asking which of my reasons are objective, why should I be interested in whether creatures relevantly different from myself can see their force? Surely a better test of my reasons is whether their force survives critical reflection on the relation between the perspective from which I take them as reasons and the world that I view from that perspective. This is a different test.[9]

Second, the agent-relative reasons that are to be seen as more the products of our own perspective are in danger of counting therefore as mere appearances. In Nagel's conception of the progress toward a more objective view, what remains for the objective view is not what originally appeared, but merely the fact that there are such (mere) appearances. In the case of the agent-relative reasons that are left behind, this amounts to the recognition that people care about this sort of thing (their own skins, perhaps), but this concern is effectively invalidated by being treated as analogous to an appearance. This is hardly the way to move if we want to undermine the pretensions of consequentialism, for we will already have admitted that the reasons that we offer as conflicting with consequentialist reasons are mere appearance. This is just what the consequentialist wants us to say.

Third, each of us, in taking the more objective view, is moving away from the subjective view from which the force of agent-relative reasons can be clearly seen. In fact, Nagel's whole apparatus has the effect of establishing that there can be no viewpoint from which the force of both sorts of reasons can be seen for what they are. If we see one clearly, we are not in the best position to see the other. But this is already to abandon what I see as a central plank in agent-relativism, namely the thought that neither sort of reason is a distortion of the other. The two sorts of reasons exist in tension, but a clear view of the agent-relative ones does not require special pleading or any other sort of messing about with the agent-neutral ones. For one can be perfectly well aware of both. The structure of Nagel's position requires him to deny this, and I think that this makes it much harder for him to mount a satisfying defense of agent-relativity. It puts unnecessary weapons in the hands of the opposition – weapons they will not be slow to use.[10] So I take this to be much the worst presupposition in Nagel's picture.

I now turn to Derek Parfit's account of agent-relativity, to which Nagel refers and which I think he takes himself to be elaborating. Parfit's version, however, raises new problems. He holds that a *theory* is agent-neutral if it gives to all agents common moral aims; it is agent-relative if it gives different agents different aims.[11] (Presumably, a theory may in these terms be mixed.) This definition, which is focused on the agent-relativity of a theory rather than that of a particular reason, has at least the merit of seeing that the event/action distinction cuts across the agent-relative/agent-neutral one. But the expression carrying the weight here is unfortunately vague, in a way that it is hard to remedy. To see this, we may notice that an agent-neutral theory may recommend as a common aim for all that children should be cared for by their parents. Even those who have no children may be enjoined here to do what they can to promote home care of children, as it were. (A childless finance minister might do this by increasing tax allowances for those who care for their own children.) An agent-relative theory might, however, require parents to care for their own children. Here the idea is that those who are parents are required to care for their own children, while those who are not parents are not required to do anything; we are dealing with an agent-relative requirement, since it gives those who are parents an aim that does not apply to those who are not. This distinction looks clear enough. But I think it will eventually collapse. Suppose we have:

Px: x is a parent
Rp: it is required that p
Cx: x cares for x's children.

Now there is a tripartite distinction between:

1. (x) (Px → R[Cx]),
2. (x) R(Px → Cx), and
3. R(x) (Px → Cx).

The first of these issues no command to those who are not parents. The command that is here is one that it is impossible for the childless to disobey or obey. This is genuine agent-relativity (for Parfit). The second is a command that those who are not parents automatically obey (I don't think this is just because we have here a material conditional made true by the falsity of its antecedent). It requires of all equally that *if they are parents* they care for their children. The third is the one that those childless people who promote child care by parents are obeying. Both (2) and (3) impose common aims on all, while (1) imposes aims on some that it does not impose on others. So (1) is the candidate agent-relative requirement, while (2) and (3) are both agent-neutral, on Parfit's definition.

The question then arises whether there is any interesting difference between (1) and (2). If there is no interesting difference here, every agent-relative requirement can be mirrored by an agent-neutral one – in fact, the difference between the agent-relative and the agent-neutral would have been shown to be insignificant. Crucially, it does not seem to be the case that a parent could claim to be obeying (2) by promoting child care by parents if he did this at the cost of caring for his own children. One is obeying (3) if one acts in this way, but not (2). So long as one is not a parent, every action one does is in accordance with (2). Somebody might choose not to become a parent in order not to be in danger of violating (2). But the same is true of (1). So there seems to be no relevant distinction between (1) and (2), even though one is on Parfit's definition agent-neutral and the other is agent-relative. All we need is a distinction between two agent-neutral requirements, (2) and (3).

The point of this is that if a theory that gives everyone the same aim (2) is effectively equivalent to one that does not (1), then the distinction between the agent-relative and the agent-neutral cannot be the same as that between theories that give common aims and those that do not, unless the agent-relative/agent-neutral distinction turns out to be of no significance. This result might please Parfit, but it is of no comfort to those who want to leave it open in the *definition* of the agent-relative whether an agent-relative requirement or option can be captured agent-neutrally.

We might hope to improve matters by looking more closely at the distinction between common and different aims. In a sense an agent-relative theory that includes agent-relative constraints on harming will give all agents a common aim, namely, not to break the constraints.[12] In another sense it gives us all different aims, since we are all jostling not to be the one who breaks them; if someone has to break them, I should strive that it not be me but you that does it. This might mean that a theory which allows (or even encourages) moral competition of this sort is to be seen as agent-relative, while agent-neutral theories will specify aims, constraints, and options all of which can be equally well recognized and acted on at once. On agent-neutral theories, we should all be able to rub moral shoulders without friction. But again there is something peculiar about the position we have got ourselves into here. We no longer seem to be anywhere near the distinction we were originally trying to capture. It would be odd to argue that agent-neutral theories can allow constraints and options, so long as they can all be exercised simultaneously. The clash between the agent-neutral and constraints or options does not lie here, but in the thought that options and constraints are in their very nature agent-relative.

So I conclude that the pioneering efforts of Parfit and Nagel are so far unsuccessful.[13] What is going on is that there is a common intuition here, which in various ways people are trying to capture, but not yet very successfully. Some are trying to capture it so as to argue that there are no agent-relative reasons, others for the opposite purpose. But the danger is that with an unsatisfactory understanding of the crucial distinction, any eventual result in favor of or against agent-relativity will be unstable. This is particularly true of the next account of agent-relativity that I will look at, namely that of Amartya Sen.[14]

Sen's influential account is designed to show that the existence of agent-relative reasons need constitute no awkwardness for consequentialism. He argues that there is agent-relativity, but that every relevant fact can be captured within an extended but still consequentialist framework. This is initially extremely improbable, to my mind; but perhaps one ought not to prejudge such matters.

Sen's discussion is in terms of values rather than of reasons. He starts by suggesting that an agent *does* things and also *views* actions and outcomes. So there is such a thing as the neutrality of a doer and the

ieutrality of a viewer, and then there will be the combination of the
wo when one views oneself as a doer. These neutralities are expressed
n the following way:[15]

Doer-neutrality (DN): $\Diamond$(A perm fA) $\leftrightarrow$ $\Diamond$(A perm fB)
Viewer-neutrality (VN): $\Diamond$(A perm fA) $\leftrightarrow$ $\Diamond$(B perm fA)
Self-evaluation neutrality (SEN): $\Diamond$(A perm fA) $\leftrightarrow$
$\Diamond$(B perm fB)

Oddly, Sen says almost nothing to defend this way of capturing what
ie is thinking of as neutrality, though everything in his analysis depends
on these formulae and there is more than one problem with them. First,
.he use of the double arrow here loses the thought that if it doesn't
matter who does the action (as in doer-neutrality) the value of the action
.hould be the same whoever is the agent. All that Sen's formulation
illows us to capture is the idea that if one action is permissible, so is
he other. I therefore think it would be better to run Sen's distinctions
n terms of an identity of value, thus:

DN: V(A perm fA) $=$ V(A perm fB)[16]
VN: V(A perm fA) $=$ V(B perm fA)
SEN: V(A perm fA) $=$ V(B perm fB)

Of these three theses any two entail the third. Given this way of
expressing Sen's distinctions, we have three corresponding relativity
:heses:

DR: V(A perm fA) $\neq$ V(A perm fB)
VR: V(A perm fA) $\neq$ V(B perm fA)
SER: V(A perm fA) $\neq$ V(B perm fB)

Each of these theses is equivalent to a disjunction:

DR: $(V[$A perm fA$] < V[$A perm fB$]) \vee (V[$A perm fA$] > V[$A perm fB$])$
VR: $(V[$A perm fA$] < V[$B perm fA$]) \vee (V[$A perm fA$] > V[$B perm fA$])$
SER: $(V[$A perm fA$] < V[$B perm fB$]) \vee (V[$A perm fA$] > V[$B perm fB$])$

There is still something wrong with the picture we are getting. The
agent-relativist is represented as denying what the agent-neutralist is
asserting. What is wrong with this is not that their positions are compatible; presumably they are not. Rather each is represented as holding
that where there is value of one sort there cannot also be value of the
other. Maybe the neutralist does hold this, but the relativist does not –

at least, not if trying to capture the intuitions with which I began this paper. Any suggestion to the contrary can only be an imposition of the consequentialist assumption that agent-relative value is a sort of distor-´ tion of agent-neutral value, so that they cannot both exist side by side. So I don't see how it can be right to start by trying to capture everything the agent-relativist wants to say using only agent-neutral value. This cannot be a fair starting point, even if we might end up there in the end; and Sen's unconscious assumption that it is fair must partly explain his conclusion that a suitably modified consequentialism can capture everything that the agent-relativist wishes to say. In my view, many agent-relativists take themselves to be describing an additional sort of value, and we completely lose this thought if we insist on describing everything using the neutralist's V. So as well as '$V(f\mathrm{A})$' standing for the value of A's doing f, we need a symbol '$V^a(f\mathrm{A})$' to stand for the (agent-relative) value for A of A's doing f. Of course we have so far given no interpretation for this symbol. We are still in the business of trying to find out what we are supposed to be looking for. Using this symbol we get:

DR: $(V^a[\mathrm{A \ perm} \ f\mathrm{A}] < V^a[\mathrm{A \ perm} \ f\mathrm{B}]) \ \mathrm{v} \ (V^a[\mathrm{A \ perm} \ f\mathrm{A}] > V^a[\mathrm{A \ perm} \ f\mathrm{B}])$

VR: $(V^a[\mathrm{A \ perm} \ f\mathrm{A}] < V^a[\mathrm{B \ perm} \ f\mathrm{A}]) \ \mathrm{v} \ (V^a[\mathrm{A \ perm} \ f\mathrm{A}] > V^a[\mathrm{B \ perm} \ f\mathrm{A}])$

SER: $(V^a[\mathrm{A \ perm} \ f\mathrm{A}] < V^a[\mathrm{B \ perm} \ f\mathrm{B}]) \ \mathrm{v} \ (V^a[\mathrm{A \ perm} \ f\mathrm{A}] > V^a[\mathrm{B \ perm} \ f\mathrm{B}])$

There remain two objectionable elements in this account, which stem from the fact that it sees all agent-relative value as concerned centrally with the contrast between different permitted actions. I would not wish to accept this as a starting point, neither the focus on actions nor the focus on permissions. With respect to action, I want to leave room for the idea that there can be agent-relative value in the completion of a project that is the agent's project but to whose completion he does not contribute. I have said a little about this above; if there are such cases their structure will be this: $V^a(p) \neq V(p)$. (Or perhaps better would be $-[V^a(p) \approx V(p)]$, if we feel that this assertion of lack of identity makes little sense, perhaps on the grounds that agent-relative and agent-neutral values are not fully commensurable.) The second objectionable element is the assumption that permissions are not distinctive acts with their own values. Sen is relying here on the common phrase 'I permitted myself'; this sort of permission may be morally indistinguishable from the act permitted, but most permissions are not like this. The permission may be right when the act permitted is wrong, and vice versa.

In fact with most of the examples the importance of permissions is negligible. With the claim that I have a reason to care for my children myself and less reason for you to care for yours, the structure is $V^a(f\text{A})$ > $V^a(f\text{B})$. One can sloppily contrast the value of my doing it with the value of my letting you do it, but the real contrast is between the value of my doing it and the value of your doing it, with both of these values being my agent-relative values. In the case of deontological constraints, where I have a reason not to twist a child's arm myself that does not convert into as strong a reason to stop you from doing so, the structure is again $V^a(f\text{A}) > V^a(f\text{B})$, and the importance, if any, of permissions is a distraction. Where reasons of autonomy give me a reason that I do the action, again we have $V^a(f\text{A}) > V^a(f\text{B})$. So there is some sort of pattern emerging here. Permissions only enter the field substantially when we come to consider tolerance. We might want to say that the value of my letting you do it is greater than the value of your doing it, especially if I can be right to let you do a wrong action. But I don't think we can assume so easily that the agent-neutralist cannot capture this sort of thought in his own terms. So though there may be a relation between the value of tolerance and that of permissions, I doubt that the whole story of tolerance will hinge on that.[17]

One should also notice that the account of agent-neutral value is spoiled by Sen's focus on permissions. Surely any consequentialist will want to admit that where the action $f\text{A}$ is heroic, we have $V(f\text{A})$ = $V(\text{A perm } f\text{A}) > V(\text{B perm } f\text{A})$. Equally, wherever B has a strong desire to do an action that A has little interest in, we surely get $V(f\text{A}) <$ $V(f\text{B})$, or $V(\text{A perm } f\text{A}) < V(\text{A perm } f\text{B})$, in a way that I think most neutralists would wish to allow. So neutralists need not assert $V(f\text{A})$ = $V(f\text{B})$ = $V(\text{A perm } f\text{A})$ = $V(\text{A perm } f\text{B})$. The whole concentration on permission, despite the potential link with tolerance, seems to me to be a mistake.

So it seems at the moment that the interesting cases are those where $V^a(f\text{A}) \neq V^a(f\text{B})$. Now normally $V^a(f\text{B}) = V(f\text{B})$; this will be so except in the special cases where A has a project that it would help if B were to do f. Otherwise $V^a(f\text{B})$ is nothing special; it is just $V(f\text{B})$ – the neutral value of B's caring for his children. But this neutral value is equally well exemplified in A's caring for *his* children. So what we should be contrasting here is the agent-relative value for A of A's caring for his children with the value of those (or any other) children being cared for by their father – A for his, B for his, and so on. This is a case where $V^a(p) \neq V(p)$.

It is possible here to confuse oneself and get stuck with the thought that the center of the problem lies with cases where $V^a(f\text{A}) \neq V^a(f\text{B})$.

But the fact that $V^a(fA) \neq V^a(fB)$ only serves to show that the valu‹ A ascribes to B's doing f is a value A can find equally in *his* doing f That value is agent-neutral value. So the real underlying contrast ⁚ between $V^a(fA)$ and $V(fA)$, or, more generally, between $V^a(p)$ an‹ $V(p)$. We are going to find this structure wherever p is among A'₂ projects, and it is especially striking when it is not among A's project‹ that p become true as a result of A's efforts.

So it seems as if the general shape of the agent-relativist's claim i₂ that there can be cases where $V^a(p) \neq V(p)$. But there is no built-i‹ temptation to suppose that in such a case A will be unable to recogniz‹ three things:

1. $V(p)$
2. $V^a(p)$
3. that $V^a(p) \neq V(p)$.

All of these things may be clear to A. And this is just what one shoulᵈ expect if the way in which I tried to motivate the idea of an agent relative reason is anywhere near the mark. Putting the matter in term₂ now of reasons of autonomy, I can accept the existence of a gap o⁚ tension between the size or strength of my agent-relative reasons an‹ the size or strength of any recognizable agent-neutral reason. But thi₂ gap need not disconcert me. I can live with it, and my recognizing ⁚ need not tear me apart. I can still find my own projects important, whil‹ recognizing that they are not agent-neutrally important.

So the right place to look for an understanding of agent-relative valu‹ is to look for discrepancies between two assessments of the one action both made by the agent. We are not to look directly for discrepancie₂ between evaluations made by the agent and by an onlooker, nor fo₂ discrepancies between the agent's evaluation of the action as done b𝐲 him and as done by another. Each can recognize the agent-relative value₂ of others; we are not restricted to noticing neutral values and our ow₂ agent-relative ones. So we can accept the reluctance of others to mak‹ sacrifices, since we discern the structure of values that supports this This shows that an attempt to establish the existence of the agent-relative is not merely an exercise in special pleading on one's own behalf. Rea‐ sons like those that protect me protect all equally, without being fo₂ that reason agent-neutral.

Instead the agent-relativist is committed to making sense of the thought that it can be important to me that this should work out right‚ though of course I know it doesn't really matter so much whether i₂ does. This pattern repeats in all the standard examples. My project'₂ being achieved may have some agent-neutral value, but it is of specia‌

importance to me. My project being achieved by me may have some agent-neutral value, but it is of special importance to me. My not doing a wrong (deontological constraint) has agent-neutral value, but it is of special importance to me. And so on. The question whether value of this type can exist is not even addressed by Sen.[18]

One significant consequence of this approach is that it raises the question whether reasons of partiality are indeed the agent-relative reasons they are often claimed to be. It seems to me possible that in these cases we do not find the structure that I am claiming to be central to the agent-relative, namely a discrepancy between two assessments both made by the agent. A father does not recognize that it matters more to him that he should care for his child than it "really" matters that he should do so. If this is right, the values here are agent-neutral. And this would create an interesting contrast between my approach and Kagan's. Kagan's consequentialist picture leads him to take the most stubborn case of a putative agent-relative value to be that associated with love and friendship, whereas on my approach[19] that is the most dubious of all the examples I have considered.

Kagan comes to focus on the value of love in the following way.[20] Defenders of ordinary morality are trying to establish the existence of options and constraints – agent-relative reasons, in fact. But in Kagan's view they are doing this while agreeing that there is a *pro tanto* reason to promote the good (the PTR).[21] So to establish that the PTR is not always overriding, it is necessary to discover a good or value: (1) that we are, after reflection, unwilling to deny or dismiss as morally illegitimate; (2) that could not be adequately appreciated from an objective point of view, because of the impartiality of that point of view; and (3) for the recognition of which a disproportionate concern with one's own interest is required.[22]

I think we should quietly forget the third of these, and be wary of the second because of the notion of objectivity that it is using. Still, Kagan considers many putative examples of this sort of agent-relative value, and rules them out in a standardly hard-nosed consequentialist way. For instance, it is nice for agents to have projects such as playing the flute or improving their backhand or attending the whole of the Ring Cycle in Bayreuth. But these projects do not go to maximize utility, and in the present state of the world there are more important things to be done. Of course a life without projects would be dull and pointless. But there is no consequentialist ban on projects. There is one project that is not only permitted but required, namely The Great Project. Pursuit of that project may require of us many sacrifices. We must be prepared to give our goods to those in need until the loss to us is as

great as the gain to them, or until our loss impairs our ability to earn
more to give. But the greatness of the sacrifice is another feature of the
present sorry state of the world, and of the unwillingness of others to
do their share. For if all were to give, each would have to give far less.
In a perfect world where all did their duty, doing one's duty would be
much less onerous, partly no doubt because the burden would be shared,
but more importantly because it would be a lesser burden for each.

The final example of a putative agent-relative value that Kagan considers is that of love or friendship. He is more sympathetic to the idea
that the value of love is the sort of value that the agent-relativist is
looking for. It is very plausible here to suggest that to love someone
requires a willingness, even a keenness, to treat that person with partial
favor. To want to treat all impartially is to love nobody. But love is an
important, perhaps a vital aspect of living a reasonable life. A world
without love would be a world that lacks something of genuine value –
something whose importance we are not, after reflection, unwilling to
deny or dismiss as morally illegitimate. But if all values were objective
and so impartial, love would be valueless. So there is at least one value
that is not objective.

Kagan's reply to this is that willingness to favor is not an essential
part of love, and is presumably therefore to be thought of as a form of
moral weakness. For him, love can be impartial – and should be, therefore. I find this reply incredibly weak. I think that the only case where
friendship and impartiality are compatible is the unusual case where one
is friends with everyone in the world. There are ethics that require this
of us (who is my neighbor?), but surely this is just because of the
partiality of love that we circumvent by loving all equally. So if the
matter is to be put in Kagan's terms, I think that the agent-relativist
will have the better of it.[23] But my main point is not to prove the existence
of agent-relative reasons, but to contrast Kagan's general approach with
the one I am trying to recommend. He focuses on reasons of partiality
whereas I am tempted to think that these are not agent-relative reasons
at all.

The main purpose of this essay has been to support a view of what
an agent-relative reason would look like if we found one, and to argue
that no extant account of the area manages to focus our attention in the
right place. Kagan takes it that the agent-relative is necessarily a distortion of the objective truth. Nagel strives earnestly to avoid saying
this, but fails. Parfit shares the right intuitions, but his attempt to characterize them is at best far too vague.[24] One might, however, ask what
I have put in place of their suggestions so far. I have offered no definition
of an agent-relative reason or value, but only held that agent-relative

lue occurs when agents rightly value the same thing in more than one
ay. As far as this goes, what is to make either sort of value *agent-*
lative? We have it that it is *qua* agents that they are doing the valuing,
t not yet that the values discovered by the valuings are in any sense
lative to the agents who discover them. On this point both Parfit and Nagel seem to do better. The reasons
at for Nagel are agent-relative are those which contain essential ref-
ence to the agent. The theories that for Parfit are agent-relative are
ose which ascribe different aims to different agents. The sense in which
mething exists only relative to the agent is clear in these views. But
I have suggested so far is that there are reasons or values that exist
tension with the (neutral) reasons or values that consequentialism
lows. Whether these reasons or values are in any significant sense
gent-relative has yet to be determined. The way it will be determined,
f course, will be by discovering that a separable group of the noncon-
quentialist reasons consists in some (not necessarily always the same)
nportant relation to the agent. This approach has the virtue of leaving
xplicit room for neutral reasons that are not consequentialist.[25]

What we may expect to discover, then, is that reasons of superero-
ation and reasons of autonomy are driven by considerations of the cost
the agent. To make the point in the case of supererogation, I favor
e view that a budding hero is justified in counting the cost of sacrifice
vice, once as a cost to someone or other and once as a cost to herself.
he question who it is to be that will pay the cost places that cost in a
ew light when the answer is "me." Here there is a clear relation to
e agent at center stage, which will justify our calling the relevant
asons "agent-relative." In the case of constraints, it is worth at least
nsidering the possibility of a similar move, which sees the reasons that
re in tension with consequentialist ones as grounded in thoughts of a
oral cost to the agent. Now is not the place to attempt to work this
ove out in full, but if anything like it can be got to run we will have
own why it is right to think of constraints as agent-relative reasons.
o I prefer to take the matter in two stages. First I try to suggest that
ere are nonconsequentialist reasons. Second I suggest senses in which
most of) these reasons are agent-relative. All those which are agent-
lative are cases where we can expect to find the common structure we
scerned above, namely that $V^a(p) \neq V(p)$.

Notes

1 The sense that I am unimportant but that my whole world is *my* world is
part of what Nagel has been trying valiantly to bring out in his contrast

between more and less objective points of view. I applaud his efforts her
even though, as I argue in J. Dancy, "Contemplating One's Nagel," *Ph*
osophical Books 29 (1988):1–16, I think them ultimately confused.

2 I do not expect all to agree with this remark. People will diverge on bo
sides. Shelly Kagan suggested to me in conversation that my idea of
tension between how much something matters and how much it matte
to me is interesting, but is just a different idea from any that Nagel wish
to discuss under the topic of agent-relative reasons. On the other sid
Philippa Foot and Stephen Darwall will be tempted to question the po
sibility of agent-neutral reasons, pursuing the idea that all reasons are
some sense agent-relative. If this idea were correct, there might be tension
but not the tension that I take myself to be describing; this would depen
on what is meant by 'agent-relative'. See, e.g., Philippa Foot, "Moralit
Action and Outcome," in T. Honderich, ed., *Morality and Objectivity:*
Tribute to J. L. Mackie (London: Routledge and Kegan Paul, 1985), pp. 2.
38; Foot, "Utilitarianism and the Virtues," *Mind* 94 (1985): 196–20
reprinted with some changes in S. Scheffler, ed., *Consequentialism and I*
Critics (Oxford: Clarendon Press, 1988), pp. 224–42; and S. Darwa
"Agent-centred Restrictions from the Inside Out," *Philosophical Stud*
50 (1986): 291–319.

3 Central discussions of reasons of autonomy include Bernard Williams
contribution to J. J. C. Smart and B. A. O. Williams, *Utilitarianism, F*
and Against (Cambridge: Cambridge University Press, 1973); B. A. C
Williams, "Utilitarianism and Moral Self-Indulgence," in H. D. Lewi
ed., *Contemporary British Philosophy,* 4th series (London: Allen and U
win, 1976), reprinted in Williams, *Moral Luck* (Cambridge: Cambrid
University Press, 1981); S. Scheffler, *The Rejection of Consequentialisn*
A Philosophical Investigation of the Considerations Underlying Rival Mor
Conceptions (Oxford: Clarendon Press, 1982); M. Slote, *Common-sen*
Morality and Consequentialism (London: Routledge and Kegan Paul, 1985
chs. 1–2; Thomas Nagel, *The View from Nowhere* (New York: Oxfoi
University Press, 1986), ch. 9; and S. Kagan, *The Limits of Moral*
(Oxford: Clarendon Press, 1989). For reasons of supererogation, see
O. Urmson, "Saints and Heroes," in A. I. Melden, ed., *Essays in Mor*
Philosophy (Seattle: University of Washington Press, 1958), pp. 198–21
J. Raz, "Permissions and Supererogation," *American Philosophical Qua*
terly 12 (1975): 161–8; Nagel, *View from Nowhere,* pp. 200ff; and Kaga
Limits of Morality. Reasons of these two sorts still constitute only oi
class of agent-relative reasons; they ground *options* not to do the actic
that would most promote the good. If there are such reasons, I have tl
option to spend money and resources on my project that could be "bette
spent on famine relief, and I have the option not to run myself into ¿
early grave in my efforts to rectify systematic social injustice. There
another putative class of agent-relative reasons, which ground *constrain*
on my freedom to do what would most promote the good. In this ess

I do not really discuss this second class of reasons at all. It is of course an open question whether what one says about the options will fit what one wants to say about the constraints.

4 Nagel, *View from Nowhere*, pp. 152–3.

5 Of course, some people would not find it odd that the agent-relative should be most securely in place; see my reference to Foot and Darwall in note 2. My point is merely that this is not what one would expect from reading Nagel's book, nor from the general tenor of the discussion of the agent-relative in the literature stemming from Scheffler, *Rejection of Consequentialism*. See for instance Slote, *Common-sense Morality*, and Kagan, *Limits of Morality*. It will be clear that my own view is that we need a theory that finds equal room for agent-relative and for agent-neutral, neither being preeminent. But I reject the consequentialist account of agent-neutral reasons.

6 Nagel, *View from Nowhere*, p. 165.

7 See Thomas Nagel, "Moral Luck," *Proceedings of the Aristotelian Society*, Supplementary Volume 50 (1976), reprinted in Nagel, *Mortal Questions* (Cambridge: Cambridge University Press, 1979), pp. 24–38.

8 In "Contemplating One's Nagel," I argue that he also runs a quite different and better conception of objectivity; but the one that I refer to in the text is the dominant one.

9 This test is the different and better conception of the objective that, as I argue in "Contemplating One's Nagel," Nagel fails to distinguish from the first.

10 A good example is Kagan's talk of distortion and bias and giving disproportionate weight to one's own interest; see Kagan, *Limits of Morality*, p. 258.

11 See Derek Parfit, *Reasons and Persons* (Oxford: Clarendon Press, 1984), pp. 54–5.

12 Agent-relative constraints occur where an agent has a reason not to do an action (e.g., twist a child's arm) over and above any reason why the action should not be done (why the arm should not be twisted). If the child's arm has got to be twisted (for the sake of some greater good, say), it is better for me that you should do it than that I should. Scheffler (*Rejection of Consequentialism*) calls this a restriction. Sometimes constraints prevent us from doing an action that would in some sense be for the best, e.g., killing an innocent being to save the lives of two others.

13 It would be a mistake to think that all I have shown is that the ways in which Nagel and Parfit run their distinction fail to serve the purposes of *my* way of approaching the nature of the agent-relative. One might make this claim if one thought that my way of motivating the agent-relative/agent-neutral distinction is just different from Nagel's, say (cf. Kagan's remark, reported in note 2). But in fact almost all my criticisms have taken Nagel's and Parfit's approaches in their own terms, and shown that the distinction as they draw it fails to serve their purposes; my attack is internal rather than external. Of

course I also think that their ways of drawing the distinction won't serve m
purposes, but that is another matter.

14 Amartya Sen, "Rights and Agency," *Philosophy and Public Affairs* 11, n
1 (1982):3–39, reprinted in Scheffler, *Consequentialism and its Critic*
pp. 187–223.

15 In these formalizations, '◇' means 'it is morally acceptable that', 'fA' mea
'A does f', '↔' means 'if and only if', and 'A perm fA' means 'A permi
himself to do f. So doer-neutrality is the claim that it is acceptable for ,
to permit himself to do f if and only if it is acceptable for him to permit
to do f. This is not exactly the way that Sen expresses the relevant formula
but I do not think that my reformulations impose any distortion of Sen
views.

16 Here we should read 'V(A perm fA)' as 'the value to be found in A
permitting himself to do f'.

17 I am here gesturing toward a much longer story about the relationship b
tween the virtue of tolerance and the existence of agent-relative reason
which I hope to tell in another place.

18 So the question whether its existence would refute consequentialism is n
resolved by Sen's showing (even assuming that he does show) that what h
thinks of as agent-relative value can be captured consequentially. The wa
in which this emerges in Sen's account depends on his notion of evaluato
relativity; I have not considered whether this notion even makes sens
though I may say that I think it is not vulnerable to the criticisms leveled a
it by Philippa Foot; see Foot, "Morality, Action and Outcome."

19 Nagel shares my suspicion here; see Nagel, *View from Nowhere*, p. 165.

20 See Kagan, *Limits of Morality*, pp. 356–85.

21 This notion of a *pro tanto* reason is just a reformulation of W. D. Ross
rather confusing talk of a *prima facie* duty; see W.D. Ross, *The Right an
The Good* (Oxford: Clarendon Press, 1930), ch. 2. We have a *pro tant*
reason to help those in need if such an action is always the better for it – i
an action that involves such help is always better than it would otherwis
have been. The PTR exists if an action that leaves the world better off i
always better than it would have been had it not done so.

22 Kagan, *Limits of Morality*, p. 356.

23 There is a further maneuver available, though Kagan does not wish to us
it (see *Limits of Morality*, p. 364n). This is to distinguish between theory o
value and theory of motivation on the lines of Parfit (*Reasons and Persons*
ch. 1) and P. Railton ("Alienation, Consequentialism, and the Demands o
Morality," *Philosophy and Public Affairs* 13 [1984]: 134–71, reprinted i
Scheffler, *Consequentialism and its Critics*, pp. 93–133). It is also to clai
that consequentialism can combine a purely impartial theory of value wit
a partial theory of motivation, i.e., one that recommends the sort of partia
motivation that is necessarily involved in love and friendship.

24 Parfit, who takes it to be *theories* that are properly to be called agent-relativ
or agent-neutral, maintains that consequentialism is probably an agent

relative theory, since in its best form it prescribes different agents different *aims*. This peculiarity is due to the way he runs a distinction between aims and outcomes. As a theory about outcomes, consequentialism might be called agent-neutral – but theories about outcomes are really neither agent-relative nor agent-neutral, since as theories about outcomes they are not in the business of giving agents aims of any sort. So Parfit's true position is that consequentialism is, if anything, agent-relative. Here, of course, he is distinguishing between consequentialism as theory of value and as theory of motivation, in the way that Kagan does not wish to do.

25　This is very important. Even if we admit that consequentialism correctly captures the nature of some moral reasons (those concerned with outcomes, presumably), we can suppose there to be other neutral reasons than these. And we might even discover that consequentialism distorts the nature of the reasons concerned with outcomes, as Foot suggests; see Foot, "Utilitarianism and the Virtues." So the question whether consequentialism is true is not the same as the question whether there are agent-relative reasons, even though the existence of such reasons would refute consequentialism.

13

The separateness of persons, distributive norms, and moral theory

DAVID BRINK

It has become commonplace in moral philosophy to claim that teleo logical moral theories, such as utilitarianism, fail to account for variou important moral phenomena recognized by commonsense morality, such as special moral obligations (e.g., obligations to intimates and promis sory obligations), moral and political rights, and distributive justice These moral failings are often traced to a common source: Teleologica theories allegedly fail to recognize or respond appropriately to the sep arateness of persons. Proper recognition of the separateness of persons it is claimed, supports a quite different, contractualist style of mora theory.

The objection focuses on utilitarianism's aggregative conception o impartiality. The utilitarian takes everyone's interests into account by aggregating their interests, balancing benefits to some against harms to others, and distributing benefits and harms so as to produce the best *total* outcome. While balancing goods and harms may be acceptable *within a life,* many think that it is not acceptable to balance goods and harms *across lives.* On the aggregative conception, individual claims may simply be outvoted by a majority. In order to respect the sepa rateness of persons, it is claimed, distributions of benefits and harms must be acceptable, in the relevant sense, to *each.* This is the contrac tualist interpretation of impartiality. Contractualist theories seek a kind of unanimity, in contrast to the majoritarianism of utilitarianism.

In this way, appeal to the separateness of persons plays both a *negative* and a *constructive* role in moral theory; it shows utilitarian and teleo logical views to be distributionally insensitive, and it motivates the dis

Work on this paper was done during a fellowship at the Center for Advanced Study in the Behavioral Sciences that was funded by an Old Dominion Fellowship from the Massachusetts Institute of Technology and by grants from the National Endowment for the Humanities (RA-20037-88) and the Andrew W. Mellon Foundation. I would like to thank these institutions for their support. I would also like to thank G. A. Cohen, Diane Jeske, Christopher Morris, Derek Parfit, Paul Pietroski, and Alan Sidelle for helpful comments and discussion. Derek Parfit's own work on some of these issues has been enormously helpful to me.

ributional claims of contractualism and other deontological theories.[1] want to reexamine this appeal to the separateness of persons in moral heory, in particular, the link between the separateness of persons, listributional norms, and different kinds of moral theory. I am skeptical hat the separateness of persons can play successfully either the negative r the constructive role.

Because these different moral theories and distributive norms provide ccounts of the foundation of moral and political entitlements, we must xamine their implications for contexts in which entitlements do not lready exist. To do this, we must focus on macro issues of just insti- utional design, because this will explain how particular entitlements are enerated, and micro questions of allocation among individuals none of vhom has a prior claim of special entitlement or desert.

1. Utilitarianism and the separateness of persons

The separateness of persons objection is usually applied to hedonistic r desire-satisfaction versions of utilitarianism, but it is supposed to pply in virtue of the utilitarian, consequentialist, or teleological *struc- ure* that these theories possess. Teleological moral theories define duty r right action in terms of promoting value or the good. Traditionally, eleological theories have been either egoistic or universalistic. Utili- arianism is a universalistic teleological theory that takes the good to be uman or sentient welfare or happiness. Utilitarianism, we noted, em- loys an aggregative conception of impartiality. Treating people im- artially involves giving everyone equal consideration, and giving equal onsideration involves taking everyone's welfare into account and bal- ncing some interests against others, if necessary, to produce the out- ome that is, on balance, best. Indeed, this interpretation of impartiality s perhaps the principal source of utilitarianism's appeal.[2] This aggre- ative conception of impartiality makes utilitarianism *person-neutral,* ecause it assigns no moral importance as such to whom a benefit or urden befalls; it is the magnitude of a good or harm, and not whose enefit or burden it is, that affects its moral importance. And person- eutrality implies an aggregative or maximizing decision procedure. If he magnitude of goods and harms is of moral importance as such, but he location of goods and harms across lives is not, we should act so as o maximize net value rather than to achieve any particular distribution.

Person-neutrality effects a kind of impartiality across lives akin to the mpartiality that *temporal-neutrality* effects within lives. Temporal- eutrality is a common view about how one rationally ought to distribute enefits and harms across different stages within the same life; it says that the temporal location of a benefit or harm within a life should no affect its rational significance. As such, temporal-neutrality implies tha I should be concerned only with the magnitude of a benefit or harm not its temporal location, and this implies that I should be impartia among the different stages of my life and maximize the total amount o welfare realized over the course of my life, rather than achieve an particular distribution.

In this way, person-neutrality is to interpersonal distribution wha temporal-neutrality is to intertemporal distribution. Indeed, many have seen the motivation for utilitarianism's person-neutrality as extending the familiar maximizing decision procedure from diachronic, intraper sonal contexts into interpersonal contexts. Sidgwick suggested this ra tionale for utilitarianism,[3] and contemporary critics of utilitarianism have followed him.[4]

But utilitarianism's person-neutral interpretation of impartiality i thought by some to be its chief defect. Its aggregative character is no sensitive to issues of distributive justice, and this reflects the fact tha it fails to recognize the *separateness of persons*. This charge has been made by various writers, including Thomas Nagel, John Rawls, Rober Nozick, and Bernard Williams.[5] As Rawls writes,

This view of social cooperation [utilitarianism's] is the consequence of extending to society the principle of choice for one man, and then, to make this extension work, conflating all persons into one. . . . Utilitarianism does not take seriousl the distinction between persons.[6]

Rawls and other critics accept intrapersonal balancing but reject inter personal balancing. But perhaps the right reaction is not to deny the parity of the intrapersonal and interpersonal cases but to extend distri butional considerations from interpersonal contexts into intrapersona ones. If utilitarianism's person-neutrality is guilty of failing to recognize the separateness of persons, perhaps temporal-neutrality is guilty o failing to recognize the *separateness of person stages*. Parity would re quire that one be concerned with the way in which one distributes good among the temporal stages of one's own life (as well as among lives and not just with maximizing total value over the course of one's life.

Friends of the separateness of persons have generally not accepted the parity of intrapersonal and interpersonal cases.[8] But they need to explain the asymmetry between intrapersonal and interpersonal distri bution. The correct explanation requires articulating the separateness of persons objection. There are metaphysical and normative aspects o the separateness of persons; together they explain the asymmetry be tween intrapersonal and interpersonal distribution.

The metaphysical separateness of persons is supposed to motivate a normative claim about the unacceptability of *uncompensated sacrifices*. Because I am a separate person, with one and only one life to lead, it may seem unreasonable to demand that I make uncompensated sacrifices. It may seem that it is reasonable to demand a sacrifice of me if and only if I receive some sufficient compensation in return. The normative separateness of persons involves the distributional constraint that sacrifice requires compensation (SRC). SRC and the metaphysical separateness of persons explains the disanalogy between intrapersonal and interpersonal distribution. If people are temporally extended but metaphysically distinct, there is automatic diachronic, intrapersonal compensation but no automatic interpersonal compensation. Compensation requires that benefactors be beneficiaries, and for compensation to be automatic benefactor and beneficiary must be the same. In the intrapersonal case one's sacrifice of one's own present good for a greater, future good is acceptable, because there is compensation later for the earlier sacrifice; benefactor and beneficiary are the same.[9] This explains why temporal-neutrality is an acceptable norm of intertemporal distribution. But in the interpersonal case, benefactor and beneficiary are different people; unless the beneficiary reciprocates in some way, the agent's sacrifice will be uncompensated. Because we are separate persons, I am not compensated when I undergo a sacrifice for a greater gain to you; your gains do not make up to me for my losses. The balancing of benefits to one person against harms to another that utilitarianism's person-neutrality requires would be acceptable if and only if there was interpersonal compensation. But this is what the separateness of persons seems to show: Because different persons are distinct beings living separate lives, there is in general no interpersonal compensation.[10] This explains what seems wrong with person-neutrality as a norm of interpersonal distribution.

This rationale for the asymmetry in intrapersonal and interpersonal distribution captures claims made by friends of the separateness of persons objection. Nagel claims that utilitarianism

ignores the distinction between persons. . . . To sacrifice one individual life for another, or one individual's happiness for another's is very different from sacrificing one gratification for another within a *single* life.[11]

A little later Nagel explains this difference by appeal to the plausibility of "the extremely strict position that there can be no interpersonal compensation for sacrifice."[12] Similarly, Nozick writes:

Individually, we each sometimes choose to undergo some pain or sacrifice for a greater benefit or to avoid a greater harm. . . . Why not, *similarly*, hold that

some persons have to bear some costs that benefit other persons more? Bu
there is no *social entity* with a good that undergoes some sacrifice for its ow
good. . . . To use a person in this way does not sufficiently respect and tak
account of the fact that he is a separate person, that his is the only life he has
He does not get some overbalancing good from his sacrifice, and no one i
entitled to force this upon him. . . . [13].

And Rawls uses similar language in explaining the separateness of per
sons objection.

Each member of society is thought to have an inviolability founded on justic
or, as some say, on natural right, which even the welfare of everyone else cannc
override. Justice denies that [for example] the loss of freedom for some is mad
right by a greater good shared by others. The reasoning which balances th
gains and losses of different persons as if they were one person is excluded. [14]

In this way, the separateness of persons objection appears to be a pow
erful objection to person-neutral moral theories such as utilitarianism

2. The Pareto interpretation of the separateness of persons

But we get a decisive objection to person-neutrality just in case th
separateness of persons objection establishes the impermissibility of *a*
balancing of one person's good against that of others. This is the *stron*
interpretation of the separateness of persons objection. [15]
    The strong interpretation requires two claims: (i) SRC's claim tha
compensation is a necessary condition of the moral acceptability of an
sacrifice; *and* (ii) the claim that sacrifice is measured by nonmoral criteri
– for instance, in terms of utilities. It seems clear that SRC's interpre
tation of sacrifice must be nonmoral if it is to support the prohibitio
on all balancing. SRC allows us to distinguish between greater an
smaller sacrifices, and the nonmoral interpretation of sacrifice tells u
to measure the size of a sacrifice in terms of the magnitude of the los
in welfare. And it seems we should measure the size of loss involved i
one distribution by comparison with people's welfare in alternative pos
sible distributions. If there are two possible policies, A and B, and m
welfare level is lower in B than in A, then the choice of B imposes
sacrifice on me. When we combine this understanding of sacrifice wit
SRC's claim that compensation is a necessary condition of the mora
acceptability of any sacrifice, we get the claim a distribution is morall
unacceptable if it imposes an uncompensated or net loss of welfare
however small – on one person in order to provide benefits – howeve
great – to others. Only in this way do we get the prohibition on a

balancing, characteristic of the strong interpretation of the separateness of persons objection.

This interpretation establishes a Pareto side constraint. There are several Pareto criteria, which can be defined in terms of people's welfare or preferences. A situation S_1 is Pareto-*superior* to another S_2 just in case at least one person would be better off in S_1 than S_2 (would prefer S_1 to S_2) and no one would be better off in S_2 (would prefer S_2). S_1 is Pareto-*inferior* to S_2 just in case S_2 is Pareto-superior to S_1. S_1 is Pareto-*optimal* just in case there is no situation that is Pareto-superior to it. S_1 and S_2 are Pareto-*incomparable* just in case at least one person would be better off in S_1 than S_2 (would prefer S_1 to S_2) and at least one person would be better off in S_2 than S_1 (would prefer S_2 to S_1). S_1 and S_2 are Pareto-*indifferent* just in case no one would be better off in S_1 than in S_2 (prefer S_1 to S_2) and vice versa. The Pareto constraint is this: only outcomes that are Pareto-superior (or -indifferent) satisfy SRC so interpreted; an outcome is unacceptable if it is Pareto-inferior or -incomparable with respect to some other alternative.[16] We get a knockdown objection to person-neutrality with an objection to all balancing, which we get by accepting the Pareto interpretation of SRC.

However, the Pareto interpretation sets up an extremely stringent distributional constraint. There are almost always multiple Pareto optima that are Pareto-incomparable. Almost all morally and politically interesting issues can be resolved only by taking actions that distribute welfare in ways that make at least one person at least a little worse off than he would have been under some alternative. Thus, the Pareto interpretation of SRC knocks out much more than person-neutrality; it knocks out any view that redistributes resources (in Pareto-incomparable ways). For instance, it will certainly knock out the kind of egalitarianism that appeals to opponents of utilitarianism, such as Nagel and Rawls. The egalitarian feature common to Nagel and Rawls is the claim that it is morally incumbent to benefit those who are worse off even if we can benefit them less than we could benefit others. And this can require not only that the better-off accept lower prospects so that the worse-off may gain but also that the better-off accept a larger absolute loss in order that the worse-off may experience a smaller absolute gain.[17]

In fact, the Pareto interpretation of SRC knocks out any view that recognizes duties of mutual aid in which benefactors are uncompensated or undercompensated. Indeed, it would seem that the only moral or political view that would satisfy the Pareto interpretation of SRC would be the sort of libertarian view that Nozick accepts that recognizes no duties of mutual aid whatsoever. But such a theory would have to assign rights to people in such a way that each person has a veto over anyone's actions, and even Nozick does not go this far, because he allows for the permissibility of market exchanges that impose negative externalities on third parties.[18]

If so, the price of treating the separateness of persons objection as a knockdown objection to the person-neutrality characteristic of utilitarianism is prohibitive. All reasonable moral theories violate the Pareto interpretation of SRC. The friend of person-neutrality should admit that teleological theories violate the Pareto interpretation of SRC and so are vulnerable to the strong interpretation of the separateness of persons objection but simply deny that this is a reasonable objection to these theories.

3. Moralizing sacrifices

Because the Pareto interpretation of SRC seems to yield an implausibly strong interpretation of the separateness of persons objection, we should reject it. The Pareto interpretation results from combining SRC with a nonmoral measure of sacrifice. A more plausible interpretation may result from combining SRC with a *moralized* account of sacrifice or of when a loss counts as a sacrifice. It implies that it is unacceptable to impose unjustified losses or burdens on one person in order that others may benefit.

Though all redistributive theories impose burdens on some so that others may benefit, not all theories impose unjustified burdens so that others may benefit. And friends of the separateness of persons objection whose own moral theories allow some interpersonal balancing may well insist that their objection should be interpreted as relying on the moralized version of SRC.

But on this interpretation the separateness of persons objection no longer presents an obviously decisive objection to person-neutral moral theories. The objection is decisive, in the way its friends believe, only on the implausibly strong interpretation of SRC that shows all reasonable moral theories to be misconceived. On the more plausible, moralized interpretation only unjustified balancing is forbidden. But it is obviously a *substantive* question when a loss or burden is unjustified and so what sort of balancing is permissible, and person-neutral theories provide one conception of when a loss counts as a sacrifice. It may be that a burden imposed in order that greater good may be done is sometimes unjustified, but this is something that has to be established. Once we drop our objection to balancing per se, it's no longer clear that person-neutrality violates SRC. Properly interpreted, the separateness of persons objection is a conversation *starter,* not the conversation stopper opponents of utilitarianism have taken it to be.

One conclusion we might draw is that critics of utilitarianism have misunderstood the explanatory asymmetries in their own criticisms. As I said at the outset, many critics want to explain specific complaints about the moral failings of person-neutrality (concerning special obligations, rights, and distributive justice) by appeal to person-neutrality's failure to recognize the separateness of persons. Perhaps they should instead reverse the order of explanation and explain how person-neutrality violates the moralized version of SRC by appeal to these claims about the specific moral failings of person-neutrality.

4. Moral asymmetry

However, the moralized interpretation of the separateness of persons need not be an explanatory dead end. Even if the moralized interpretation does not itself establish when a loss or burden is justified, it may still make some moral structures more plausible than others. For it seems to be a presupposition of deciding when a burden or sacrifice is justified that not all burdens are morally on a par, and this may threaten moral theories that assign no intrinsic significance to different kinds of burden or sacrifice.

A libertarian rights theory that assigns each individual a veto on actions of others that affect his welfare and so forbids all (nonvoluntary) balancing treats all burdens or sacrifices as if they were on a par morally. It does not see any moral difference between the small burdens that duties of mutual aid impose on the superrich and the serious harms to the destitute that such duties aim to mitigate. But once we begin to distinguish between justified and unjustified sacrifices, as the moralized interpretation forces us to, we are likely to see an asymmetry here. So, even if such libertarian theories do not flout any formal feature of SRC, the moralized interpretation of SRC may make such theories seem very implausible.

In a similar way, the focus on when a sacrifice is justified may make some forms of person-neutrality seem implausible. For some person-neutral theories see no loss as intrinsically more significant than any other loss. To be sure, all person-neutral theories require that for a sacrifice to be justified, it must produce at least as large a benefit to someone. But on familiar hedonistic or desire-satisfaction assumptions about value, no kind of loss is *intrinsically* more important than another; a loss of any kind, K_1, can always be balanced by a sufficient number of benefits of any other kind, K_2. Of course, the principle of diminishing marginal utility will tend to constrain the inequalities that efficiency allows. But diminishing marginal utility sets in at different points for different people, and a sufficiently large pool of small beneficiaries can make even a large sacrifice by a small group efficient. So, for instance, it seems possible in principle that a loss of some significant good (e.g., freedom of speech) to one person could be counterbalanced by a large number of comparatively minor gains (e.g., freedom from unwanted disturbance) to others. As long as some sorts of losses are intrinsically more important than others, these sorts of person-neutral conceptions of the moralized interpretation of SRC will be implausible.

When we think about the moralized interpretation of SRC we are likely to think that some sacrifice or losses are morally more significant than others and, in particular, that burdens on those who are worse off are harder to justify than are burdens to those who are better off. In this way, we are likely to think that there is a moral asymmetry in "top-down" and "bottom-up" sacrifice. Call this the *moral asymmetry thesis*.

Moral asymmetry explains the egalitarian appeal to the separateness of persons objection. For both Rawls and Nagel recognize that their forms of egalitarianism require the better-off to forgo benefits – indeed, sometimes very large benefits – they would otherwise enjoy in order that the position of the worse-off be improved – even if the improvement is fairly small. They can and do defend *this* sort of balancing by appeal to the moral asymmetry of top-down and bottom-up sacrifices. Moreover, they seem to think that moral asymmetry and the sort of balancing that it requires follow from the right conception of the contractualist requirement that just distributions must be acceptable to each affected party.

Consider Rawls's difference principle. It requires maximizing the position of the worst-off. Rawls defends the difference principle only as applied to the basic structure of society; he does not defend it as a general distributional principle.[19] However, he allows that someone might well extend the argument of justice as fairness to rightness as fairness,[20] and the egalitarian thrust of the difference principle obviously has wider appeal. I shall discuss the difference principle as a general distributional norm that applies to a variety of institutional mechanisms and social policies that determine people's entitlements. In order to distinguish this somewhat wider view from Rawls's difference principle I shall refer to it as *maximin* (the name Rawls uses for the decision theoretic principle used to derive the difference principle from the original position).

It is worth noting that 'worst-off' functions within maximin and the difference principle as a definite description, picking out those individ als who occupy the worst-off representative position under different distributions, and so may refer to different individuals in different possible distributions (or worlds). It does not function as a rigid designator picking out the same individual in all possible worlds.[21] The contractualist nature of the justification of the difference principle is clear. Rawls represents the principles of just institutional design, including the difference principle, as the result of a contract that all would have agreed to under fair conditions. In order to make the contractual circumstances fair, Rawls represents contractors as equal moral persons, and this, he believes, requires placing them behind a veil of ignorance in the original position. The difference principle is acceptable, in the relevant sense, to each just in case it would be chosen in the original position.

The fact that the difference principle reflects the moral asymmetry thesis is revealed most clearly by considering the difference principle's plausibility independently of the contractual argument.[22] In defending the difference principle in preference to utilitarianism, Rawls writes,

[Utilitarianism implies that] we are to accept the greater advantages of others as a sufficient reason for lower expectations over the whole course of our life. This is surely an extreme demand. In fact, when society is conceived as a social system designed to advance the good of its members, it seems quite incredible that some citizens should be expected . . . to accept lower prospects of life for the sake of others.[23]

If this is an appeal to the Pareto interpretation of SRC, then it is an objection to all balancing, including the balancing that the difference principle and, more generally, maximin require. For, as Nozick notes, the better-off can complain about the difference principle that it asks them to accept lower prospects for the sake of others.[24] Presumably, Rawls is appealing to the moralized interpretation of SRC, rather than the Pareto interpretation.[25] He denies that the sacrifices the difference principle requires of the better-off and those that utilitarianism may require of the worse-off are morally comparable. He thinks that the top-down sacrifices that the difference principle requires are justified. He asks us to consider two representative persons A and B, where B is the worst-off member of society and A is among the best-off.

Now B can accept A's being better off since A's advantages have been gained in ways that improve B's prospects. If A were not allowed his better position, B would be even worse off than he is. The difficulty [for the difference principle] is to show that A has no grounds for complaint. Perhaps he is required to have less than he might since his having more would result in some loss to B. Now what can be said to the more favored man? To begin with, it is clear that the well-being of each depends on a scheme of social cooperation without whic no one could have a satisfactory life. Secondly, we can ask for the willin cooperation of everyone only if the terms of the scheme are reasonable. Th difference principle, then, seems to be a fair basis on which those better er dowed, or more fortunate in their social circumstances, could expect others t collaborate with them when some workable arrangement is a necessary conditio of the good of all.[26]

As Nozick rightly complains, this defense of the difference principle i inadequate.[27] Precisely because the well-being of each depends upon . scheme of mutual cooperation, the mutual interdependence that Rawl mentions establishes no asymmetry in A's and B's positions.

Rawls's considered reply to the better-off must be different. Rawl denies that the better-off have any moral claim to their benefits; this i the point of his claim that we should treat the distribution of natura talents, as well as the distribution of social advantages, as a commor asset.[28] The better-off are better off largely by virtue of natural anc social advantages that they have inherited. Because these advantage are the products of natural and social lotteries that are outside a person' control, no one is entitled to benefit from employment of these advan tages unrestrictedly. So the better-off have no prior claim to a large share of the benefits of social cooperation with the worse-off. They are allowed to benefit from the productive employment of their natural anc social assets only on morally acceptable terms.[29] And Rawls thinks tha morally acceptable terms must reflect the moral asymmetry in top-dow» and bottom-up sacrifices.[30] The worse-off have moral priority over the better-off simply by virtue of being worse off. It is an unjustified sacrifice which Rawls thinks utilitarianism may allow, if the worst-off – who are worst off through the operation of morally arbitrary factors – are mad worse off for the sake of still greater benefits to the better-off. By contrast, it is not an unjustified sacrifice if the better-off – who are bette» off through the operation of morally arbitrary factors – are asked tc accept somewhat lower prospects for the sake of benefits to those whc are worse off.

In *The Possibility of Altruism* Nagel suggests that the separateness o persons implies that we must try to solve the "combinatorial problem' about how to balance individuals' competing claims and interests in ; way that is acceptable from each person's point of view.[31] A prope» model, Nagel claims, would derive distributional norms from a choice situation in which "the chooser expects to lead *all* of the lives in question not as a single super-life but as a set of individual lives."[32] Such a model he thinks, would support moral asymmetry.

Perhaps the model is no more than an image, but it seems to me a useful one, for it renders plausible the extremely strict position that there can be no interpersonal compensation for sacrifice. If one works from that position, then one can arrive at a result similar to that which Rawls derives from his construction. That is, one will feel that first priority must be given, in any principle of combinatorial weighting, to improving the lot of those in the population who are worst off. . . .[33]

In his essay "Equality," Nagel links acceptability to each, moral asymmetry, and egalitarianism. Egalitarianism, Nagel claims, requires results that are in some sense acceptable to everyone. Where outcomes represent improvements to some that are not Pareto improvements, no result is completely acceptable to everyone. What we must make do with, Nagel claims, is the outcome that is the least unacceptable to the person to whom it is most unacceptable. The unacceptability of someone's position is a function of both her relative level of well-being (her complaint is worst, along this dimension, if she is the worst-off person; her complaint is least serious if she is the best-off person) and the size of her loss (i.e., the amount by which she is worse off than she would have been under some alternative). This kind of egalitarianism, Nagel claims, rests on a sense of *moral priority* or *urgency* that attaches to the claims of the worse-off.[34]

Moral asymmetry plays a similar role in T. M. Scanlon's contractualist version of egalitarianism in his essay "Contractualism and Utilitarianism." Scanlon's preferred statement of contractualism is this:

An act is wrong if its performance under the circumstances would be disallowed by any system of rules for the general regulation of behavior which no one could reasonably reject as a basis for informed, unforced general agreement.[35]

Just as Rawls intends his two principles of justice to apply to the basic structure of society, not to particular actions or outcomes, the objects of reasonable rejection by Scanlon's contractors are principles, not particular actions or outcomes. However, I think that the contractualist idea applies to the determination of entitlements generally, and so my discussion will extend Scanlon's ideas more widely.[36]

According to Scanlon, contractualism reflects the need to justify one's actions to others on grounds that they cannot reasonably reject.[37] This need might be thought to reflect the moralized interpretation of SRC. In situations where no one outcome is preferred by all, there is a sense in which no outcome is acceptable to all, because every outcome imposes losses on some. But we can accept the moralized interpretation of SRC's claim that no one should have to accept unreasonable or unjustified burdens. This is naturally expressed in contractualist vernacular as the claims that an outcome or principle is unacceptable if it can be reasonably rejected and that it is acceptable or permissible if no one can reasonably reject it.

But what would count as reasonable grounds for rejection? Scanlon suggests, "Under contractualism, when we consider a principle our attention is naturally directed first to those who would do worse under it."[38] We may wonder why the worse-off are the natural focus. Why not just look to how significantly a principle or outcome affects anyone's welfare? The focus on the worse-off must reflect a belief in the moral asymmetry of the claims of the better-off and worse-off.

But how should we give priority to the worse-off? Scanlon considers assigning the worst-off a veto, as maximin does, and rejects this as extreme. But his objection seems to be not to the use of a veto per se; he seems willing to assign the biggest complaint a veto, provided we measure the size of a complaint in the right way. He suggests that in assessing a person's complaint about a distribution we should take into account the size of her relative loss and her absolute level of well-being as well as her relative level of well-being.[39]

5. Contractualism, moral asymmetry, and minimax complaint

Indeed, all three views direct our attention to the worst complaint; they disagree over how to measure the size of complaint. Maximin says that the size of someone's complaint is a function of (i) her relative level of well-being; the worst complaint belongs to the person or position that occupies the worst position under the various alternative outcomes. According to Nagel, the size of someone's complaint is a function of (i) her relative level of well-being and (ii) the size of her loss (i.e., the amount by which she is worse off than she would have been under some alternative).[40] According to Scanlon, the size of someone's complaint a function of (i) her relative level of well-being, (ii) the size of her loss, and (iii) her absolute level of well-being.[41] It is unclear exactly how these different measures of the size of a complaint are to be integrated so as to yield a single assessment of the size of a complaint, but these details need not concern us here. The important point is that all three agree that we should make the worst complaint as small as possible, though they measure the size of a complaint in different ways. In this way, each gives the biggest complaint a kind of veto.[42] Following Derek Parfit, will call this general claim that all three share *minimax complaint*, because it instructs us to minimize the maximum complaint.[43]

Moreover, all three views link three moral ideas: (a) the contractualist idea that the permissibility of a distribution requires that it be acceptable in the relevant way to each affected party; (b) the moral asymmetry thesis, according to which the claims of those who have bigger complaints or are in some way worse off are morally more urgent such that we must often benefit those whom we can benefit less; and (c) a form of egalitarianism that relies on minimax complaint. The reasoning linking the three theses seems to be something like this. Contractualism implies that an outcome or distribution must be acceptable to each. But because there are multiple Pareto optima, no distribution will be complaint-free. Given moral asymmetry, we approximate unanimity by focusing on the complaints and preferences of those who are in some way worse off, for they have a bigger, more urgent complaint. But then one should focus on the biggest complaint; this is the morally most urgent claim. As minimax complaint claims, this complaint should be made as least bad as possible.

6. Moral asymmetry and minimax

However, these three theses are not so tightly linked. When we moralize sacrifice, we may be led to accept the moral asymmetry of top-down and bottom-up sacrifice, and moral asymmetry does undermine certain versions of utilitarianism and libertarianism. To this extent, the separateness of persons objection, properly interpreted, may support some form of egalitarianism. However, minimax complaint is an implausible distributional norm, not required by moral asymmetry.

The appeal of minimax is that by giving the person or group with the worst complaint a veto it gives clear expression to moral asymmetry. The worst complaint is morally more urgent than other complaints; we should always alleviate it first. Losses may not be imposed upon the person or group with the worst complaint, and there is a positive obligation to raise the prospects of the worst complaint as high as possible.[44]

It is worth noting that 'the worst complaint' functions within minimax complaint, as 'worst-off' person or position does within maximin, as a definite description, picking out those individuals whose complaint best satisfies the criteria measuring the size of a complaint, and so may refer to different individuals in different possible worlds.

The different versions of minimax incorporate different measures of the seriousness of complaints. Maximin is that version of minimax complaint that measures the size of a complaint in terms of one's relative position. It gives the person or group with the worst relative level of well-being a veto; we are to minimize the seriousness of that complaint by maximizing the prospects of the worst-off. In many cases we may

agree that the better-off should forgo benefits so that the condition
the worst-off can be improved. But maximin requires that all but
worst-off forgo all benefits, however large, so that the worst-off
improved, however little. In particular, maximin can require that
worst-off be marginally improved even if this means that those o
marginally better than the worst-off forgo a much larger improveme
Consider the alternative distributions in Diagram 13.1.[45]

	A	B
Smallest Loss	5	40
Best Worst-off	6	7

Diagram 13.1

Maximin requires Best Worst-off, rather than Smallest Loss, ev
though B loses much more under Best Worst-off than A does und
Smallest Loss. We may not think that this is right. B may seem to ha
a legitimate complaint against Best Worst-off.

The friend of maximin may wonder why A's situation cannot be i
proved more efficiently. But these alternatives need not be unrealisti

First, if Best Worst-off involves redistribution, there may be h
transfer costs (e.g., because of bureaucratic transfer mechanisms).
a large loss to the better-off may make for a small improvement to t
beneficiaries of the redistribution.

Second, the goods distributed may not be perfectly divisible. Suppc
Smallest Loss and Best Worst-off represent the results, in terms
further life expectancy in years, of two different distributions of t
same scarce medical resource. Imagine A and B are individuals and t
question is how to distribute a single pill. In Smallest Loss B gets t
pill; in Best Worst-off A gets the pill. A's condition is marginally wo
so that he would die somewhat sooner without the pill; but because
condition falls below a critical threshold, his benefit from the treatme
would be much smaller. Here too we may think that B has a reasona
argument for Smallest Loss.

Third, more or less divisible resources may produce differential be
efits to differently situated people. Consider the impact of two differe
health-care policies on two different conditions that afflict equal numb
of people (Diagram 13.2). Assume that condition B is only margina
less severe than A, but can be treated much more easily and successful

	A-Patients	B-Patients
Smallest Loss	5 years	40 years
Best Worst-off	6 years	7 years

Diagram 13.2

Though Best Worst-off maximizes the prognosis of the worst-off patients, patients with condition *B* can fairly complain about Best Worst-off and demand Smallest Loss.

In these cases someone who is marginally less worse off than the worst-off seems to have a reasonable complaint about maximin, because it imposes a much larger comparative loss on her; she is made to forgo a much larger benefit by adopting maximin than the worst-off secures under maximin. One way to avoid these objections is to include the size of someone's loss in measuring the seriousness of her complaint. This is basically Nagel's view; we might call it *minimax weighted loss*. On this view, we assign the worst complaint a veto and maximize the situation of the person with the worst complaint, where the size of the complaint is a function of both (i) the person's relative social position and (ii) the size of her loss.[47]

This may still not capture all that seems relevant to assessing the size of a complaint. The significance of a person's relative social position and of the size of her loss may be affected by her *absolute* level of well-being. We may be less likely to give priority to smaller losses of the worst-off over the significantly larger losses of the somewhat better-off if the somewhat better-off are still leading miserable lives or if the worst-off are very well off indeed. Similarly, we may be less impressed with a large loss to someone whose level after the loss is still (absolutely) very high.

A natural conclusion is to include absolute level of well-being as a measure of the size of a person's complaint. This, I think, is Scanlon's view. We might call the version of minimax complaint that measures complaints this way *tri-measure minimax complaint*. According to it, we assign the worst complaint a veto and maximize the situation of the person or group with the worst complaint, where the size of a complaint is a function of (i) a person's relative social position, (ii) the size of her loss, and (iii) her absolute level of well-being.

Tri-measure minimax complaint is perhaps the most plausible version of minimax. But my discussion will focus on the general structure of minimax theories rather than any particular version. They all claim that

losses may not be imposed upon the person or group with the wors
complaint and that the worst complaint should be minimized.

If we restricted our attention, as Nagel recommends, to individua
pairwise comparisons, then some version of minimax complaint migh
seem an appropriate distributional principle. When one thinks simp
of contests between individual complaints, moral asymmetry implies tha
the most serious complaint should be minimized and that the wors
complaint should, therefore, be given a veto.

But this restriction to individual pairwise comparison ignores the *cu
mulative* moral force of individual complaints. Where one complain
stands against a great many complaints that are individually somewha
less serious, it is less clear that the individually most serious complain
should always win.

All of our examples so far have concerned *same-number* comparison
in which we have varied only absolute and relative position and size c
loss. Now consider a *different-number* comparison between two edu
cational policies for the handicapped (Diagram 13.3). Assume that w
have a fixed number of resources to devote to special education. Als
assume, somewhat artificially, that we can quantify both the severity c
handicaps and the amount of benefit that different policies would pro
duce. One handicap is marginally more severe and also more rare
Because this handicap is more severe, it is harder to overcome than th
other, and so education of these children is more resource-intensive
One policy (Hardship) gives educational priority to those with the wors
handicap, while the other (Benefit) gives priority to the larger grou
with the smaller handicap.

	A-Children	B-Children
Benefit	x improve by 5	500x improve by 20
Hardship	x improve by 20	500x improve by 6

Diagram 13.3

Condition *B* is much more common than condition *A,* but *A*-childre
have a bigger complaint than *B*-children. *A*-children are marginall
worse off, and they stand to lose marginally more if Benefit is enacte
(15) than *B*-children do if Hardship is enacted (14). It follows tha
Hardship maximizes the good of those with the worst complaint, whethe
we measure the seriousness of complaints by maximin, minima
weighted loss, or tri-measure minimax. So all three versions of minima

agree in requiring Hardship. But representatives of *B*-children can fairly complain about Hardship and demand Benefit. Though Hardship can be defended by noting that the complaint of *each A*-child is worse, individually, than that of any *single B*-child, it implies a much greater total loss than Benefit, and one can arguably claim that *B*-children possess a greater *collective* complaint.

Or we might take a structurally isomorphic case and vary the details. We might consider a different-number variation on the two health policies (Diagram 13.4).

	A-Patients	*B*-Patients
Benefit	*x* get 5 years	500*x* get 20 years
Hardship	*x* get 20 years	500*x* get 6 years

Diagram 13.4

Condition *B* is much more common than condition *A*, but *A*-patients have a bigger complaint than *B*-patients. Assume that *A*-patients and *B*-patients are at the same absolute position where further years of life are substantial goods, say, 25 years old. *A*-patients are marginally worse off, and they stand to lose marginally more if Benefit is enacted (15 years) than *B*-patients do if Hardship is enacted (14 years). It follows that Hardship maximizes the prognosis of those with the worst complaint, however we measure the seriousness of complaints. And so all three versions of minimax agree in requiring Hardship. But the patients with condition *B* can fairly complain about Hardship and demand Benefit. Though each *A*-patient can defend Hardship by noting that his complaint is worse, individually, than that of any single *B*-patient, Hardship implies a greater total loss, and *B*-patients can arguably claim to possess a greater collective complaint.

By giving those with the greatest individual complaint a veto, minimax complaint does not record the moral significance of any less serious losses and so is unable to see how a much larger number of such losses might render justified some losses to those with the worst individual complaints. This reflects its fundamentally antiaggregative character.[48] But in this respect, minimax holds those with less severe complaints – even if the complaints are only marginally less severe and no matter how many of them there are – hostage to improvements to those with more severe complaints – no matter how small a number they are. This seems to be a good illustration of the dictatorship of the worst (individual) complaint. Though the dictatorship of the worst complaint may be more benign than other forms of dictatorship, it is still unreasonable. Moral asymmetry reflects the fact that some complaints are morally *more* urgent than others. But moral asymmetry is itself a scalar phenomenon. If so, it seems inappropriate to give any one complaint, even the worst complaint, an absolute veto.

Numbers may not always be decisive. It may be false that there is always some number of less serious claims that would outweigh some smaller number of more serious claims. No number of minor perquisites (e.g., snowmobiles) to those with much less serious complaints is going to make up for significant losses (e.g., lower levels of nutrition or basic medical care) to those with the worst complaints. But, as in the cases I've considered, numbers do sometimes seem decisive, and are perhaps always relevant. If so, then we cannot accept any version of minimax that gives the worst complaint a veto across the board.

This shows that we need to distinguish moral asymmetry and minimax complaint. Minimax complaint presupposes and so implies moral asymmetry, but moral asymmetry does not imply minimax complaint. Moral asymmetry requires that we give moral priority to those who have bigger complaints, but only minimax complaint is antiaggregative. We can accept moral asymmetry without accepting minimax complaint; and if we do accept the former, we should reject the latter. On no reasonable way of measuring the seriousness of complaints should we give a veto to the worst (individual) complaint. Other things being equal, many only marginally less severe complaints ought to combine to outweigh a few marginally worse complaints.

We can and should still try to justify actions to each individual, as contractualism claims. But such a justification can appeal to group complaints as well as individual complaints. If moral asymmetry is correct, we can justify asking someone to make a sacrifice in same-number cases by showing that another individual has a more serious complaint about any alternative than he does to this sacrifice. But in different-number cases we can justify asking someone to make a sacrifice by showing that the alternatives impose significant sacrifices, and so generate significant, even if marginally less serious, complaints on a much larger number of people. Though our complaints may be individually somewhat smaller than yours, *as a group* we may have a bigger complaint. If so, the antiaggregative character of minimax complaint represents an implausible interpretation of the moralized version of SRC and so an implausible moral response to the separateness of persons.

7. Teleological ethics re-examined

hat does this conclusion imply about the negative role that the sep-
ateness of persons is supposed to play in moral theory? Does the
oralized interpretation of the separateness of persons objection un-
rmine utilitarianism and other teleological moral theories? The mor-
zed interpretation of SRC suggests the moral asymmetry thesis, and
oral asymmetry seemed to support minimax theories that assign the
orst complaint a veto. But whether or not we accept moral asymmetry,
e should not accept minimax complaint. But if we reject minimax
omplaint, the moral appeal to the separateness of persons loses its
tiaggregative punch. If the separateness of persons loses its antiag-
egative punch, it's no longer clear that the separateness of persons
ojection, even in its moralized form, is compelling. *How* teleological
eories are to be squared with the separateness of persons depends on
ether we accept moral asymmetry.

8. Moral asymmetry?

we let the numbers count *and* we reject moral asymmetry, utilitar-
ism and other teleological theories are easily reconciled with the
parateness of persons. For then a sacrifice is justified just in case it is
ficient, that is, if and only if it produces at least as large benefits to
me as it imposes burdens on others. But we saw (in Section 4) that
rson-neutral moral theories do not seem to moralize sacrifice in a
ausible way if they count no kind of loss as intrinsically more serious
an another. In this way, hedonistic and desire-satisfaction utilitarian-
n do not seem to moralize sacrifice in the right way.

These claims may seem to commit us to moral asymmetry, because
oral asymmetry just is the view that losses to those who are in some
ay worse off are morally more serious than losses to those who are
ss badly off in such a way that it's morally required to benefit the
orse-off even if we can confer a smaller benefit on them than we could
the better-off. But we could distinguish some kinds of losses as
trinsically more serious than others without embracing moral asym-
etry. To see this, consider Nagel's claims about egalitarianism. He
troduces egalitarianism, by contrast with utilitarianism, as relying on
claim about the urgency of certain needs.

[egalitarianism] also resembles utilitarianism formally, in being applied first
the assessment of outcomes rather than actions. But it does not combine all
ints of view by a majoritarian method. Instead, it establishes an order of

priority among needs and gives preference to the most urgent, regardless
numbers.[49]

Later he illustrates the egalitarian commitment to asymmetry with th
example of a parent's choice between a move to the country that wou
benefit her first child who is normal and happy and enjoys the outdoo
and a move to the city that would benefit her second child who suffe
from a painful handicap and would be helped by the availability of speci
medical and educational facilities in the city. Nagel asks us to assum
that the move to the country would provide a somewhat greater bene
to the first child than the move to the city would provide to the secor
child.

If one chose to move to the city, it would be an egalitarian decision. It is mo
urgent to benefit the second child, even though the benefit we can give him
less than the benefit we can give the first child.[50]

These claims about the greater urgency of the needs of the worse-c
may seem equivalent to moral asymmetry. However, Nagel's claims he
are ambiguous in ways that threaten the equivalence. His first clai
connects egalitarianism with a notion of moral priority or urgency th
attaches to kinds of needs and benefits;[51] call this *urgency of needs*.
implies, among other things, that we should meet a more urgent nee
before a less urgent one. His second claim connects egalitarianism wi
a kind of urgency and priority that attaches to people or social pos
tions;[52] call this *urgency of person or position*. Of course, the two kine
of urgency are connected. Having a more urgent need that is unme
ceteris paribus, makes one's position more urgent, because it makes or
worse off or gives one a bigger complaint. For the most part, and f
most of my discussion, these two kinds of urgency go together. But th
can come apart, and it is important to decide whether to recogniz
genuine urgency of person or position, that is, such urgency as cann
be explained in terms of urgency of needs. Urgency of person or positior
as distinct from urgency of needs, would give the person with a bigg
complaint a stronger moral claim to any kind of benefit than a persc
with a smaller complaint has to any kind of benefit. But this is a ve
strong claim; it would imply that it is morally required to confer a trivi
benefit on someone who is worse off even at the cost of not meeting a
urgent need of someone who is marginally better off. If we find th
doubtful, as I do, then we should not recognize urgency of person c
position.

But it is only urgency of person or position that clearly impli
moral asymmetry. If we accept urgency of person or position then w
must accept moral asymmetry's claim that we should benefit tho

ho are worse off or have a bigger complaint even though we can
enefit them less than we could benefit others. But urgency of needs
oes not obviously imply this. The crucial question is whether the
rgency of a need affects the size of the benefit we confer by meeting
he need. Only if the answer is no does the greater urgency of some
eeds imply moral asymmetry. But this is not clear. We might distin-
uish the value of meeting needs and other goods and claim that by
eeting a need we confer a greater benefit than by providing other
oods. In a similar spirit, we might distinguish some needs as more
rgent or basic than other needs, and we might think that the urgency
r basicness of a need reflects the size of the benefit we confer by
eeting it. But if this is how we understand the greater urgency of
ome needs, recognition of their urgency does not demand moral
symmetry. For the demand to meet more urgent needs first can be
xplained entirely in person-neutral terms; by meeting more urgent
eeds first, we confer a greater benefit and promote more value. If
o, then we may admit the greater urgency of some needs without
et being committed to Nagel's precise claims about the case of the
andicapped child. We might admit that a larger share of the hand-
apped child's basic needs remain unmet, in comparison with the
ealthy child, and conclude that nondivisible resources (as in Nagel's
xample) should be directed toward improving the situation of the
andicapped child – but precisely because this is the most beneficial
se of scarce nondivisible resources. If we really had a clear case
where we would be doing more good for the healthy child than we
ould do for the handicapped child, then perhaps it would be less
lear that there was a moral requirement to benefit the handicapped
hild nonetheless, as moral asymmetry would require.

The greater urgency of certain needs (say, those of the handicapped
hild) seems fairly robust. For instance, we do not think that the greater
rgency of the needs of the worse-off is hostage to facts about the
iminishing marginal utility of meeting less urgent needs and desires of
he better-off. So a person-neutral account of the greater urgency of
ome needs in terms of the greater value of meeting them cannot rest
n traditional hedonistic or desire-satisfaction theories of value or wel-
are. It must rest, instead, on objective or normative, rather than purely
onative, claims about value or welfare. So the strategy of accommo-
ating these claims about the greater urgency of the claims of the worse-
ff without commitment to moral asymmetry is available only to person-
eutral moral theories incorporating objective or normative assumptions
bout value and not to more traditional hedonistic or desire-satisfaction
orms of utilitarianism.

9. Moral asymmetry within a teleological theory

I have tried to suggest how some of our egalitarian intuitions may
accommodated by suitable adjustments in our evaluative assumptio
If so, we need not accept moral asymmetry. A teleological theory co
accommodate a kind of moral urgency, which the moralized version
the separateness of persons supports, along traditional lines, provid
it employs the right structure within its theory of value. But I have o
raised a question about the need for moral asymmetry. Because I
uncertain about moral asymmetry, I propose to see if a teleologi
theory could accommodate it.

The *prima facie* difficulty is that moral asymmetry implies that t
rightness of an act is not directly proportional to the value the
produces, and this seems inconsistent with traditional formulations
the teleologist's conception of the relation between the good and t
right.

We might try to construct a moral theory that is otherwise teleologi
by attending to the virtues and vices of minimax complaint. This the
would incorporate moral asymmetry by looking to the size of an in
vidual's complaint and giving priority to those who have more seric
complaints, but it would reject minimax's antiaggregative features. L
like traditional teleological theories, it would allow the moral importan
of a benefit or harm to be affected not simply by its magnitude but a
by the size of the complaint of the person whom the benefit or ha
befalls; but, unlike minimax complaint, it would aggregate over co
plaints and benefits and harms. We might call this view *weighted co*
plaint minimization, or simply complaint minimization. As a fr
approximation, it says that it is permissible to demand a sacrifice
someone if and only if the consequences of doing so generate complai
at least as small as any alternative. Complaint minimization must ta
into account (a) the number of complaints and (b) the size of individ
complaints – where the size of individual complaints might be measure
as tri-measure insists, in terms of the (i) relative position, (ii) size
loss, and (iii) absolute level of well-being. Some version of compla
minimization promises to integrate minimax's claims about moral asy
metry without its antiaggregative character.

One may wonder whether complaint minimization can count as
teleological theory. For complaint minimization takes the value to
promoted to be the satisfaction of complaints in proportion to the
seriousness, and the seriousness of a complaint is a moral property
that complaint; whereas teleological theories are often assumed to defi
the moral property of rightness in terms of the promotion of son

nonmoral value(s). This assumption is sometimes taken to follow from the claim that teleological theories, unlike deontological theories, must specify the right in terms of the good and specify the good independently of the right.[53]

But teleological theories should eschew these constraints; they need only define the right in terms of the good and conceive of the good as *distinct* from the right. Unless the good is distinct from the right, defining the right in terms of the good will be circular. But if the right that the teleologist defines in terms of the good is all-things-considered permissibility, then she can define the good in any other way, without circularity. In particular, the teleologist can give an account of the good in terms of moral properties, even right-making properties, so long as these are not themselves all-things-considered right-making properties. If so, this answers the *prima facie* difficulty for incorporating moral asymmetry within a teleological theory. For complaint minimization does make all-things-considered rightness directly proportional to moralized value, and the moralization of value does not itself disqualify a theory as teleological.

Of course, complaint minimization, as it stands, is seriously incomplete. It does not provide a metric for integrating the three measures of the seriousness of a complaint nor a metric for integrating number of complaints and size of complaints. Some complaints may be lexically prior to others so that no number of less serious complaints of a certain type (e.g., snowmobile deprivation) could outweigh any number of more serious complaints of a certain kind (e.g., nutrition or education deprivation); but other complaints, though more serious than some, will not be lexically prior to them.[54] For the time being, I must treat complaint minimization as if it were an intuitionistic doctrine (in Rawls's sense), because I am not in a position to state the principles that articulate these metrics.[55] But this is not to say that such weighting and priority principles cannot be constructed. Presumably a less abstract investigation of situations in which the different variables pull in different directions would aid the construction of such principles.

10. Contractualism re-examined

I have questioned whether the separateness of persons can play the negative role of undermining all utilitarian and teleological moral theories. Can it play the constructive role of supporting contractualist moral theories? Rawls, Nagel, and Scanlon all think that the separateness of persons provides support for contractualism, and they link contractualism with moral asymmetry and moral asymmetry with some form of minimax complaint. The reasoning linking these ideas seems to be this. The negative role for the separateness of persons is supposed to convince us that we must eschew the majoritarianism of teleological views for the kind of unanimity of contractualism. Rather than seeking the largest balance of benefits over harms across lives, we should seek distributions that are, in the relevant way, acceptable to each.[56] But because there are multiple Pareto optima, no distribution is complaint-free. We must moralize complaints and sacrifices, and when we do this we are led to moral asymmetry. Given moral asymmetry, the next-best thing to unanimity is for us to focus on the complaints and preferences of those who have a bigger, more urgent complaint. But then one should focus on the biggest complaint; this is the morally most urgent claim. As minimax complaint claims, this complaint should be made as least bad as possible.

I have raised questions about moral asymmetry and argued that we should reject minimax complaint. Whether rejection of minimax complaint casts doubt on the contractualist interpretation of the separateness of persons depends on how we formulate contractualism. Because I'm confident only that we should reject minimax complaint, I'll concentrate on the relation between contractualism and minimax complaint. I think contractualism can be articulated in ways that are not committed to minimax complaint.

Rawls's version of contractualism clearly eschews unanimous agreement among actual people with self-knowledge and established preferences. This sort of *ex post* agreement is not only impractical, because there are multiple Pareto optima,[57] it is not the right sort of contract to yield a theory of justice. Such a contract must be *moralized;* we want to know what terms of interaction people would agree to under fair conditions that abstract from people's features that are arbitrary from the moral point of view.[58] This is Rawls's reason for making the agreement an *ex ante* agreement among individuals who are ignorant of their actual characteristics and positions. Rawls's use of the original position in the contractual argument registers the need for a moralized agreement in an especially clear way and accounts, I believe, for much of the appeal of his contractual argument.

The thickness of the veil of ignorance that Rawls employs in the original position seems to ensure that it makes no difference to the choice made in the original position who has entered it. Because Rawls's veil abstracts from features of individuals that set them apart, the choice in the original position can be represented as a problem in individual decision theory under special circumstances, rather than a normal contract among several parties with conflicting interests.[59] As such, it provides a clear way to model the question of when a loss or sacrifice is justified.

A nonmoralized *ex post* unanimity condition results, we have seen, in a Pareto constraint that gives each person a veto. This naturally lends itself to a ban on aggregation and interpersonal balancing. And this, we have seen, imposes an intolerable distributional constraint. The explicit moralization of Rawls's contract makes it less clear that the relevant kind of unanimity is incompatible with aggregation.[60] It's simply not clear that an individual trying to advance his prospects, subject to ignorance about which possible life he will lead, would choose to maximize the minimum relative position, regardless, among other things, of the number of occupants of the various relative positions. So it is doubtful that the difference principle or maximin would be chosen over complaint minimization by parties in the original position.[61]

Scanlon thinks Rawls weakens his argument against aggregative views, such as average utilitarianism, by exchanging an *ex post* agreement among different individuals with conflicting interests for the *ex ante* choice of a single self-interested individual under ignorance.[62] Scanlon's idea seems to be that by reducing an interpersonal combinatorial problem to a problem of one person weighing and combining different possibilities for himself we lose objections to interpersonal balancing that an *ex post* agreement brings out, because we are no longer required to justify distributive norms to each affected party.[63]

But there is a justification that can be offered to each affected party for whatever distributive norm would be chosen in the original position, namely, that this is the norm that he would have agreed to in fair initial conditions. If a party does not accept this justification, because he's not interested in what would be chosen in these circumstances, then we can dismiss his complaint as that of someone who is not interested in morally justifying his conduct to others, much as we might reject the complaint of someone whose objection to a distribution relies on the nonmoralized Pareto interpretation of SRC.

Scanlon's contractualism is in pretty much the same boat, though this may be less clear because the moralization of his contract is somewhat less prominent. For reasons that need not concern us, Scanlon formulates his version of contractualism in terms of principles or outcomes not being rejectable, rather than in terms of their being acceptable.[64] But he recognizes that some parties would refuse assent to an *ex post* agreement that imposed any burden on them – even if every alternative agreement imposed far greater burdens on others – if only because they were not interested in finding terms of interaction that could be justified to all. This is the force of his trying to identify distributive norms that

cannot be *reasonably* rejected.[65] But this raises the question of what
would count as reasonable grounds for rejecting a distributive norm or
outcome. This seems to be a moral question, in part because it involves
determination of when a sacrifice or burden is morally unjustified. But
whereas Rawls's version of contractualism provides a reasonably clear
way to model this question – namely, in terms of what any arbitrary
individual would choose behind a thick veil of ignorance designed to
exclude morally arbitrary information – Scanlon offers fairly little
guidance.

So the abstract statement of contractualism does not tell us how to
evaluate the reasonableness of a complaint or a rejection of an outcome
or principle; *a fortiori* it does not tell us that we should not aggregate
complaints in determining their reasonableness. This is clear on one
natural paraphrase of Scanlon's contractualism. Because contractualism
is motivated by the "desire to justify one's actions to others on grounds
that they could not reasonably reject,"[66] we might naturally formulate
it as the claim that

(a) An action, outcome, or principle that one favors is permissible
if and only if *others* cannot reasonably reject it.

But (a) has no antiaggregative commitments. A distributive norm that
minimizes the individually worst complaint may be reasonably rejectable
by others collectively. However, Scanlon sometimes formulates contractualism as

(b) An action, outcome, or principle is permissible if and only if
no one can reasonably reject it.

Formulation (b) seems to be ambiguous between (a), which does not
rule out aggregation, and

(c) An action, outcome, or principle is permissible if and only if
no single individual can reasonably reject it.

If an individual can reasonably reject an action, outcome, or principle,
because he is a member of a large class of people with serious individual
complaints, then even (c) carries no antiaggregative punch. Formulation
(c) will rule out aggregation only if the only ground an individual has
for reasonable rejection is the size of his own complaint, that is, only
if (c) is interpreted as

(d) An action, outcome, or principle is permissible if and only if
*no one person has a bigger complaint about it than someone (else)
does about some alternative.*

Formulation (d) alone would imply minimax complaint. But none of the more abstract statements of contractualism and its appeal commits us to (d).

These are reasons to separate the three layers of Scanlon's position – contractualism, moral asymmetry, and minimax complaint. Given the underlying motivation of justifying one's actions to others, the most natural formulations of contractualism are (a) and (b). They imply neither moral asymmetry nor a ban on aggregation; they are compatible with any form of teleological theory. But just as the question when a sacrifice is justified may lead us to deny that all benefits and losses are morally on a par, the criterion of reasonable rejectability may lead us, as Scanlon believes, to focus on those who are in some way worse off and have larger complaints. But even if we accept moral asymmetry and its relevance to the reasonableness of a person's complaint, this doesn't prohibit us from aggregating. Indeed, if we're concerned to justify our conduct to others, we should allow that others may have a collective complaint that is larger than the complaint of the person with the worst individual complaint. So we can and should reject the third layer of Scanlon's view – minimax complaint – even if we accept the first two layers. Moreover, the first two layers of Scanlon's view are compatible with a teleological view such as complaint minimization.

Nagel contrasts the unanimity that egalitarianism seeks with the majoritarianism of utilitarianism; whereas majoritarianism is aggregative, the requirement of unanimous acceptability is antiaggregative.[67] It is true that utilitarianism is aggregative. Moreover, it is true that unanimity is antiaggregative if the agreement is not moralized. But this sort of unanimity implies the Pareto constraint, and this leads to the intolerable distributional constraint that condemns Nagel's egalitarianism as much as utilitarianism.

Nagel acknowledges this and suggests that the pairwise comparison that minimax complaint invokes is the closest that we can come to unanimity.[68]

So let me return to the issue of unanimity in the assessment of outcomes. The essence of such a criterion is to try in a moral assessment to include each person's point of view separately, so as to achieve a result which is in a significant sense acceptable to each person involved or affected. Where there is a conflict of interests, no result can be completely acceptable to everyone. But it is possible to assess each result from each point of view to find the result that is least unacceptable to the person to whom it is most unacceptable. This means that any other alternative will be more unacceptable to someone than this alternative is to anyone. The preferred alternative is in that sense the least unacceptable, considered from each person's point of view separately. A radically egalitarian policy of giving absolute priority to the worst-off, regardless of numbers, would result from always choosing the least unacceptable alternative, in this sense.[69]

But it is puzzling to claim that minimax complaint is the closest that we can come to unanimity.[70] For minimax complaint involves, as we have seen, the dictatorship of the worst complaint. This may be a benevolent dictatorship, or one that is morally required (though I have denied this), but it is a dictatorship. It would be natural to construct a spectrum of voting procedures, running from dictatorship, at one pole, through majorities and various supermajorities to unanimity, at the other pole. But if we do this, it seems implausible to think that minimax complaint is the closest we can come to unanimity, because dictatorship seems to be the farthest thing from unanimity.

Of course, it's true that both unanimity and dictatorship distribute vetoes. But unanimity gives each a veto, whereas dictatorship gives only one a veto. It would seem that we come closer to giving everyone a veto (unanimity) by giving some, collectively, a veto (as in various kinds of majorities) than by giving one a veto (as in dictatorship).

Nagel's claims are perhaps more plausible when we see that he is moralizing the unanimity condition by appeal to moral asymmetry. He suggests that we trade in the notion of what is acceptable for what is not unacceptable. Then the closest we can come to unanimity is to find what is least unacceptable. But because of moral asymmetry, a burden that befalls someone who is worse off or has a bigger complaint is, *ceteris paribus*, morally more unacceptable than one that befalls someone who is better off. If so, it might seem that a distribution that minimizes the maximum complaint is least unacceptable and so closest to unanimity.

But this follows only if we have *already* restricted ourselves to pairwise comparisons. If we have not, then it's open to us to think that in determining the unacceptability of a distribution we can count not only how big a complaint an individual has but also how many individuals have a complaint about that distribution. But this would be to assess the unacceptability of a distribution according to complaint minimization, not minimax complaint.

Nagel suggests one other line of argument from a unanimity condition, moralized by moral asymmetry, to minimax complaint. One way of formulating moral asymmetry, as we have seen, is in terms of the greater moral urgency or importance of certain needs, when compared with other needs and goods. Now we might think that moral asymmetry, so understood, requires a lexical voting procedure and that minimax complaint secures a kind of unanimity within such a procedure.

Each individual's claim has a complex form: it includes more or less all his needs and interests, but in an order of relative urgency or importance. This determines both which of them are to be satisfied first and whether they are to be satisfied before or after the interests of others. Something close to unanimity is being invoked. An arrangement must be acceptable first from the point of view of everyone's most basic claims, then from the point of view of everyone's next most basic claims, etc.[71]

Notice, however, that this view does not rule out aggregation *within* a level of urgency. If there are conflicts at the most basic level, then the least unacceptable distribution would presumably be the one that minimized failure to meet these most basic claims. But perhaps minimax complaint is not intended to be antiaggregative in this sense; perhaps it is intended to be antiaggregative only *across* levels of urgency. This links a kind of unanimity with a kind of prohibition on aggregation.

But the obvious question is why we should adopt this lexical voting procedure. The lexical character of the procedure ensures that no single most basic need can go unmet in order to meet any number of less basic needs. But why should we employ this procedure as a general matter? Nagel seems to think that the lexical procedure follows from recognition of moral asymmetry. But all asymmetry claims is that, other things being equal, it's morally more important to satisfy a more basic need than a less basic need. But other things may not be, and often seem not to be, equal when we pit one basic need against many only marginally less basic needs. Moral asymmetry is a scalar phenomenon. Though we acknowledge that a single less urgent need makes a smaller claim than a single more urgent need, we should recognize that the less urgent need does make a counterclaim. But then when we turn from same-number cases to different-number cases, it seems reasonable to recognize a greater counterclaim. Though the many make counterclaims that are individually smaller, they make a counterclaim that is collectively greater. If so, the right response to moral asymmetry should be aggregative in the way complaint minimization is.

Minimax complaint does not fall out of contractualism or moral asymmetry without additional premises. One kind of egalitarianism requires minimax complaint and not simply moral asymmetry. But Nagel has offered no argument for linking this kind of egalitarianism with contractualism and moral asymmetry.

We might summarize the relations among contractualism, moral asymmetry, and minimax complaint as follows. Because contractualism and moral asymmetry are not committed to minimax complaint, our worries about minimax complaint threaten neither moral asymmetry nor contractualism. So our worries about minimax complaint do not threaten the contention that the separateness of persons plays a constructive role in moral theory by providing a motivation for contractualism. But it is important to note that, given the moralized understanding of SRC and, consequently, of the kind of unanimity that contractualism seeks, the separateness of persons does not itself support a distinctively nonteleological form of contractualism. This is not simply the claim that contractualism and teleological ethics are compatible, because a form of utilitarianism could, in principle, be agreed to in the right sort of contract.[72] Rather, I agree with critics of utilitarianism that a suitably moralized contract should rule out traditional utilitarian aggregation in which no kind of loss is intrinsically more significant than another.[73] But I insist that a suitably moralized contract must produce distributional norms that do aggregate over losses or complaints that have been suitably weighted according to their moral significance.

11. Conclusion

My concern here has been with abstract structural issues about the relationship between the separateness of persons, moral theory, and distributive norms. The separateness of persons objection purports to show that there is something wrong with the structure of utilitarian or teleological moral theories and that we should accept instead a distinctively nonteleological form of contractualism. The only version of the test the separateness of persons objection imposes that such theories obviously flunk is the strong version that rests on the Pareto interpretation of SRC. But because every reasonable moral theory flunks that test, it is no objection to teleological theories.

However, there is another, more plausible version of the separateness of persons objection that rests on a moralized version of SRC. And the moralized interpretation of SRC may seem to undermine utilitarianism and support contractualism. The moralization of SRC suggests the moral asymmetry thesis that top-down sacrifice is less serious than bottom-up sacrifice. Moral asymmetry may seem to demand that we make affairs least unacceptable to those for whom they are most unacceptable. This leads to minimax theories that assign the worst complaint a veto. Because minimax theories are antiaggregative, this interpretation of the separateness of persons may seem to be a good objection to utilitarian and other teleological theories. It may also seem to support a version of contractualism. The contractualist demands that we combine the points of view of different persons not in an aggregative fashion but in a fashion that makes distributions acceptable in the relevant way from each point of view. Because of conflicts among different points of view, no distribution will be acceptable to each point of view. We need to moralize the kind of unanimity that contractualism seeks, and we do this by appeal to moral asymmetry. But when we try to find the least unacceptable distribution, moral asymmetry seems to tell us to focus on those with the biggest complaints and to make them as small as possible.

However, minimax theories are not the right way to represent moral asymmetry. Though they measure the seriousness of a complaint differently, they all give a veto to the worst complaint, and this establishes the dictatorship of the worst complaint. And the dictatorship of the worst complaint fails to register the moral significance of complaints other than the worst complaint. Because, other things being equal, many only marginally less severe complaints can combine to outweigh a few marginally worse complaints, we should reject the antiaggregative character of minimax and aggregate over benefits and harms that have been suitably weighted for their importance. Teleological views can make these claims, even if they are not available to traditional hedonistic and desire-satisfaction versions of utilitarianism. If so, the separateness of persons objection, even in its most plausible form, does not undermine all teleological moral theories. Moreover, any suitably moralized interpretation of unanimity should allow such aggregation. If so, the versions of contractualism that can be motivated by the separateness of persons are not distinctively nonteleological. This means that the separateness of persons can play neither the negative nor the positive role that its friends have claimed it does.

Notes

1 In a similar way, McKerlie distinguishes the "positive connection" and the "negative connection" that might be claimed to hold between the separateness of persons and moral theory; see Dennis McKerlie, "Egalitarianism and the Separateness of Persons," *Canadian Journal of Philosophy* 18 (1988):205–26.

2 Contrast Scanlon's suggestion that the appeal of utilitarianism lies in its account of moral motivation in terms of sympathy and benevolence; see T. M. Scanlon, "Contractualism and Utilitarianism," in A. Sen and B. Williams, eds., *Utilitarianism and Beyond* (Cambridge: Cambridge University Press, 1982), p. 115.

3 Henry Sidgwick, *The Methods of Ethics*, 7th ed. (Chicago: University of Chicago Press, 1907), pp. 381–2, 418.

4 John Rawls, *A Theory of Justice* (Cambridge, Mass.: Harvard University Press, 1971), pp. 23–4.

5 Thomas Nagel, *The Possibility of Altruism* (Princeton: Princeton University Press, 1970), pp. 134, 138–42; Rawls, *Theory of Justice,* pp. 23–9, 187–8; Robert Nozick, *Anarchy, State, and Utopia* (New York: Basic Books, 1974), pp. 31–4; and Bernard Williams, "Persons, Character, and Morality," reprinted in his *Moral Luck* (Cambridge: Cambridge University Press, 1981), p. 3.

6 Rawls, *Theory of Justice*, p. 27; cf. pp. 29, 187–8.

7 One way in which distribution might be important is compatible with temporal-neutrality. A life might be worse if it contained a highly inegalitarian distribution of goods. Perhaps a good life is a kind of organic whole whose value is not reducible to the sum of the value of each of the parts. Cf. G. E. Moore, *Principia Ethica* (Cambridge: Cambridge University Press, 1903), secs. 18–22; and C. I. Lewis, *An Analysis of Knowledge and Valuation* (La Salle: Open Court, 1946), pp. 491, 494–5. If an arrangement of goods is itself an important good within a life, then temporal-neutrality's commitment to maximization of value over the course of one's life will itself require a certain distribution.

8 Except perhaps Williams, "Persons, Character, and Morality," pp. 8–13.

9 This defense of temporal-neutrality depends on the assumption that it is persons, rather than person stages, that are the normatively relevant units. For discussion and defense of this assumption, see my "Rational Egoism and the Separateness of Persons," in J. Dancy, ed., *Reading Parfit* (Oxford: Basil Blackwell, 1993).

10 I will not here question the assumption that interpersonal compensation is problematic. But this assumption deserves scrutiny. If we accept the plausible claim that the relation that matters in discussions of personal identity is psychological continuity, then the welfare of distinct people is arguably interdependent in a way that makes possible some forms of interpersonal compensation. Cf. my "Rational Egoism, Self, and Others," in O. Flanagan and A. Rorty, eds., *Identity, Character, and Morality* (Cambridge, Mass.: MIT Press, 1990); and Derek Parfit, *Reasons and Persons* (Oxford: Clarendon Press, 1984), ch. 15.

11 Nagel, *Possibility of Altruism*, p. 138.

12 Ibid., p. 142.

13 Nozick, *Anarchy, State, and Utopia*, pp. 32–3.

14 Rawls, *Theory of Justice*, p. 28.

15 My reading of the separateness of persons objection might be compared with Parfit's Objection to Balancing; see Parfit, *Reasons and Persons*, sec. 115.

16 Notice that my discussion does not use the actual situation as a baseline for assessing Pareto-superiority, -optimality, -inferiority, -incomparability, or -indifference. In the process of determining entitlements, none yet exist; so it's inappropriate to use the status quo as a baseline. The baseline must be alternative possible distributions.

17 Thomas Nagel, "Equality," reprinted in his *Mortal Questions* (Cambridge: Cambridge University Press, 1979), pp. 116–27, esp. 123–5.

18 Contrary to what Nozick explicitly claims (*Anarchy, State, and Utopia*, p. 161). Think about how operation of the market within a system of private property rights in the means of production and bequest produces concentrations of property rights that adversely affect the bargaining position of people not party to those market exchanges (e.g., future members of the

working class). These negative externalities of the market show that voluntary market exchanges are not always Pareto improvements. Nozick must also resist the implication of the Pareto interpretation of SRC that Pareto improvements are sufficient grounds for demanding a (compensated) sacrifice, for he presumably believes that nonvoluntary Pareto improvements are impermissible.

Insofar as a libertarian view is (imperfectly) motivated by the Pareto interpretation of SRC, it seems to assume that something like the state of nature serves as a baseline in terms of which Pareto-superiority, -inferiority, and -indifference are to be measured.

19 Rawls, *Theory of Justice*, pp. 7, 17.
20 Ibid., p. 17.
21 Consider three possible distributions.

	A	B	C
Distribution 1	5	7	9
Distribution 2	8	8	7
Distribution 3	9	7	5

Suppose (1) is the actual world. *A* is worst off in (1). Maximizing the position of the worst-off is to be understood as requiring that we move from (1) to (2), where *C* is the worst-off. Thus, "the worst-off" does not refer to the same person in all worlds, and maximin does not require us (always) to maximize the position of the person who is worst off in the actual world (thus, maximin does not treat [3] as preferable to [1]). This shows that the difference principle treats "the worst-off" as a definite description, rather than a rigid designator.

22 Insofar as the moral asymmetry thesis both supports the difference principle and is relevant to its stability in a well-ordered society, it is relevant to the contractual argument for the difference principle. But I think the relationship between moral asymmetry and the difference principle is easier to see (even if only initially) in the noncontractual setting.

23 Ibid., p. 178.
24 Nozick, *Anarchy, State, and Utopia*, p. 197.
25 Cf. Rawls, *Theory of Justice*, p. 176.
26 Ibid., p. 103.
27 Nozick, *Anarchy, State, and Utopia*, pp. 192–6. Also notice that because 'worst-off' functions as a definite description, rather than a rigid designator, it is not necessarily true that B would have been even worse off than he is if the difference principle had not been adopted, because someone else might occupy this worse worst-off position. What is true is that *someone* would

have been even worse off than B is if the difference principle had not been adopted.

28 Rawls, *Theory of Justice*, pp. 15, 101–2, 107.

29 Nozick, of course, rejects this first part of Rawls's reply. He suggests, perhaps, that treating the distribution of natural endowments as a common asset wrongly involves giving others property rights in your person (cf. *Anarchy*, p. 229), and he explicitly asserts that one's entitlements need not be "deserved all the way down" in order to be legitimate (ibid., p. 225). But neither of these claims seems to affect Rawls's point. The claim that people's talents should be treated as a common asset does not give the community property rights to individuals' talents; to treat natural talents as a common asset is only to see a social product that takes individuals' unearned natural talents as inputs as an appropriate object of equitable distribution. In doing so, we do not deny that individuals are entitled to their natural abilities; we do not give the community the right to compel individuals to employ their talents productively; we do not give the community the right to deny individuals the opportunity to employ their talents productively; and we do not even deny individuals the right to benefit from the productive employment of their talents; we deny only that individuals are entitled to all the benefits that they can get others to concede to them from the productive social employment of their talents.

30 Cf. Nagel, *Possibility of Altruism*, p. 142. Also see Thomas Nagel, *Equality and Partiality* (New York: Oxford University Press, 1991), p. 79.

31 Nagel, *Possibility of Altruism*, pp. 141–2.

32 Ibid., p. 141.

33 Ibid., p. 142.

34 Nagel, "Equality," pp. 123, 125, 117–18.

35 Scanlon, "Contractualism and Utilitarianism," p. 110.

36 My focus will not be on individual, discrete actions and outcomes – the focus that Rawls and Scanlon rightly resist – but on institutional mechanisms and policy decisions that generate entitlements and significantly affect people's life prospects. For instance, Nozick's objection that liberty upsets patterned principles (*Anarchy, State, and Utopia*, 160–4) seems to assume that patterned principles directly regulate the justice and injustice of particular, discrete transactions among individuals. Rawls or Scanlon can reply that contractualist principles regulate directly matters of institutional design, rather than particular transactions (cf. *Theory of Justice*, pp. 87–8). The worries that I shall raise for views like those of Rawls and Scanlon do not make this mistake, but focus on the implications of these views for institutions and policies that determine entitlements and affect people's life prospects.

37 Scanlon, "Contractualism and Utilitarianism," p. 116. Cf. Rawls, *Theory of Justice*, pp. 16, 173; Nagel, "Equality," p. 123.

38 Scanlon, "Contractualism and Utilitarianism," p. 123.

39 Ibid.

40 Nagel, "Equality," p. 125.

41 Scanlon, "Contractualism and Utilitarianism," p. 123.

42 Nagel is willing to let the claims of those with the biggest complaints be overridden in some circumstances, but he seems to regard this as an anti-egalitarian element in his views ("Equality," pp. 124–5). Also, after noting that his own view is fundamentally antiaggregative, Scanlon allows that the question how "aggregative considerations can enter into a contractualist argument is a further question too large to be entered into here" ("Contractualism and Utilitarianism," p. 123). These qualifications on the antiaggregative character of their views make it difficult to know whether my criticisms would trouble them. Insofar as they take this antiaggregative feature to be a principal virtue of their positions and reject person-neutral views because these views are aggregative, they should have difficulty accepting my conclusions.

43 My discussion of minimax complaint owes much to lectures Parfit gave at Harvard in the spring of 1989, which are developed in his book manuscript, "On Giving Priority to the Worse Off."

44 Presumably, friends of minimax complaint would endorse the *lexical* version of minimax complaint: First, we minimize the maximum complaint; then, subject to this constraint, we minimize the next-worst complaint; and so on until, subject to the constraints imposed by previous stages, we minimize the smallest complaint (cf. Rawls, *Theory of Justice,* p. 83).

45 Rows indicate distributions under different norms or policies, while columns indicate persons or groups. Unless otherwise indicated, the size of different groups is the same. The numbers measure life prospects, or significant effects on life prospects, by whatever nonmoral index the reader thinks appropriate (e.g., utilities or primary goods).

46 The Smallest Loss and Best Worst-off counterexample is a case in which "chain-connection" does not hold (cf. ibid., p. 80). Rawls claims that the difference principle applies even in cases (worlds) where chain-connection does not hold (ibid., pp. 80–3).

Of course, *Theory of Justice* does stress practical as well as theoretical virtues in theories of justice (e.g., ibid., pp. 90, 95, 138, 140, 142, 318, 320, 501). This practical focus may allow Rawls to discount unrealistic counterexamples to the difference principle. But we can address issues of practicality *after* trying to settle theoretical issues. Moreover, the theoretical differences between maximin and, more generally, minimax complaint and their rivals do have significant practical implications.

47 I shall not discuss the version of minimax complaint in which the size of complaint depends on the size of a person's relative loss ([ii]) alone, because I don't think it captures the intuitions that motivate moral asymmetry. As such, this version of minimax complaint has no egalitarian commitments. It would appear to preclude all egalitarian transfers from the better-off to the worse-off that reduce the total social product. Thus, for example, it would condemn Distribution 2 in

	A	B
Distribution 1	2	100
Distribution 2	31	70

whereas any robust version of moral asymmetry would presumably insist on it. This version of minimax complaint resembles Gauthier's view, though he treats the state of nature as the baseline in assessing losses, as I do not. See David Gauthier, *Morals by Agreement* (Oxford: Clarendon Press, 1986), pp. 14, 133–46.

48 Nagel, "Equality," p. 123; Scanlon, "Contractualism and Utilitarianism," p. 123.

49 Nagel, "Equality," pp. 116–17.

50 Ibid., p. 124.

51 Ibid., p. 117.

52 Ibid., pp. 117–18, 122–5.

53 Cf. Rawls, *Theory of Justice,* pp. 24–5, 30–1.

54 Cf. ibid., pp. 42–3.

55 Cf. ibid., p. 34.

56 Ibid., pp. 16, 173; Nagel, "Equality," p. 123; Scanlon, "Contractualism and Utilitarianism," p. 119.

57 Rawls, *Theory of Justice,* pp. 136, 140.

58 Ibid., pp. 12, 120.

59 Ibid., pp. 17, 119, 121, 138, 139.

60 Indeed, the difference principle itself requires aggregation as long as representative social positions (e.g., the worst-off) are sufficiently coarse-grained as to include subgroups at different levels of well-being and the level of a representative position is defined as the average of the levels of its subgroups.

61 Rawls argues against unrestricted utilitarianism on the ground that it is not a stable distributional norm, because its stability would require those whose interests might be sacrificed in order to maximize total or average utility to identify their interests with the interests of others in a way that is psychologically unrealistic, as well as morally unattractive (*Theory of Justice,* pp. 177, 500). But when we notice that maximin involves a dictatorship of the worst complaint, we may doubt its stability. For its stability would seem to require the entire population of those who are marginally less worse off than the worst-off – no matter how large this population is – to identify their interests completely with those of the worst-off – no matter how small a population this is.

62 Scanlon, "Contractualism and Utilitarianism," pp. 124–5.

63 This is similar to the idea, which some have accepted, that if we model (i) the interpersonal combinatorial problem on (ii) the problem of how an

individual would combine the interests of different individuals if she imagined living these lives *seriatim,* then we are committed by temporal-neutrality to utilitarianism's person-neutrality. Lewis endorses this way of modeling the interpersonal combinatorial problem; see Lewis, *Analysis of Knowledge and Valuation,* pp. 546–7. Nagel and Hare both find utilitarian commitments in this model. See Nagel, *Possibility of Altruism,* pp. 138–9; and R. M. Hare, *Moral Thinking* (Oxford: Clarendon Press, 1981), pp. 110–11. But the model does not require the utilitarian conclusion. It would do so only if (iii) the individual treated these distinct lives (to be lived *seriatim*) as if they were parts or stages of one single superlife. Then the requirement of temporal-neutrality (see Section 1 of this chapter) would require utilitarianism's person-neutrality. But the question is precisely whether it is reasonable to understand (ii) as (iii).

64 Scanlon doesn't want to say that a distribution is permissible if it imposes severe hardships on self-sacrificing people who are willing to accept them, as we would have to if the operative notion was acceptability. Because people could reasonably reject such burdens, even if they do not, contractualism won't permit this distribution if it's formulated in terms of reasonable rejectability ("Contractualism and Utilitarianism," pp. 111–12).

65 Ibid., p. 111.

66 Ibid., p. 116.

67 Nagel, "Equality," pp. 117, 123.

68 Cf. ibid., p. 117.

69 Ibid., p. 123.

70 Cf. McKerlie, "Egalitarianism and the Separateness of Persons," pp. 218–20.

71 Nagel, "Equality," p. 117. Notice that it is urgency that attaches to needs, rather than persons or positions, that Nagel appeals to here.

72 Of course, Rawls and Scanlon concede *this* (*Theory of Justice,* pp. 15–16; "Contractualism and Utilitarianism," p. 110), but they think a version of minimax complaint is the most plausible result of the right sort of contract.

73 In this way, my views about the relation between contractualism and teleological ethics are quite different from those of John Harsanyi in "Morality and the Theory of Rational Behavior," reprinted in A. Sen and B. Williams, eds., *Utilitarianism and Beyond* (Cambridge: Cambridge University Press, 1985).

14

Harmful goods, harmless bads

LARRY TEMKIN

1. Introduction

The Slogan: One situation *cannot* be worse (or better) than another if there is *no one* for whom it *is* worse (or better).

Like certain other slogans – for example, Each person is deserving of equal consideration and respect – the Slogan enjoys widespread acceptance. It underlies many arguments in philosophy and economics, and those appealing to it span the range of theoretical positions, including deontological, consequentialist, and rights-based views. In addition, as with some more famous slogans, most believe that the Slogan expresses a deep and important truth. So, like a powerful modern-day Occam's razor, often the Slogan is wielded to carve out, shape, or whittle down the domain of moral value.

Unfortunately, the Slogan is almost always invoked both implicitly and rhetorically. Perhaps it has been thought to be an ultimate moral principle – that which provides the justification for *other* claims, but which cannot, and need not, *itself* be justified. More likely the Slogan has been thought so obvious as to not even require explicit acknowledgment let alone explication or defense. After all, one might rhetorically ask, how *could* one situation be worse than another if there is *no one* for whom it *is* worse?

In this article I shall present considerations relevant to assessing the Slogan and the arguments invoking it. My central claims are three. First, widespread agreement about the Slogan is more apparent than real. The Slogan is a very confusing claim, subject to many interpretations with

I am grateful to the National Humanities Center for its support, and also to my colleagues at Rice University and members of the Triangle Circle Ethics Group in Chapel Hill. Among those who have generously commented on earlier drafts of this essay are Michael Bayles, John Broome, Tyler Cowen, Jonathan Dancy, James Griffin, Shelly Kagan, John O'Connor, Bill Rowe, and Thomas Scanlon. Special thanks are due to Derek Parfit, whose suggestions greatly influenced this work, and to Thomas Nagel, whose comments on another work of mine, many years ago, first prompted the writing of this essay.

different implications. Hence, uncritical acceptance of the Slogan covers up the fact that no single position is being invoked or agreed upon. Second, substantive interpretations of the Slogan are neither obvious nor uncontroversial. Thus, rhetorical appeals to the Slogan are unwarranted in support of significant moral positions. Third, even if there are some plausible interpretations of the Slogan, the Slogan does not support most of the particular positions it has been thought to support.

In sum, I shall argue that the Slogan and the arguments invoking it are at best misleading and at worst mistaken. Minimally, then, the Slogan requires explication and defense heretofore lacking. In addition, most positions appealing to it must either be rejected or supported on other grounds.

The paper is divided into eight sections. In Section 2 I present some of the arguments invoking the Slogan. In Section 3 I briefly comment on a recent argument attacking the Slogan. In Section 4 I distinguish several ways of interpreting the Slogan, and note the avenue most worth pursuing. In Sections 5–7 I look at three theories of the good to see if any support the Slogan and the arguments invoking it. In Section 8 I discuss some other interpretations of the Slogan, along with reasons for its great appeal. I end by noting that there *may* be a kernel of truth the Slogan awkwardly expresses which *is* both deep and important. However, this fact, if it is one, does not undermine my central claims.

2. Cases where the Slogan is implicitly invoked

Let me indicate some of the cases where the Slogan seems to have been implicitly invoked.

(1) Locke's theory of acquisition holds that people have a property right to any unowned thing they mix their labor with "at least where there is enough and as good left in common for others."[1] Nozick writes of this position that "the crucial point is whether appropriation of an unowned object worsens the situation of others."[2] The implication is that as long as there is no one for whom acquiring the property is worse, it cannot be bad.

(2) Nozick follows Locke when he writes, "A medical researcher who synthesizes a new substance (out of easily obtainable materials) that effectively treats a new disease and who refuses to sell except on his own terms does not worsen the situation of others by depriving them of whatever he has appropriated."[3] Here, Nozick implicitly relies on the Slogan to support his position that the researcher does nothing wrong if he keeps his product off the market.[4]

Similarly, though the point of Nozick's Wilt Chamberlain example is that liberty upsets patterns, much of its force seems derived from the Slogan. Thus, Nozick writes:

Each of these persons *chose* to give twenty-five cents of their money to Chamberlain. They could have spent it on going to the movies, or candy bars.... Can anyone else complain on grounds of justice?... After someone transfers something to Wilt Chamberlain, third parties *still* have their legitimate shares, *their* shares have not changed.[5]

Again, the implication is that if no one is worsened by the exchange, it cannot be bad.

(3) A situation is *Pareto-optimal* if no one's lot could be improved without worsening the lot of someone else. Most economists think a non-Pareto-optimal situation is inefficient. Some take a much stronger position. They think that whenever we could improve the lot of some, without worsening the lot of anyone else, it would be irrational, and wrong, not to do so. Clearly, this position presupposes the Slogan. After all, if a non-Pareto-optimal situation *could* be better than a (more) Pareto-optimal one, though there was no one for whom it was better, it need not be either irrational or wrong to fail to transform the former into the latter.

(4) The Slogan also explains why some find Rawls's Difference Principle (DP) more plausible than egalitarianism, and others find it too egalitarian to be plausible. When DP allows vast gains for the better-off to promote tiny gains for the worse-off, it is often defended by invoking the Slogan. Likewise, DP is criticized via the Slogan for failing to permit gains to the better-off that are not accompanied by gains to the worse-off.[6]

(5) Consider Diagram 14.1.

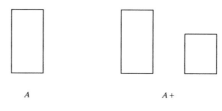

A   A +

Diagram 14.1

In discussing such a diagram, Derek Parfit wrote:

Let us compare A with A +. The only difference is that A + contains an extra group, who have lives worth living, and who affect no one else.... [I]t seems [hard]... to believe that A + is *worse* than A. This implies that it would have been better if the extra group had never existed. If their lives are worth living, and they affect no one else, why is it bad that these people are alive?[7]

Here, too, the Slogan seems to be invoked, for the question is, how could $A+$ be worse than A when there is no one for whom it is worse?[8]

(6) Similarly, I think the Slogan underlies the thinking of most non-egalitarians.[9] Consider Diagram 14.2.

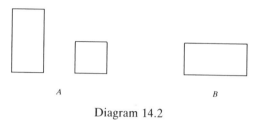

Diagram 14.2

Let A represent a world where half are blind, B a world where all are. One *could* transform A into B by putting out the eyes of those with sight. However, many find the view that this would improve the situation in even one respect more than incomprehensible, they find it abominable. That B is more equal than A gives one *no reason at all*, they think, to transform A into B; and only a hardened misanthrope, or someone motivated by the basest form of envy, could think otherwise. After all, they ask, how *could* B be better in *any* respect, if there is *no one* for whom it is better?[10]

(7) In "Rights, Goals, and Fairness," Thomas Scanlon observes, "rights . . . need to be justified somehow, and how other than by appeal to the human interests their recognition promotes and protects? This seems to be the uncontrovertible insight of the classical utilitarians."[11] Many extend Scanlon's view to argue against the intrinsic value of respecting rights. Thus, it is contended that since the whole point of a system of rights is (must be?) to promote and protect human (or sentient) interests, there is not reason to respect (apparent) rights in those (rare) cases where doing so fails to promote or protect anyone's interests. Analogously, many claim there is nothing intrinsically bad about violating (apparent) rights when this benefits some and harms no one. These claims derive much of their force from the Slogan, according to which a situation where rights are respected (or violated) *cannot* be better (or worse) than one where they are not, if there is *no one* for whom it *is* better (or worse).

(8) Finally, we may note that standard objections to rule-utilitarianism, virtue-based, and deontological theories often parallel those noted against equality and rights-based theories. That is, they

involve constructing cases where no one benefits and some are harmed, or where some benefit and no one is harmed, if only one does or doesn't (a) follow the rule, (b) act virtuously, or (c) do one's duty. Once more, the force of these objections rests on an implicit appeal to the Slogan.

These are merely some of the many positions implicitly invoking the Slogan. The list is by no means exhaustive. As we shall see, one should be wary of any appeals to the Slogan. Hence, one must seek other justifications for the positions one finds plausible.[12]

3. The Non-Identity Problem

In "Future Generations: Further Problems," Derek Parfit presents the *Non-Identity Problem*, an ingenious argument that challenges the Slogan. A variation of it is depicted in Diagram 14.3.

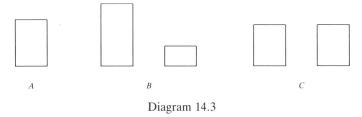

A   B   C

Diagram 14.3

Let *A* represent a generation contemplating two policies. On the *live-for-today* policy, they have children immediately, and deplete the natural resources for current uses. *B* would result; *they* would be better off, but their children would fare less well. On the *take-care-of-tomorrow* policy, they postpone having children a few years, and conserve their resources. *C* would result; *they* would fare slightly less well than they do now, but the children they have would fare as well as they.

Most believe the take-care-of-tomorrow policy should be adopted. But this is incompatible with the Slogan given two plausible assumptions: (*P*) the children born in *B* would be *different people* from the children born in *C* (being conceived several years later they would come from different sperm and ova, be raised by older and wiser parents, etc.), and (*Q*) one cannot harm or act against the interests of someone who will never exist and, more particularly, one does not harm someone by failing to conceive her (so, by refraining from sex for a month, a woman does not harm any of the millions of people who might have existed if she had had sex and conceived).[13] Given these assumptions,[14] there is *no one* for whom the live-for-today policy would be worse: not the parents, who fare better in *B* than in either *A* or *C;* not the children in

, because *they* wouldn't exist if the take-care-of-tomorrow policy was adopted; and not the children in *C*, because they don't exist and never will exist if the live-for-today policy is adopted. On the other hand, if the take-care-of-tomorrow policy is adopted there *will* be someone for whom it is worse, namely the parents. Thus, unless we alter our judgment about which policy is better, the Slogan needs to be revised, if not rejected.

I have discussed Parfit's argument with many nonphilosophers as well as philosophers. Almost all find it perplexing. Most, at least initially, try to undermine it. Some question assumption *P* (often on [weak] theological grounds), others assumption *Q*. Some simply insist something *must* be wrong with the argument, though they know not what!

Among those accepting Parfit's argument, few believe the Slogan should be rejected outright. They point out, rightly, that the most Parfit *establishes* is that there is a limited and fairly peculiar range of cases where the Slogan does not apply. These are cases where future generations are involved, and, more particularly, cases where one's choices determine *who* comes to be. In most cases of moral concern these conditions do not obtain, and for such cases, it is contended, the Slogan remains plausible.[15]

These reactions are not atypical.[16] They point to both the strength and widespread appeal of the Slogan, as well as the need to supplement Parfit's argument if, as I believe, appeals to the Slogan should be resisted.

4. Interpreting the Slogan

The Slogan is ambiguous. For example, it might be used as shorthand for any of the following claims.

1. One situation *cannot* be worse (or better) than another *in any respect* if there is *no one* for whom it *is* worse (or better) *in any respect*.

2. *One situation cannot* be worse (or better) than another *in any respect* if there is *no one* for whom it *is* worse (or better) *all things considered*.

3. *One situation cannot* be worse (or better) than another *all things considered* if there is *no one* for whom it *is* worse (or better) *in any respect*.

4. *One situation cannot* be worse (or better) than another *all things considered* if there is *no one* for whom it *is* worse (or better) *all things considered*.

In this essay, my concern is with the Slogan understood as shorthand
for (1). Interpretation (2) is not plausible, and (3) and (4) are much
weaker and less interesting than (1). More importantly, (3) and (4)
would not license many conclusions for which the Slogan has been
invoked.[17]

The nonegalitarian who insists that there is *no reason at all* to put
out the eyes of the sighted uses the Slogan to support the view that
equality has *no* intrinsic value. At best, (1) could support such a
conclusion. Interpretations (3) and (4) could not. In fact, (3) and (4)
are compatible with equality being the most important ideal. They
merely rule out the conclusions that equality is all that matters and
that equality matters more than everything else combined. Such conclusions are not terribly interesting and one need hardly invoke the
Slogan to support them.

Similarly, few would deny that keeping one's promise or respecting
rights or acting virtuously is not always the best thing to do all things
considered. More interesting are the claims that there is *no* reason to
keep one's promise or respect rights or act virtuously, in cases where
there is no one for whom it is better. I believe opponents of deontological, rights-based, and virtue theories often invoke the Slogan to
support the latter, stronger claims. Again, at best (1) could support such
claims, (3) and (4) could not.

Finally, I think Nozick's Wilt Chamberlain example is intended to
illustrate not merely that voluntary transactions that leave no one worse
off are acceptable all things considered, but that there is *nothing* wrong
with them, that is, *no* reason to prevent them. Here, too, the Slogan
could only support such a view interpreted as (1).

Another reason for focusing on (1) is that (3) and (4) derive much of
their plausibility and rhetorical appeal from (1). After all, if one situation
could be worse than another in some respect, even if there was no one
for whom it was worse in even one respect (and hence all things considered), then why couldn't it be worse all things considered? Presumably the one situation *would* be worse than the other all things considered
if there was no respect in which it was better, or if the respect(s) in
which it was better were not sufficient to outweigh the respect(s) in
which it was worse. Surely there is no *a priori* reason to rule out such
possibilities if (1) is false.

Together, the preceding makes plain the Slogan's full force. It isn't
merely that one situation *is* never worse than another if there is no one
for whom it is worse – as if this might be true in some respects, but not
"all things considered." Rather, it is that one situation *cannot* be worse
than another if there is no one for whom it is worse – as if there is no

·espect in which this might be so, and hence no question that in some ·ases the positive features might outweigh the negative ones. It is this ;trong position, expressed by (1), that underlies and explains people's ;onfident rhetorical uses of the Slogan.

In what follows, then, I shall understand the Slogan as shorthand 'or (1), unless otherwise noted. Doing so will be sufficient to establish ny central claims. In fact, I believe the considerations adduced also provide reason to be skeptical of (3) and (4), though this is not to leny that in *most* cases situation *A* will not be worse (or better) than ;ituation *B* all things considered, if there is no one for whom it is worse (or better).

The Slogan is most naturally interpreted as making a claim about what .s relevant to a situation's being good. This means that (1) is itself subject to interpretation, as the content and implications of the Slogan will lepend on one's theory, or theories, of the good. Thus, appearances to the contrary, people endorsing the Slogan are in fact endorsing very lifferent positions if they hold different theories of the good.[18] This will pecome clearer, along with its importance, as the essay progresses.

To assess properly the Slogan and the arguments invoking it, it is necessary to consider whether any plausible theories of the good support them. In the next sections, I shall focus on three candidates: the *Mental State Theory,* the *Subjective Desire-Fulfillment Theory,* and the *Objective List Theory.* Though other alternatives are possible, I believe that my arguments could be applied to plausible alternatives, and hence that the theories considered are sufficient for my central claims.

Two asides before turning to Section 5. First, one benefit from assessing the Slogan is that it forces us to get clearer about theories of the good and to make important distinctions easily neglected. As we shall see, one may usefully distinguish between theories about *self-interest,* which tell us what is good or bad *for* someone, and theories about *outcomes,* which tell us what makes an outcome good or bad. Unfortunately, perhaps partly due to the Slogan's appeal, the differences between these theories are often blurred or overlooked. I believe that some theories put forward as ·"theories of the good" are most plausible as theories about self-interest, while others are most plausible as theories about outcomes. Correspondingly, some theories that are easily dismissed as "full theories of the good" may yet deserve attention when "properly" interpreted. In addition, the most plausible "full theory of the good" may be different from, but include elements of, each such theory.

Second, although sufficient for my present purposes, Sections 5–7 raise more questions than they answer, and at that they raise but a small portion of the unresolved questions regarding theories of the good.

Unfortunately, this crucially important area has been sorely neglecte(
It warrants, and would surely repay, much more attention than I ca
give it in this essay.

5. The Mental State Theory

Let us begin with the Mental State Theory (MST) of the classical uti
itarians. According to this theory, *only conscious states have intrins*
value or disvalue, and everything else has value or disvalue only to th
extent that it promotes positive or negative conscious states.

At first, MST *seems* to support the Slogan.[19] Consider, for exampl(
Diagram 14.4.

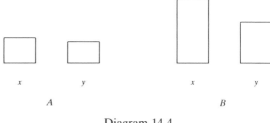

x   y   x   y

A   B

Diagram 14.4

If the column heights represent conscious states (where the taller th
column the higher the quality of people's conscious states), then a(
cording to MST there would be *no* reason to regard the greater inequali(
in *B* as bad, since there is *no one* whose conscious states it affec(
adversely, and hence, no one for whom it is worse.[20] Here, MST seen
not only to yield the Slogan's results, but to account for those resul(
and, correspondingly, for the Slogan itself.

I believe MST represents a significant insight of the classical utilita
ians. It is arguable, for example, that ice cream, tropical paradises, an
Beethoven's symphonies, as well as rotten eggs, desert wastelands, an
screeching brakes, only have their value or disvalue in virtue of the(
effects on conscious states. Indeed, it is arguable that *most* things onl
have value or disvalue in virtue of their effects on conscious state
Nevertheless, MST goes too far in claiming that *only* conscious stat(
are intrinsically valuable. Surely this position is implausible as a fu
theory about outcomes. If it were true it would undermine virtuall
every ideal.

Consider Diagram 14.5 and the conception of *proportional justic(*
according to which there ought to be a proportion between faring we
and doing well.

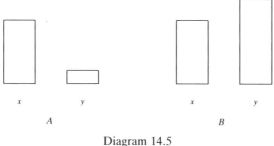

Diagram 14.5

Let *A* and *B* represent alternative afterlives, with the *x* columns representing the saints' conscious states, and the *y* columns the sinners'. Furthermore, assume *A* accurately reflects how the two groups "should" fare according to proportional justice and their earthly lives. Clearly, in accordance with proportional justice, *A* would be better than *B*.

Is this implausible? Many, including Aristotle, Kant, and Ross, have thought not. Yet on MST not only would *B* be better, there would be no respect in which it was worse.

Most would find this hard to accept. They believe there would be *something* morally bad about the evilest mass murders faring better than the most benign saints, even if there was *no one* for whom it was worse.[21]

It might be contended that there *is* someone for whom *B* is worse than *A* (at least in one respect), namely us, the observers who are bothered by *B*.[22] Strictly speaking this is correct, but irrelevant. Our concern is with how *A* and *B* themselves compare. To assess this from the perspective of MST, we must restrict our attention to the conscious states of those who are actually in *A* and *B*. To include our reactions as observers would not be to assess the situations themselves, but to assess another, wider, situation, one that merely included the original situations among its components. Of course, it might be claimed that there *is* no respect in which *B* is worse than *A* considered by themselves, and hence that the only reason *B* is worse than *A* (at least in one respect) is that we, the observers, are bothered by *B*. However, despite the claims of Hobbes and others,[23] many believe this gets things backward. Thus, most advocates of proportional justice would deny that *B* is worse than *A* because they find it objectionable. Rather, they would contend, the reason they find *B* objectionable is that injustice is bad. Thus, most who believe that *B* is worse than *A* in at least one respect would insist that this would be so even if there were no observers "offended" by the situation, or even if the only observers were indifferent to injustice or perhaps even relished it.[24]

These considerations suggest that unless one is willing to reject pro-

portional justice entirely and abandon the view that there is *some* respect
in which *B* is worse than *A* (considered by themselves), one must reject
the Slogan as supported by MST. To the question "how *could* one
situation be worse than another if there is *no one* for whom it *is* worse?"
one might respond, "it could be worse if it were worse regarding proportional justice." This would express the view that conscious states are
not all that matters – proportional justice does too. Naturally, an egalitarian could make a similar response.

Analogous remarks could be made about freedom, autonomy, virtue,
duty, or any other ideal. Consider Diagram 14.6, where the column
heights again represent the quality of conscious states.

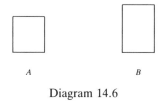

Diagram 14.6

If in situation *A* people were free, autonomous, virtuous, or dutiful,
and in situation *B* people were much less so, *A* might be preferred to
B by those who value the ideals in question. Rejecting the Slogan as
supported by MST, they would contend that in addition to conscious
states we (should) also care about people's freedom, autonomy, virtue,
or duty fulfillment.

Ironically, the Slogan as supported by MST would even be rejected
by the classical utilitarians themselves, who would undoubtedly judge
the live-for-today policy of Section 3 worse than the take-care-of-
tomorrow policy, as it is worse in terms of both total and average utility.
But of course this judgment cannot be made if one situation cannot be
worse than another if there is *no one* for whom it *is* worse in terms of
their conscious states.

So, among those who would reject the Slogan as (apparently) supported by MST would be the proponents of proportional justice, equality, freedom, autonomy, virtue, duty, and even maximizing total or
average utility. This does not mean, of course, that one *should* care
about *each* of these ideals. No positive argument has been offered in
support of them. But unless one is willing to reject them *all*, one cannot
reject *any* merely because it entails that one situation could be worse
than another though it is not worse for anyone's conscious states. *Other*
reasons must be found to oppose the ideals one finds implausible.

Most agree that MST has serious shortcomings as a full theory of the good. But many would disagree on exactly where MST goes wrong. Though easily ignored, the source of this disagreement is important. To illustrate it, let us invoke the distinction noted at the end of Section 4 between theories about self-interest and theories about outcomes. Recall that the former tell us what is good or bad *for* someone,[25] the latter what makes an *outcome* good or bad. Unfortunately, the precise relationship between these is not evident, and failure to carefully distinguish them has been the source of much confusion, as well as, perhaps, the Slogan's appeal.

Some who reject MST object to it as a theory about outcomes, though not as a theory about self-interest. They think it plausible that something can only be good or bad *for* someone insofar as it affects her conscious states, but deny that only conscious states are intrinsically good or bad. For example, advocates of proportional justice could agree that sinners faring better than saints needn't be worse *for* anyone, yet insist that such a situation might still be bad, because proportional justice has value beyond its being good *for* people.

On the other hand, some who reject MST object to it as a theory about outcomes *because* they think it inadequate as a theory about self-interest. For example, some believe that freedom is good *for* people, beyond its influence on conscious states. So, they might regard a world with higher conscious states but less freedom as worse than one with lower conscious states but more freedom precisely *because* they believe people are better off in the latter than the former.

Naturally, one might reject MST for both reasons, thinking it goes wrong as a theory about self-interest *and* as a theory about outcomes, without the latter being due *only* to the former.[26]

Each of these reasons may underlie Nozick's example of the experience machine. He writes:

Suppose there were an experience machine that would give you any experience you desired. . . . Would you plug in? *What else can matter to us, other than how our lives feel from the inside?* First, we want to do certain things, and not just have the experience of doing them. . . . [Second,] we want to *be* a certain way, to be a certain sort of person. Someone floating in a tank is an indeterminate blob. . . . We learn that something matters to us in addition to experience by imagining an experience machine and then realizing that we would not use it. . . . Perhaps what we desire is to live (an active verb) ourselves, in contact with reality. (And this, machines cannot do *for* us.)[27]

Most agree with Nozick. Even if some would plug themselves in, most would think it bad if everyone were to do so, even if there was no one for whom it was worse in terms of the quality of their conscious states. However, is this because conscious states are not all that matter for (a) the "badness" of outcomes, or (b) what makes someone's life good or bad? Though this issue has largely been overlooked, I suspect some think the former, some the latter, and some both.

MST was first offered as a full theory of the good. Believing that only the quality of conscious states was relevant to the good for both individuals *and* outcomes, the classical utilitarians saw no need for different theories of the good. Regrettably, many have unwittingly followed their path, assuming the same theory would suffice for self-interest, outcomes, and the full theory of the good. Thus, convinced of MST's implausibility as a full theory of the good, many dismissed it without pursuing the source of its shortcomings. This is unfortunate, for on reflection I think some would agree that while MST is *not* an adequate theory about outcomes, it *is* an adequate theory about self-interest. That is, it is arguable that one of the great insights of the classical utilitarians was not only that *most* things are only good insofar as they promote positive mental states, but the further point that *nothing* is good *for* someone, i.e. in her self-interest, except insofar as it positively affects the quality of her conscious states.

The foregoing is not only of general importance, it directly bears on our central issue. According to the Slogan, one situation *cannot* be worse than another in even one respect, if there is *no one* for whom it *is* worse in even one respect. This implies that one's theory of outcomes must be a direct function of (perhaps, in a sense, supervenient on) one's theory of self-interest. Clearly, however, to accept MST as a theory about self-interest while rejecting it as a theory about outcomes is to deny the relation in question. More specifically, it is to insist that some factors can be relevant to the goodness of outcomes other than those relevant to what is good *for* people. Thus, on the view in question, one must reject the Slogan and the arguments invoking it, at least on its most natural and straightforward interpretation.[28]

Interestingly, once one distinguishes between theories about self-interest and theories about outcomes one may wonder why the Slogan seemed plausible in the first place. After all, while the quality of people's lives will certainly play a (and perhaps the) major role in the goodness of outcomes, why should the correct theory about outcomes be dependent on the correct theory about self-interest in the way the Slogan would have us believe?

Still, if one thinks MST fails as a theory about self-interest, one may yet believe that the correct theory about outcomes will involve an alternative to MST that does support the Slogan. Let us next consider if a Subjective Desire-Fulfillment Theory yields this result.

6. The Subjective Desire-Fulfillment Theory

1 this section, I note many unresolved questions facing the Subjective Desire-Fulfillment Theory (SDFT). Minimally, this shows that rhetorical appeals to the Slogan are (currently) unjustified insofar as they ultimately rest on SDFT. I next suggest that even if its problems can be met SDFT probably does not support the Slogan. I end by arguing that even if some plausible version of SDFT supports the Slogan, it will not support the particular arguments that in fact invoke the Slogan.

Let me begin by briefly presenting the Subjective Desire-Fulfillment Theory and noting its main attractions. SDFT holds that something will be good or bad for someone insofar, and only insofar, as it promotes or contravenes the fulfillment of her desires; where, roughly, the value of fulfilling an agent's desires is ultimately derivable from her desires themselves. So, on this view, the agent is, within certain limits discussed below, the ultimate arbiter of her own good. What she desires is good for her and, importantly, it is her desiring it that makes it so.

Some are attracted to SDFT by the following sort of case. Suppose Jones was deeply committed to *his* helping the advance of science. Convinced that a unified field theory must be true, he devotes his life to seeking one and, because of his eminence, most scientists follow his example. At the time of his death Jones is a contented man, universally respected for the advances it is thought he has made. Unfortunately, the search for the unified field theory is later recognized as one of the worst turns in the history of science. Moreover, historians and scientists agree that Jones's publications and stature probably set back the advance of science a hundred years or more.

Some think such a turn of events would be worse for Jones, even though it would not affect his conscious states. He would have failed in one of the ways he most wanted to succeed. Unlike MST, SDFT can capture this view, for although the later developments would have no bearing on Jones's conscious states, they would have a bearing – a powerfully negative one – on the fulfillment of his deepest (self-regarding) desires.

Similarly, some are attracted to SDFT because it can account for the view that even if no one's mental states are adversely affected, there would be something wrong with slandering another, deceiving another, making a promise to someone dying and then counting it as of no weight, and plugging everyone into Nozick's experience machine. This is because most have strong desires that would be contravened by such actions.

In addition, some are attracted to SDFT by theoretical considerations

about the relationship between conscious states and desires. They be
lieve conscious states are not *themselves* good or bad. Rather, they think
that whether a conscious state is good or not depends on whether it
plays a role in fulfilling some desire.

One important implication of SDFT follows directly from the Jones
and dying promise cases, and indirectly from the others. One cannot
ignore past desires merely because they are past or even because the
desirer has died.[29]

Despite its attractions I have great reservations about SDFT both as
a theory about self-interest and as one about outcomes. Let me indicate
some of these and then argue that even if my worries can be allayed
SDFT probably will not support the Slogan or the way it has been
invoked.

Some profess difficulty in understanding how something could be
intrinsically good or bad without being good or bad *for* someone. Confronted with MST's shortcomings, they are driven to and find comfort
in SDFT, according to which someone can be made worse off by the
contravening of her desires even if she is never aware this has happened
and it has no effect on her conscious states. For my own part, I confess
the latter view seems no less mysterious than the former. Surely, in the
clearest, most straightforward sense, the person *herself* won't be harmed
if, after she is dead, someone slanders her. *She* is no longer around to
be harmed. Exactly where, when, and how is the damage done, such
that *she* is now worse off than she was before? The mystery is perhaps
less gripping when the person is still alive, but it is not less puzzling.

Perhaps we are to understand such claims counterfactually. Slander
is worse for someone if it is true that had she learned of it she would
have been worse off. Yet how does the truth of that counterfactual
actually make her worse off? If a tree had fallen on Sue she would have
been worse off, but that doesn't make her so.

A Subjective Desire-Fulfillment Theorist might respond: "Granted,
it may sound a bit odd to say someone can be harmed by events not
affecting her conscious states. But this merely shows there is *some* force
to MST. Having seen in Section 5 that MST is implausible, the correct
conclusion to draw is that there are *different* ways something can be
worse for someone. And, on reflection, we see that something can be
worse for someone by contravening her desires."

This may be the correct conclusion to draw from Section 5, but it is
neither obvious nor forced on us. Why not grant, with the Mental State
Theorist, that something can only be worse *for* someone insofar as it
hurts her conscious states, but reject the view that something can only
be morally *bad* if it is bad *for* someone? Why shouldn't we say, for

example, that contravening Sue's desires is bad, even if, because she is dead, it isn't worse *for her?* Notice, this would be consistent with holding that the action only *is* bad because Sue had the desires she did.

Since all might agree that (a) acting against the desires of the dead isn't worse for them in terms of their conscious states, (b) nevertheless we ought not to so act, and (c) our so acting might only *be* bad because of desires they had while alive, it may seem inconsequential whether we describe such actions as bad because they contravene desires or because they are worse *for* people. There are two reasons to reject this. First, recognizing actions or outcomes as bad though not worse for anyone enables us to see the weakness of the Slogan and the arguments invoking it. Second, accepting the view that contravening desires is actually worse for people enables one to sidestep the explanation called for on the alternative view as to *why* contravening desires is bad.

When I slander the dead is this bad because (a) contravening desires is intrinsically bad,[30] (b) slander is intrinsically bad, (c) contravening desires and/or slandering fail(s) to show proper respect due someone with a moral personality, (d) doing so fails to properly express my moral personality, or . . . ? I don't know the full answer to this question, but it is not evident that the "badness" of my action lies in my harming the person whose desire I have contravened or, for that matter, in anyone's being left worse off than they were before.

Another worry regarding SDFT is whether a plausible account can be given of which desires are to count as being better or worse for someone when they are fulfilled or contravened. Should it be her *actual* desires or her *conditional* ones – those she *would* have if she were unrushed, clear-thinking, fully informed, and so on. Similarly, should it be her *global* desires – the deepest desires she has about her life as a whole – or her *local* desires – the particular desires one has at each moment of one's life? Moreover, what are we to say when someone's desires are the result of "distorting" influences? What if the "distorting" influences are the factors usually involved in "normal" social conditioning? On SDFT it is crucial that one be able to identify those desires the fulfillment of which promotes someone's good. But, on an SDFT – unlike an objective theory – it is unclear how one could plausibly do this.

The preceding worries mainly concern SDFT's plausibility as a theory about self-interest. Even if they could be allayed, SDFT seems implausible as a theory about outcomes.

According to SDFT, someone will be worse off if, after she is dead, events conspire to undermine the ends she seriously pursued.[31] Yet, throughout history people have earnestly promoted ends we do not share. Does this mean we *ought* to consider what would best promote the ends of, for example, the devoted Spartans, monarchists, Jacobeans, and Pilgrims, in deciding what to do? This seems implausible.

Interestingly, if we retain SDFT as a theory about self-interest yet reject it as a theory of outcomes, the result is a position almost the obverse of the Slogan. Instead of an outcome only being good or bad if it is good or bad *for* people, an outcome's being good or bad *for* people (e.g., Spartans) need not be relevant to *its* being good or bad.

Many of my worries dovetail with standard worries about subjective theories. For example, many believe we need not count the desires of sadists and bigots – past or present – even if they are deeply committed to advancing pain or prejudice. Similarly, many think ignoring the starving's desire for food would be worse than ignoring an equally strong desire for money to build a telescope, even if the telescope builder were the one starving and would herself prefer money for the telescope to food.[32] It is unclear how SDFT can capture these sentiments without invoking an objective element.

More importantly, for many, SDFT cannot accommodate our deepest views about the nature and foundations of moral value. This is not the place to rehash the arguments for or against objectivity in ethics. Suffice it to say, many would insist that if morality is not to be a vain and chimerical notion it cannot be our desires for freedom, justice, or autonomy that make them good, otherwise if we came to desire slavery, injustice, or external controls it would then be true that *those* were good.[33]

This last point is worth special emphasis. People differ markedly in what they value. Where some would trade losses in freedom, autonomy, equality, or justice for gains in conscious states, others would not; where some would agree with Mill that the discontented genius is better off than the contented simpleton, others would not; where some would value freedom more than justice, others would not; and so on. On SDFT nothing precludes such disagreements. To the contrary, SDFT would support each side where disputes arose. But, of course, such disagreements *need* not occur. If, perchance, everyone preferred one alternative to another, then on SDFT it would be *that* alternative which was better, *whichever* one it was. Indeed, an alternative that no one desired would be an alternative in no way good.

On an objective theory there is room for saying that everyone is mistaken in what they value. On a subjective theory, where what makes something good is that people desire it,[34] such a claim seems indefensible. The upshot of this is important though not surprising. SDFT has room for whatever ideals people desire. Yet, as a subjective theory, it leaves no room for the objectivity or intrinsic value of *any* ideal. Thus, even if SDFT supported the Slogan, one could not appeal to it to undermine the intrinsic value of certain ideals, without committing oneself to the ultimate subjectivity of *all* our ideals.

Of course one might claim that an unrushed, clear-thinking, fully informed person *must* rationally prefer some of the positions noted above. But first, unless the good is objective there seems little to recommend this. In fact, if anything, it seems these issues are ones about which there is room for rational disagreement, even though, on an objective theory, there may be one "best" answer. Second, in the absence of independent arguments for the rationality of certain positions such a claim will be of no help in adjudicating between rival positions, as everyone can avail himself of the claim that *his* position would be preferred by unrushed, clear-thinking, fully informed people (like himself). And third, once such independent arguments have been presented I suspect the boundary into objectivity will have been crossed and SDFT will have been left behind.

So far, I have merely raised serious questions about SDFT. Still, I hope to have said enough to remind the reader that SDFT is hardly self-evident. It follows that even *if* SDFT supported the Slogan – a big if – this would not license the rhetorical appeals to the Slogan that abound in philosophy and economics. At best the Slogan would remain controversial, awaiting the resolution of the problems facing SDFT, or still another argument, independent of both MST and SDFT, that has yet to be given.

One question about which there is much dispute is whether SDFT should be *restricted* – only attaching weight to the fulfillment of an agent's self-regarding desires, her desires about how *she* herself fares and how *her* life progresses – or *unrestricted* – also attaching weight to an agent's other-regarding desires, her desires about how *others* fare and how *their* lives progress, as well as any desires she may have about the world per se.[35] Now in general any desire intimately connected with one's deepest projects and commitments will count as self-regarding in the relevant sense. Still, whether a particular desire is self-regarding is not simply a matter of the desire's strength. People can have strong desires about others (e.g., that their children fare well), or weak desires about themselves (e.g., that their meal be tasty).

The dispute between restricted and unrestricted SDFTs deserves separate attention for two reasons. First, its root may partly lie in a failure to distinguish between a theory's plausibility as a theory about self-interest or outcomes and its plausibility as a full theory of the good. Second, reflection on the dispute suggests that, setting aside the issue of controversiality, SDFT does not support the Slogan.

Consider two cases. Case 1 is put by Derek Parfit in *Reasons and Persons*. He writes:

> Suppose that I meet a stranger who has what is believed to be a fatal disease. My sympathy is aroused, and I strongly want this stranger to be cured. Much later, when I have forgotten our meeting, the stranger is cured. On the Unrestricted Desire-Fulfillment Theory, this event is good for me and makes my life go better. This is not plausible. We should reject this theory.[36]

Case 2 may be put as follows. Suppose Jean has a strong other-regarding desire that certain graves be well tended. And suppose Liz could, with equal ease, fulfill either this strong desire or Jean's much weaker self-regarding desire for some suntan oil. Assuming Liz had no duty to do the latter, most would agree that *if* she were going to fulfill one of the desires it would be better to fulfill the strong one.

Reflecting on case 1, many are drawn to the conclusion that a restricted SDFT is more plausible than an unrestricted one. Reflecting on case 2, many are drawn to the opposite conclusion. There is an element of truth to both positions, but its exact nature is easily (and too often) overlooked.

Case 1 illustrates that an unrestricted SDFT is implausible *as a theory about self-interest*.[37] Case 2 illustrates that a restricted SDFT is implausible *as a theory about outcomes*. Together, then, cases 1 and 2 suggest that neither a restricted nor an unrestricted SDFT is plausible *as a full theory of the good*. But this does not show that each should be rejected out of hand. It remains possible that a restricted SDFT is plausible as a theory about self-interest, an unrestricted SDFT is plausible as a theory about outcomes, and neither is more plausible than the other *simpliciter*.

An unrestricted SDFT will count certain things as good or bad that we do not think are good or bad *for* anyone. This shows we must either reject the unrestricted SDFT, even as a theory about outcomes, or reject the Slogan. Similarly, a restricted SDFT fails to count as good for people certain factors we regard as good. This shows we must either reject the restricted SDFT, even as a theory about self-interest, or reject the Slogan. Thus, once one gets clear about the strengths and weaknesses of the two views, one sees that neither a restricted nor an unrestricted SDFT will plausibly support the Slogan.[38]

I have argued that SDFT is at best controversial. I have also argued that neither a restricted nor an unrestricted SDFT will support the Slogan. Let me conclude this section by noting that even if some version of SDFT were both to prove ultimately true and to support the Slogan, it would not support the numerous arguments implicitly invoking the Slogan.

On any plausible version of SDFT one will want to count as good *for* someone the satisfaction of those desires intimately connected with her deepest projects and commitments. Thus, recall how SDFT answers Nozick's challenge about the experience machine. On such a theory there would be good reason not to plug ourselves in because, as Nozick rightly observes, among our deepest desires are the desires to "do certain things . . . to *be* a certain way . . . and to live (an active verb) ourselves, in contact with reality." Well similarly, on SDFT there would be good reason to strive for freedom, justice, autonomy, and so on, because those too count among (some) people's deepest desires.

Consider again Nozick's Wilt Chamberlain example. While on SDFT it might be true that Chamberlain's receiving a million dollars could not be bad if there was no one for whom it was worse, the if clause would not be fulfilled. As long as there are (or have been) people for whom the advance of equality is among their deepest projects and commitments, there *will be* someone for whom the situation in question is worse in terms of the contravening of their relevant desires.[39] Hence, on SDFT, the Slogan would not support the kind of position Nozick has put forward. Similar remarks would apply to each of the arguments noted earlier that implicitly invoke the Slogan. One must look elsewhere for a position supporting both the Slogan and arguments invoking it.

7. The Objective List Theory

Let us next consider the Objective List Theory (OLT), which regards some things as intrinsically good or bad independently of people's desires or conscious states. This theory can avoid most problems facing MST and SDFT while capturing much of their appeal.

OLT can count as objectively good most of the pleasures MST counts, but it needn't count *all* pleasures as such. Thus, for example, it can avoid the unpalatable view that even the sadist's pleasures are good.

Similarly, OLT can count as good the fulfillment of desires plausibly counted as such by SDFT, yet (a) disregard the desires of sadists and bigots, (b) discount the unshared desires of past generations that are not independently binding, (c) accord weight to some, but not necessarily all, unrestricted desires, and (d) regard some alternatives as better or worse for people independently of their desires or how they were formed.

Most importantly, OLT provides (or would if it could be adequately worked out) the foundation for moral values that many think necessary if morality is not to be a vain and chimerical notion. After all, as we noted earlier, many believe that unlike most other factors, the goodness of moral ideals cannot be based on people's desires or conscious states.

There are, then, powerful attractions to OLT both as a theory about self-interest and as one about outcomes. But OLT also has problems – including the profoundly deep one of determining the *correct* objective list for self-interest or for outcomes. Rather than minimize this problem, I believe it is partly because well-meaning, conscientious, and seemingly rational people differ markedly on this issue that rhetorical appeals to the Slogan should be rejected. This will be developed further below, but first let me suggest that once one moves to OLT there seems to be little, if any, reason to be wedded to the Slogan.

Once we recognize that some things are intrinsically valuable independently of people's desires or conscious states it seems an open question what the full range of objective values would involve regarding their nature, content, or relation to sentient beings. Though presumably there will be some essential connection between our nature and the boundaries of moral value, why must it be one of *benefit,* for either us or others? Why *can't* the boundaries of the objectively good extend beyond what is good *for* someone – perhaps focusing on our capacity *to lead* a *morally* good life, as well as on our capacity *to have* a *prudentially* good life?

To be sure, an objective list for outcomes would include many factors on an objective list for self-interest. But there seems to be plenty of room for the former to be broader than the latter – that is, to include some factors, like certain moral ideals, that are not necessarily good *for* anyone.

Consider a typical list of ideals some have thought objectively valuable: utility, autonomy, freedom, rights, virtue, duty, equality, justice. Cases can be constructed for each of these ideals where violation of the ideal would not be worse for anyone in terms of their desires or conscious states. Given this, how should an Objective List Theorist respond?

One might insist that in such cases there is no respect in which the frustration of the ideal is bad. This supports the Slogan, but require leaving *every* moral ideal off the objective list for outcomes. Few would accept this response. Certainly most who have invoked the Slogan have not, and would not, accept it as undermining the objectivity of virtually all moral ideals.

Alternatively, one might argue that some ideals are good *for* people even when they do not promote higher conscious states or greater desire fulfillment. For example, it might be urged that freedom and autonomy are objectively good *for* people in the sense imagined. This would enable one to retain the Slogan without rejecting the objectivity of *all* our ideals.

I am dubious of this position. I find it at least as plausible to claim that freedom and autonomy are objectively good beyond the respects in which they benefit people as to claim that they are good *for* someone even if she doesn't desire them and they are worse for her conscious states. Still, even granting the position in question, at most it shows that there is *some* reason – and not the best, I think – to include such ideals on our objective list for outcomes. It assuredly does *not* show that the Slogan should be retained, and that ideals lacking this feature must, perforce, be left off.

Consider again our earlier example about the saints and sinners. Even if we don't believe with Kant and others that *A*, the situation where everyone "gets what they deserve," is better all things considered than *B*, the situation where the evilest mass murderers fare better than the most benign saints, is there *nothing* morally bad about the latter situation? *No* respect in which *B* is worse than *A*?

Or consider two societies, *C* and *D*. Society *C* is composed of equally deserving members where all are treated fairly and equally. Society *D* is composed of equally deserving members where most are treated as well as the people in *C*, but a few enjoy special rights and privileges as part of a hereditary aristocracy.[40] I, for one, am inclined to think *C* would be better than *D* all things considered. But even if this is too strong, is there no respect in which *D* is worse than *C*? Is there *nothing* morally bad about some equally deserving people being treated better than others?[41]

To grant that there is *some* respect in which *B* is worse than *A,* or *D* is worse than *C* is to grant a place for justice or equality on the correct objective list for outcomes, even though there is no intimate connection between the value of these ideals and their being good *for* people. This in turn is to reject the Slogan. How *could* one situation be worse than another if there is *no one* for whom it *is* worse? It could be worse if it is worse with respect to justice or equality, but more or less equivalent with respect to other ideals.

Of course, it is one thing to believe the correct objective list for outcomes will include ideals like justice and equality. It is quite another to *prove* this must be so. But in this respect ideals like justice and equality fare no worse than any other ideal. For example, that utility is always good *for* people, and hence would appear on the correct objective list for self-interest, is certainly no *proof* that it must appear on the objective list for outcomes. Indeed, this might be disputed by those mainly concerned with proportional justice.

Undoubtedly, then, it will be far from easy to construct and justify the correct objective list for outcomes. But if this *can* be done, I suspect many ideals on the list will be there for Kantian reasons, because they express respect for moral agents, whether ourselves or others, or perhaps for the moral law itself.[42] (To be indifferent between the sinners faring better than the saints and the saints faring better than the sinners is, in a deep and fundamental way, to fail to express a preference for good over evil.) Such Kantian notions are, of course, extremely elusive. All the more reason careful reflection and argument is needed in this area.

These remarks bear on my earlier suggestion that even if freedom and autonomy are, in a sense, objectively good for people, this is probably *not* the best reason for including them on the objective list for outcomes. Several attempts have been made recently to argue for the objective value of freedom, autonomy, or rights.[43] It is telling that *none* of these attempts appeals to the supposed fact that these ideals are objectively good *for* people. Instead, the arguments have been couched almost exclusively in Kantian terms, for example in terms of expressing respect for moral agents or of treating people as ends in themselves. But then, if these are appropriate reasons for including an ideal on the objective list for outcomes, it seems they might also warrant the inclusion of ideals like duty, justice, or equality, though they either do not have, or share to the same extent, the added feature of being objectively good *for* people.

It seems, then, the correct objective list for outcomes (if there is one) will include ideals not justified by their being good *for* people. Correspondingly, it seems that like MST and SDFT, OLT will not support the Slogan.

Of course one could always retain the Slogan by claiming that failure to show proper respect for moral agents or the moral law is bad *for* someone, for example the person to whom the respect *is* due and the agent herself whose wrongful action fails to respect her own worth as a moral agent. However, I believe this confuses issues, blurring an important distinction between harming someone and failing to respect someone. It also suggests that in acting wrongly we invariably harm ourselves,[44] which seems too easy a route to a conclusion so many great philosophers have tried, without success, to arrive at. Still, setting these worries aside, this move saves the Slogan only by robbing it of its teeth. For the advocate of any plausible ideal could make such a move – that is, claim that there would always be *someone* for whom the violation of her ideal would be worse (the violator if no one else). Thus, the Slogan could not be used to support any of the particular conclusions for which it has been invoked. This is, I think, the right conclusion, but not the most plausible way of arriving at it.

I have not argued that any particular ideals *must* appear on the correct objective list for outcomes. (Though admittedly I would be surprised if ideals like justice and equality, which many have thought lie at the core of morality, were not to appear.) Rather, I have tried to show that once one moves in the direction of an Objective List Theory it becomes an open question which ideals really belong on such a list and why.

That there is substantial disagreement about the correct objective list for outcomes, or even self-interest, underscores the importance of careful thought and argument about the nature of these lists. Of course, one might simply *insist* that the Slogan *must* be right, and hence that ideals like justice and equality must be rejected. But to do so would probably be wrong and certainly be unwarranted. Such an assertion begs the questions that most need addressing. Instead of advancing the level of moral argument it cuts off debate where it needs to begin. In sum, until significant reasoning about the nature and foundation of the correct objective lists establishes otherwise, arguments based on rhetorical appeal to the Slogan should be rejected.

8. Conclusion

The Slogan has been appealed to without argument by philosophers and economists across the ideological spectrum. In this essay, I have shown that despite, or perhaps because of, its widespread and uncritical acceptance, there is no single position represented by the claim that one situation *cannot* be worse than another if there is *no one* for whom it *is* worse. The most natural and straightforward interpretation of the Slogan asserts a significant but purely formal relationship between theories about self-interest and theories about outcomes. Thus, the substantive content of the Slogan will depend on these theories. But these are theories about which there is much disagreement. Correspondingly, many who think they agree in accepting the Slogan are in fact committing themselves to very different positions.

In this essay, I have also assessed whether a Mental State Theory, a Subjective Desire-Fulfillment Theory, or an Objective List Theory would plausibly support either the Slogan or the arguments invoking it. My arguments suggest, first, that none of these theories would justify rhetorical appeals to the Slogan. Second, that the most plausible versions of these theories would probably not support the Slogan. And third, even those versions of the theories that (might) support the Slogan, would not support most of the particular arguments that have invoked the Slogan.

In sum, once one distinguishes between theories of the good pertaining to self-interest and theories of the good pertaining to outcomes, there is good reason to doubt the Slogan, and even better reason to reject the arguments rhetorically invoking it. Thus, in the absence of an argument for the Slogan yet to be given, one must seek other justification for the positions one finds plausible.

Sparked by the arguments of this essay, several alternative principles have been offered as related to the Slogan.

> P_1: If in situation Y there is no one who is worse off than he is in X, then in bringing about X, rather than Y, I have violated no one's rights.
>
> P_2: Whether one situation is better or worse than another *for* someone is always relevant to whether that situation is better or worse.[45]

Several claims might be made regarding the relation between the Slogan and P_1 or P_2. It might be claimed that despite my assertions to the contrary few, if any, ever accepted the Slogan; what they accepted instead was P_1 or P_2. Alternatively, it might be claimed that P_1 or P_2 is what advocates of the Slogan understand it to mean, that is, that the correct interpretation of the Slogan just is P_1 or P_2. Finally, it might be claimed that while many in fact accepted the Slogan, what they should have accepted instead (and perhaps did accept as well) was P_1 or P_2.

For the purposes of this essay let me simply state, without argument, my reaction to these claims. First, I deny the first claim. Over the past years I have met many who think the Slogan expresses an important truth, and who are loath to give it up despite my arguments. Second, while there might be a connection for some between the Slogan and P_1 or P_2, I do not believe the Slogan is plausibly interpreted as P_1 or P_2. At the very least, the Slogan would be a *very* misleading way of expressing either P_1 or P_2. Third, to those who insist on interpreting the Slogan as P_1 or P_2, or who advocate P_1 or P_2 as preferable to the Slogan, I grant that P_1 or P_2 may be more plausible than (alternative interpretations of) the Slogan, but I point out that unless they are interpreted so as to be trivially true, and therefore uninteresting, neither P_1 nor P_2 justify rhetorical appeals to them.[46] Finally, and most importantly, P_1 and P_2 are much weaker than the interpretation of the Slogan I discussed, and whatever their ultimate plausibility, neither would support the particular conclusions for which the Slogan has been invoked.[47]

It is, I think, impressive testimony of the Slogan's seductive power that it seems to have tremendous force whenever it can be invoked to support one's position. Indeed, I suspect many who would be unmoved by the Slogan if it were employed against something they favor – perhaps justice, rights, or duty – nevertheless find it convincing when employed against something they reject – say, virtue, equality, or rule-utilitarianism.[48] Moreover, most who have read this essay continue to assert that surely there must be some cases, or some interpretation, that makes invoking the Slogan appropriate. Let me close, therefore, with three comments as to why people may have found the Slogan plausible. The first has already been touched on and can be dealt with briefly. The others require a bit more treatment, but important lessons can be learned from each.

First, it was an important step in moral philosophy when classical utilitarians emphasized the extent to which the value of things depended on their being good or bad *for* sentient beings. On reflection, it seems true of most everything that it only has the value it does because of the way it affects conscious states or the fulfillment of desires. Faced with this tremendous insight, it is easy to suppose that what is so of most things must be true of everything. Moreover, it may seem that only by accepting this view can one avoid the Pandora's box of intuitionism in ethics. It is only when one looks closely at the moral ideals and the different theories about self-interest and outcomes that one begins to doubt the legitimacy of this position and the range of its use.

A second reason some may have adopted the Slogan is by drawing questionable conclusions from misleading cases. For example, all agree that putting out people's eyes would be wrong, even if that were the only way of achieving equality. Moreover, for most, this judgment is *so* firm, they might naturally conclude both that there is nothing to be said for the ideal of equality, and that the truth of the Slogan accounts for this fact. But, natural or not, this conclusion is highly suspect.

In such examples our other ideals are either silent or line up squarely against equality. Our concerns about utility, perfectionism, humanitarianism, and rights combine to yield our strong unequivocal judgments. But these are *all-things-considered judgments,* perfectly compatible with equality being one ideal, among others, deserving of value. And, in cases where our other ideals diverge, equality often seems to rightly make a difference.

It is all too common in moral philosophy to dismiss *in toto* any position with implausible implications. Unfortunately, this often results in ignoring significant insights the position expresses. Equality is not the only ideal that would, if exclusively pursued, have terrible implications. The same is true of justice, freedom, utility, and so on. This does not show that our ideals are implausible. It shows that morality is complex.

The final reason I want to suggest for the Slogan's attraction can only be dealt with briefly here. Basically, it is that some may be associating the Slogan with what may be called the *individualistic* approach in ethics, according to which individuals are the proper objects of moral concern, not groups or societies. On this view, unlike the *global* or *holistic* approach, it doesn't matter what happens to a group or society per se – whether it is left intact, slightly modified, or entirely transformed – all that matters is what happens to the present, future, and (perhaps) past individuals who are or would be affected by that group or society.

I believe there is much to be said for the individualistic approach. In fact, I suspect that global or holistic approaches are generally mistaken in moral philosophy, whether embodied in a principle like Rawls's maximin principle, with its focus on the worst-off *group,* or in a principle like average utilitarianism, with its focus on the average level of *society.* I cannot defend these claims here,[49] but if they are right, they may help to explain why the Slogan seemed to pose a special threat to egalitarianism.

I believe that most have thought, wrongly, that the egalitarian's concerns are global in nature, that is, that egalitarian judgments are fundamentally about how *societies* fare with respect to inequality, as if inequality is bad because it is bad for a *society* to be unequal. So, the egalitarian seemed to be in a position analogous to someone who cared about what happens to *France,* over and above the extent to which sentient beings are affected by events involving France.

Naturally, the individualistic approach opposes such a view. And the Slogan can be used to express this opposition. The rhetorical question, How *could* one situation be worse than another if there is *no one* for whom it *is* worse? *can* be taken to express the individualist's position that *societies* are not the proper objects of moral concern, people in societies are.

I believe, then, that insofar as it is taken to express the individualistic approach, the Slogan does challenge views like average utilitarianism and like egalitarianism as it has normally been thought of. However, my own view is that the common conception about egalitarianism is badly mistaken. On my view egalitarianism is not global, it is individualistic.[50] More generally, I believe that most ideals can be properly understood individualistically. So, for example, the utilitarian, the egalitarian, and the person who cares about proportional justice can all agree that sentient individuals are the proper objects of moral concern. Where they disagree is in their answer to the question, What is it *about* sentient individuals one should care about? Is it *only* their utility, or is it also their share in the distribution of goods, either relative to others, or relative to what they deserve?

I conclude that insofar as the Slogan is taken to express the individualistic approach it may express (though no doubt misleadingly) an important truth about morality. So, in one respect, people's intuitive reactions to the Slogan may be justified after all. However, the truth the Slogan expresses is not uncontroversial. More importantly, it will not support the particular conclusions for which the Slogan has been invoked. The central results of the essay stand.

Notes

1 See Locke's *Second Treatise on Civil Government*, secs. 26–33 (the passage in quotes comes from sec. 26).

2 Robert Nozick, *Anarchy, State, and Utopia* (Oxford: Basil Blackwell, 1974), p. 175.

3 Ibid., p. 181.

4 Interestingly, among those rejecting Nozick's conclusion most insist that it is precisely because the medical researcher does worsen the situation of those he deprives of his medicine that he acts wrongly in keeping his product off the market. This is, I suspect, further indirect support for my claim regarding the widespread appeal of the Slogan, as it suggests (though does not entail) that most who reject Nozick's conclusion do so not because they reject the Slogan but rather because they think Nozick has misapplied it. In any event, whether or not Nozick has misapplied the Slogan it does seem he has appealed to it, and that is all I am concerned with for my present purposes.

5 Ibid., p. 161.

6 Actually, Rawls's lexical version of the Difference Principle allows some gains of the sort in question, but in general Rawls wants to rule out any inequalities that do not "maximize, or at least contribute to, the long-term expectations of the least fortunate group in society." John Rawls, *A Theory of Justice* (Cambridge, Mass.: Harvard University Press, 1971), p. 151; see also pp. 64–5, 78–9, 83, and 150.

7 Derek Parfit, "Future Generations: Further Problems," *Philosophy and Public Affairs* 11, no. 2 (spring 1982), pp. 158–9.

8 Parfit's own views have changed since publishing "Future Generations: Further Problems." He now has other arguments to support the claim that $A +$ is not worse than A that do not appeal to the Slogan. Nevertheless, there was a time where he did implicitly appeal to the Slogan in the manner suggested. Moreover, I am convinced that many of those who accepted Parfit's claims about how A and $A +$ compare did so because of their implicit acceptance of the Slogan. (I know I did originally, as did many of my students and colleagues.)

9 Variations of the following reasoning are found in most writings against equality, and when lecturing on equality I have almost invariably encountered some version of it. W. D. Falk strongly endorsed such reasoning in the spring of 1980 (in conversation), and numerous others have since.

10 One can see how these considerations might drive one toward nonegalitarianism, but they might also drive one toward a version of egalitarianism that distinguishes between (a) cases where the plight of the worse-off is partly a function of the inequality – were the inequality removed in an appropriate

way they would be better off; and (b) cases where the plight of the worse-off is not a function of the inequality – were the inequality removed they would not benefit, or perhaps not exist at all. A view maintaining that inequality is only objectionable in the former cases could accommodate the Slogan, and hence avoid these objections. (Though, in the end, I think such a view faces grave difficulties, and gives up more than the egalitarian wants to.)

11 Thomas Scanlon, "Rights, Goals, and Fairness," in S. Hampshire, ed., *Public and Private Morality* (Cambridge: Cambridge University Press, 1978), pp. 93–111.

12 One anonymous critic has suggested that the Slogan is *really* only relevant to case 5 (Parfit's example from his Mere Addition Paradox), that in fact Parfit "invented" the problem I am concerned with, and hence that this essay will only be of interest to Parfit followers. Frankly, I am flabbergasted by such claims. First, to say that Parfit "invented" the problem is to suggest that the problem is only a pseudo-problem, that were it not for Parfit's troublesome arguments there would *be* no problem. But surely this is mistaken. I readily grant that prior to Parfit I, and others, were oblivious to the worries illuminated by the Mere Addition Paradox and the Non-Identity Problem; but this only means that Parfit discovered a problem, not that he *invented* one. The problem is a deep and genuine one, whether it was previously recognized or not. Second, I am convinced the critic is mistaken in thinking the Slogan only applies to case 5. To be cautious, let me grant my critic that there may be other reasons that *also* underlie cases 1–8; still, I am confident that for many people the Slogan gives cases 1–8 much of their appeal. Having lectured on inequality for many years I have confronted numerous variations of case 6, and subsequent discussions have left no doubt in my mind that many people's views about inequality are influenced by the Slogan's appeal (cf. note 9). Moreover, I know for a fact that I invoked the Slogan in presenting objections of the sort suggested in case 8 (cf. note 48), and I doubt that I am the only person to have done so. Finally, I take some consolation in knowing that my critic is simply mistaken in his or her assessment of who might be interested in this essay. I have found this essay's topic to generate intense debate among diverse audiences in three different countries, most of whom, surely, are not "Parfit followers."

Ironically, contra the claim discussed above, several people have suggested that most of the positions noted in this section (i.e., cases 1–8) are equivalent and, more specifically, reduce to an objection against equality. This, too, is surely mistaken. Though each position appeals to the Slogan for support, the claim that equality is not intrinsically valuable is markedly different, and has different implications, from the corresponding claims about rights, virtues, duties, and rules. Similarly, while Nozick's and Parfit's positions *seem* to entail that equality is not intrinsically valuable (but see note 10), the latter position does not entail the former ones. For example, Parfit's position entails the rejection of both average utilitarianism and certain applications of the maximin principle, but neither rejection is entailed by the position that equality is not intrinsically valuable. Moreover, while Nozick's position is analogous to Locke's, it neither entails, nor is entailed by Parfit's.

Of course, anyone invoking the Slogan is committed to whatever the Slogan entails. But this does not show that every position appealing to the Slogan is equivalent.

13 An average ejaculation contains between 120 and 750 million sperm cells. If one thinks of all of the partners a woman might have sex with during the time each month when she is fertile, and if one thinks that each sperm would combine with her ovum to create a unique individual, the number of possible people she might conceive each month is astronomical. It is surely implausible to think that she acts against each of their interests if she refrains from sex. Moreover, while it might be true that if she had had sex with Tom she might have conceived a particular individual, Tom Jr., it seems implausible to contend that she acted against Tom Jr.'s interest when she had sex with her husband Barry, and conceived Barry Jr. instead.

14 I shall not defend these assumptions. They are defended ably by Parfit. See "Future Generations: Further Problems," esp. pp. 113–19.

15 At one stage I think this was Parfit's own view of the matter. (Based on conversation. Also, this partly explains how, in the same article, he could both present the Non-Identity Argument and later implicitly appeal to the Slogan in the Mere Addition Paradox when comparing A with $A+$.)

16 In conversations with Douglas MacLean and Shelly Kagan, both reported encountering the same reactions in people they talked to about the Non-Identity Problem. Kagan, in fact, reported that both he and Annette Baier inclined toward Parfit's original view that the Slogan only fails in the peculiar range of cases Parfit described.

17 Some readers may wonder why I bother to distinguish among (1)–(4) and defend my understanding of the Slogan as shorthand for (1). Jonathan Dancy, for example, suggested in correspondence that I might do away with this section as it "merely lists interpretations of the Slogan which have tempted nobody." I wish Dancy were right, but experience has taught me he is not. This section was only added to the essay after earlier drafts elicited numerous comments and questions about the best way of interpreting the Slogan. Indeed, in the face of my arguments a number of people claimed the Slogan *should* be interpreted as (3) or (4) rather than (1). Obviously, for the reasons given in the text, I think they are mistaken. Still, I think this section will help avoid unnecessary errors or confusion.

18 Jonathan Dancy has questioned this claim. He wonders whether supporters of the Slogan are really holding different views, depending on their theories of the good, or whether they merely have different reasons for the same view. This may be a terminological issue, but for reasons implied later I take it that the practical, substantive implications of the Slogan will be very different depending on the theory of the good underlying it, and I also take

it that two views or positions are distinct from each other if their implications are different.

19 I emphasize the word 'seems' here because some readers have been misled by my claims regarding the connection between MST and the Slogan. It is not my view that MST *actually* "supports" or "accounts" for the Slogan, only that it may *appear* to, given the evaluations it yields to certain situations. The main point of this section is to show that however plausible it may seem, the appearance in question is illusory.

20 As the reader may note, I am here considering what MST would say about A and B considered *just by themselves*. I am ignoring the effects of A and B on the conscious states of us, as observers, who may care about equality. For our present purposes there are good reasons to do this, some of which are noted below in my discussion of proportional justice.

To ensure that my example is relevant to the Slogan as I am interpreting it, (i.e., as shorthand for [1]), I am assuming that the greater inequality in B hasn't by itself caused negative conscious states (envy?) that happen to be outweighed by other positive conscious states present in B but not in A. Perhaps the worse-off group is separated by an ocean and unaware of the better-off group. Perhaps they are Mental State Utilitarians who do not care about inequality per se, and hence are unequivocally pleased by what they take to be uniform improvement for the better.

21 Situation B isn't worse for the saints. By hypothesis they fare as well in B as in A. And it certainly isn't worse for the sinners! Hence there is no one for whom it is worse. (We may suppose, if we want, that the saints are blissfully unaware of how the sinners are faring, though if they are truly *saints* this supposition may be unnecessary. I leave God and His feelings out of this discussion [perhaps He doesn't exist]; but notice, on the view being called into question, what reason could He have for preferring A to B, when there is no one for whom B is worse?)

22 One critic, who shall remain nameless (for his own protection!), has suggested that this paragraph be removed as it merely serves to ward off "an absolutely stupid objection." I have some sympathy with this claim, if not its tact, but having confronted the objection in question on *numerous* occasions I am afraid the paragraph serves a useful function.

23 Recall Hobbes's famous claim "whatsoever is the object of any man's Appetite or Desire, that is it, which he for his part calleth Good." This claim is endorsed by John Mackie, *Ethics* (Harmondsworth, England: Penguin Books, 1977), and too many others to bother citing.

24 I have contended that, on MST, we should assess how situations compare considered by themselves. It is worth observing that the Slogan would lose its force – from which the central claims of this article would follow – if, in assessing situations, appeals were made to how observers would react or, for that matter, to what a rational impartial spectator would say. The reasons for this are (implicitly) given in Sections 6 and 7, so I shall not duplicate them here.

25 Which is, of course, very different from telling us what makes someone good or bad.

26 There may be other reasons for rejecting MST as well, but this need not concern us here.

27 Nozick, *Anarchy, State, and Utopia*, pp. 42–5, his emphasis.

28 The reason for this tag will become clear in the final section of this essay.

29 The reason for this is put nicely by Parfit. He writes, "These . . . Theorists count it as bad for me if my desire is not fulfilled, even if . . . I never know this. How then can it matter whether, when my desire is not fulfilled, I am dead? All that my death does is *ensure* that I will never know this. If we think it irrelevant that I never know about the non-fulfillment of my desire, we cannot defensibly claim that my death makes a difference." *Reasons and Persons* (Oxford: Clarendon Press, 1984), p. 495.

The implications of this position extend beyond the central concerns of this essay. It has long been thought an essential feature of utilitarianism that it is a forward-looking doctrine, and this has been counted among both its greatest strengths (accounting for some of its reformist implications and its independence from prevailing codes and norms) and its greatest weaknesses (because of its disregard for past histories, promises, contracts, etc.). But the forward-looking aspect of utilitarianism is not a function of its formal features either as a maximization doctrine or as one concerned solely with the consequences of actions.

So *classical* utilitarianism was essentially forward-looking, because it accepted MST, and because one *cannot* affect past states of consciousness. However, one *can* affect whether certain past desires are fulfilled, because even self-regarding desires can be about the future and one's relation to it. So, combined with SDFT, utilitarianism *needn't* be essentially forward-looking.

R. M. Hare was one of the first to both recognize and accept the implications in question. He writes, "to frustrate a desire of mine is against my interest even if I do not know that it is being frustrated, or if I am dead." Later he adds, "for what it is worth I will record my opinion that the dying man's interests *are* harmed if promises are made to him and then broken, and even more that mine are harmed if people are cheating me without my knowing it." "Ethical Theory and Utilitarianism," in H. D. Lewis, ed., *Contemporary British Philosophy* (London: George Allen and Unwin, 1976), pp. 130–1.

30 Here, as elsewhere, I am assuming the person in question had a "self-regarding" desire that they not be slandered. The meaning and importance of this assumption will become clearer below.

31 Assuming the person had a deep desire to make a lasting contribution toward those ends or ideals.

32 This example is taken from Thomas Scanlon's "Preference and Urgency," *Journal of Philosophy* 72, no. 19 (November 1975): 655–69.

33 This parallels the view that many have toward the age-old *Euthyphro* ques-

tion: "Is what God commands good because He commands it, or does He command it because it is good?" Many think that if morality is not to be a vain and chimerical notion it must be the latter and not the former. Otherwise God could command us to murder and murder would then be good.

34 I use this as shorthand for the more cumbersome: "what makes something good is that it figures in the fulfillment of someone's desires."

35 The desire that the moon be made of green cheese is "other-regarding" in the sense it is being used here as is the desire that one's children fare well.

36 Parfit, *Reasons and Persons*, p. 494.

37 Parfit is clear about this. He does not claim for his example more than it shows. Others, I suspect, have been less careful in their thinking.

38 The argument regarding the restricted SDFT might be put as follows. Suppose one accepts the view that a restricted SDFT is plausible as a theory about self-interest, but believes, in case 2, that Liz should fulfill Jean's other-regarding desire about the graves rather than her self-regarding desire about the suntan oil. One should then reject the Slogan, for while tending the graves would be better than getting the lotion there may be *no one* for whom it *is* better and, indeed, someone for whom it is worse – namely, Jean, whose self-regarding desire for the suntan oil goes unfulfilled. (For the sake of this example I am assuming that the people in the graves had no desires one way or the other about the tending of their graves. In other words, I take it that Liz might base her actions solely on the nature of Jean's desires without needing to appeal to its really being better for the people in the graves.)

The above point is generalizable. Although a restricted SDFT is more plausible than an unrestricted one as a theory about self-interest, there are cases where we think the right way of respecting someone, or acting on her behalf, would be to do what she would most want us to do rather than what would be best *for her*. Often, this involves giving weight to some of her strong unrestricted desires (even in cases where she would never learn of our action). Thus, on a restricted SDFT an element enters into our assessment of alternatives beyond what is best *for* the particular people in those alternatives. Hence, a restricted SDFT will not support the Slogan.

I leave to the interested reader the construction of the analogous argument regarding the unrestricted SDFT.

39 The crucial point here is the one noted above, that on any plausible version of SDFT one will want to count as good *for* someone the satisfaction of those desires intimately connected with her deepest projects and commitments. One might try to deny this, but I do not see how to distinguish in a non-*ad hoc* and non-question-begging way between, say, the deep projects and commitments of one who cares about advancing equality or justice and those of one committed to advancing science or writing a masterpiece to be read and admired for generations to come.

40 This need not cause envy or resentment among the others. I am assuming this to be the case in my example. The people may simply be indifferent to

the practice or, as with many in England or Sweden, they may rather fancy it.

41 These remarks parallel Thomas Scanlon's in "Nozick on Rights, Liberty, and Property," *Philosophy and Public Affairs* 6, no. 1 (winter 1976):3–25. He writes: "If the evil of being relatively disadvantaged justifies eliminating inequalities by redistribution . . . it may be asked whether it does not provide an equally strong reason for simply worsening the position of the better off when redistribution is not possible. This may sound irrational, but in the case of many social inequalities, for example, distinctions of rank or social caste, egalitarian demands for the elimination of non-redistributable advantages are not implausible. In other cases, where we think that non-redistributable advantages should not be eliminated, this is not because these advantages are consistent with pure egalitarianism, but because we temper the demands of equality with other considerations. Equality is not our only concern." Pp. 9–10.

42 I believe that on most plausible theories of self-interest to express respect for moral agents or the moral law in a Kantian sense will not necessarily be good *for* anyone (though it usually will). I briefly discuss the contrary view below.

43 See, for example, the writings of Nozick, Dworkin, Fried, and Donagan.

44 Strictly speaking, this would only follow if failing to respect others, or the moral law, always involved failing to respect ourselves. But I think this is precisely what Kant and his followers would want to say. On a deontological or agent-relative view, the focus is always on the agent, on what I do, rather than on the outcome, or what happens. For Kant, when I fail to respect others this is wrong not because of the bad effects this has for them, but because I have failed to act in accordance with a good will, which means I have failed to act in accordance with the moral law that I prescribe to myself. Correspondingly, the wrongness of my action will be intimately bound up with my failing to respect my moral personality as a free and autonomous member of the realm of ends. On the view under discussion this would necessarily have to be regarded as being worse for me. (I take it a similar claim would need to be made about virtue theories. According to virtue theorists we are blameworthy whenever we evidence a bad character by [voluntarily] failing to act virtuously. Presumably, all such actions would have to be regarded as harmful to the agent. This is a conclusion Aristotle would embrace, but one that cannot simply be asserted.)

45 P_1 was suggested by Bill Rowe, P_2 by Thomas Hill, Sr.

46 It may seem otherwise, particularly in the case of P_2. But though I myself think P_2 is probably true, its spirit is more controversial than first appears. Most who accept P_2 believe utility is intrinsically good. Correspondingly, they use P_2 to express their view that whatever *other* factors may *also* be relevant to a situation's being good, to the extent one situation is better than another for someone, it must be, to that extent, better. But I take it this is precisely what Kant, among others, would deny. (Recall Kant's claims that

"the sight of a being adorned with no feature of a pure and good will, ye enjoying uninterrupted prosperity, can never give pleasure to a rationa impartial spectator," and that the "good will is the indispensable conditior even of worthiness to be happy.") Thus, in the saints and sinners example noted earlier, I think Kant would deny that the sinners faring well is in one respect good, though in another bad. Rather, I think Kant would insist that the situation where the sinners fare better than the saints is wholly and unequivocally worse than the situation where everybody receives what he deserves.

It is not only advocates of proportional justice who must deny the spirit of P_2. Considering our obligations toward future generations, some believe that certain lives are so diseased or deprived that even if they are worth living, and so of value for the people whose lives they are, it would have been better in itself – even apart from their effects on others – if those lives had never been led. (See the work of Gregory Kavka.) Others believe that even if lives worth living are never intrinsically bad, many such lives are not intrinsically good (though they have subjective value for the possessors of such lives, they do not make the world better from the impersonal [objective] moral point of view). (See Derek Parfit's work.) On reflection, I think advocates of both positions must reject P_2.

47 In this respect, of course, they are no worse off than the interpretation I discussed. But neither are they better off.

I suspect some people may have been partly attracted to the Slogan because they accepted both P_1, and P_3: One situation cannot be worse than another if no one's rights would be violated in bringing the one situation about rather than the other. However, P_3 is not plausible. And in any event, insofar as P_1 and P_3 imply the Slogan, together they are subject to all the problems this essay raises.

48 I confess, much to my chagrin, that only after working on this essay did I realize that I had been implicitly invoking the Slogan against positions I rejected long after I had dismissed similar arguments made by others against equality. Of course, I did not then realize, as I now do, that an implicit appeal to the Slogan underlay both kinds of arguments. (My embarrassment is only slightly lessened by the fact that I appear to have plenty of company. For example, as my earlier remarks suggest, I think both Nozick and Parfit implicitly invoke the Slogan in some cases, despite explicitly rejecting it [or, perhaps, alternative interpretations of it] in others.)

49 I argue for them in my book *Inequality* (New York: Oxford University Press, 1993).

50 This view is defended in my work on inequality (ibid.).